CW01213402

From the Corn Laws to Free Trade

From the Corn Laws to Free Trade

Interests, Ideas, and Institutions in Historical Perspective

Cheryl Schonhardt-Bailey

The MIT Press
Cambridge, Massachusetts
London, England

© 2006 Massachusetts Institute of Technology

All rights reserved. No part of this book may be reproduced in any form by any electronic or mechanical means (including photocopying, recording, or information storage and retrieval) without permission in writing from the publisher.

MIT Press books may be purchased at special quantity discounts for business or sales promotional use. For information, please e-mail ⟨special_sales@mitpress.mit.edu⟩, or write to Special Sales Department, The MIT Press, 55 Hayward Street, Cambridge, MA 02142.

This book was set in Palatino on 3B2 by Asco Typesetters, Hong Kong and was printed and bound in the United States of America.

Library of Congress Cataloging-in-Publication Data

Schonhardt-Bailey, Cheryl, 1961–
From the corn laws to free trade : interests, ideas, and institutions in historical perspective / Cheryl Schonhardt-Bailey.
   p. cm.
Includes bibliographical references (p.) and index.
ISBN 0-262-19543-7 (alk. paper)
1. Corn laws (Great Britain)—History—19th century. 2. Free trade—Great Britain—History—19th century. 3. Great Britain. Parliament—Voting—History—19th century. 4. Great Britain—Politics and government—1837–1901. I. Title.

HF2044.S36 2006
382'.71094109034—dc22   2006043343

10 9 8 7 6 5 4 3 2 1

To my children
Hannah and Samuel,
For your faith

Contents

Preface   ix

1 Introduction: The Puzzle   1

2 Interests, Ideas and Institutions Simplified: A Demand- and Supply-Side Perspective   31

I The Demand Side: The League, the Landowners, and Free Trade   47

3 Lessons in Lobbying for Free Trade: To Concentrate or Not   49

4 Nationalizing the Interest in Free Trade   75

5 The Waning Demand for Protection: Portfolio Diversification of Landowners   107

6 Votes in Parliament, Dissected into Ideology, Party, and Interests   127

II The Supply Side   155

7 Conservatives Who Sounded Like Trustees but Voted Like Delegates   157

8 Repeal in Historical Context: Key Parliamentary Debates on the Corn Laws before 1846   191

9 Free Trade's Last Hurdle: Why the Lords Acquiesced   227

10 Feeling the Heat of the League? How Local Newspapers Affected MPs' Voting on Repeal   263

11 Concluding Thoughts on Repeal and the Road to Democratic Reform in Nineteenth-Century Britain   283

Appendix 1 Summary Table of All Regression Variables and Further Details on Measuring District Trade Orientation   293
Appendix 2 Speakers 22 January to 15 May 1846 in the Debates on the Customs and Corn Importation Bill   301
Appendix 3 Characteristics of Members of Parliament, 1815 to 1828   317
Appendix 4 Details of Parliamentary Proceedings, 1814 to 1846   331
Appendix 5 Details of Members of Parliament Sampled for Newspaper Analysis   339
Notes   359
References   389
Index   409

Preface

The idea for this book originated in 1986 and 1987 when I was a graduate student at the University of California, Los Angeles. In an international political economy seminar, I first encountered the story of Britain's conversion to free trade in the mid-nineteenth century. At that time, hegemonic stability theory was the most prominent (at least among IPE scholars) analytical framework for understanding Britain's departure from protection for agriculture (as seen in the repeal of the Corn Laws). I wrote a seminar paper in which I argued that domestic economic interests, and not the structure of the international system, provided the best explanation for the policy shift to free trade. I recall writing that first paper and feeling as though I had opened a Pandora's box of interrelated and overlapping issues, all of which conspired against a simple explanation for the policy shift.

Britain's repeal of its protectionist Corn Laws continued to puzzle and intrigue me (primarily because I was sure that my seminar paper was wholly inadequate). I abandoned my Soviet Union program of study in favor of a Ph.D. dissertation on repeal. John Zaller and Barbara Geddes helped me to discover the joys of empirical analysis and hypothesis testing, but this presented the problem of data collection. I traveled to Britain for what was intended to be four months of field work, but a romantic interest in a certain British economic historian (also my landlord) led me to marry, relocate, and start a family in Britain. (I never imagined that the puzzle of repeal would eventually lead my children to call me "mummy.")

Meanwhile, my intellectual interest in repeal ended (temporarily) with the completion of my Ph.D. in 1991. The dissertation offered an extensive (and data-rich) economic-interest explanation for the policy shift, but it paid scant attention to the role of ideas and institutions. Much to the chagrin of my supervisor, David Lake, I did not turn the dissertation into a book—basically because I doubted that the sum offered more than three of the core chapters, which had been published separately as articles. (As indicated in various notes in this book, parts of chapters 3 and 4 were published in the *American Political Science Review* and *World Politics*. A fragment of chapter 6 was published in *Parliamentary History*, while the more complete version appeared in the *British Journal of Political Science*.)

In 1995, I returned to the story of repeal when I edited four volumes on Britain's conversion and adherence to free trade in the nineteenth century—*Rise of Free Trade* (Schonhardt-Bailey 1997). Having trawled through a mountain of primary-source documents relating to British trade policy from 1814 to 1906, I could no longer dismiss my earlier (and convenient) notion that ideas were unimportant in explaining the policy shift to free trade. But the methodological challenge was how to model and measure the role of ideas (and, more broadly, ideology) within a policy setting in which I believed that economic interests played a key role. Two possible avenues were (1) more careful dissection of the roll-call votes to measure the ideological motivations of Members of Parliament and (2) a thorough analysis of the parliamentary debates leading up to and including the year of repeal (1846). For the former, I relied on an adaptation of Keith Poole and Howard Rosenthal's NOMINATE scores (with, I might add, generous assistance from Keith Poole in adapting NOMINATE to the Parliament of 1841 to 1847), and for the latter, I discovered the delights of computer-assisted content analysis in a little-known software called Alceste. This software made it possible for me to analyze over 3,000 pages of parliamentary debates on trade policy over the period from 1814 to 1846. Readers who wish to examine these debates may find the complete set on the data page of my Web site, ⟨http://personal.lse.ac.uk/schonhar⟩.

Around the same time, Iain McLean shared with me early versions of his interpretation of repeal, which hinged on Sir Robert Peel, the Duke of Wellington, and the House of Lords and was later published in his book *Rational Choice and British Politics: An Analysis of Rhetoric and Manipulation from Peel to Blair* (2001). In a somewhat related vein, Ken Shepsle encouraged me to think more carefully about the institutional setting in which both interests and ideas might interact. Institutions, it seemed, were also central to the policy shift to free trade. It slowly dawned on me that the true story of repeal probably required some understanding of how economic interests interacted with ideas and the institutional setting of mid-nineteenth century Britain. While attractive for some purposes, the simplicity of economic interests no longer provided me with an adequate explanation for repeal of the Corn Laws.

In the late 1990s, I decided to return to repeal in full force with the hope that I could somehow bring together (both theoretically and empirically) interests, ideas, and institutions in a single framework for understanding the policy shift to free trade. Whether I have succeeded in the pages that follow is for the reader to decide.

The long gestation period for this book has meant that I have acquired a number of debts of gratitude. I have benefited from the comments of various audiences, including numerous annual meetings of the American Political Science Association and the European Public Choice Society; the University of Sussex (1996); the "1846 Freedom and Trade 1996: A Commemoration of the Repeal of the Corn Laws" conference in Manchester (1996); the "Instituting Trade: Trade Policy and Nineteenth-Century Political Institutions" mini-conference at the Center for Political Economy, Washington University (1997); the Rational Choice Group, hosted in Brian Barry's living room (1997); the Royal Institute of International Affairs; the London School of Economics Government Department Seminar; the Leitner Program in International and Comparative Political Economy, Yale Center for International and Area Studies (2003); and the Richard Cobden Bicentenary Conference, hosted in Cobden's home in Sussex (2004). A number of individuals have, moreover, kindly provided me with detailed comments, helpful suggestions, and where necessary, unreserved criticisms. These include Nick Allum, Brian Barry, Lance Davis, Jeff Frieden, Barbara Geddes, Miriam Golden, Judy Goldstein, Bernie Grofman, Arye Hillman, Tony Howe, Doug Irwin, Chai Lieven, Fiona McGillivray, Tim McKeown, Iain McLean, Helen Milner, Michael Munger, Angela O'Mahoney, Bob Pahre, John Petrocik, Ron Rogowski, Howard Rosenthal, Ken Scheve, Ken Shepsle, Heidi Ullrich, Eric Uslaner, and Daniel Verdier. I am also grateful to John Covell (MIT Press senior editor) for his enthusiasm and support for this book and to the reviewers of this book for their helpful suggestions.

Because I have sought to measure empirically the three I's (interests, ideas, and institutions) in the context of repeal, this book contains a variety of methodologies, including descriptive statistics; cross-tabulations; linear, logistic, and multinomial logistic regression; NOMINATE; and computer-assisted content analysis (Alceste). But numbers (particularly en masse) can be boring, and so I have tried to present the results graphically wherever possible. In the early years, Craig Schonhardt (my brother) helped me to prepare the graphs, and in the later stages, Mina Moshkeri of the LSE Design Unit spent endless hours preparing the many graphs for this book. I am extremely grateful to Craig and Mina for their patient assistance over the years.

A number of bodies have generously provided funding for this project, including the UCLA Center for International and Strategic Affairs, the UCLA Political Science Department, the Nuffield Foundation, the LSE Staff Research Fund, and the LSE Suntory and Toyota International Centre for Economics and Related Disciplines (STICERD). I would not have been able to embark on this project let alone bring it to fruition without this funding.

I owe a very special thanks to the late W. O. Aydelotte, who dedicated his academic life to compiling a massive dataset on the MPs of the 1841 to 1847 Parliament. Considering that his dataset was compiled in the 1960s, both his data collection and his methodological pursuits were path breaking. My gratitude also extends to Mrs. Aydelotte, who located the names of MPs and sent them to Iain McLean, who in turn shared them with me. Without the names of the MPs, I would not have been able to complete the analysis of the critical roll-call votes on repeal.

Others lent a hand to this book in an essential but perhaps less direct way. Here I refer to the friendship and support of other women political scientists who also balance motherhood with research. For Barbara Geddes, Fiona McGillivray, and Frances Rosenbluth, I hold special affection and gratitude. I must also note the words of the late Susan Strange, who in her 1995 International Studies Association presidential address shared her personal story of having six children. She encouraged young women political scientists not to defer motherhood for too long. Feminists were not pleased with her remarks, I am told, but her words gave me the courage to take a leap of faith into motherhood, and for that I am deeply grateful.

Finally, I have left the dearest to the last. Four men have—in very different ways—provided me with strength, patience, and the intellectual wherewithal to complete this book. First, my late father, Ray Schonhardt, had a motto: "If it's worth doing, it's worth doing right." Well, Dad, it took me awhile, but this book is about as right as I can get the story of repeal. Second, Gordon Bannerman has been (and continues to be) an outstandingly committed and diligent research assistant. The detailed appendices to this book, in particular, are testament to his excellent skills as an historian. Third, if ever there was a model supervisor and mentor, David Lake would be it. Never once has David stinted in offering me advice in all aspects of my research and career. For his guidance, wisdom, and friendship over the past nineteen or so years, I am tremendously grateful. And fourth, my husband, Andrew Bailey, is my number one pillar of support. For many years, he has skillfully and patiently helped me to enter data, interpret stacks of computer printouts, edit text (over and over again), and tease out the logic of difficult arguments and even has found time to deal with diapers, laundry, and dinners while I sit at the computer. Most importantly, he has encouraged me to persevere with this project and has provided me with a comfortable and loving environment in which to do so.

This book is dedicated to our children, Hannah Louise Schonhardt Bailey and Samuel John Schonhardt Bailey. My dears, your prayers and your affection got me through the final stages of this project. Hugs and kisses to you both.

1   Introduction: The Puzzle

The Puzzle

As far as puzzles go, Britain's repeal of the protectionist Corn Laws in 1846 ranks among the best.[1] Rarely do we find a case in which political representatives acted seemingly against not only their own economic and political interests but also against the mandate on which many of them were elected. This case is fascinating and intriguing because its central puzzle has not yet been adequately explained. Britain's bold move to free trade in 1846 was both unprecedented and unilateral; moreover, it violated the core protectionist ideology of the Conservative party while simultaneously undercutting the economic interests of the ruling landed aristocracy. The Conservatives entered government in 1841 with a strong and (what appeared to be) unified commitment to protecting agriculture, and yet their leader, Prime Minister Sir Robert Peel, completely reversed this stance within five years. About a third of the Members of Parliament (MPs) in his party followed Peel by supporting his repeal legislation, while the rest remained firmly committed to protecting agriculture. Within a month of gaining repeal, the Peel government fell,[2] and the Conservatives remained divided and for the most part out of office for decades. Given the disastrous political fallout from repeal, why did some MPs choose to support it? Equally intriguing is why the House of Lords, a chamber of unelected landowning aristocrats, failed to halt repeal by invoking its veto. At the heart of the puzzle is the question of why both houses of Parliament enacted a policy that appeared to harm their own economic interests *and* more broadly those of the larger landed aristocracy. Linked to this puzzle are related questions. Why did a ruling party leader, *along with* a large portion of his political party, endorse a remarkable policy that would bring down the government and send a fractured party into political hibernation for a generation? Why, moreover, would a long tradition of Conservative ideology in which protectionism was core suddenly undergo a metamorphosis? Finally, why would an upper chamber that saw itself as a check on wayward "democratic" forces in the lower chamber nonetheless fail to use its power of the veto? At the heart of these questions lies a thicket of overlapping and intertwined interests, ideas, and institutions, which no account of repeal has yet managed fully to explain.

The findings of this book tell a simple but compelling story: economic interests accounted for the momentum behind repeal, a momentum that overshadowed almost all else. Indeed, as part of a broader impulse toward democratic reform, these same interests, left unsatisfied, could have snowballed into revolution—as Peel and others feared (and as happened just two years later in France). Interests account for most of the dynamics of repeal, but they do not on their own explain why reform rather than revolution emerged in mid-nineteenth-century Britain. To understand that last (quite important) fraction of the whole, we require an understanding of how the engine of interests was shaped by the forces of ideas and institutions.

This is a book about an anomaly of spectacular proportions. For more than 150 years, researchers have sought to unravel the puzzle of repeal. Indeed, this anomalous case continues to spark the curiosity of leading political scientists on both sides of the Atlantic into the twenty-first century (McLean 2001; Shepsle 2003). This book seeks to resolve this puzzle by explaining how and why interests, ideas, and institutions interacted to produce the abrupt shift to free trade. But its novelty extends beyond that. Using a variety of methodological tools to measure both quantitative and qualitative data, I show how the main concepts at stake may be quantified and studied systematically to gauge when and under what circumstances each matters. Perhaps most important, my analysis specifies the *interactive* effects of interests, ideas, and institutions. It demonstrates when interests matter more than ideas (and vice versa), when and how institutions constrain interests, and when and how interests and ideas force institutions to change. In short, it provides a causal map for the interplay between interests, ideas, and institutions. This map, in turn, speaks to the current debate in political science on the relative importance of these factors, a debate that animates large segments of the discipline of political science.

Interests, Ideas, and Institutions in Current Debates

A number of authors have recently sought to unpack the competing and complementary effects of interests, ideas, and institutions with respect to policy or institutional changes (Blyth 2002; Lieberman 2002; Golob 2003), but as yet, theory and empirical work in this area are only beginning to establish a footing. Inasmuch as disagreements about the relative importance of interests, ideas, and institutions will invariably prod researchers to specify more carefully how these influences interact, this area of study will no doubt grow. At present, the debate surrounding interests, ideas, and institutions is disparate and disjointed, and so finding a common thread is difficult. Three current controversies in different subfields of political science illustrate how this book can be said to contribute to our understanding of how interests, ideas, and institutions (the three *I*s) interact.

Comparative Politics and Beyond: Questions of Methods and Theory

In comparative politics, researchers have sought to overcome methodological and theoretical barriers to integrating the three *I*s. In his survey of the subfield, Laitin appeals to comparativists to acquire skills in multiple methodologies—namely, statistics, formal methods, and the narrative (Laitin 2002). He offers some examples of how this tripartite methodology might unfold and argues that by integrating, rather than specializing in, methods, comparativists may achieve scientific progress (Laitin 2002, 659).

The appeal itself, however, may be seen as yet another installment in the tussle between quantitative and qualitative methods, with political scientists in comparative politics and other subfields echoing the same concerns and some offering suggestions for integration (King, Keohane, et al. 1994; Laitin, Caporaso, et al. 1995; Eichengreen 1998). In the midst of this tussle lies the underlying conflict over weighting interests, ideas, and institutions. At the risk of oversimplification, researchers who engage statistics in their work also tend to highlight the role of interests. Researchers who are studying ideas and ideology, meanwhile, acknowledge that people often care about more than pecuniary self-interest; they also care about the environment, family values, national security, human dignity, and so on. But these ideas are difficult to operationalize and test, particularly compared with interest-based motivations. Hence, a qualitative approach is often preferred by these researchers. Finally, while institutional models help us to understand how interests are aggregated (or not) and how informational asymmetries affect outcomes, the lack of consensus on whether institutions are exogenous or endogenous (or both) and thus the difficulty in empirically testing their effects have created a methodological quagmire for those studying institutions (a point taken up below).

Returning to Laitin's appeal, there is much to be said for research that integrates multiple methods into a single and coherent analytical framework. This books offers an example of how a variety of methodological approaches (including statistics, a touch of formal methods, and some narrative) can be employed to answer different questions, all stemming from a single puzzle. Moreover, several of the chapters employ a new methodology—computer-assisted content analysis—which in effect quantifies qualitative (textual) data.

A second but related hurdle facing comparativists is what Hall (1997, 196) describes as a "heuristic limitation of considerable significance"— namely, the failure of "the vast majority of analyses produced by [comparative] political economists" to consider how the *process* of political conflict and political debate affects the formation of interests and coalitions of interests (Hall 1997, 196).[3] Because the process of political conflict and political debate can, in itself, shape the policy outcome (in some cases, like repeal, quite profoundly), merely identifying fixed, exogenous variables is ultimately of limited value. Individuals have multiple and sometimes conflicting interests, and their interests may become malleable in the process of political conflict, as I suggest in chapter 4. In a related vein, politicians play two roles that often collide. These two roles—the delegate (representing the interests of constituents) and the trustee (representing the larger societal welfare)—are just as relevant to contemporary politics as they were to nineteenth-century British MPs (chapters 6, 7, and 8). By definition, delegates pursue policies that serve the interests (normally economic) of their constituents, while trustees pursue policies that fulfill some idea of what constitutes the broader societal welfare. Understanding how these roles collide and evolve over time—and how they ultimately shape the policy outcome—requires an examination of the compromises that politicians make in the course of political conflict and political debate. Of key importance to the case of repeal of the Corn Laws is the compromise that some MPs made with respect to their perceived roles as both delegates and trustees. An analysis of the parliamentary debates on repeal reveals the story of *pivotal MPs who came to vote as delegates but justify these votes in terms of their perceived roles as trustees.*

Rational-Choice and Historical Institutionalism: A Question of Causality

Rational-choice institutionalism and historical institutionalism tend to agree that institutions basically consist of routines within organizations that structure and constrain the information, beliefs, incentives, choices, and, ultimately, payoffs to individuals and groups (Pierson and Skocpol 2002, 706; Weingast 2002, 661). Yet the two approaches disagree quite markedly on the appropriate time horizon for studying institutions, the extent to which institutions are exogenous or endogenous, and the relevance of "processes over time" (Pierson and Skocpol 2002, 698). On the one hand, rational-choice institutionalism has contributed extensively to our understanding of the effects of, for example, parliamentary systems, divided government, elections, and constitutions on political outcomes.[4] In short, it has enabled us to understand better the exogeneity of institutions. The approach has, however, recently begun to explore why institutions form at all, why they take the form that they do, and why they survive over time. In other words, rational-choice institutionalists have begun to model the endogeneity of institutions.[5] In contrast, a core focus of historical institutionalism is the rise and decline of institutions, and as such, the approach claims to "take time seriously" by studying institutional development in the long run (Pierson and Skocpol 2002, 695). Historical institutionalists accuse rational-choice theory of failing to move beyond micro-level, short-run analyses of institutions—in effect, of failing to conceptualize institutions as part of a broader society, within which other institutions and societal groupings operate. In the words of historical institutionalists, "Politics ends up sliced and frozen into artificial moments on the slide of a powerful but tightly focused microscope" (Pierson and Skocpol 2002, 717). Finally, the familiar quantitative and qualitative clash emerges in the preferred methodologies of the two approaches, with rational-choicers favoring quantitative and formal methods and historical institutionalists more comfortable with qualitative methods.

The gap between the approaches remains wide, but inasmuch as Weingast's survey characterizes the endogeneity of institutions as the future direction of rational-choice theory and anticipates some integration of rational-choice and historical institutionalism, there appears to be some mellowing of the rigidities that separate the two approaches. This book makes a small step toward bridging rational-choice and historical institutionalism in two ways. First, it characterizes repeal as partly the product of medium- to long-term changes in the demand for free trade. These changes in turn (1) transformed how both MPs and peers perceived their roles as representatives, (2) created two latent factions within the Conservative party, a process that led to the party's disastrous fissure, and (3) forced MPs and peers to accept repeal as the necessary concession by the landed aristocracy to retain their control of Parliament. The book examines how both interests and ideas shaped the development of the British constitution, the Conservative party, and parliamentary democracy more broadly in nineteenth-century Britain. And so *the "demand" for reform in Britain shaped the institutional setting, but, just as important, the institutional setting channeled this demand into a particular outcome that was repeal and not revolution.* The demand-side part of the argument cannot, moreover, explain the abrupt reversal in 1846 of the pivotal MPs, the Peelites. To understand this sudden and dramatic reversal, we must shift from a macro- to a micro-level: we need to know what forced Peelites to move from full support for protection in 1845 (and before) to full support for free trade in 1846.

This micro-level analysis illustrates a second way that this book helps to bridge rational-choice and historical institutionalism—its methodology. The motivation for employing computer-assisted content analysis to examine the *whole* of the parliamentary debates from the introduction of repeal by the government and its ultimate passage in both houses of Parliament was to uncover the catalyst, or unique idea, for the abrupt reversal of the Peelites. However, whatever new idea that might be uncovered as "unique" in 1846 can be said to be so only if it failed to appear in any of the debates on trade policy in the previous several decades. (Simple research design suggests that the effect of a stimulus on a particular response is better demonstrated by sampling a number of preresponse settings rather than just one.) Hence, by employing the microscope of rational-choice institutionalism several times before the critical policy shift in 1846, we gather a number of powerful and tightly focused images of the institutional context in which MPs considered trade policy. Taken together, these images paint a larger picture of how this institutional context changed during a time of rapid industrialization and widespread civil unrest (including the 1832 Reform Act agitation, Chartism, and so on).

Roll-Call Voting: Why Do Legislators Vote the Way They Do?

The fundamental question of why legislators vote the way they do has produced a lively debate among both political scientists and economists. At the heart of the debate is the question of the relative importance of constituents' economic interests, the personal ideology of legislators, and partisanship. There are two fundamental unresolved issues in this debate. The first issue is the centuries-old tension between the delegate and trustee modes of representation. As mentioned earlier, delegates are said to represent the interests (normally economic) of their constituents (Mayhew 1974), whereas trustees represent what they deem to be the national or wider public interest (Hill 1929; Eulau 1962; Davidson 1969; Uslaner 1999). With deliberate oversimplification, delegates are motivated entirely by the interests of their constituents, while trustees are motivated entirely by their own ideological predisposition. But as I discuss in chapter 6, empirical analyses of roll-call votes suggest that legislative behavior cannot be understood in a monocausal framework. Rather, it must be understood with reference to the combined influences of constituency preferences, legislators' personal ideology, and political-party allegiance (Levitt 1996; Jenkins 2000). Measuring the extent to which these factors weigh on the decisions of legislators raises a second issue of contention—namely, methodology. In the cogent words of Barbara Geddes (2003, 175–212), "The approach you choose affects the answers you get"—though in this case, it may be said that the chosen *methodology* may be driving conflicting results. On the one hand are those who use some form of a linear model to derive regression coefficients to measure the effects of interests, ideology, and party on roll-call votes (Peltzman 1984; Kalt and Zupan 1990; Snyder and Groseclose 2000, 2001) and who generally find interests or party to have greater influence than personal ideology. On the other hand are those who use a spatial model—most notably Poole and Rosenthal's NOMINATE (or DW-NOMINATE) (Poole and Rosenthal 1997; McCarty, Poole, et al. 2001)—to capture the structure of legislative voting behavior and who find the single most important factor to be the legislator's personal ideology.[6]

While this book does not purport to resolve these underlying areas of contention, it does inform the debate in three ways. First, chapter 6 presents a methodological framework for disentangling the relative influences of constituency interest, MP personal ideology, and MP party on roll-call votes in the British Parliament of 1841 to 1847. Drawing on the insights and methods applied to the American Congress, I identify and measure the interplay between interests, ideology, and party loyalties from 1841 to 1846 that provide a basis for understanding how the pivotal MPs came to reverse their position on repeal. Second, this book places an analysis of the roll-call votes within a demand-side and supply-side framework, in which interests, ideas, and institutions factor prominently. As an example, not only do I examine the interaction of constituency interests, MP personal ideology, and MP party, but I also explore how these factors were shaped by exogenous changes in institutions (such as the 1832 Reform Act) and how one of these factors—constituency interests—in turn shaped the institutional conflict over repeal that emerged between the House of Commons and the House of Lords. Third, inasmuch as methodology underpins much of the controversy over legislative voting behavior, I introduce a new method for capturing the intentions and motivations of legislators—analyzing the content of their speeches. While others have explored this avenue (Austen-Smith and Riker 1987, 1990; Austen-Smith 1990),[7] American political scientists do not appear to have subsequently taken up Austen-Smith and Riker's interest in legislative debates, in contrast to recent work by European political scientists (including Laver, Benoit, et al. 2003). One possible reason might be that in the American case, committees are fundamentally important in shaping legislation and so floor debate might be said to be less important to the final outcome. In comparison, no equivalent committee structure existed in the British Parliament of the nineteenth century, and so floor debate can be said to have been more relevant to the final legislative outcome. The content of parliamentary debates is analyzed extensively in this book (chapters 7, 8, and 9), and as a result I am able to obtain an understanding of the process by which the pivotal MPs came to change their position on repeal. Perhaps more intriguingly, content analysis of the debates, merged with more traditional content analysis of local newspapers, allows me to measure the effects of constituency interests *and ideas* on both how MPs voted and the rationale they gave for how they voted.

This discussion in no way exhausts key debates in political science in which interests, ideas, and institutions are contested. These examples do, however, help to motivate both the substantive and methodological content of this book. Repeal, in short, provides an outstanding case specimen with which to investigate the interaction of interests, ideas, and institutions. In the search for the holy grail of politics—namely, a general theory of the interaction of the three *Is*—the study of repeal may very well provide a small, first step. We now turn to set the prehistory, or backdrop, for this investigation.

The Backdrop for Repeal[8]

1815 and the Sliding Scale

Government regulation of exports and imports of corn was well established long before the nineteenth century (Barnes 1930). The Corn Laws of the seventeenth and eighteenth centuries had a dual purpose: they sought to prevent "grain from being at any time, either so dear that the poor cannot subsist, or so cheap that the farmer cannot live by growing of it" (Smith n.d., quoted in Fay 1932, 34). The Napoleonic wars brought a fundamental change in the history of the Corn Laws. During the war years, agriculturists enjoyed high grain prices, but with the peace prices fell dramatically.[9] In response, Parliament enacted the Corn Law of 1815, which allowed free entry when the price of corn was above 80 shillings per quarter and prohibited entry when the price fell below 80 shillings. Some argue that this new legislation, unlike that of the earlier Corn Laws, was "defiantly protective": "It sought to fasten on a country at peace the protection furnished by a generation of war" (Fay 1932, 35).[10] Others maintain, however, that fear of scarcity drove government policy. Rapid population growth and a dependence on foreign corn are said to have justified a policy of self-sufficiency based on concerns for national security (Hilton 1977, 20–26).[11] A third rationale for the move to protection is that the government hurriedly passed the legislation to gain the support of landowners as it scrambled to pay its war debt.[12]

The 1815 law suffered from two basic flaws: it generated no government revenue from protection, and it was too rigid. Public petitions of distress that resulted from the 1815 law were directed to a Select Committee of the House of Commons, whose report was drafted by William Huskisson. In the report, Huskisson called for a return to the "practically free" trade that existed before 1815 (Fay 1932, 80). The Act of 1822 allowed wheat to be imported when the domestic price reached 80 shillings per quarter, but when the price fell to 70 shillings, imports were again prohibited. Between 1822 and 1828, the price never reached 80 shillings, and thus the act never came into effect. In 1822, David Ricardo proposed that protection should be withdrawn gradually, beginning with a fixed duty of 20 shillings and lowered by annual reductions of 1 shilling until it reached 10 shillings, where it would then remain.[13] By 1827, discussion was not of free trade in corn but rather of the choice between a fixed duty (as Ricardo had suggested) or a sliding scale (as Huskisson, president of the Board of Trade, proposed). The fixed duty avoided the problem of averaging prices, which any sliding scale would face. George Canning (Foreign Secretary)[14] and others stressed that a fixed duty would not allow flexibility in times of scarcity, posing the likelihood that the government would be forced to suspend the duty during such times.[15] Other politicians favored the sliding scale because it, unlike the fixed duty that was favored by the "cold-blooded political economists," was based on "experience" and not "theory."[16] Huskisson's justification for the sliding scale was that it remedied the worst feature of 1815—rigidity. The agriculturists rejected Huskisson's 1827 bill, however, on the grounds that his pivot point of 60 shillings (from which the duty of 20 shillings would gradually descend) would afford them inadequate protection. In drafting the 1827 bill, Huskisson and the Duke of Wellington (to become Prime Minister in 1828) became embroiled in a fundamental disagreement: the former sought to move toward freer trade in corn, while the latter sought to consolidate protection for agriculture.[17] In 1828, Huskisson and Wellington agreed on a sliding-scale tariff for corn, so that as the price rose, the duty would fall. Fay described the 1828 sliding scale as "Huskisson's sliding scale spoiled" (Fay 1932, 84). While Huskisson suggested a pivot point of 60 or 62 shillings, the 1828 act legislated 66 shillings. According to the 1828 act, when the price of British wheat was 52 shillings per quarter or below, the duty would be 34 shillings, 8 pence; as the price rose, the duty would fall to 1 shilling when the price hit 73 shillings. The 1828 scale also differed from Huskisson's in that it introduced large jumps in the scale (a 13 shillings, 8 pence, duty at a price of 69 shillings and a 1 shilling duty at a price of 73 shillings). Speculators took advantage of the rapid descent of the scale when prices were high, withholding sales until the price rose 1 or 2 shillings to avoid the payment of duties. In spite of this defect, the 1828 act continued to operate until Peel introduced a modified sliding scale in 1842. Peel's sliding scale differed from both the 1827 bill and the 1828 act in that it abolished the pivot point. Peel also lessened the incentive for speculation by smoothing out the scale at the lower end and reducing the maximum duty to 20 shillings when the price hit 51 shillings or below.

In brief, 1815, 1828, and 1842 were the years of significant changes in the Corn Laws. Paralleling the history of Corn Law legislation were major demographic and economic changes that cut against the fabric of protection for food. From 1811 to 1841, the population of Great Britain increased from 12.6 million to 18 million, and British farmers were becoming less able to provide sufficient supplies for the home market. This said, while Britain had not been self-sufficient in corn since the early 1760s, British agriculturists "still managed to feed every year on the average all except about 700,000 and as late as 1831–1840, all except about 1,050,000 of the population" (Chaloner 1968, x). A second factor proved more fatal to the Corn Laws—the growth of British manufacturing industry and export trade, especially in textiles. More particularly, as the industrial prosperity and export boom of the early 1830s began to weaken, industrialists became increasingly vocal about "unfair" protection enjoyed by the agriculturists. Beginning in 1836, an economic downturn together with a series of poor harvests sparked the industrialists into action. High food prices and unemployment gave impetus both to the middle and working classes, the former organized as the Anti-Corn Law League and the latter as the Chartist movement.

The League Machine
The Anti-Corn Law League was the first modern and national-level political pressure group to emerge in Britain.[18] It began in London in 1836 as the Anti-Corn Law Association, but by 1838 had found its natural base in Manchester. The leaders of the League were manufacturers and professionals engaged in export trade, most of whom were concentrated in the county of Lancashire. Foremost among its leaders were two cotton textile manufacturers—Richard Cobden and John Bright. In the course of the struggle against the Corn Laws, both were to become Members of Parliament—Cobden for Stockport and Bright for Durham. Another key MP in the Corn Law struggle was Charles Villiers, Member for Wolverhampton. It was Villiers who became famous for his annual motions for repeal of the Corn Laws, which began in 1838 and continued to 1846.

Historians refer to the League as "the most impressive of nineteenth-century pressure groups, which exercised a distinct influence on the repeal of the Corn Laws in 1846" (Howe 1984, p. 208).[19] It was called the "League machine," whose organization "presents one of the first examples of a recurring feature of modern political life, the highly organised political pressure group with its centralised administration and its formidable propaganda apparatus" (McCord 1958, 187). The *Times* even led with an article announcing the League as "a great fact" (Prentice

1968, 1: 149–152).[20] The two key features of the League's operational strategy were its nationwide propaganda and electoral registration campaigns. The League raised substantial subscriptions to finance its propaganda campaign. It maintained a small army of workers and speakers, who toured the country distributing numerous tracts (most notably, the famous *Anti-Corn Law Circular*)[21] and giving thousands of speeches on the virtues of free trade and the evils of protection. The registration campaign was the League's tool for replacing protectionist landowners in Parliament with free-trade supporters. After electoral losses for free traders in 1841 and 1842, the League focused its energy and resources on returning a free-trade majority in the anticipated general election of 1848. To achieve this, its leaders adopted a tactical strategy that included manipulating the voter registers and employing propaganda devices with existing voters. Looking toward the 1848 election, the League sought to add as many free traders and delete as many protectionists from these registers as possible. The latter they accomplished by making objections against thousands of protectionists at the annual revisions of the registers. The former required a different tactic—exploiting a feature of the Reform Act of 1832 (which effectively enfranchised the middle class). This feature was the 40 shilling county-property qualification, which Bright referred to as "the great constitutional weapon which we intend to wield."[22] While the 40 shilling qualification had been in place since 1430, the increase in county seats from 188 to 253 (an increase from roughly 29 percent to 38 percent of the total seats) magnified the importance of the 40 shilling franchise in the 1832 Reform Act.[23] The League used the 40 shilling qualification to create several thousand new free-trade voters in county constituencies with large urban electorates, constituencies whose representation was increased by the Reform Act. Leaguers even urged parents to create a nest-egg for a son by making him a freeholder: in Cobden's words, "it is an act of duty, for you make him thereby an independent freeman, and put it in his power to defend himself and his children from political oppression."[24] In spite of Appeal Court rulings in February 1845 and January 1846 that votes created by the 40 shilling freehold qualification were valid, protectionists continued to challenge the constitutionality of the League's registration campaign, and Leaguers continued to defend their activities.[25]

The propaganda and registration campaigns, moreover, were brought together to further the political success of the League. As its agents distributed propaganda tracts to every elector in twenty-four county divisions and 187 boroughs, they submitted to the League headquarters consistent and complete reports on the electorate in their districts. These reports provided the League with a comprehensive picture of the electoral scene throughout England, thereby allowing it much greater knowledge of and control over electoral districts than either the Conservatives or Liberals possessed "with their more limited and local organisation" (McCord 1958, 147–150). The earlier distribution of propaganda tracts thus provided the League with an extensive database from which they could inflict political pressure on Members of Parliament, who were concerned with their bids for reelection in the anticipated 1848 election.

By 1844, the League had established itself as a formidable political and ideological force for free trade. Its registration campaign in the counties created a remarkable number of free-trade electors, as chapter 2 (table 2.1) details. Chapters 3 and 4 further describe the impressive organizational and ideological successes of the League. By 1844, the defensive Anti-League (or Agricultural Protection Society),[26] however, emerged in response to the League, yet this group of protectionist landowners and farmers never obtained the same momentum or backing as the League. According to Chaloner, the Anti-League "failed to make an impression on British agricultural policy because Conservative politicians were reluctant to speak or vote against Sir Robert Peel until 1846, and it cannot be said that its literary contribution was as solid or as logical as that of the Free Traders" (Chaloner 1970, 146). In financial terms, while the League grew from a £5,000 annual fund in 1839 to one of £250,000 in 1845, the latter year saw the core of the Anti-League (the Essex Agricultural Protection Society) scraping together the paltry sum of £2,000 to fund its campaign (McCord 1958; Crosby 1976).

A second challenge to the League was the Chartist movement. The Chartists were an organized working-class movement that sought parliamentary reform, arguing that reform must encompass the entire social and political horizon. In contrast, the League chose a single-issue strategy to gain repeal. Clashes between the Chartists and the League often erupted into open hostility and violence, as Chartists viewed Leaguers as traitors to the reform movement, and conversely, Leaguers criticized Chartists for pushing unrealistic reforms and thereby threatening to sabotage their focused strategy.[27]

Peel's Motion to Repeal

Clearly, momentum was building for repeal, but the governing Conservative party, led by Sir Robert Peel, had committed itself to protection when entering office in 1841. Conservatives had, moreover, unanimously defended this policy against a number of radical-led motions for repeal in the years leading up to 1846. But Peel persuaded his cabinet colleagues to reverse their position on repeal in the late autumn of 1845, thereby paving the way for his introduction of the repeal legislation in January 1846. Unlike McLean (2001, 33–56), this book does not aim to understand the psychology of Peel's reversal.[28] Rather, my intent is to unravel the motivations of those who followed him and, in particular, those Conservatives (MPs and peers) who had been, up to 1846, steadfast defenders of a policy of protection for agriculture. Peel's motion in January 1846 sets the stage for their conversion, and as such, his three-hour speech was vital.

Peel's speech in the first reading of the repeal legislation[29] provided a multifaceted justification for repeal. For the nation as a whole, Peel argued that the principle of free trade was welfare-enhancing because it would (1) allow Britain to retain its preeminence in world trade (thereby staving off foreign competition); (2) be a winning strategy, regardless of whether other countries reciprocated with lower duties; and (3) not result in a loss to public revenue, as the trade and industrial prosperity combined with the new income tax would offset the lost income from duties. Quoting League sources, Peel explained why he believed that the prosperity following the 1842 reduction of duties could not continue without further liberalization.

At the heart of Peel's speech was a plea to the opposing manufacturing and agricultural interests to accept a policy of mutual concessions. He urged manufacturers to forfeit their remaining protective duties on woolens, linen, silks, and other manufactured goods to adhere to the general rule that no duty should exceed 10 percent (15 percent for silks). He introduced a further simplification of the tariff code and reduced tariffs on a number of other items (shoes, spirits, and sugar). His greatest hurdle, however, was to gain the support of the agriculturists. Duties on certain foods (butter, cheese, hops, and fish) would be reduced, while those on others (meat, beef, port, potatoes, vegetables, bacon, and other nongrains) would be abolished. Grain protection would be abolished as of 1849. After discounting the link between bread prices and wages, Peel sought to address two issues associated with the clash of interests. First, in regard to class conflict, Peel argued that agitation had grown to such an extent that the government had no option but to act to appease the industrial and working classes. Second, the "heavy" financial burden of the landowning classes was lessened by a number of incentives to agriculturists—a consolidation of the highways system, relief to rural districts from pauperism, a number of expenses shifted from the counties to the Consolidated Fund, and finally loans for agricultural improvements at moderate interest rates.

While this detailed and comprehensive rationale for repeal was intended to convert as many wavering and even hostile MPs as possible, it fails to speak to the political *process* that unfolded in Parliament over the next several months. That is, it provides no clue about which, if any, of Peel's many appeals bore fruit. To gain some insight into Peel's assessment of the *process* of repeal, three of his postrepeal statements require attention. First, in Peel's final speech as Prime Minister, before being ousted in early summer 1846, Peel credited Richard Cobden, Anti-Corn Law League leader, with the success of repeal (quoted in Prentice 1968, 339–340):

I must say, with reference to hon. gentlemen opposite, as I say with reference to ourselves, neither of us is the party which is justly entitled to the credit of [repeal]. There has been a combination of parties, and that combination, and the influence of government, have led to their ultimate success; but the name which ought to be, and will be associated with the success of those measures, is the name of the man who, acting, I believe, from pure and disinterested motives, has, with untiring energy, by appeals to reason, enforced their necessity with an eloquence the more to be admired because it was unaffected and unadorned—the name which ought to be associated with the success of those measures, is the name of RICHARD COBDEN.

This statement can be read as testament both to the free-trade ideals propagated by Cobden and, by inference, to the organization to which he invested his free-trade campaign—the Anti-Corn Law League.

In a second statement two years after repeal, Peel shifted attention from the free-trade ideals behind repeal to focus on the political importance of the interests clamoring for repeal. At this point, the passage of repeal can be seen as part of a more elaborate exercise in concessionary politics.[30] The following quote from Cobden's biographer, Morley (1881, 1: 407) provides a telling portrayal of Peel's reaction to the Revolution of 1848 in France:

It was just because the sober portion of the House of Commons were aware from how limited and exclusive a source they drew their authority, that the League represented so formidable, because so unknown, a force. The same thought was present to the reflective mind of Peel. Cobden tells a story in one of his speeches which illustrates this. One evening in 1848 they were sitting in the House of Commons, when the news came that the government of Louis Philippe had been overthrown and a republic proclaimed. When the buzz of conversation ran round the House, as the startling intelligence was passed from member to member, Cobden said to Joseph Hume, who sat beside him, "Go across and tell Sir Robert Peel." Hume went to the front bench opposite, where Sir Robert was sitting in his usual isolation. "This comes," said Peel, when Hume had whispered the catastrophe, "this comes of trying to govern the country through a narrow representation in Parliament, without regarding the wishes of those outside. It is what this party behind me wanted me to do in the matter of the Corn Laws, and I would not do it."

Peel suggested that he sought repeal to "satisfy the wishes of those outside"—the middle-class industrialists. He implied that a "narrow representation in Parliament"—control of Parliament by the landed aristocracy—required that concessions be made to satisfy interests clamoring for reform. The alternative, he implied, was that pressures for reform might have become overwhelming, as the French case exemplified. Peel and his supporters took to heart Cobden's remark in December 1845 (when it was becoming evident that Peel's government would move for repeal) that "We should have liked to have had another year of qualification for counties. If we had had another year or two, we could have shown the monopolist landowners that we can transfer power in this country from the hands of a class totally into the hands of the middle and industrial classes of this country" (quoted in Searle 1993, 43). As Searle and other historians conclude, "As it was, Peel, through his timely concession, brought the League's campaign to an abrupt halt before the registration drive and the purchase of 40 s. freeholds had got into full swing. The outcome was a Parliament still heavily under aristocratic control" (Searle 1993, 43). In sum, repeal was an attempt to moderate the mounting pressures for parliamentary reform: by satisfying the middle-class industrialists with repeal, the drive to gain control of parliamentary seats would cease, and, moreover, the working-class Chartist movement (seeking more radical reform of Parliament) would lose momentum.

Finally, Peel died suddenly in 1850,[31] but his memoirs were published by his trustees a few years later. Many sections of these memoirs are devoted to repeal, and one would expect to find a full account of his motives behind repeal and perhaps also his perspective on the *process* that led to its passage. Instead, we find that Peel's account of repeal is presented as a collection of personal correspondence and cabinet memoranda, prefaced with two items. First, he presented his 1847 letter to his Tamworth constituency, providing a reasoned explanation of repeal based on the economic merits of free trade and the positive, though limited, experiences with liberal economic policies passed in 1842. (Taking this at face value—and ignoring all the subsequent documents—one might interpret free-trade ideology as the prime motivator for Peel.) Second, he justified the subsequent collection of documents (in lieu of a personal narrative) as containing "a more faithful narrative and explanation of that which took place than any that memory could supply" (Peel 1857, 98). He then (perhaps inadvertently) teased future historians to decipher from the subsequent documents (running to 250 pages) the motives of his government and the supporters of repeal (Peel 1857, 107):

In giving these documents at length, I may perhaps overrate their importance, and unduly to assume that the interest which at one time they might have derived from party excitement will survive its abatement. They are, however, the materials from which the future historian will extract that which is worthy of permanent record, and from which, with the aid of other contemporary evidence, he will pronounce his judgment on the motives and conduct of public men.

From these documents, however, *many* theories for repeal might be constructed—and, indeed, they have. Peel, in effect, almost deliberately launched a century and a half of competing explanations for the underlying causes of repeal. Indeed, the vast array of documents emanating from the Anti-Corn Law League, the Anti-Anti-Corn Law League, the classical economists, the parliamentary debates, and so on has provided academics with a mountain of conflicting evidence from which to glean truth from fiction. So how have they fared?

Explanations of Repeal

The Political Struggle and a Timely Concession
Elsewhere I have surveyed explanations for repeal and its aftermath (Schonhardt-Bailey 1997, 1: 1–51), and so the following provides only of an overview of the debate. A good beginning is the conclusion of the first historian to document repeal—Archibald Prentice—who just

a few short years after repeal compiled a comprehensive two-volume (nearly 900-page) history of the Anti-Corn Law League. Characterizing the campaign in terms of class struggle, he concluded in 1853 that (Prentice 1968, 2: 444)

> Not one of the ruinous results prophecied, have occurred from the repeal of the Corn Laws; and those who laboured for the destruction of those poverty-creating enactments, can now look with deep satisfaction on the improved condition of the great mass of the people, emancipated from a cruel subjection to class interests.

The bitter class fury to which Peel claimed he responded with the repeal legislation is obvious from this conclusion. A little over 100 years later, historians continued along much the same lines, with McCord remarking that repeal "marked a further diminution in the control of national affairs by the aristocracy." He argued that "repeal carried further one of the results of the Reform Act of 1832; the new influences of modern Britain, whose importance had received partial recognition in 1832, had forced a way into the governing group for their representatives" (McCord 1958, 215). More recently, Searle has embellished this distinctly *political* explanation for repeal, characterizing the League as "an assault by an 'excluded' urban elite on the social dominance and virtual monopoly of political power of the aristocratic Establishment" (Searle 1993, 19). At the heart of this establishment was the "territorial constitution," or the landed basis of the British constitution. As discussed further in chapter 7, the rationale for the territorial constitution was that those individuals most affected by government policy (understood to be landowners) should be the ones to dictate those policies. And for these landowners, free trade represented a threat not only (and perhaps not even foremost) to their wealth but to their social and political status. For the Conservative party, in particular, protection for agriculture was the cornerstone to the territorial constitution. At least, this was the traditional view of Conservatives. Yet as early as 1843, Peel began to raise the possibility of other ways to ensure the preservation of the territorial constitution (or territorial aristocracy), as evidenced by his last sentence in the following quote (cited in Searle 1993, 42):

> I believe it to be of utmost importance that a territorial aristocracy should be maintained. I believe that in no country is it of more importance than in this, with its ancient constitution, ancient habits, and mixed form of government. I trust that a territorial aristocracy, with all its just influence and authority, will

long be maintained. I believe such an aristocracy to be essential to the purposes of good government. The question only is—what, in a certain state of public opinion, and in a certain position of society, is the most effectual way of maintaining the legitimate influence and authority of a territorial aristocracy.

Thus, while Peel—and indeed all Conservatives—remained firmly wedded to the territorial constitution, the link between this and protection began to undergo scrutiny and in 1846 finally broke, as chapter 7 documents.

In the end, Peel and his followers are deemed to have sacrificed protection to preserve their privileged status. Whether this then "ushered in an 'Indian summer of the British aristocracy'" or "was 'tantamount to accepting the middle-class view of the national interest, which placed the needs of consumers and the prosperity of producers before the unearned incomes of the landlords'" is a debate among historians that this book does not address (Searle 1993, 44). What *is* relevant here is that political scientists and economic historians have repeatedly challenged (or deliberately ignored) this *political* interpretation of repeal.

Repeal as the Product of Free-Trade Ideology
As suggested above, the documentary evidence from repeal (including Peel's own memoirs) has invited scholars to construct a number of competing hypotheses. In contrast to the political explanation, a number of economists and political scientists have argued that it was the economic logic of free trade that ultimately persuaded both Peel and his followers. Kindleberger, for example, faulted a number of "economic theories of representative democracy"[32] for failing to account for repeal. He credits Ricardo, Cobden, and others with bringing about repeal. Repeal constituted "the intellectual triumph of political economists...[who] represented a rapidly rising ideology of freedom for industry to buy in the cheapest and sell in the dearest market." Moreover, the other European countries formed "a single entity which moved to free trade for ideological or perhaps doctrinal reasons. Manchester and the English political economists persuaded Britain which persuaded Europe, by precept and example."[33] In a related vein, Rohrlich has asserted that it was not so much liberalism per se that led to repeal but rather the emergence of market liberalism within a uniquely British "economic culture."[34] For Rohrlich, repeal occurred as British society as a whole rapidly shifted its beliefs about political economy. Finally, Howe credits the permanence of free trade with its ideological appeal to common British voter:

Britain's loyalty to free trade in the long run is... primarily to be explained by the early appeal of free trade to her politicians as an ideology and practice of state autonomy, and the subsequent centrality of free trade to the values and opinions of the electorate. Free trade in the 1840s may have been an essential component of the evangelical world-view, but after 1846 it was also propagated as a value to which all Victorians... subscribed, and whose longest adherents were Liberal and Labour working-class voters.[35]

Hence, in the views of Kindleberger, Rohrlich, and Howe, free-trade ideology caused a general shift in the cultural orientation of the British public.

A slightly different approach is taken by Irwin and Hilton, who focus predominantly on Peel's conversion. Irwin argues that Peel's change of mind was not a matter of shifting from protection to free trade but rather from believing that agriculture was an exception to the general rule of free trade to believing that free trade should *include* agriculture. In his view, both ideology and the experience of the 1842 reforms helped to persuade Peel.[36] Hilton lends a moral tone to Peel's conversion, arguing that Peel came to believe that repeal was morally imperative for the British state.[37]

All these authors maintain that the driving force behind repeal was not politics or economic interests but rather the persuasive logic of Manchester school liberalism.

Economic Interests and Repeal

Interest-based explanations for repeal divide into two levels—micro-level analyses of key actors or groups (industrialists, landowners, and the Anti-Corn Law League) and macro-level analyses of Britain's relative gains (or losses) from free trade. At the micro-level, Anderson and Tollison argue that the Anti-Corn Law League served as an agent for the cotton textile industry. In their view, the League sought primarily to retard the passage of factory legislation, and repeal was only secondary to that goal. In contrast to this view, chapter 3 finds that free-trade interests had actually spread throughout the country (both from export-sector deconcentration and geographic deconcentration).[38] At the same time, the leading export industry (cotton textiles) had become both industrially (among firms) and geographically more concentrated. Thus, the organization of the League benefited from the best of both worlds—a deconcentrated export sector and a concentrated leading export industry. Moreover, in chapter 5 we find that because landowners' portfolios had become increasingly diversified, with income from rent invested in railway and industry shares, their resistance to agricultural free trade had lessened.[39]

At the macro-level, Stein poses a stark dilemma between absolute gains and relative gains from trade.[40] Britain did indeed enjoy absolute gains from free trade, but these were purchased (in Stein's view) at the expense of forgoing relative gains that a protectionist policy would have delivered. Cain and Hopkins extend Gallagher and Robinson's theory of "free-trade imperialism," arguing that Britain's ultimate goal in repeal was to persuade rival countries to forgo industrialization in favor of agricultural production by opening the British market to their agricultural exports.[41] For them, as for Lake and James, repeal was intended not as unilateral policy but rather as a way to preserve an industrial monopoly.[42] For Lake and James, Britain exercised its hegemonic leadership by inducing other countries—and particularly the United States—to follow its lead. They argue that repeal constituted a subtle and indirect form of coercive hegemonic leadership: it allowed Britain to alter the incentives of American producers to facilitate the emergence of the free-trade coalition. In contrast, Pahre downplays the significance of repeal, arguing that British free trade began in the 1820s, not the 1840s (Pahre 1997). For Pahre, relative gains from free trade are closely tied to a hegemon's external security arrangements—namely, whether it leads a large military coalition. Because Britain lacked allies after the Napoleonic wars (when the Quadruple Alliance fell apart), it ascertained that a large military establishment would provoke others to enhance their own military security. It therefore chose a policy of military restraint and economic openness. For the authors who focus on the macro-level, domestic interests and politics were shaped by Britain's concern with its relative position in the international arena. For the micro-level group of authors, on the other hand, Britain's shift in policy was the product of domestic pressures.

A Story of Institutions
Verdier rejects entirely that repeal was an economic struggle. He contends that repeal was an institutional struggle over the relative power of Parliament and the cabinet (Verdier 1997, 4: 312):

The repeal of the Corn Laws took place amidst a long-standing dispute between the frontbench and the backbench of the Conservative party on the nature of the party as a policymaking organisation. The backbench saw the party as an electoral organisation with little policymaking extension and thus limited rights to invoke voting discipline. The party for them was a convenient way of stabilising logrolling among particular, locally-entrenched interests. In contrast, the frontbench viewed the party as a full-fledged policymaking institution, requiring voting discipline from its members for the passage of measures of a general character.

This intrapartisan political struggle is said to have represented a choice between two different regime types: "the centralized, rigid, dogmatic system of party government which eventually stabilized in late-Victorian Britain, or the decentralized, penetrated, clientelistic, graft-ridden system which thrived in the USA" (Verdier 1997, 4: 312).

As this brief survey illustrates, the causes of repeal are much disputed. Segments of the political interpretation have been taken up by the economic interests perspective, inasmuch as class and sectoral interests clearly overlap. But other explanations for repeal reject—directly or indirectly—the notion that repeal was a concession by the aristocracy to retain control of Parliament. We are left in a fog of conflicting arguments and conflicting evidence. The mountain of evidence that has puzzled and intrigued scholars for over 150 years has also allowed them to become stuck in that area of knowledge and argumentation that is of greatest interest or familiarity. No scholar to date has attempted systematically to examine the evidence to obtain a more informed judgment as to the appropriate weights that should be assigned to interests, ideas, and institutions. Moreover, no one has taken this exercise one step further to gauge the interactive effects of interests, ideas, and institutions on the repeal of the Corn Laws.

Identifying the Relevant Interests, Ideas, and Institutions

Simply identifying which interests, ideas, and institutions mattered for repeal is a worthwhile task but ultimately is of limited value. Most social scientists would accept that all three factors matter, though to varying extents. This book details *how*, *when*, and *why* interests, ideas, and institutions came to play a part in repeal. It also maps out a dynamic between these three factors that culminated in the perplexing policy outcome.

Until now, I have assumed that interests, ideas, and institutions are all concepts with which readers are familiar. To a large extent, this is probably true, but for the sake of clarity, it is worth explaining these terms as they are used in this book. It should also be stated that my application of these terms is targeted at the case of nineteenth-century

Britain; however, as will be seen, a number of features from this application can easily extend to a broad array of political settings.

Interests

In a political economy setting, interests are usually either economic or political. Economic actors seek to maximize their income (or wealth) while political actors maximize the probability of gaining or retaining public office.[43] To a greater or lesser extent, policy preferences derive from actors' interests—meaning that interests (economic or political) can be mitigated by other factors, including ideology, party affiliation, and institutional constraints. Preferences thus derive from interests but are not synonymous with interests. As Milner aptly notes, "Interests are the stable foundation on which actors' preferences over policy shift as their situation and the policy area vary."[44] Interests are simply one of the essential raw ingredients from which preferences are formed. More vividly, they may be seen as the engine that drives preferences.

In the case of repeal, the two sets of interests at loggerheads were those of industrialists (who sought free trade in agriculture as a means to expand Britain's export trade) and landowners (whose economic, social, and political status was intimately connected with protection for agriculture). Chapter 3 shows how the industrialists were able to organize for collective action in the Anti-Corn Law League as a result of a unique configuration of concentrated and dispersed interests. This chapter presents a modified version of the public-choice interest-group model that integrates concentrated and deconcentrated interests with successful lobbying. Effective free-trade lobbying required the political fusion of the economic interests representing two fundamental changes in nineteenth-century Britain's economy: (1) geographic concentration of the core export industry (cotton textiles) and (2) deconcentration of the broader export sector both geographically and in terms of industrial structure. Empirical evidence from both national and individual levels supports the contention that the timing and political success of the Anti-Corn Law League required the combined forces of core export interests and the more diverse and geographically more evenly distributed interests of the export sector as a whole.

Over roughly the same time period, the policy preferences of landowners on average became slightly less protectionist as their incomes became less tied to agricultural rents. Chapter 5 provides evidence to suggest that MPs from constituencies with more such diversified landowners were also more likely to support free trade, thus demonstrating a link between a reduced demand for protection and support for repeal. The driving force behind the diversification of the asset portfolios of landowners was the rapidly emerging capital market, evidenced in the 1830s by the spread of stock-market activity throughout Britain. The combination of a large role for direct investment (in the form of direct ownership of industrial production by landowners) and the development of securities markets enabled some profit-maximizing landowners to switch into industrial investment, which in turn influenced their trade preferences. Support for this argument is found from analysis of data from both the individual level (death-duty registers) and aggregate level (income-tax-return schedules).

Finally, chapter 6 dissects the influences of constituency interests, party, and ideology on the votes of MPs before and as they considered repealing the Corn Laws in 1846. While the Conservative party shared a distinct ideology, it was also a coalition of two interest-based alliances. The Non-Peelite Conservatives represented mostly (protectionist-oriented) agricultural districts, while the Peelites represented districts with more free-trade leaning (and more diversified) interests. Before 1846, Peelites voted according to a general Conservative ideology, but in 1846 an abrupt change occurred: the pivotal Peelites appear to have eschewed Conservative party unity and their own personal ideology in favor more of the preferences of their constituents. Repeal appears to have gained passage as these MPs switched from voting more as trustees to voting more as delegates.

In sum, then, interests—or more specifically, *changes* in the composition of interests—account for the net increase in demand for free trade from the late 1830s and early 1840s. A purely demand-side perspective of repeal might stop at this point, as the focus on interests is relatively elegant, and testing hypotheses derived from such a model is methodologically manageable.[45] Interests describe very well the engine or the force that drove repeal to the doors of Parliament. They cannot, however, tell us why a Conservative government that was committed to protection would suddenly and dramatically reverse its course in 1846 and thus suffer disastrous consequences to itself and its party as a result. Interests inform us of the "necessary" conditions for repeal (for instance, as will be described in chapter 2, the conversion of more and more Liberals to free trade) but say nothing about the "sufficient" conditions. In this context, an account of the sufficient causes of repeal would require (1) a rationale for the *abrupt* reversal of that portion of the Conservative party that supported Peel's legislation (the Peelites) and (2) an understanding of the origins of the split in the Conservative party over repeal, in particular how the Peelites managed to reconcile their support for repeal with a Conservative ideology in which protection for agriculture had been paramount and how the Lords—a chamber of landowning aristocrats who were by definition immune from electoral constraints—came to endorse repeal, in spite of its constitutional veto power.

Ideas and Ideology
Ideas are not ideologies, since the latter usually implies some fairly coherent collection of the former. My intention is not to ring fence ideas from ideologies but rather to analyze the uses to which ideas *and* ideologies are put—particularly in shaping policy preferences. Shepsle depicts ideas as "the hooks on which politicians hang their objectives and by which they further their interests" (Shepsle 1985, 233). Chapter 4 shows how these hooks might work in lobbying behavior as groups appeal to nongroup members with the use of popular images and myths. Yet chapter 4 and later chapters illustrate that ideas are not mere fig leafs for interests. Ideas form a critical component of the mix that comprises actors' preferences. If interests may be seen as the engine that drives preferences, ideas comprise both the intellect and emotion that *inspire* actors.[46]

Ideas such as "anti-aristocracy" and the inherent "morality of free trade" inspired the message of the Anti-Corn Law League (chapter 4), thereby contributing significantly to its success. The Anti-Corn Law League invoked a particular strategy (which I call "nationalizing the interest") in which it appealed to the general British public to support repealing the Corn Laws. Key to this strategy was the use of unifying themes or ideas, particularly ones that were linked to the broader societal welfare. This chapter explores how the League exploited this strategy and lays the groundwork for more empirical examinations of the effects of the League's efforts on MPs and peers in part 2 of this book.

The League also embodied the idea of democratic change in the composition of Parliament. Indeed, this would have been the likely result of its registration campaign. Repeal became intertwined with the drive to replace protectionist MPs with free-trade MPs and thereby erode (if not destroy) the aristocratic control of Parliament. In short, repeal promised to serve as the mechanism for (at least partial) democratic reform of Parliament, a prospect that alarmed Peel and the Lords and put them on a defensive footing. The League thus convinced both

Peel and the Lords that repeal was a concession worth making to stave off more radical reform.

Applying computer-assisted content analysis, chapter 7 shows that to push the wavering Peelite Conservatives over the brink, a supply-side reinterpretation of repeal itself was required. Peel offered a somewhat vague reinterpretation when he introduced the repeal bill, characterizing repeal as a means to preserve the landed basis of Parliament. Peelites immediately latched onto this reinterpretation as it offered them a way to represent more faithfully their constituents' interests *and* appear to remain faithful to Conservatism. That is, the reinterpretation of repeal allowed Peelites to vote more as delegates (representing the increasing free-trade orientation of their constituencies) but to justify their betrayal of a protectionist Conservative ideology in the language of disinterested and moral trustees whose motive was only to promote the nation's economic and social well-being. In spatial terms, this reinterpretation of repeal constitutes a second dimension that split the Conservatives on the question of how best to preserve the landed basis of Parliament.

One simplistic "ideas" interpretation of the Peelites might suggest that they converted to repeal entirely from loyalty to Peel and the desire to maintain political stability, while a second equally simplistic "interests" interpretation might suggest that the Peelites—and indeed most Liberal MPs—acquiesced in the face of constituency pressures. The findings of chapter 7 tell a more subtle story of the interaction of ideas and interests, and perhaps most important, it shows us *how* each mattered in this setting.

The astute critic might argue that a simpler account of repeal might conflate the ideas propagated by the League with the changing constituency interests to sustain a demand-side model of repeal. It could be argued that the addition of a supply-side perspective is unnecessary and that all that is needed is to interpret constituency demands as stemming from both ideas and interests. In this view, Peelites might be argued to have reversed their stance as a result of the intense lobbying of the League. In short, *ideas* stemming from constituents, rather than their interests, may have converted the pivotal MPs to free trade. Chapter 10 tests this hypothesis explicitly by measuring the free-trade ideas that MPs were exposed to in their constituencies from 1841 to 1846 and then linking this to their voting records in Parliament. I use local newspaper coverage of trade policy in 1841 and 1846 to compare the prevalence of free-trade ideas in the districts of Peelites and Non-

Peelite Conservatives to examine the change from 1841 to 1846. The results provide empirical evidence of the increased intensity in lobbying by the Anti-Corn Law League from 1841 to 1846, thereby increasing the demand for repeal. Yet it is also found that Peelites did not experience any dramatic changes in the ideas to which they were exposed in their constituencies—more to the point, the effect of free-trade ideas on the voting behavior of Peelites appears to be almost nonexistent. This strengthens the argument that the abrupt reversal of the Peelites was not simply the product of demand-side pressures.

Institutions

One can hardly quibble with Douglass North's classic definition of institutions as "the rules of the game in a society or; more formally, the humanely devised constraints that shape human interaction" (North 1990, 3). Narrowing this somewhat, the primary focus here is on legislative institutions and how these shaped political behavior. For instance, the Reform Act of 1832 both afforded more representation to the middle-class industrialists *and* shaped the particular lobbying strategy (the use of the 40 shilling freehold) of the League. This particular institutional configuration thus gave rise to a particular form of free-trade lobbying (chapter 4). Unlike the standard rational-choice view of institutions as exogenous, however, I examine how institutions evolve over time—namely, how MPs and peers came to perceive their parliamentary behavior as increasingly more constrained by public opinion. As this constraining force of public opinion became more evident to MPs and peers, they (somewhat grudgingly) came to accept a more delegate-oriented mode of political representation.

Chapters 7, 8, and 9 show that both houses of Parliament became increasingly constrained by a public opinion clamoring for representatives to behave more as "delegates" and less as "trustees." Indeed, this institutional shift extended as far as to halt the Lords from playing its role as a "veto player." Chapter 9 analyzes the debates on repeal of the Corn Laws in the House of Lords in May and June 1846. At issue is the puzzle of why a chamber consisting of aristocratic landowners (whose income was largely derived from agricultural rents) would accept a policy of free trade in agriculture. Chapter 9 finds that support for the free-trade legislation in the upper chamber was motivated largely by political self-interest (that is, by voting for repeal, peers conceded the economic privilege of protection to stave off democratic reform of Parliament) and by the idea that radical reform of Parliament was imminent if repeal failed. This chapter presents the first extensive empirical analysis of the repeal legislation in the House of Lords and produces findings that contradict some of the prevailing historiography. Together with the analyses of the debates on trade policy in the House of Commons from 1814 to 1846 (chapters 7 and 8), we find empirical support for the growing acceptance by MPs and peers of the importance of public opinion in constraining the policy-making ability of legislators (construed as a progression from the trustee to the delegate form of representation). The message of chapter 9 is that while the Lords held an institutional veto over the Commons, it failed to invoke its veto because it was constrained by public opinion. Thus, together with the Commons, the Lords were pushed to rethink their roles as representatives. No longer could they formulate policy without considering the opinions of "the masses out-of-doors." Subtly but forcefully, Parliament was slowly evolving toward a more delegate mode of representation.

Final Remarks

The main argument of this book is that interests drove repeal to the doors of Parliament, ideas inspired constituents and legislators alike to endorse free trade (in spite of what may have been contrary or conflicting interests), and institutions shaped *and* were shaped by the interests and ideas that drove repeal. In short, repeal must be understood as the product of interests, ideas, *and* institutions. Interests, it should be conceded, account for a good deal of the story. They tell us how repeal came to emerge as an issue of public policy and how it was elevated to the public agenda. Most important, the interests of constituents underpin the motivations of the Peelites. The findings in chapter 6, for instance, call into question the presumed "independence" of the Peelites as they voted for repeal. Statistical analysis of their votes show that insofar as Peelites voted as trustees, they did so only up to 1846. Their conversion to repeal did not demonstrate their commitment to beliefs independent of their constituents; rather, their conversion reflected a departure from voting more as trustees to voting more as delegates.

Yet interests alone do not account for the passage of repeal *in 1846*, nor can one rely on an interest-based argument to argue that repeal was inevitable at some point in mid-nineteenth-century Britain. It was not inevitable that a Parliament of landowning aristocrats would acquiesce to repeal. Indeed, in late December 1845, when it became all but certain that a motion to repeal would be introduced in early 1846, Leaguers still anticipated a "great parliamentary struggle," and if this struggle failed in the short-term, Leaguers were "fully prepared, and with ample means" to continue their campaign "for *five more years if necessary*" (Prentice 1968, 417). Even those at the heart of the League were uncertain as to its likely success in 1846, as the ultimate passage of repeal in 1846 hinged on the parliamentary arena. Interests bring us to the brink of repeal, but they cannot account for the final outcome; for that, we require an analysis of the ideas and institutions within the parliamentary arena.

The configuration of interests in mid-nineteenth-century Britain was, moreover, highly divisive. Class conflict was rampant. Industrialists, whose economic and political power threatened the ruling landowning aristocracy, ignited repeal with this class conflict, thereby making repeal a critical juncture in the process of democratic reform in Britain. Extending the lesson of repeal to other settings, then, it is likely that in cases of divided and conflicting interests (akin to Britain in the early 1840s), the importance of ideas—and possibly also institutions—will be elevated. Ideas may indeed become hooks on which political actors advance their interests (as exemplified by the League and the Peelites), and actors within legislative institutions who seek stability (and thereby self-preservation) may endorse policy that appears to be far from their ideal point (as exemplified by the Lords). Others have alluded to the notion that certain configurations of interests make ideas more prominent,[47] but far less common are empirically driven expositions of the interaction of interests, ideas, and institutions. This book provides such an exposition.

More speculatively, the case of repeal illustrates that interests alone do not necessarily predict policy outcomes, although they provide much of the explanatory framework. We may conjecture that when interests are majoritarian (that is, when a clear majority supports the general thrust of the policy), those interests will likely tell us most of what we want to know about the policy outcome. But when interests are highly conflicted and decidedly lopsided, one or both sides will be more likely to look to ideas to gain advantage. Moreover, highly charged interests may even force stability-seeking actors within institutions to make concessions, thereby forcing institutional evolution.

If ideas can be said to play a pivotal role in policy making, how do we predict *which* idea out of a population of at least $N > 1$ might take hold? Why did antiaristocracy and the morality of free trade feature prominently in League propaganda, and why did the idea of the territorial constitution become the rationale that Peelites used to justify their betrayal of the cause of protection? Very simply, some ideas are more attractive than others because they fit with the objective of self-interested political actors. Class conflict served to rally both the middle and working classes around repeal, and Peelites' reinterpretation of Conservative party ideology (the product of the reinterpretation of the territorial constitution) served to advance the interests of the Peelites. In both cases, ideas were selected because they served an immediate purpose—to advance underlying interests.

Finally, while the literature on institutions and democracy continues to mount (Acemoglu and Robinson 2005, Milner and Kubota 2005), scholars do not often try to demonstrate which institutions are relevant to policy changes,[48] how they become relevant, and how they interact with interests and ideas. In the case of repeal, the Reform Act of 1832 gave momentum to the lobbying efforts of the League, and these lobbying efforts, in turn, subsequently shaped parliamentary democracy in Britain. Perhaps most intriguing of all is that interests, on their own, may well have created a revolutionary setting similar to that which occurred in 1848 France. But the particular ideas used and the institutions in which these interests sought repeal served in the end to mitigate a potentially explosive outcome. Ideas and institutions in mid-nineteenth-century Britain served to move the discontent of industrialists toward reform rather than revolution. Hence, while it might be said that much of the dynamics of repeal can be understood by mapping the constellation of interests, the precise outcome—that is, that small perturbation left unaccounted for by interests—can sometimes matter. Sometimes, it can mean the difference between revolution and reform. And so understanding how these ideas and institutions came to matter in the final outcome becomes fundamentally important to understanding not only repeal but also democratic reform in modern Britain.

2

Interests, Ideas, and Institutions Simplified: A Demand- and Supply-Side Perspective

Demand-Side and Supply-Side Models

Demand-Side Models

Theories of repeal have generally focused on interests, ideas, or institutions, as noted in chapter 1. Another way to conceptualize the plethora of competing explanations for repeal is to characterize them as *demand-side* or *supply-side* in their focus. In demand-side theories political representatives translate into policy the new set of preferences that arise from exogenous changes in the interests, partisanship, or ideas of their constituents.[1] The simple assumption is that legislators are motivated by the desire to remain in office. To stay in office, they need to be reelected, and to be reelected, they need to satisfy the preferences of a relevant constituency. In short, legislators are motivated by what Mayhew famously described as the "electoral connection" (Mayhew 1974).

For instance, British MPs may have acted as conduits for free-trade interests that were created from industrialization (Thomas 1939; Brock 1941; Anderson and Tollison 1985; Cox 1987; McKeown 1989; Schonhardt-Bailey 1991a, 1991c, 1994) or have reflected a liberal shift in ideas or ideology (Kindleberger 1975; Rohrlich 1987; Hilton 1988; Howe 1997). There are, however, at least two potentially faulty assumptions of a pure demand-side model. First, it assumes that politicians are no more than passive recipients of constituency or political party pressures. However, representatives often confront conflicting pressures between their constituencies and their party and between their own ideological predisposition and the wishes of their constituents or party. Hence, the reconciliation of these differences requires initiative and activity—not passivity. Second, the model sometimes assumes that the institutional setting in which policy is made (in this case, Parliament) has no significant bearing on the policy outcome. Yet in many cases, institutional features that give rise to strategic behavior by political leaders[2] may ultimately determine the success or failure of a policy.

In the case of repeal, demand-side explanations have successfully captured many of the necessary causes but have struggled to capture the sufficient ones. In particular, these models offer no clear rationale for *why* the Peelites suddenly reversed their position on repeal. Although chapters 5 and 6 provide evidence that differences in constituency types likely made Peelites less wedded to protectionism than Non-Peelite Conservatives (NPCs), constituency type cannot account for the very *swift* reversal of their policy stance. In other words, it is difficult to point to an abrupt transformation in free-trade interests and lobbying activity that could fully explain why Peelites supported protection up to 1845 and then shifted swiftly to free trade in 1846. We can infer that growing free-trade interests pushed Peelites towards repeal, but this does not tell us what actually pushed them over the edge to support repeal. To know this, we must look to the actual setting in which the conversion occurred—the institutional setting of Parliament.

Supply-Side Models

Supply-side theories of policy making tend to focus on the institutional setting in which legislators operate (Krehbiel 1991, 1998; Cox and McCubbins 1993; Stewart 2001),[3] but ideas can also form the linchpin of a supply-side theory of policy making (Baumgartner and Jones 1993; Bawn 1999). Most recently, McLean (2001) has argued that Peel astutely maneuvred his cabinet into a position of accepting what they had previously vehemently opposed—repeal. Part of his story rests on Peel's employing of clever ministerial tactics to engineer his reappointment by the Queen in late 1845 and on a cabinet that was willing to support repeal. The second part of McLean's story is that Peel is said to have altered the choice set of his cabinet and backbench MPs from the single dimension of repeal to a multiple one that linked repeal to the Irish potato famine.

McLean's (2001, 36) argument warrants attention, as he purports to test the relative influences of constituency interests and ideology (the latter defined as "public order and the Queen's government") in the policy shift to repeal. He concludes that "Interests and ideology both played a great part. But for elites as well as for legislators, ideology was probably the greater" (McLean 2001, 53). McLean's argument hinges on Peel, whom he argues acted "heresthetically"—that is, Peel divided the majority in favor of protection by persuading some of them that repeal was necessary to assuage starvation and the possibility of civil unrest arising from the Irish potato famine. Thus, "Peel seized the Famine heresthetically as an issue on which to change the dimensionality of politics, and hence force repeal through, which he could not otherwise have done" (McLean 2001, 53). McLean tests this argument by examining correspondence between Peel and cabinet members in the critical months leading up to Peel's formal introduction of the repeal legislation in January 1846. He then applies logistic regression to test whether Peel's emphasis on the famine can explain the conversion of the Peelites in the Commons to free trade. He obtains rather poor results for this test: his best-performing model for English Conservative MPs fails to account for the votes of 55 (64 percent) Peelites and 27 (14 percent) Non-Peelite Conservatives on the final reading of repeal.

In contrast to McLean's findings, chapter 6 finds strong evidence to suggest that Peelites shifted their votes in accordance with the interests of their constituents, *not* in accordance with MPs' personal ideology. Yet while my analysis of the roll-call votes tells us what the Peelites did (they shifted from voting as trustees to voting as delegates), it does not tell us *why* they did so. Perhaps the famine provided cover for their free-trade votes—or perhaps some other dimension provided similar cover. Only further evidence—such as the written record—can shed light on the motivations of the Peelites. Indeed, if evidence exists to support McLean's claim for the introduction of a "famine dimension" into the debates over repeal, this should be found in the statements of MPs themselves.

The Argument

Repeal cannot be fully explained by either a demand- or supply-side explanation alone. Rather, both are needed to understand why repeal occurred and particularly why it occurred in 1846.

Demand-Side Pressure
In the several years leading up to repeal, free-trade interests had intensified, partly the result of the geographic concentration of the cotton textile industry. These interests had, moreover, spread more widely, owing to the deconcentration of the broader export sector both

geographically and in terms of industrial structure. (Chapter 3 documents the spread of free-trade interests.) Thus, intensified and more widely spread free-trade interests increasingly became politicized under the leadership of the Anti-Corn Law League. Meanwhile, the policy preference of (some) landowners became less protectionist as their asset portfolios became more diversified (documented in chapter 5). The net increase in free-trade interests served to convert more Liberal MPs to repeal, as seen in their roll-call votes: Liberal support for repeal grew from 71 percent of MPs in 1843 to 81 percent in 1844 and 89 percent in 1845.[4] The demand-side effect on Conservative MPs was not, however, sufficient to *convert* them to free trade. Indeed, no more than four Conservative MPs voted for free trade in the divisions on repeal from 1842 to 1845. Yet as chapters 5 and 6 demonstrate, Peelites represented constituencies with some free-trade leanings (relative to those of NPCs), and so, as delegates, they most likely faced more free-trade pressures. In short, *the demand-side shift brought more Liberals into the repeal camp and brought Peelites nearer to the brink of converting to repeal.*

Spatial voting models provide a useful way to conceptualize the effects of demand-side changes on legislative voting behavior. On various occasions before January 1846, MPs were asked to consider a vote to cease protection for British agriculture. The two options—repeal or the status quo (protection)—are depicted along a single horizontal trade-land dimension in figure 2.1.[5] (The designation of *trade* and *land* represents the underlying conflict over the orientation of Britain's national economic interest.) The ideal point of the median Liberal (M_L), Peelite ($M_{Peelite}$), and Non-Peelite Conservative (M_{NPC}) is mapped spatially along the line. The MP who is indifferent to repeal or protection is situated at the cut point. All MPs to the left of the cut point voted for repeal, and all those to the right voted against (that is, for the status quo—SQ). Figure 2.1 illustrates the spatial positions of MPs on the issue of repeal just before 1846.

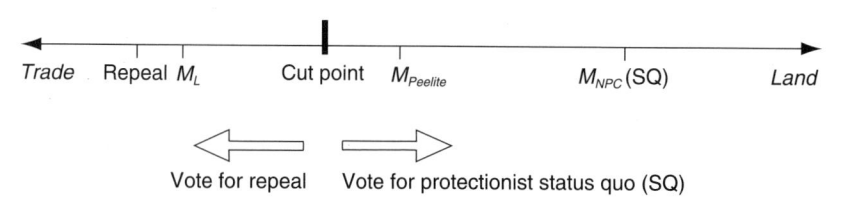

Figure 2.1
The prevailing trade-land dimension in Parliament, pre-1846

Demand-side pressures, driven (in the short-term) by the lobbying efforts of the Anti-Corn Law League (Schonhardt-Bailey 1991a), pushed the median Liberal MP further from indifference and toward repeal. Feeling these same pressures, the ideal point of the median Peelite moved gradually away from that of the median Non-Peelite Conservative.[6] As noted in chapter 1, Cobden famously remarked that the Corn Laws had been repealed too soon, meaning that the demand-side pressures that pushed for repeal were gaining momentum in transforming the landed basis of Parliament. Once Cobden realized that Peel would likely introduce repeal before the next election, he noted: "We should have liked to have had another year of qualification for counties [from the League registration campaign]. If we had had another year or two, we could have shown the monopolist landowners that we can transfer power in this country from the hands of a class totally into the hands of the middle and industrial classes of this country" (Searle 1993, 43). Cobden was referring to the League's longer-term strategy for repealing the Corn Laws by creating an elected free-trade majority in Parliament. To this end, the League campaigned to create new free-trade electors by purchasing 40 shilling freeholds (a feature of the 1832 Reform Act), while it also sought to reduce the number of protectionist electors by challenging their qualifications on the electoral registers (Schonhardt-Bailey 2001; McCord 1958; Prentice 1968). Table 2.1, derived from the testimony of Leaguers before a parliamentary committee in 1845, illustrates the success of the League for 1845 alone as it sought to transform the English electorate into a free-trade majority. In that year, the League challenged, on average, 11 percent of the eligible voters in constituencies that contained just over a quarter of the total English county electorate, with an end success rate of 50 percent. The dual strategy of the League is most striking in Lancashire South and Lancashire North. In the former, the League struck off almost 8 percent of the electorate, but between 1841 and 1845 the electorate increased almost 21 percent, much of this owing to the 40 shilling freehold registrations. In Lancashire North, the League struck off 5.5 percent of the electors, while their 40 shilling campaign contributed to an overall increase of almost 5 percent of the electorate. Indeed, if one adds the change in the electorate in 1844 and 1845, claimed by the League to be the result of their activity, it equals 19 percent of the electorate in Lancashire South and 16 percent in Middlesex in 1841. Moreover, at a by-election in Lancashire South in 1844, the Conservative candidate beat the Liberal candidate by just 598 votes. So the success of the League in

Table 2.1
League and protectionist activity in challenging electors

League activity in challenging electors

Constituency	Registered Electors 1841	Registered Electors 1845	Change	Change (percentage)	League Activity in the Year 1845 Electors Challenged	Electorate in 1845 (percentage)	Electors Struck Off	Electorate in 1845 (percentage)	Success Rate (percentage)
Warwickshire North	6,786	6,291	−495	−7.29%	650	10.33%	106	1.68%	16.31%
Staffordshire North	10,020	10,050	30	0.30	2,013	20.03	1,000	9.95	49.68
Gloucestershire East	7,971	8,069	98	1.23	919	11.39	413	5.12	44.94
Buckinghamshire	6,107	5,884	−223	−3.65	1,000	17.00	51	0.87	5.10
Lancashire South	18,148	21,940	3,792	20.89	2,896	13.20	1,722	7.85	59.46
Cheshire North	5,832	6,380	548	9.40	1,167	18.29	509	7.98	43.62
Cheshire South	6,972	7,940	968	13.88	415	5.23	246	3.10	59.28
Westmoreland	4,480	4,480	0	0.00	306	6.83	51	1.14	16.67
Hampshire South	5,591	5,791	200	3.58	80	1.38	36	0.62	45.00
Somerset East	9,759	9,655	−104	−1.07	537	5.56	373	3.86	69.46
Middlesex	13,919	13,679	−240	−1.72	1,944	14.21	1,119	8.18	57.56
Staffordshire South	8,469	8,560	91	1.07	837	9.78	484	5.65	57.83
Lancashire North	10,032	10,507	475	4.73	643	6.12	582	5.54	90.51
Surrey East	6,222	n.a.	n.a.	n.a.	367	n.a.	n.a.	n.a.	n.a.
Yorkshire West Riding	30,998	n.a.	n.a.	n.a.	22	n.a.	n.a.	n.a.	n.a.
Leicestershire South	4,854	n.a.	n.a.	n.a.	1,370	n.a.	30	n.a.	2.19
Cambridgeshire	n.a.	3,888	n.a.	n.a.	95	2.44	31	0.80	32.63
Total[a]		124,114			13,502	10.97%	6,723	5.46%	49.79%

Interests, Ideas, and Institutions Simplified

Protectionist activity in challenging electors

Constituency	Protectionist Activity in 1845			
	Electors Challenged	Electorate in 1845 (percentage)	Electors Struck Off	Electorate in 1845 (percentage)
Warwickshire North	n.a.	n.a.	n.a.	n.a.
Staffordshire North	n.a.	n.a.	n.a.	n.a.
Gloucestershire East	301	3.73%	103	1.28%
Buckinghamshire	n.a.	n.a.	n.a.	n.a.
Lancashire South	2,128	9.70	734	3.35
Cheshire North	950	14.89	106	1.66
Cheshire South	n.a.	n.a.	n.a.	n.a.
Westmoreland	n.a.	n.a.	n.a.	n.a.
Hampshire South	n.a.	n.a.	n.a.	n.a.
Somerset East	n.a.	n.a.	n.a.	n.a.
Middlesex	n.a.	n.a.	n.a.	n.a.
Staffordshire South	n.a.	n.a.	n.a.	n.a.
Lancashire North	n.a.	n.a.	n.a.	n.a.
Surrey East	n.a.	n.a.	n.a.	n.a.
Yorkshire West Riding	n.a.	n.a.	n.a.	n.a.
Leicestershire South	n.a.	n.a.	n.a.	n.a.
Cambridgeshire	n.a.	n.a.	n.a.	n.a.
Total	3,379	9.29%	943	2.59%

Table 2.1
(continued)

Source: Report from the Select Committee on Votes of Electors, *Parliamentary Papers* VIII 1846, pps. 190–194, 208, 220, 256, 299, 309–312 and 327–328. Evidence of W. W. Burrell, Richard Helps, Henry Lucas, Colin Campbell Macauley, Charles Bradford Passman, George Whateley, and George Wilson.

Notes: Total county electorate of England was said by the Anti-Corn Law League to be 445,630, so these counties equal 28 percent of the total. In addition, in Lancashire North the League is said to have gained (by claims and objections) 957 votes in 1843 and 553 votes in 1844. In Lancashire South the League is said to have gained 1,741 votes (by strike off and new votes) in 1844. In Middlesex the League is said by George Wilson to have gained 466 votes in 1843 and 1844 and 651 votes by new claims in 1845. In some counties, the total votes "struck off" figure for the League may include votes gained by new entries to the register by League supporters.

a. Totals do not include Surrey East, Yorkshire West Riding, and Leicestershire South.

the following year in striking off 1,722 electors in that constituency was presumably not irrelevant to the prospects of the sitting MPs.

Whether the League could have gained a numerical majority for free trade in Parliament is open to speculation. Given a restricted franchise and the property qualifications of 1832, its successes under these circumstances were remarkable. To put into perspective the threat from the League's electoral strategy, in the 1841 general election the Conservatives had gained fifty-three seats from their "opponents" (Blake 1974, 281) and were thus able to form the government. In the constituencies listed in table 2.1, the League's strategy posed a direct challenge to twenty-six Conservative MPs (half the swing in 1841).

MPs (particularly in marginal constituencies) quite rightly had reason to fear the League. As Cobden wrote to T. Hunter[7] on 12 March 1846: "In fact there are not a hundred men in the Commons, or twenty in the Lords, who at heart are anxious for total repeal. They are coerced by the out-of-doors [public] opinion, and nothing but the dread of the League organisation enables Peel to persevere. But for our forty-shilling freehold bludgeons, the aristocracy would have resisted the Government measure almost to a man" (Morley 1881, 370). In carrying repeal, Peel preempted the League's efforts. Subsequently, the Anti-Corn Law League was disbanded, and so the registration campaign and all the fervor of the League's efforts died. It was precisely this demand-side pressure that Peel sought to stave off by conceding to repeal. As Prest (1977, 133) notes,

The entire period between 1832 and 1847 can be interpreted as one continuous registration battle, which Peel joined in when he appreciated its importance, and then lost. Peel surrendered in 1845–6, as soon as he saw the battle turning against him, without giving the constituency agents on his own side the chance to fight back against the League and with the League's own weapons.... The consequence was that for nearly twenty years successive Whig governments came under so little external pressure that they were able, in effect, to extend a truce to the Conservatives.

More vividly, Peel's response to the overthrow of the government of Louis Philippe in 1848—in which he is said to have retorted that "this comes of trying to govern the country through a narrow representation in Parliament, without regarding the wishes of those outside. It is what this party behind me wanted me to do in the matter of the Corn Laws, and I would not do it" (Morley 1881, 1: 407) (see chapter 1)—reveals the determination of Peel not to allow repeal to give rise to pressures for parliamentary reform.

Supply-Side Shift

Peelites in 1846 thus became torn between, on the one hand, representing the increasing free-trade-oriented interests of their constituents and, on the other hand, remaining loyal to a Conservative ideology that sought to defend traditional British institutions, including protection. As Lord Ashburton commented in 1841, "I am aware to what extent our Conservative party is a party pledged to the support of the land and that, that principle abandoned, the party is dissolved" (quoted in Gash 1965, 137–138).

The relationship between constitutional conservatism and agricultural protection was a simple one: "protecting agriculture preserved the landed basis of the British constitution" (Gambles 1999, 58). Conservatives were particularly concerned that the 1832 Reform Act "had transformed both the nature of representation and the electoral pressures on the tariff through the primacy of the sectional interests of urban manufacturers and creditor interests in the reformed political nation" (Gambles 1999, 57). Hence, free trade was seen as divisive and therefore contrary to the responsibilities of government, which included balancing the various interests in society. Protection, on the other hand, allowed government to use the tariff as a tool to balance economic interests, particularly between landowners and manufacturers.

At the heart of conservatism was the concept of the "territorial constitution" or "territorial aristocracy," which was grounded in works of prominent seventeenth- and eighteenth-century writers. For instance, Daniel Defoe maintained that freeholders were "the proper owners of the country" while others were merely "sojourners, like lodgers in a house," and again, "I make no question but property of land is the best title to government in the world" (Defoe 1702, 16, quoted in Namier 1930, 21). The rationale for the territorial constitution was that those individuals most affected by the policies of government should be the ones to dictate those policies. In other words, as land was argued to be fixed and capital mobile,[8] the interests of landowners were deemed to have a permanent role in the British constitution.[9] The territorial constitution did not mean, however, that the landowning aristocracy had carte blanche to disregard the interests of all other sections of society. Rather, other sections of society, along with the colonies, were said to be represented "virtually" in Parliament. MPs were intended to represent all their constituents, voters and nonvoters alike. Yet as the landowning aristocracy endorsed Edmund Burke's advocacy of the *trustee* mode of representation[10]—which maintained that landowners, who held "real" property, had a greater claim to governing than manufacturers (Gambles 1999, 58–59)—there is an unresolved tension in how MPs might faithfully represent ("virtually") the interests of all sections of society while at the same time ensuring that landowners themselves would not suffer undue losses.

With the move toward "individual" as opposed to "virtual" representation in 1832, Conservatives feared a constant clash between and among land, capital, and labor for "the governing dynamic of a landed nobility and gentry...was, as Goulburn reminded [Peel] in 1845, the only barrier...against the revolutionary effects of the Reform Bill" (Macintyre 1989, 143). Free trade, in their view, would serve to deepen this clash further: "Political protest was explained as a direct consequence of a social and economic crisis of distribution which free-trade political economy seemed to compound" (Gambles 1999, 57). Hence, protection served to stabilize the inevitable social unrest that resulted from encroachments on the territorial basis of Parliament, while free trade would only exacerbate these tensions. Moreover, protection provided a means to reequilibrate divergent economic interests.

As Peelites observed the growth of interests linked to manufacturing and trade—partly in their own districts but also throughout the country—the pressure for repeal mounted. For Peelites to justify their support for repeal in terms of the interests of their constituents would, however, wholly cut against the grain of Conservatism. Indeed, it is likely that most Peelites would have rejected the Liberal notion of legislators as delegates, and thus we should not expect them to refer to constituency interests as justification for their repeal votes. Rather, they would likely have sought other compelling reasons to justify their abrupt reversal. Perhaps most important, they would have sought to square these reasons with their Conservative ideology.

Before 1846, Peelites voted according to their Conservative (protectionist) ideology, but in January 1846, Peel offered them a way to embrace their constituents' interests *and* appear to remain faithful to Conservatism. If protectionism could be legitimately excluded from the umbrella of traditional institutions, then Conservatives who voted for repeal (Peelites) could profess to be adhering to the respected trustee mode of representation rather than caving in to popular demand, as a delegate might do.[11] Peel characterized repeal as a means to preserve the traditional institutions of the British government—and, in particular, the aristocracy. It would ensure peace between the commercial and aristocratic classes, thereby ensuring the nation's welfare and stability. While all Conservatives agreed on the preservation of the territorial constitution, Peelites came to believe that repeal offered a new means to that end. In a broader perspective, Peel's willingness to concede on repeal can be traced to lessons learned from the 1832 Reform Act. In his 1834 Tamworth Manifesto, Peel argued for the widening of the social foundations of the Conservative party and urged Conservatives to control rather than to halt democratic reform. As Gash (1965, 140) notes, "Peel's approach to the mercantile and industrial interests... was essentially conciliatory and comprehensive."

Defense of the "territorial constitution" was only one of several justifications that Peel employed to argue for repeal, however. Indeed, one could say that he adopted a "shot-gun"[12] approach to his advocacy of repeal (see chapter 1)—but it was this theme that resonated with the Peelites since it appealed to their Conservative ideology. This form of argumentation provided Peelites with the nudge to push them into the repeal camp. Peelites did not follow Peel in a herdlike mentality: they followed Peel because his rationale for repeal offered a Conservative cover to enable them to align with their increasingly free-trade-oriented constituencies.

In short, a shift in constituency demands was necessary but not sufficient to convert a majority of MPs to repeal. Even if all Liberal MPs voted for repeal (which, in the end, all but six did)[13] (Aydelotte n.d.), repeal could not have passed in the 1841 to 1847 Parliament without the support of some Conservative MPs. To push the wavering Conservatives to free trade, the definition of repeal required reinterpretation so that it could be seen to be compatible with Conservative ideology. Peel provided this reinterpretation when he introduced the repeal legislation, and Peelites latched onto this reinterpretation as political and ideological cover for their free-trade votes. By trumpeting themselves as loyal to the longer-term preservation of the territorial constitution and judging that repeal was a necessary concession to ensure this outcome, Peelites could vote as delegates without having to justify themselves as such.

Figure 2.1 illustrates the demand-side pressures placed on MPs, and figure 2.2 illustrates the final supply-side shift to repeal. The horizontal line in figure 2.2 represents the initial single trade-land dimension, while the line at 45 degrees represents the new dimension of the "territorial constitution." The key feature is the movement of the median

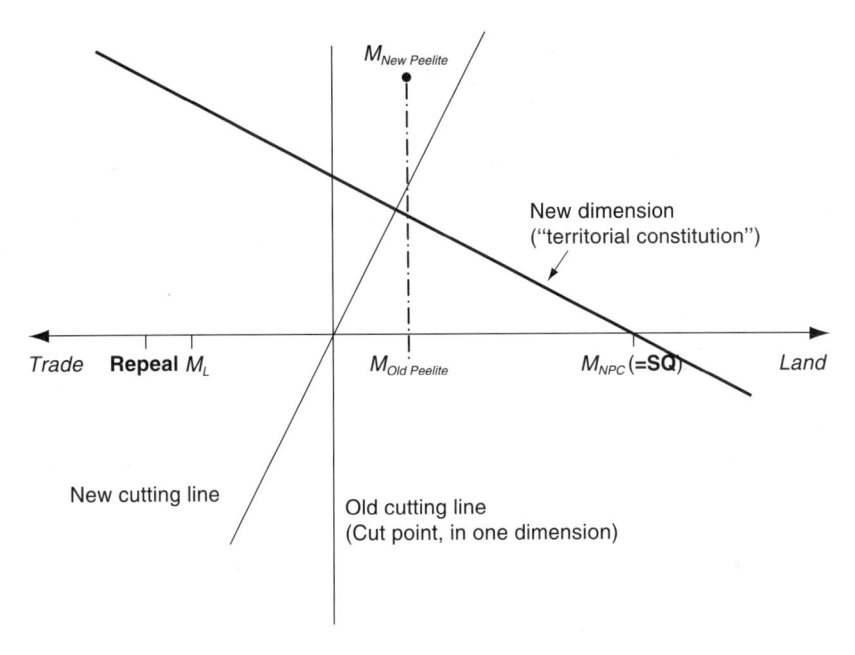

Interests, Ideas, and Institutions Simplified 43

Figure 2.2
Shift of the Peelites: Introducing a new dimension

Peelite from an ideal point to the right of the cutting line, or cut point (that is, against repeal) in one dimension to an ideal point to the left of the new cutting line (for repeal) in two dimensions.[14] In one dimension, the median Peelite was nearer to repeal than the median Non-Peelite Conservative but was nonetheless well to the right of the cutting line. By raising the profile of the territorial constitution, the second dimension served to divide the Conservatives. Toward the left side (and to the *left* of the new cutting line, though the exact position is unimportant), Peelites argued for repeal as a means to defend the landed basis of Parliament, while at the extreme right (and still to the right of the cutting line), NPCs firmly defended protectionism as core to the preservation of that same end. This new dimension was, in effect, a dimension of means rather than ends. A "dimension of means" raises the question of whether the territorial constitution was mere rhetoric or whether this justification for repeal offered an actual alternative to the "old" interpretation of repeal. The answer is that this new dimension contained *both* rhetoric and reality. The territorial constitution provided Peelites with a persuasive argument for their conversion to repeal, and to the extent that this rhetoric gave Peelites greater freedom to vote more as delegates, the reality of repeal may well have lengthened the tenure of aristocratic control of Parliament. Repeal offered a concessionary means to moderate—but not halt—the impetus for democratic reform. For NPCs, repeal represented the end of the landed aristocracy's economic *and* political monopolies, while for Peelites it meant the end of the economic monopoly and a reprieve on the political monopoly. Stated differently, in the short term, the territorial constitution offered Peelites a convenient rhetorical device, but in the long term, repeal may have provided some breathing space for the landed aristocracy to adapt to democratic change.

Note from figure 2.2 that the only group of MPs affected by the second dimension were the Peelites. NPCs and Liberals remained unaffected by the new dimension. The median Liberal MP supported repeal because it benefited the interests of British manufacturing and trade, while the median NPC opposed repeal because it harmed the interests of landowners. Non-Peelite Conservatives also opposed repeal because they believed that free trade would undermine their notion of the territorial constitution. Thus, the second dimension intersects their ideal point on the first dimension.

Three points should be highlighted. First, Peel did not rest his argument for repeal solely—or even predominantly—on the defense of the territorial constitution. Peel's arguments and justifications for repeal were multifaceted, as described in chapter 1. Hence, it is difficult to spot any "heresthetics"[15] in Peel's mention of the territorial constitution. Contrary to McLean's view, this book finds that Peel did not singlehandedly redefine repeal to gain support. Rather, the Peelites magnified the theme of the territorial constitution.[16] Second, it is impossible to know with certainty the extent to which Peelites latched on to the territorial constitution idea as a matter of convenience or as one of conviction. The argument is that the idea served as a convenient cover for voting behavior that veered toward the representation of constituents' interests. It is entirely plausible that Peelites truly believed that repeal would ensure the preservation of the territorial constitution and that the increasingly free-trade-oriented nature of their constituencies was a sheer coincidence. This is plausible but unlikely. Third, the defense of the territorial constitution may be seen as a new dimension (or more simply, a new idea) that offered a reinterpretation of repeal.

Findings We Should Expect (and a Recap)

The remaining chapters in this book endeavor to test aspects of this demand- and supply-side approach by drawing on a variety of methodologies (including statistical and textual) and both quantitative and qualitative data. In part 1 (chapters 3 through 6), I examine the demand-side pressures for free trade. As noted earlier, chapter 3 finds that the demand for protection had declined by the early 1840s, owing to the portfolio diversification of (some) landowners into nonagricultural ventures, and chapter 4 finds that changes in the structure of the British economy (particularly its export sector) helped to intensify and spread more widely its free-trade interests. In short, landowners were becoming less wedded to protectionism at about the same time as manufacturers were clamoring more loudly and effectively for free trade. Chapter 5 examines how this clamoring transformed into a unique form of lobbying as the Anti-Corn Law League engaged in a strategy of "nationalizing the interest"—that is, appealing to the general British public to support repealing the Corn Laws by linking repeal to unifying themes, such as democratic reform and antiaristocracy. Finally, chapter 6 provides an empirical test of the effect of demand-side pressures on the votes of MPs in the lead-up to repeal and on repeal itself. This chapter finds evidence to suggest that in 1846, the pivotal MPs—the Peelites—abruptly shifted from voting as trustees to voting as delegates. In other words, they (like their Liberal counterparts) shifted their voting behavior to reflect the net increase in constituency demand for free trade. The role of economic interests is prominent in these chapters, although ideas are found to be critical to the lobbying of the League and Conservative ideology severely constrained the voting behavior of Peelites before 1846. The key defining institution in the demand-side story is the 1832 Reform Act, which gave rise to the politicization of middle-class interests and shaped the lobbying strategies of the League.

In part 2 (chapters 7 through 9), I focus more on the parliamentary setting to explore the supply-side aspect of repeal. Chapter 6 details how MPs actually voted on repeal but does not tell us *why* the Peelites abruptly shifted from voting as trustees to voting as delegates. Chapter 7 is the first of three chapters that use computer-assisted content analysis to analyze the speeches of MPs and peers in their entirety. The analysis reveals that a reinterpretation of repeal allowed Peelites to vote as delegates but to justify their betrayal of a protectionist Conservative ideology in the language of disinterested and moral trustees whose motive was only to promote the nation's well-being. Chapter 8 tests the robustness of the findings in chapter 7 by asking whether Peel's reinterpretation of repeal as a policy that would preserve the territorial constitution was indeed unique to 1846. I find that this rationale was not articulated as a theme in any of the debates on trade policy in the thirty years prior to 1846, which lends significant weight to my argument that while demand-side pressures were necessary for repeal, the final explanation for repeal must hinge on the introduction of a second dimension of argumentation, thereby splitting the Non-Peelite Conservatives from the Peelites. Chapter 9 explores the institutional conflict between one legislative chamber (the Commons) perceived as caving in to popular demand and one (the Lords) that perceived itself as immune to pressure from "out-of-doors." The latter, whose members were prominent landowning aristocrats, vehemently opposed repeal and had within its powers to veto the legislation. Why did the Lords then fail to veto repeal? This chapter examines how demand-side pressures for parliamentary reform ultimately persuaded peers to accept the lesser of two evils—repeal over democratic reform. The contribution of this chapter is that it allows us to trace how institutions such as Parliament can be constrained and ultimately shaped by economic interests. Finally, chapter 10 plays devil's advocate. It asks whether it might have been the ideas and arguments of the League and not changes in the economic make-up of their constituencies that persuaded Peelites to change their position. While the results of this analysis of newspaper coverage in local constituencies clearly illustrate the increased intensity in lobbying by the League from 1841 to 1846 (thereby increasing the demand for repeal), they also find that the effect of free-trade ideas on the voting behavior of Peelites was almost nonexistent.

I

The Demand Side: The League, the Landowners, and Free Trade

3 Lessons in Lobbying for Free Trade: To Concentrate or Not

Introduction

This chapter presents a modified version of the endogenous-protection literature that integrates concentrated and deconcentrated interests with successful lobbying. It is suggested that effective free-trade lobbying required the political fusion of the economic interests representing two fundamental changes in nineteenth-century Britain's economy: (1) geographic concentration of the core export industry (cotton textiles) and (2) deconcentration of the broader export sector both geographically and in terms of industrial structure. Empirical evidence from both national and individual levels supports the contention that the timing and political success[1] of the Anti-Corn Law League required the combined forces of core export interests and the more diverse and geographically more evenly distributed interests of the export sector as a whole.

Within the endogenous-protection literature conflicting interpretations exist among theorists regarding the importance of concentrated versus deconcentrated interests in successful lobbying. Yet these seemingly conflicting interpretations may be integrated. I discuss two general types of (de)concentration: industry (de)concentration (of capital, labor, or output) and geographic (de)concentration (of industries or industry "interests" across or within a geographic area). Effective lobbying by the League was the political outcome of the fusion of these two types of concentration in two contrasting forms: (1) industrial and geographic concentration of the core export industry (cotton textiles) and (2) deconcentration of the broader export sector, both geographically and (in terms of industrial structure) into a larger number and broader array of composite industries. Empirical evidence from both the national and individual levels supports the contention that core export interests were necessary to create the political machinery of the League but were not sufficient to expand this to create the necessary political influence at the national level—something that required political pressure to spread across a larger number of parliamentary constituencies. The organizational success of this lobby required the combined forces of core export interests and the more diverse and geographically more evenly distributed interests of the export sector as a whole. It was the growing concentration of the former and the increasing deconcentration of the latter that explain the timing and the organizational success of the Anti-Corn Law League free-trade lobby.

Interest-Group Theory

The endogenous-protection literature (Olson 1965; Lavergne 1983; Baldwin 1985)[2] maintains that the propensity to organize for collective action can be measured by characteristics of a particular industry. It is traditionally argued that the greater the share of production by the industry's top firms (the greater the industry concentration), the more likely they are to organize, since the largest firms will accrue a larger share of the total gains and therefore be willing to bear a disproportionate share of the costs of organizing. Moreover, industries with a large number of firms usually experience the free-rider problem, making organization more difficult. The probability of organizing, ceteris paribus, is therefore inversely related to the number of firms in the industry. Proponents of the theory also maintain that because geographic concentration reduces transportation, information, and other costs that inhibit organization, the more geographically concentrated the industry, the greater the probability that its firms will organize.

Authors generally consider both industry and geographic concentration as key indicators of potential political leverage, although they are often divided on the combined effects of the two forms of concentration. The theoretic logic underpinning industry concentration (traditionally based on the four-firm concentration ratio) relies on Olson's argument that concentrated industries are better positioned to overcome the free-rider problem, given the (usually) small numbers of firms and their unequal size. According to Olson, where the number of actors in a group is small, each actor's contribution to provision of the good makes a perceptible difference in the quantity of the good provided, and large firms in industries with unequal distributions of firm sizes will tend to receive a proportionately larger share of the good and therefore may contribute to its provision despite the existence of free riders (Olson 1965).

Concentrated industries, according to Olson, may experience fewer difficulties in organizing for collective action. However, other theorists argue that geographically deconcentrated industries are more successful in obtaining their political objectives. Pincus (1975), for example, finds that industries that are geographically more evenly distributed (and thus possess constituents in a larger number of electoral districts) lower the bargaining costs among legislators. Lower bargaining costs imply that fewer compromises are required—hence an easier passage into protective legislation. Pincus (1975, 769) explains that, "In a system of geographical representation...transfer costs arose and it was costly for a senator to vote other than in his constituents' direct interests. The more even the distribution of pressure on the single issue, the less wastage there was in the course of transfers of pressure, one senator to another. From a given total of pressure, the highest possible duty would have resulted when the pressure was evenly distributed over the senators." Moreover, he combines industry concentration with geographic deconcentration to form a revised model of interest-group activity. In his study, Pincus (1975, 757) finds that "the ideal industry pressure groups had low proprietorial income shares and geographically concentrated production units, but...political effectiveness required the group to speak for many establishments with output spread fairly evenly across states." Industries that are large and geographically deconcentrated, in Pincus's view, are more likely to obtain favorable legislation. More recently, Busch and Reinhardt argue that geographic concentration refers to grassroots activism and should thus be considered a demand-side pressure, while political concentration (namely, the dispersion of employment across electoral districts) constitutes a "supply side story about electoral representation" (Busch and Reinhardt 2003, 2).

Empirical tests of the effects of industry (de)concentration and geographic (de)concentration on tariff structure have produced mixed findings. For instance, Baldwin (1985) and Lavergne (1983) reject both measures of concentration as poor predictors of tariff legislation. Caves (1976) finds only qualified support for industry concentration, although when he includes other measures, he concludes that the interest-group model performs quite well overall. In comparison, Pincus's (1975) positive empirical findings for industry concentration as well as geographic deconcentration diverge markedly from those of his contemporaries, although other studies have tended to endorse his basic premise. Paul Godek (1985) gives evidence of a positive relationship between geographic and industrial concentration and trade restrictions—but within a framework more directly concerned with exploring the effects of industry structure on tariffs versus quotas. Specifically, Godek finds positive relationships between (1) geographic-concentration industry size and quota levels and (2) higher levels of industry concentration (fewer firms) and tariff levels. More recent authors have tended to find that geographically concentrated industries are more politically active (Hansen 1990; Milner 1997a, 1997b; Busch and Reinhardt 2000).

The critical point of contention hinges not on industry concentration but on geographic concentration. Olson argues that industry concentration combined with geographic *concentration* leads to successful lobbies, since the latter makes organizational efforts less onerous. Pincus argues that industry concentration plus geographic *deconcentration* lead to successful lobbies. He is less concerned about the difficulties that geographically deconcentrated groups incur in organizing and more concerned with degrees of political effectiveness once organized. Alternatively, if organization is initially achieved by the fusion of two groups—a leading export industry exhibiting both geographic and capital concentration and a broader export sector more deconcentrated in terms of the number of composite industries and the geographic spread of those industries (incorporating the leader as one of its constituent industries)—we may accept Pincus's argument without contradicting Olson's. The fusion of industry and sector is critical to overcoming the problem of organization created by Pincus's model of geographic deconcentration. I address the problem of how deconcentration enhances organizational ability (and hence political strength) by examining the coexistence of geographic and capital concentration in the leading export industry and deconcentration (both geographically and by number of industries) in the broader export sector.

An Extension of Interest-Group Theory

The analysis of interest-group activity in this chapter differs from the standard approach in two ways. First, free trade, rather than protection, is identified as the quasi public good. Unlike models that link collective action with the provision of trade protection, models concerned with the effects of collective action on trade liberalization may include not only the static gains from policy change but also the gains accruing from external scale economies. Rather than assuming (as neoclassical growth theory does) constant returns to scale, economists have argued that the most important benefits of trade liberalization result from increasing returns to scale to productive factors at the industry level. Drawing on the endogenous-economic-growth literature (originating with the work of Grossman and Helpman 1988, Krugman 1988, and Baldwin 1989), which stresses increasing returns to scale and therefore the dynamic gains resulting from trade liberalization, the dynamic gains from liberalization should correlate with industry size and capital concentration. With increasing returns to scale, the standard argument that protective forces enjoy an inherent advantage over free-trade forces (given the concentrated benefits and dispersed costs associated with protective legislation) (e.g., Lavergne 1983, 19–20) is turned on its head. Increasing returns to scale from trade liberalization suggest that manufacturers for export would benefit from the one-time (static) upward shift in sales accruing from trade liberalization and that they (and especially the largest exporters) would benefit even more from the externalities accruing from their ability to exploit a larger share of the world market—that is, from the dynamic dimension of liberalization. Pincus's argument may therefore be amended as follows: the ideal free-trade pressure group should consist of a key export industry that exhibits both capital and geographic concentration, combined with deconcentration at the export-sector level, both geographically and by number of composite industries. Increasing returns to scale mean that individuals with interests at the key export-industry level benefit disproportionately but that nevertheless the small, less capital-concentrated exporters also reap the rewards of larger absolute sales, plus some of the externalities associated with a (marginally) larger market share.

A second dimension that differs from standard interest-group theory is the focus here on the timing of pressure-group activity. Why is it that the League emerged in the late 1830s rather than decades earlier when manufacturing had already surpassed agriculture as the dominant sector in the British economy?[3] Rather than adopting a static view in determining which industry characteristics contribute to or detract from organizational efforts, I trace the progression of organization to discern the factors that catalyze it.[4] Some authors have attempted to measure the dynamic determinants of tariff legislation (Baack and Ray 1983), but virtually nonexistent are attempts to analyze the effects of *changes* in industry and geographic concentration on organization—that is, the dynamic elements of organization, especially of free-trade forces.

In brief, this chapter extends the interest-group approach to emphasize the mix between industry—here, specifically capital—concentration and geographic deconcentration of the broader export sector. This view differs from Pincus's model in that (1) by examining a free-trade instead of a protection lobby, it adds the dimension of increasing returns to scale from liberalization and therefore broadens the analysis to include the effects that potential dynamic gains may have had on exporters' incentive to lobby and (2) it examines the effects of changes over time in industry and sectoral structure on organizational ability. It seeks to extend Pincus's model to include the issue of organizational ability within a context of geographic deconcentration.

Concentration and Deconcentration in Nineteenth-Century Britain

Industry concentration is often derived from the concentration ratio of the top four firms in a given industry. Unfortunately, firm-level data for British industries in the early to mid-nineteenth century are sparse at best and simply unavailable for most industries. Studies in economic history have, in part, explored the question of industry concentration, but even these remain limited primarily to the cotton textile industry.

However, inferring from equipment type and employment figures, a tentative consensus has emerged within this literature on the increasing geographic concentration of cotton textile-industry activity into Lancashire during the second quarter of the nineteenth century. Evidence from the economic-history literature is piecemeal but illustrative. For instance, while the total number of cotton power looms in England more than doubled between 1835 and 1850, Lancashire's share of this total increased from 67.5 to 79.1 percent (Fang 1978). Moreover, Von Tunzelmann (1978, 236–239) finds that for the period from 1835 to 1846, Lancashire increased its share of the nation's total employment in cotton mills from 66.7 to 72.3 percent. During the same period, Lancashire also expanded its share of the nation's total horsepower in the cotton industry from 64.4 to 69.3 percent, expanding further to 74.8 percent in 1856.

Even Gatrell (1977), who claims that the cotton-textile industry remained broadly capital-deconcentrated during the early nineteenth century, acknowledges a trend toward *geographic* concentration into

Lancashire (and particularly Manchester) from the mid- to late 1830s onward. From the Factory Inspector's reports of 1835 and 1841, Gatrell finds that a "trend towards the more intensified use of capital [in Lancashire] may be inferred from the fact that labour increased by some 53 per cent and horsepower by some 64 per cent between 1835 and 1841. Something like two-thirds of power and two-fifths of labour were added before the end of 1838" (Gatrell 1977, 101).

Taylor (1949) more fully endorsed the trend toward geographic concentration in his study of cotton manufactures in Lancashire, Cheshire, Derbyshire, and Yorkshire from 1825 to 1850. Taylor found that the industry had become largely concentrated in the Lancashire coalfield (or "districts easily served by it") as a result of the growing replacement both of water power by steam engines and of hand looms by power looms. The greater availability of capital and improved transport facilities, in turn, helped to explain the emergence of steam engines and power looms in Lancashire.

In contrast, evidence of industry concentration in cotton textiles is less conclusive, in large part the result of limited surviving data. Cottrell (1980), however, provides some evidence of industry concentration and attributes it to rapid changes in technology: "From the 1830s weaving began to be a mechanized process. This led to the demise of the hand loom and the water-powered rural spinning mill.... As a result of these developments, fixed capital invested in the manufacturing branches of the Lancashire cotton industry increased from approximately £14.8 million in 1834 to £31 million in 1856. An investment in a 'typical' mill of the 1830s amounted to between £20,000 and £50,000, and at the beginning of the decade Manchester mills were employing on average 400 hands as opposed to half that number two decades before" (Cottrell 1980, 23).

Lloyd-Jones and LeRoux (1980, 1982) examine more explicitly the changing industrial structure in Manchester, using labor as a proxy for capital. They argue that the structure of the city's cotton industry from 1815 to 1841 was shaped by the demise of small firms (150 and fewer employees) and the entry of medium to large firms (151 to 500 and over 500 employees, respectively). These authors find that the median size of the labor force per firm rose from 54 employees to 174 and that the number of small firms decreased from 28 percent to 12 percent, while medium-size firms increased from 27 percent to 56 percent. While recalculations of the authors' data cast doubt on the relevance of their division between medium and large firms,[5] not to mention the list of further methodological and theoretical problems noted by at least one economic historian (Bailey 1984), they do not call into question the sharp increase in average firm size. Moreover, Howe (1984) supports Lloyd-Jones and LeRoux's observation of the growing dominance of medium and large firm size. While his study of the structure of the cotton industry in the 1840s is not primarily concerned with industry concentration, Howe essentially extends Lloyd-Jones and LeRoux's premise to other textile activities (calico printing and bleaching) and to noncotton textiles (flax, silk, and worsted). Defining small firms as those employing capital near £10,000, medium to large from £50,000 to £200,000, and giants at £500,000, Howe finds that "only in woollens did the 'democratic' structure of numerous small units survive" (Howe 1984, 5).

Although it is difficult to translate these studies into a single framework for understanding industry concentration, the important conclusion is the agreement on the increasing geographic concentration of the cotton industry in Lancashire. Accordingly, this chapter does not contribute "new" data on capital concentration in Lancashire; rather, I accept the general consensus and test the impact of capital concentration on lobbying efforts, using proxy variables. In contrast to the emphasis on the cotton-textile industry, economic historians have tended to ignore the development of Britain's other export industries and therefore cannot provide us with comparable evidence on the export sector as a whole.[6] Because much of the firm-level data necessary for such analysis do not exist, alternative means for exploring the structure of Britain's export sector are developed. In brief, this chapter seeks to establish something closer to a national picture of the export sector's geographic and industry (interest) (de)concentration and thus achieve a better understanding of the relationship between export interests and pressure-group activity.

Concentration, Deconcentration, and the Anti-Corn Law League

Geographic and industry concentration of the textile industry by itself does not amount to an explanation of the emergence of the Anti-Corn Law League. A deliberate link must be made between this concentration and free-trade pressure-group activity by the League. To do so, we must examine the League's organizational management and the geographic distribution of subscriptions to the League.

Chapters 1 and 2 describe the League's registration campaign and note that historians have often described the League as the first modern pressure group to emerge in Britain. Crucial to its organizational success was its efficient administrative structure, a structure supported and operated by a concentrated core of export-oriented free-trade supporters. This centralized administration—the financial core of the League—was situated in Manchester and operated by a nexus of that city's manufacturing and professional elite. McCord notes that the League's efficiency may indeed "be traced in great part to the business-like character" of this commercially minded group of individuals (McCord 1958, 172–173).[7] Of critical importance is that the businesslike characters of the League council were also its chief financial supporters. According to Howe (1984, 209–210), "The initial membership of the Manchester Association and of the League were both heavily recruited from the textile masters, together with merchants and professional men.... [Their] greatest contribution to the success of the League was financial. In its ability to call on vast funds over short periods, the League exceeded all other nineteenth-century pressure groups." Howe notes that 56 percent of the subscriptions over £100 came from Lancashire in 1844 and that 70 percent came from that county in 1846 (Howe 1984, 212). Table 3.1 illustrates the distribution of subscriptions to the League by city, county, and region. Although this list is by no means comprehensive, it does depict Lancashire as the dominant contributing county and (in subscriptions per person) Manchester as the leading contributing city.[8]

Considering the general consensus in the economic-history literature on geographic concentration of the leading export industry in Lancashire (more specifically, Manchester), one can easily surmise that this concentration of capital enhanced that geographic area's ability to function as the financial and operational core of League activities. Manufacturers, merchants, and professionals in Manchester were able to draw on this concentrated core of potential free-trade beneficiaries to initiate and propel League efforts at gaining repeal. More specifically, increased geographic concentration of industry capital acted as a barrier to entry and thus meant greater benefits accruing from free trade to key actors in this region—hence, a stronger incentive for these actors to lobby for free trade. Moreover, if we add the dynamic dimension of trade liberalization, the incentive to lobby increases substantially since these key actors stood to gain even more from the

Table 3.1
Subscriptions to the Anti-Corn Law League

City (in order of increasing subscription per 100 population)[a]	A	B
Newcastle-upon-Tyne, Northumberland, NE	0	0
Rotherham, Yorkshire, NE	0	0
Wednesfield, Staffordshire, M	0	0
Willenhall, Staffordshire, M	0	0
S. Shields, Durham, NE	0	0
N. Shields, Northumberland, NE	0	0
Durham, Durham, NE	0	0
Wednesbury, Staffordshire, M	0	0
Kingston-upon-Hull, Yorkshire, NE	0	0
Brighton, Sussex, SE	0	0
Gateshead, Durham, NE	0	0
Stoke-on-Trent, Staffordshire, M	0	0
Shelton, Nottinghamshire, M	0	0
Saddleworth, Yorkshire, NE	0	0
Hanley, Staffordshire, M	0	0
Barton, Lincolnshire, EA	0	0
Great Grimsby, Lincolnshire, EA	0	0
Selby, Yorkshire, NE	0	0
Gainsborough, Lincolnshire, EA	0	0
Thorne, Lincolnshire, EA	0	0
Oughtibridge, Yorkshire, NE	0	0
Exeter, Devon, SW	.01	.18
Bath, Somerset, SW	.09	.81
Beverley, Yorkshire, NE[b]	.10	—
Dudley, Staffordshire, M	.19	2.88
Leigh, Lancashire, NW	.22	8.74
West Bromwich, Staffordshire, M	.25	.88
Birmingham, Warwickshire, M	.28	3.88
Burslem, Staffordshire, M	.31	8.47
Ross-on-Wye, Herefordshire, M[b]	.37	—
Wolverhampton, Staffordshire, M	.41	10.59
Newcastle-under-Line, Staffordshire, M	.51	10.99
Bilston, Staffordshire, M	.55	31.98
Macclesfield, Cheshire, NW	.66	9.54
Sheffield, Yorkshire, NE	.90	11.20
Wigan, Lancashire, NW	1.51	82.70
Bristol, Somerset, SW	1.56	14.11
Stockport, Cheshire, NW	1.79	22.48

Table 3.1
(continued)

City (in order of increasing subscription per 100 population)[a]	A	B
Nottingham, Nottinghamshire, M	2.70	19.92
Otley, Yorkshire, NE[b]	2.73	—
London, Middlesex, SE	2.98	44.53
Oldham, Lancashire, NW	3.19	65.83
Warrington, Cheshire, NW	3.79	93.68
Preston, Lancashire, NW	5.88	169.05
Bolton, Lancashire, NW	6.67	84.63
Blackburn, Lancashire, NW	7.19	209.17
Bury, Lancashire, NW	8.27	147.66
Liverpool, Lancashire, NW	8.73	74.08
Rochdale, Lancashire, NW	12.76	475.40
Ashton-under Lyne, Lancashire, NW	19.98	341.43
Leeds, Yorkshire, NE	26.07	368.38
Manchester, Lancashire, NW	30.60	178.70

Note: Column A gives subscriptions to the League for 1843 to 1846 in pounds per 100 of total population for each town. Column B gives the same subscriptions in pounds per 100 individuals listed in the town's commercial directory as having an occupation.
a. NE = North East, M = Midlands, SE = South East, EA = East Anglia, SW = South West, NW = North West.
b. No occupational totals could be obtained to compute figures for Beverley, Ross-on-Wye, or Otley.

permanent increase in the long-run growth rate of output resulting from trade liberalization.

Export-Sector Deconcentration

At the same time that capital investment in the cotton-textile industry was becoming concentrated geographically in Lancashire, Britain's overall export sector was becoming less concentrated, both geographically and in terms of the share accounted for by the various export industries. Davis (1979), in an examination of Britain's exports by commodity type (a proxy for the industries themselves), argues that the Industrial Revolution temporarily disrupted Britain's trend toward export deconcentration. Consequently, exports were highly concentrated in one industry—textiles. By the mid-nineteenth century, as Europeans developed their own cotton mills and large ironworks, Britain's comparative advantage over Europe had shifted from the export of finished manufactures (especially textiles) into the export of semifinished goods. Thus, Britain's exports to Europe increasingly consisted of such items as yarns, iron billets, bars and girders, and spinoffs from raw materials like wool, cotton, and hides (Davis 1979, 34).

Figure 3.1 illustrates the growth in exports of semifinished products (such as iron and steel; cotton, woollen, and linen yarns; and copper products). Moreover, a comparison of 1846 with 1825 British Customs records reveals 154 new categories of export (excluding new classifications of textiles) and only fourteen discontinued categories. Of the 154 new additions to Britain's export trades, semifinished products feature quite prominently. Figure 3.2 presents concentration indices calculated for the export sector from 1815 to 1880. Most striking is the abrupt reversal in trend beginning in 1830: whereas from 1815 to 1830, Britain's export concentration index decreased from 64.5 to 54.1 (became more concentrated), by 1845 it had climbed to 68.5 (became less concentrated) and continued increasing for several more decades. Further, an examination of Britain's export-concentration indices for the next one hundred years (to 1980, in five-year increments) provides added significance to the 1830 to 1845 shift. First, while exports clearly became less concentrated from 1830 to 1890, no subsequent trend is evident, as the index fluctuates within a narrow band ranging from the high 80s to low 90s. Second, a comparison of the 1830 to 1845 shift in index against every fifteen-year period from 1815 to 1980 (again in five-year increments) found the change from 1830 to 1845 to be statistically significant at the .0001 level (second only to the shift between 1840 and 1855).

Figures 3.1 and 3.2 indicate that at the aggregate level, Britain's export sector most definitely had resumed its pre-Industrial Revolution trend toward diversification.[9] These figures do not, however, provide us with any evidence of a parallel trend toward geographic deconcentration of export-sector interests. For some gauge of these interests, we require data at the micro level and by geographic location.

City directories offer one means of studying the economic interests of nineteenth-century Britain's populace, at least insofar as these interests may be assumed to correspond with each individual's occupational categorization. In spite of their incompleteness and inevitable inaccuracies,[10] these directories provide us with as near an approximation of the economic interest composition of various nineteenth-century cities and towns as is possible. (The appendix to this chapter elaborates on the procedure used for sampling from these directories.)

The Demand Side

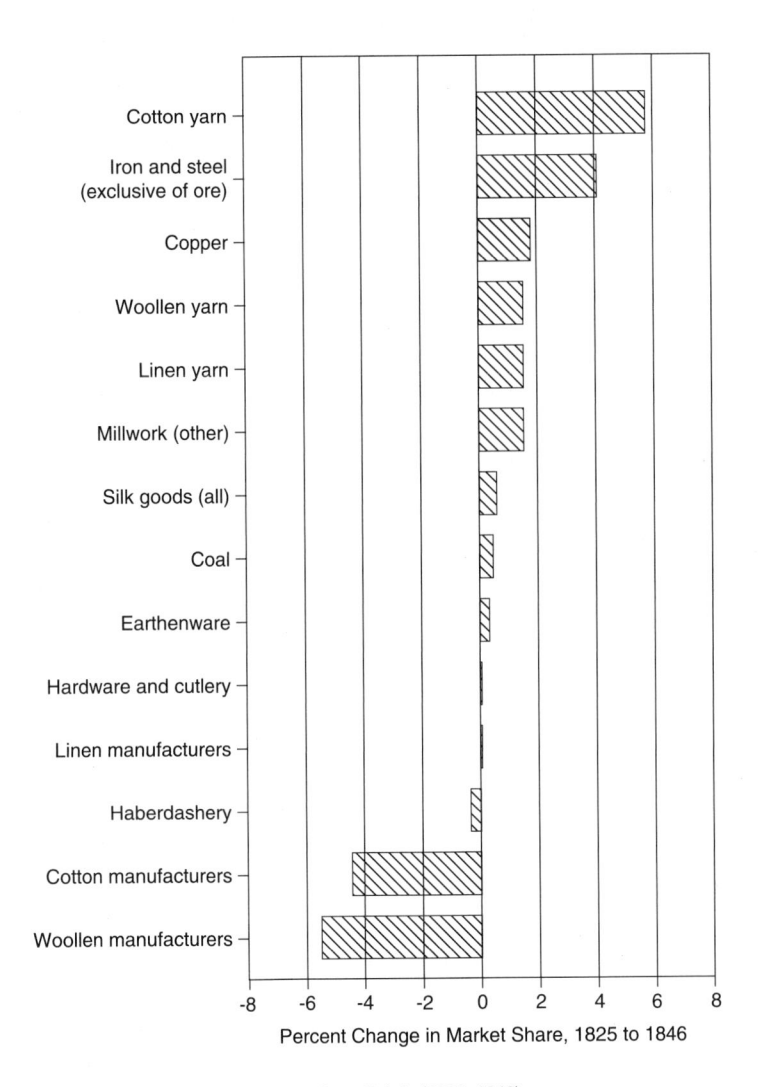

[Bar chart showing Percent Change in Market Share, 1825 to 1846, for the following categories (approximate values):
- Cotton yarn: +6
- Iron and steel (exclusive of ore): +4
- Copper: +2
- Woollen yarn: +2
- Linen yarn: +2
- Millwork (other): +2
- Silk goods (all): +1
- Coal: +1
- Earthenware: <+1
- Hardware and cutlery: 0
- Linen manufacturers: 0
- Haberdashery: +1
- Cotton manufacturers: -4
- Woollen manufacturers: -5]

Percent Change in Market Share, 1825 to 1846

Source: Great Britain (1825–1846).

Note: Declared values are used instead of official values (ie values fixed in the early eighteenth century) since rapidly falling prices for cotton goods during this period seriously distort the comparison among export commodities. For further discussion of declared versus official values, see Davis (1979).

Figure 3.1
Change in export market share of leading British industries between 1825 and 1846

Source: Derived from Mitchell (1988, 481–485).

Note: Mitchell's classifications within the export sector include coal, iron and steel, machinery, ships and boats, nonferrous metals, cotton goods, wool goods and chemicals. Concentration indices are calculated from the index of qualitative variation (IQV).

$$IQV = \frac{k(N^2 - \Sigma f^2)}{N^2(k-1)}$$

k = number of categories (here k = number of categories of exports (y))
N = number of cases (here N = 100%)
Σf^2 = sum of the squared frequencies

here $f^2 = \Sigma\left[\left(\left(\frac{y}{\Sigma y}\right) *100\right)^2\right]$

IQV is defined as the ratio of the amount of variation actually observed in a distribution of scores to the maximum variation that could exist in that distribution. The index varies from zero (no variation) to one (maximum variation) (Healey 1984, 66–69).

Figure 3.2
Concentration of the British export sector, 1815 to 1880

Samples from the city directories demonstrate the trend toward geographic dispersion of export-sector interests, both absolutely and relative to the import-competing interests (the landed aristocracy and gentry). Geographic concentration indices for the occupational categories given in the appendix indicate that the interests of all occupations became less concentrated except for one category—the landed aristocracy (Schonhardt-Bailey 1991b).

In the 1820s, the landed elite was by far the most concentrated group, and by the 1840s, they had become geographically even more concentrated. In contrast, all other categories of occupations had become less concentrated. In particular, professionals aligned with manufacturing and the retail specialty trades and the service sector were the two leading categories of geographic dispersion.

It should be emphasized that the concentration measures used here refer only to towns and cities and not to rural areas. Consequently, this urban sample allows us to conclude that declining numbers of landowners (relative to other occupations) were concentrating into fewer towns and therefore would very likely have been less able to exert political pressure.[11] In contrast, increasing numbers of export-oriented interests were present in a larger number of towns and were likely to have demonstrated a commensurate increase in political influence. A caveat to this is that under the unreformed (pre-1832) Parliament, a landowner's political influence was not necessarily limited to residence in the borough—although with the elimination of many pocket boroughs in the 1832 reform, such influence would have become less common.

Two distinct trends toward deconcentration in the British economy between the mid-1820s and the mid-1840s are thus observed: (1) national-level export-sector diversification into a broader range of export trades and (2) geographic deconcentration of industry interests as categories of occupations spread more evenly throughout the country. Simply put, industry interests extended to new trades for export and simultaneously became geographically more dispersed. Additionally, an examination of the total occupational distribution illustrates the expansion of (potential) export interests into the professions and retail-specialty trades (Schonhardt-Bailey 1991b). Meanwhile, however, the import-competing interests of the landed elite became geographically more concentrated than they already were, and they declined in their share of the total occupational distribution.

Deconcentration and the Anti-Corn Law League

Together with its concentrated organizational core, the League pursued a nationwide propaganda campaign (part of its nationalizing the interest strategy, as detailed in the next chapter) and an electoral registration campaign (as discussed in chapters 1 and 2). It would be difficult to offer direct evidence to bridge the massive national propaganda and voter-registration campaigns to the deconcentrated interests of the export sector. However, one might surmise that this national network, emanating from Manchester, was directed toward a more receptive audience than it would have enjoyed in the 1820s. Scores of new export trades had, by the 1840s, created countless new interests in trade expansion as well as interests in, if not across-the-board liberalization, certainly in strongly opposing the continued protection of British agriculture. Geographically, these interests were spread far more evenly, therefore creating more constituencies to which the League could propagandize and influence voter-registration lists. A wider constituency base, moreover, also allowed the League to present itself to parliamentary members as a national lobby with widespread electoral support. At the same time, the landed elite's core of support had both declined relative to other occupations and become more concentrated geographically. In brief, the League had the best of both worlds—a concentrated core of financial and organizational support combined with a national network scheme addressing itself to newly awakened interests in the repeal of protection for agriculture.

An Empirical Test

A successful empirical test should link both the diversification of export interests and concentration of the core export industry in Lancashire to the Anti-Corn Law League. Beginning with diversification, I examine (1) the relationship between export interests in the 1840s and League subscriptions and (2) the relationship between the *growth* in export interests (occurring between the mid-1820s and the mid-1840s) and League subscriptions. The former may be considered the static dimension; the latter a more dynamic dimension.

Both the static and dynamic dimensions are tested using four distinct but overlapping groups of occupational interests. The two dimensions differ in that the static interest groups draw only from the 1840s directories, whereas the dynamic groups measure the *difference* in occupational structure between the 1820s and 1840s. Interest group A constitutes the most narrowly defined export-industry interest group and is defined as export-oriented manufacturers plus professionals engaged directly in the export trade. The group is given as a percentage of the sum of all the occupational groupings. Interest-group B broadens group A to include professionals not explicitly linked to export trades (agents, brokers, merchants) as well as retailers, specialty trades, and service-sector occupations. Group B attempts to measure the combined strength of actual and highly probable export-oriented interests—that is, individuals likely to have been closely linked to the export sector. Interest-group C adds to group B manufacturers whose activities were directed primarily toward the domestic market. Interest-group D combines all manufacturing interests together. Groups A, B, C, and D are each given as a proportion of the sum of all occupations.

The dynamic interest-groups measure changes over time in the percentages of the population falling into each of the four groupings. For instance, by subtracting group A's percentage of the total occupations in the 1820s from its percentage of the total occupations in the 1840s, the dynamic measure of interest-group A indicates the change in strictly export-oriented interests from the mid-1820s to the mid-1840s, measured as a percentage of the total employed population.

Tables 3.2 and 3.3 give the results of linear regressions of each interest group and change in interest group, respectively, on League subscriptions. (See book Appendix 1 for a summary list of the variables used in this and other chapters.) Unfortunately, the geographical concentration of capital offers no empirical data that are suitable for statistical analysis and therefore has to be proxied. Considering the earlier discussion of concentration of the textile industry into Lancashire, the proxy is constructed as a dichotomous variable with the dummy assigned to all towns inside Lancashire. Hence, I do not demonstrate the *direct* statistical link between geographic concentration and League contributions.

The emphasis of the analysis is on the relative strengths of the interest groups as derived from slope estimates. While the overall explanatory performance of the equations is just about acceptable for historical data such as these (with regression coefficients ranging from .21 to .34), estimations of fit are not sufficiently different among the regressions to offer insight into the validity of the competing hypotheses. Moreover, while it may be useful to note that the dummy

Table 3.2
Coefficient estimates for the relationship between export-sector interest groups in the mid-1840s and subscriptions to the Anti-Corn Law League

Variable	Interest Group A Coefficient	Interest Group A Standard Error	Interest Group B Coefficient	Interest Group B Standard Error	Interest Group C Coefficient	Interest Group C Standard Error	Interest Group D Coefficient	Interest Group D Standard Error
Subscription per 100 in population:								
Constant	−0.19	—	−2.55	—	−6.89	—	−1.19	—
Interest group[a]	5.70	8.15	6.20	11.99	11.22	12.78	6.89	7.86
Dummy variable[b]	7.77*	2.32	7.53*	2.31	7.15*	2.34	7.58*	2.92
R^2	0.243		0.238		0.249		0.249	
Subscription per 100 in commercial directory:								
Constant	12.07	—	−78.87	—	−135.51	—	4.86	—
Interest group[a]	34.36	123.26	154.84	179.23	211.03	191.15	44.55	119.29
Dummy variable[b]	141.11*	35.14	139.43*	34.49	132.22*	34.95	140.0*	34.79
R^2	0.316		0.329		0.338		0.318	

Source: Commercial directories from the 1840s.
Note: $N = 38$. Interest group A = export-oriented manufacturers and professionals aligned with manufacturing, B = A + nonaligned professional and retail trades, C = B + manufacturers supplying domestic markets, D = A + manufacturers supplying domestic markets.
a. Each interest group is expressed as a proportion of the sum of all occupations as listed in the appendix to chapter 3.
b. A proxy for export sector capital concentration in Lancashire.
*Statistically significant at $p < .01$.

Table 3.3
Coefficient estimates for the relationship between the growth in export-sector interest groups between the mid-1820s and the mid-1840s and subscriptions to the League

Variable	Group Change A Coefficient	Group Change A Standard Error	Group Change B Coefficient	Group Change B Standard Error	Group Change C Coefficient	Group Change C Standard Error	Group Change D Coefficient	Group Change D Standard Error
Subscription per 100 in population:								
Constant	2.44	—	1.86	—	1.81	—	2.13	—
Interest group[a]	7.19	8.35	4.8	8.47	1.39	10.46	3.75	8.9
Dummy variable[b]	7.01*	2.56	7.27*	2.56	7.22*	2.58	7.04*	2.62
R^2	0.228		0.218		0.21		0.214	
Subscription per 100 in commercial directory:								
Constant	39.36	—	27.49	—	27.12	—	34.96	—
Interest group[a]	151.99	124.16	116.62	126.34	81.74	156.71	100.76	133.04
Dummy variable[b]	131.26*	38.04	136.75*	38.21	134.66*	38.71	130.55*	39.14
R^2	0.326		0.312		0.299		0.306	

Source: Commercial directories from the 1820s and 1840s.
Note: $N = 33$. Groups are as in table 3.2.
a. Each interest group is defined as in table 3.2.
b. A proxy for export-sector capital concentration in Lancashire.
*Statistically significant at $p < .01$.

is consistently significant at the .01 level and the interest groups consistently statistically insignificant, note also that (1) I could have predicted a strong statistical performance for the dummy, given evidence that the textile manufacturers in Lancashire as individuals contributed most to the League, and that (2) historical data such as were used to construct the interest group variables are rarely in a form likely to produce statistical significance in regression analysis. Hence, I provide a tentative analysis of the relative strengths of the interest groups by exploring the variations both among the interest-group slope coefficients and between these coefficients and the Lancashire dummy slope coefficients.

The Lancashire dummy slope coefficient in both the static and dynamic regressions provides statistical confirmation that Lancashire residents contributed substantially more to the League than non-Lancashire residents. Interpreting this variable as a proxy for capital concentration, the slope coefficient suggests that this extra capital translated into contributions to the League inside Lancashire amounting to, ceteris paribus, over £7 per person—or £135 per working person—*more than* those outside Lancashire (see table 3.2). More revealing, however, are the contrasts among the various groups of occupations in table 3.2.

For both the static 1840s set of regressions, the largest contributions came from towns with a high proportion of interest-group C—that is, exporters, marginal exporters, and domestic-market manufacturers. Indeed, the largest contributors were towns situated in Lancashire with exporters, marginal exporters, and domestic-market manufacturers constituting a high percentage of the population. Nonetheless, the strength of the coefficient for group C illustrates the importance of diversification of export interests at the national level so that even the towns outside Lancashire with populations of diversified export interests were important contributors to the League. (For example, for each 10 percent increase in diversified export interests in the country's working population, a town would, ceteris paribus, contribute about £21 more to the League.)

In the dynamic regressions (table 3.3), the extension of export interests to a greater number of occupations from the 1820s to 1840s (group-change B, C, and D) appeared far less important than the increase in occupations most directly tied to exports (group-change A). Clearly, the growth of the narrowest group of export interests (group A) had the greatest influence on League contributions, although the growth of the actual and highly probable export-oriented interest group (group-change B) also demonstrated an influence on League contributions. The broadest group (group-change C, derived from group C) showed the least impact on League contributions—a finding that initially might seem *not* to support the deconcentrated-export-interests hypothesis. However, considering that the interest groups were constructed as percentages of the total population, the group of occupations that was most directly associated with exports (group A) constituted a smaller percentage of the population and thus allowed a greater margin for growth than did the larger initial percentages of the remaining groups (all of which included occupations given in interest-group A plus other occupations less directly tied to exports). We may conclude, then, that the strong performance of the narrower group of export interests emphasizes the importance of the *growth* in those interests closely associated with the export trade (group-change A), as well as interests with a highly probable link to the export trade (group-change B). Growth of the most broadly defined group (group-change C)—which already included the largest percentage of the population—was, not surprisingly, the weakest performer. However, the impressive performance of this group in the static measures suggests that while the *level* of export-interest geographic deconcentration certainly contributed to support for the League, the effect of the *growth* of this deconcentration was either less important than its actual level or was important but requires a measure other than change in the percentage of the population to capture its effect (for example, one that could capture the effect of individuals falling within group C who over time moved into the narrower group A).

Briefly stated, the regression results illustrate the impact of both diversified export interests and of geographic concentration of capital in Lancashire on the Anti-Corn Law League. It was not the core export industry alone that best accounts for League financial support but rather the combined clout of interests within this industry plus the more geographically diversified export sector, including the groups newly created and less directly associated with the export interests.

Conclusion

The emergence of the Anti-Corn Law League as a free-trade pressure group is best explained not by the standard Olson interest-group model but rather as the combination of two concurrent changes in the nineteenth-century British economy. First, geographic concentration of the textile industry into Lancashire acted both to concentrate resources available for launching the free-trade campaign and to concentrate the expected benefits accruing from free trade, hence motivating this core of industrialists to bear a disproportionate burden in supplying the free-trade public good. Second, an increase in the number of industries comprising the export sector, combined with geographic deconcentration of export-oriented interests, enhanced the political leverage of the League by broadening its base of support. Its propaganda and voter-registration campaigns thereby enjoyed a geographically broader base of support, and, equally important, the free-trade message of the League would certainly have appealed to the recently expanded number of occupations (interests) connected to the export trade.

More broadly, this chapter has portrayed the emergence of a free-trade pressure group as the united force of concentrated and deconcentrated interests. Whereas concentrated industry interests willing to bear a disproportionate share of the burden easily overcame the free-rider problem through their smaller numbers and concentrated benefits from liberalization (both static and dynamic), their narrow political base of support required a broader constituency to lobby effectively for liberalization. This emerged as the economy diversified its exports and as export interests became more geographically widespread.

Appendix

Publishers issued two common types of directories for nineteenth-century cities and towns—commercial directories and trade directories. Commercial directories may be likened to modern-day white pages, since they list individual names, addresses, and occupations (or titles). Trade directories correspond to our yellow pages, as they list beneath each trade the names and addresses of the tradesmen. A third type of directory, the court directory (which was only occasionally available), listed the local aristocracy, gentry, and clergy. Here, a city's court directory was subsumed under the trade-directory classifications, with the total number of aristocracy and gentry coded as a separate category under the particular city's trade directory. While elsewhere I use the combined data from both sets of directories (Schonhardt-Bailey 1991b), for simplification the regression results are given here only for the commercial directories.

A sample size of 5 percent was drawn from the commercial directories (white pages) for each city; however, for cities with over ten thousand listings, I drew a sample of 2.5 percent and then doubled the numbers under each occupational category. (For a few small villages, I drew at least thirty-five individuals or the standard 5 percent—whichever was larger.) Actual total numbers of individuals were counted under each category of the trade directories (yellow pages). Samples were drawn from all cities publishing directories for both the mid-1820s and the mid-1840s. The key reference listing all available city directories before the 1850s was Norton (1950). I also consulted the London Guildhall Library's current listings for additional directories.

In Schonhardt-Bailey (1991b), I give the county and regional breakdown of the city directory samples. Figure 3.3 provides a map of the distribution. Not surprisingly, the industrial areas were overrepresented, and the agricultural areas underrepresented. For the purposes of this chapter, however, underrepresentation of agricultural regions is of little concern, since their absence biases the sample against the geographic deconcentration hypothesis rather than in favor of it (that is, if we think of the country as divided into two types of regions—agricultural and industrial/commercial—then regardless of whether geographic deconcentration were to extend to the agricultural regions, it would not diminish findings demonstrating that deconcentration occurred within the more industrial and commercial portions of the country).

The hundreds of various occupation types were grouped into fifteen categories, as follows.

Export-Oriented Manufacturers

1. *Manufacturing, export of light goods* Bleachers, bobbin makers, canvas manufacturers, cloth dressers, cotton manufacturers, cotton dealers, dyers, hat manufacturers, linen drapers, milliners and dressmakers, needle and pin makers, thread manufacturers, woolen cloth manufacturers, and so on.

2. *Manufacturing, export of heavy goods* Brass founders, braziers, coppersmiths, tinplate workers, iron founders, tool manufacturers, and so on.

3. *Manufacturing, semiexport (serving the home market as well as foreign markets)* Brush manufacturers, cabinetmakers, coal dealers, leather cutters and manufacturers, earthenware dealers and manufacturers,

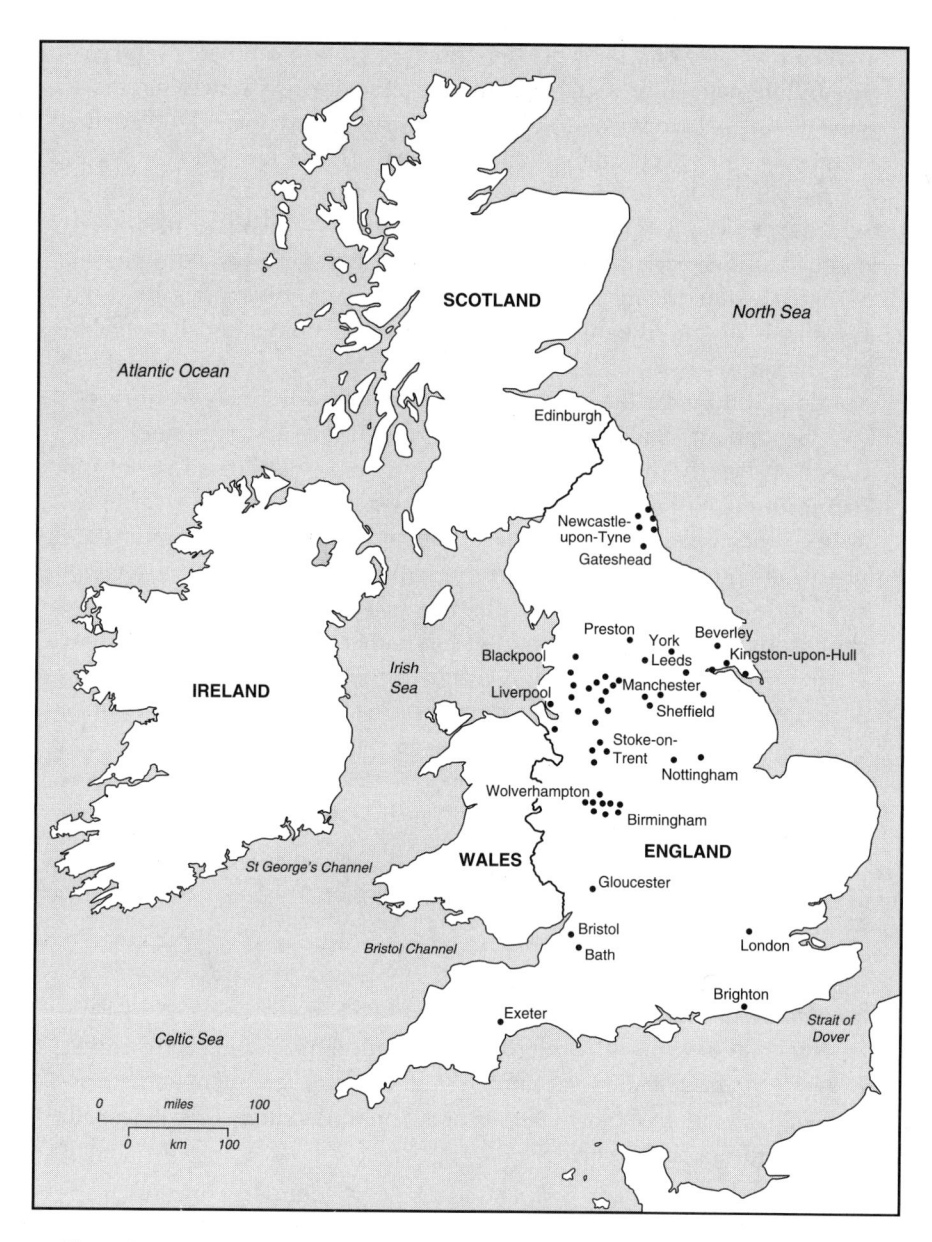

Figure 3.3
City Directories for mid-1820s and mid-1840s

glass manufacturers, gunmakers, hardware dealers, hosiers and glovers, lead merchants, rope and twine manufacturers, watch and clock manufacturers, and so on.

Professionals

4. *Professional, nonaligned* Academy owners, accountants, agents, architects, attorneys-solicitors, auctioneers, bankers, barristers, brokers, commissioners, consuls, clergy, insurance agents, merchants, publishers, pawnbrokers, surgeons, and so on.

5. *Professional, aligned with manufacturing* Warehouse owners, clothing brokers, cotton brokers, engineers, stock and share brokers, and so on.

6. *Professional, aligned with land* Surveyors, land agents, and so on.

Agricultural

7. *Agriculture, farming.*

8. *Agriculture, semiexport (serving domestic market as well as foreign markets)* Bacon, ham, and cheese factors, gardeners and seedsmen, oil merchants, seed merchants, and so on.

9. *Agriculture, serving domestic market* Bakers, butchers, cattle dealers, wheat and flour merchants, corn millers, fruiterers, grocers, poulterers, and so on.

Miscellaneous

10. *Manufacturing, serving domestic market* Basketmakers, blacksmiths, boot and shoe makers, bricklayers and builders, confectioners, engravers, gas light makers, whitesmiths and bellhangers, and so on.

11. *Other retail, specialty trades, service sector* Artificial limb makers, animal preservers, booksellers and stationers, tea and coffee dealers, druggists, eatinghouse keepers, haberdashers, news vendors, shopkeepers, victuallers, and so on.

12. *Fishing and shipping* Fishing gear makers, fishmongers, boat builders and owners, ship builders and owners, and so on.

13. *Widows and spinsters.*

14. *Aristocracy, landowners, gentry, titled men of independent means.*

15. *Military.*

These categorizations clearly are problematic, as room for subjective estimation was quite broad. Moreover, the problems in trying to ascertain from national-level export totals the export interests of individuals in particular cities are obvious. My estimates of the interests of individuals' occupations were based on 1825, 1830, 1835, 1840, and 1846 export records (Great Britain 1825–1846).

The list of League subscriptions was obtained from two sources: (McCord 1958; Prentice 1968). My sample is limited to cities publishing commercial or trade directories for years circa 1825 and 1846. These cities, the counties and regions in which they fall, and their per capita subscriptions to the League are given in table 3.1.

4 Nationalizing the Interest in Free Trade

Ideas and Interest Groups

In the previous chapter, we analyzed the emergence of the Anti-Corn Law League. This chapter explores the means by which the League spread its free-trade message throughout Britain, thereby intensifying the demand-side pressure for free trade. Interest-based approaches (most of which adopt a demand-side perspective) generally seek to explain why some groups are more successful than others in shaping public policy. These approaches devote far less attention to how groups communicate with nongroup members—that is, how they appeal to the general public for support.[1] In this chapter, we find that such appeals are often based on unifying themes or ideas, particularly ones that are linked with the broader societal welfare. Thus, it is the use of ideas,[2] ceteris paribus, that enables some groups to succeed where others fail.

This chapter examines how and under what conditions an economic interest group (such as the League) might persuade nongroup members to support the group's policy objective. Ideas are central to facilitating and shaping the ways in which interest groups appeal to the general public. Some interest groups are able to *nationalize their interest* by using ideas or ideologies to gain support for their policy objective (support that is not available from interests alone).[3]

The concept of nationalizing the interest can be used to *compare* the success and failure of interest-group lobbying, as I have done elsewhere.[4] This chapter, however, focuses exclusively on one case of nationalizing the interest—the Anti-Corn Law League and repeal.

Nationalizing the Interest

Nationalizing the interest means that parochial interests create the appearance (which may or may not be based in fact) that their political objective is (or should be) shared by the larger citizenry (or by a particular social or economic class): the particular is represented as the general. The goal in representing the particular as the general is to create a large (even national) following. However well groups pursue the interests of their members, they will not gain the support of the general public without some recourse to ideology or, at a minimum, ideas.[5] Ideology persuades the general public to support or to become indifferent to the group's policy preferences; that is, it makes the policy goal palatable to nonmembers of the group. Groups that nationalize the interest may even use ideological persuasion to *shape the economic interests* of individuals, particularly insofar as changes in policy (such as economic-policy reform) make it difficult for individuals to calculate their actual interests. Bates and Krueger (1993, 456) emphasize the importance of ideology in shaping individuals' interests:

> A result of this uncertainty [in economic-policy reforms] is that people can be persuaded as to where their economic interests lie; wide scope is thus left for rhetoric and persuasion. In such situations, advocates of particular economic theories or of ideological conceptions of how economies work can acquire influence.... Under conditions of uncertainty, people's beliefs of where their economic interests lie can be created and organized by political activists; rather than shaping events, notions of self-interest are instead themselves shaped and formed. In pursuing their economic interests, people act in response to ideology.

In other words, *economic interests will be more successful in obtaining their political objectives when, as a collectivity, they are able to "nationalize the interest."* When all else is held constant, groups that do not engage in a nationalizing the interest strategy would be expected to fare less well in the policy arena.

Interest-Based versus Ideology-Based Groups

E. E. Schattschneider (1960) argued that interest-based and ideology-based groups are distinguished by whether members can expect to benefit personally from the goal of the group. For example, the members of the National Association of Manufacturers expect to benefit personally from policies promoted by the association, while the members of the American League to Abolish Capital Punishment do not ex-

The Demand Side   77

pect to escape execution as a result of membership, since membership includes *anyone* opposed to capital punishment, not just those persons on death row (Schattschneider 1960, 26). According to Schattschneider, interest-based groups provide exclusive benefits to members, while ideology-based groups provide nonexclusive benefits. Yet this distinction becomes blurred if one considers the "logic" of collective action (Olson 1965), since interest-based and ideology-based groups both provide public and possibly also private goods. An interest-based group provides both a public and a private good. Favorable corporate tax policy, for example, may benefit all businesses, regardless of whether they contribute to the corporate lobby organization, while selective incentives (special publications, credit cards, newsletters, access to information and other resources) are enjoyed by contributing members only. Likewise, the goals pursued by ideology-based groups (such as the abolition of capital punishment, a clean environment, and a nuclear-free world) can be enjoyed by contributors and noncontributors alike (depending on whether the goal is valued by the noncontributor) and the enjoyment by one individual does not detract from that of another. They may also provide private goods to contributing members, such as newsletters, invitations to special events, a sense of personal gratification, and so on. Yet the distinction between interest-based and ideology-based groups has less to do with the exclusivity of benefits and more to do with the tendency of the interest-based groups to "rationalize their special interests as public interests" (Schattschneider 1960, 25). Interest-based groups may thus obfuscate the exclusive returns expected from the policy objective to individuals who do not share these returns (nongroup members). At this point, interest-based groups may invoke ideas or ideology as a tool of obfuscation: they may engage in a strategy of nationalizing the group's interest. Ideology-based groups, on the other hand, begin and end their appeal with the tool of ideology, while interest-based groups begin with shared interests and then invoke the tool of ideology only when and as necessary. Interest groups that use ideas or ideology to obfuscate the special benefits (generally economic gain) accruing to their members are indeed exploiting the ideology in pursuit of (an) ulterior motive(s).[6]

Conditions for Nationalizing the Interest

Why are some interest groups more successful at nationalizing the interest than others? At least three conditions favor some groups over others: (1) the existence of positive externalities to the special benefit that is sought by the group, externalities that may be linked to an idea or ideology; (2) good organization and strong leadership; and (3) a conducive institutional environment. Condition 1 is unique to the concept of nationalizing the interest, while conditions 2 and 3 are widely accepted as keys to successful lobbying. Organization, leadership, and conducive institutions can surely be helpful, but not all three are absolutely essential. What *is* essential, however, is condition 1—the existence of positive externalities.

Positive Externality A positive externality, or spillover, from a policy outcome is some benefit that accrues to noninterested, nonmembers of the particular group that desires the policy. (For the sake of simplicity, some homogeneity of interests among group members is assumed so that aggregation of interests is unproblematic.) While the tangible benefit may be difficult or impossible to measure, the *idea* or image behind it is appealing to most people. This idea or image is generally couched in terms of the broader societal welfare: a prosperous economy, national pride, family values, and a clean environment are all potential positive externalities. Consider contemporary farmers' groups that seek to obtain or retain trade protection. Appeals to the public are phrased in terms of the broader societal welfare: "self-sufficiency in agriculture is necessary for the nation's security" (Winters 1990; Ruppel and Kellogg 1991); "agriculture must be protected as an environmentally friendly 'green' industry" (Anderson 1992); and "the family farm must be protected in order to preserve traditional rural values" or "the countryside." A statement by the European Union (EU) Farm Commissioner invokes positive externalities to defend Common Agricultural Policy (CAP) subsidies: "If European society is interested in the European model of agriculture, meaning that agricultural output is not measured only in cereals or beef but also in the landscape and the environment, it needs to pay the additional cost" ("Farmer Franz Fischler Digs In" 1998). The French are particularly adept at invoking positive externalities to defend their status as a main beneficiary of CAP subsidies, arguing that these subsidies are part of the "spirit and heritage" of the EU ("The EU's Coming Wrangle for Reforms and Spoils" 1999). Because the French see themselves as a farming nation (though only a small fraction of the workforce is devoted to farming), they are sympathetic to their farmers as "they burn down buildings, block motorways, dump tonnes of imported fruit and vegetables on the streets and stage other violent demonstrations in defence of what they consider their right to cash from the public purse" ("Not All as Cosseted as Consumers Say" 1998).

William Browne's (1992, 11–15; 2001, 50–60) depiction of the myths behind American agricultural policy offers an apt illustration of how American farmers also invoke positive externalities to garner support for agricultural subsidies. He maintains that American farmers perpetuate the idea that family farms are central to the nation's cultural heritage, purporting that farms are necessary for preserving individual liberties in capitalist societies and family farms are "repositories for family values and hence for traditional ways of defining personal loyalties within a framework of community" (Browne 1992, 11). As a consequence, "agrarian populist arguments have...been applied to public policy as reasons to preserve family farms or, more frequently, to preserve farming as a way of life in general" (13). It is precisely the ambiguity of the ideas and images behind the "agrarian ideal" that makes them so politically attractive, for as Browne (1992, 13–15) notes,

> They are contested symbols, vague images of how agriculture ought to be, or once was. Their lack of specificity means that competing political interests can easily appropriate them.... There is irony in the fact that an agrarian philosophy that stresses the importance of community and the public good should be used to promote the interests of a few.

Because American farming lobbies use family values and community spirit as images or ideas, they have been successful in persuading urban consumers to pay higher prices for subsidized food. In this case, "ideas have power" (Browne 2001, 50). They inspire consumers to think beyond the immediate consumption value of food.

But how do these images or ideas actually work to persuade nongroup members to accept the policy objective of the interest group? How do ideas become "inspirational"? Kenneth Shepsle (1985, 233) depicts the role of ideas quite simply as "the hooks on which politicians hang their objectives and by which they further their interests." But how exactly do these hooks work? In the examples given above, ideas hook nongroup members by getting them to think of the price paid for a commodity as including a package of goods, not just the one item. That is, the commodity becomes multidimensional. The package price includes not just the food product but other items as well, such as supporting the family farm, preserving the countryside, and alleviating rural poverty. The positive externalities from the policy outcome thus provide the ideas that transform a commodity valued by a single dimension (private consumption) to one with value in other dimensions. For instance, when the Anti-Corn Law League failed to persuade nonagricultural workers that their real wages would rise as a result of repeal, it sought to persuade them to see free trade not in terms of wage issues but rather in terms of fighting against a landowning aristocracy (the monopolists), as is shown later in this chapter. The job of interest groups engaged in nationalizing the interest is to (1) convince nongroup members that the commodity (or more broadly, the policy outcome) is multidimensional and (2) persuade them of the value of the other bits of the package. In terms of trade protection, for example, nongroup members then become willing to pay more for the same product (say, food) because they give higher salience to the other bits of the package (say, the environment or family values).

Interest groups are not alone in appealing to positive externalities for support. Political parties may use it to enlarge their membership, or as one author aptly puts it: "National societal goals transcending group interests offer the best sales prospect for the party intent on establishing or enlarging an appeal previously limited to specific sections of the population" (Kirchheimer 1990, 54). Political leaders may also appeal to positive externalities to garner support for their policies. Positive externalities may be linked to a specific idea or to a wider ideology, but in either case they are seen to enhance the broader societal welfare.

Leadership and Organization Interest groups that enjoy strong leadership and good organization are better situated to nationalize the interest. The importance of leadership is fairly self-evident, for "the best ideology, in terms of internal logical consistency and emotional appeal, is as nothing without committed apostles to spread it" (Hinich and Munger 1994, 21). Group *leaders*, therefore, almost certainly will be true believers in the ideology they invoke to nationalize the interest. Almost as self-evident is the need for organization, since only when ideologies are backed by organizations will they take hold. Sartori boldly states that "no idea has ever made much headway without an organization behind it.... Wherever ideologies seem to be important in politics they have a firm organizational basis.... Ideological persuasion requires a powerfully organized network of communications" (Sartori 1990, 169–170).

Undoubtedly, leadership and organization are vital, but it is difficult to quantify how much of each is actually required for a successful nationalizing the interest strategy. The Anti-Corn Law League enjoyed superb leadership and an unprecedented organizational apparatus—and it succeeded in its policy objective of repeal. During Britain's era of proposed Tariff Reform, the Free Trade Union exhibited rather average leadership and never attained the national organization of the League—and yet it too succeeded in persuading the electorate of its free-trade goal (Schonhardt-Bailey 2001). (Inasmuch as the Union sought to preserve a policy while the League sought to change policy, it might be said that the former faced an easier task than the latter.) In brief, while some leadership and organization are necessary, extraordinary quantities of either do not appear essential.

Institutions Three institutions are relevant for nationalizing the interest. Changes in the franchise, the party system, and governmental agencies or departments can each (or in concert) facilitate or block the efforts of interest groups that attempt to nationalize the interest. For instance, laws that enfranchise new groups of individuals (the middle class, the working class, or women) will undoubtedly provide a window of opportunity for those individuals to nationalize their interests. This may arise as a consequence of a newly enfranchised group sharing some common idea of what contributes to the broader societal welfare: middle-class voters might share an antipathy toward aristocratic traditions; working-class voters might share a commitment to fair practices in the workplace; and women voters might share a commitment to nondiscrimination in employment. "Antiaristocracy", "workers' rights," and "women's rights" then become ideological fodder for much narrower goals of economic interest groups.

A polity in which parties are highly ideological can limit the opportunity for interest groups to nationalize the interest, since party cleavages may dominate the ideological debate. Conversely, a polity of ideologically weak parties may allow interest groups more freedom to exploit ideology as they seek to nationalize their interest. This assertion makes sense if one assumes that an equilibrium level of "ideologizing" exists in any polity and that, in the first instance, political parties provide the bulk of the ideological thinking. If parties sacrifice ideology for the economic interests of their members, an "ideological vacuum" is created. This in turn creates an opportunity for interest groups to fill the vacuum through a strategy of nationalizing the interest.

If, moreover, we accept that some political parties are more ideological than other parties (Bell 1960; Duverger 1961; Waxman 1968;

Kirchheimer 1990; Lijphart 1990; Lipset and Rokkan 1990; Mair 1990; Schonhardt-Bailey 1998), and we assume that an equilibrium level of "ideologizing" exists in any polity, it becomes clear that the less the ideological content of political parties, the greater the opportunity for interest groups to nationalize the interest. Specifically, if interest groups operate in a polity dominated by highly ideological parties, their ability to adopt a strategy of nationalizing the interest is circumscribed. Conversely, where parties represent the interests of their members over ideology, an ideological vacuum may arise that interest groups may exploit. In this sense, the *party* institutional context constrains or enhances the ability of interest groups to nationalize their interest.

Finally, inasmuch as ideas and ideologies become embedded in institutions and thereby "take on a life of their own" (Goldstein 1993), we should expect that this would have repercussions for interest groups that seek to exploit ideologies. When ideologies become embedded in governmental agencies or departments, they acquire added legitimacy, which in turn can benefit interest groups that seek to exploit these same ideologies and hinder groups whose goals conflict with these ideologies.

Other Factors Just as some policies (like international trade) have greater scope for nationalizing the interest than others,[7] some types of groups will be more likely to use the strategy than others. Groups comprised of "insiders" (individuals who are either part of or have easy access to the policy-making elite) tend not to engage in nationalizing the interest, since to do so would dilute their privileged access to the policy makers. "Outsider" groups (those that have little or no direct access to policy makers) are more likely to seek to nationalize their interest as a way of placing greater political pressure on policy makers. The Anti-Corn Law League and Protectionist MPs, respectively, provide a perfect example of the propensity of outsiders to nationalize their interest while insiders relied on their presumed strength in Parliament.

This distinction between insider and outsider groups parallels Schnattschneider's (1960, 38–39) observation that it is the (initially) weak, rather than the strong, who seek the involvement of more and more people in a conflict:

The notion of "pressure" distorts the image of the power relations involved [in political conflicts]. *Private conflicts are taken into the public arena precisely because someone wants to make certain that the power ratio among the private interests most immediately involved shall not prevail....* Since the contestants in private conflicts are apt to be unequal in strength, it follows that *the most powerful special interests want private settlements* because they are able to dictate the outcome as long as the conflict remains private.... Therefore, it is the weak, not the strong, who appeal to public authority for relief.

While the designation of weak and strong groups can lead to circularity in predicting policy outcomes (the strong win because they are strong), the private versus public debate helps us to see the link between policy type and group type. That is, policies that are narrow, highly technical, or secretive have little scope for public debate[8] and have insider groups that are more likely to hold sway. Hence, one would not expect to find a nationalizing-the-interest strategy at work. On the other hand, policies where the debate is open to the public have more outsider groups and therefore are where we would expect to find the groups engaging in nationalizing the interest. Very often policies and groups do not separate into these two general types, and so we find insider and outsider groups competing against one another. In this case, nationalizing the interest may be a way for an outsider group to counter the insider-access advantage.

The Endogeneity and Exogeneity of Individuals' Preferences
To better understand individuals' preferences, we must investigate how actors—particularly interest groups—might exploit ideas to further their interests. But first we must have a clear notion of how individuals construct their policy preferences.

Individuals' Preferences Think of interests and ideology as two dimensions of individual preferences. That is, an individual may be motivated primarily (or even entirely) by economic interests, so that she advocates only those policies for which she perceives a clear and immediate economic benefit. At the other end of the spectrum is an individual who is entirely altruistic, so that she advocates policies that she discerns as benefiting society as a whole or a disadvantaged section of society. (For purposes of simplification, all dimensions of ideas and ideology are collapsed onto a single dimension.) Figure 4.1 captures these two extremes in motivation.[9] In figure 4.1a, the individual is motivated by economic interests alone. Her ideal line (in bold) designates her interest-motivated preference on a particular policy. Her preference function, or utility function, is greatest on this line. Her utility declines with distance from her ideal line, so that a policy that falls

a. Preference from interests only

Interests

Only interests matter

u_0
u_1
u_2

Ideal line

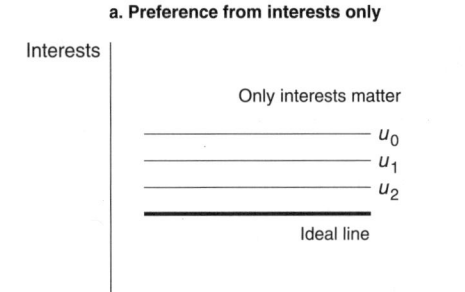

Ideas or Ideology

b. Preference from ideas or ideology only

Interests

Only ideas or ideology matter

u_2 u_1 u_0

Ideal line

Ideas or Ideology

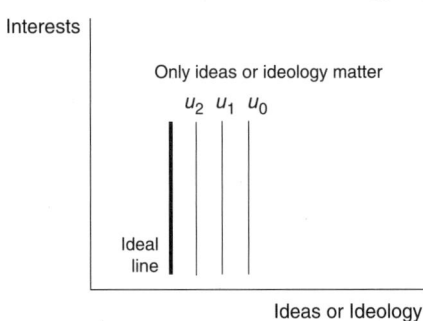

Figure 4.1
Two extremes for policy preferences

on, say, u_0 is preferred less than all others nearer to her ideal line. Note that the indifference curves, or lines above the ideal line, are flat, meaning that the ideas or ideology dimension has no bearing on her preference. The story is reversed in figure 4.1b, where the individual is motivated solely by ideas or ideology. (Ideally, the lines would be drawn in a three-dimensional space, with utility representing the third dimension.)

Most individuals fall somewhere in between these two extremes, with economic interests and ideological beliefs together shaping policy preferences. In figure 4.2, we see three types of policy preferences where interests *and* ideas or ideology both have salience. In figure 4.2a, interests and ideas or ideology are weighted equally in deciding the policy preference. In figures 4.2b and 4.2c, the two dimensions have different salience, so that the indifference curves are ellipses. In

a. Interests and ideas are equally salient.

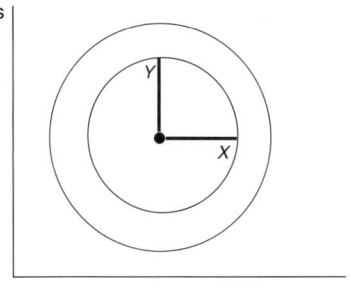

b. Interests are more salient.

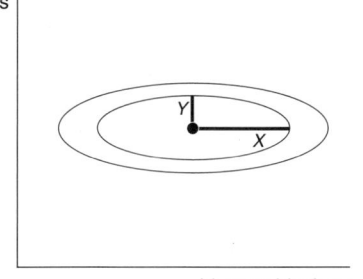

c. Ideas are more salient.

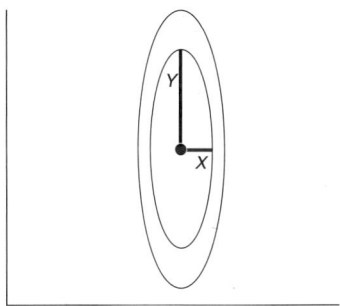

Figure 4.2
Variations in salience of interests and ideas or ideology

figure 4.2b, economic interests are more important to the individual's policy preference, so that the curves are squeezed from the sides, forming a horizontal ellipse. As economic interests become relatively more important (and ideas or ideology relatively less important), the ellipse flattens further, so that at the extreme, we return to the flat curves in figure 4.1a. The same applies to the vertical ellipse in figure 4.2c. The bold lines extending from the first indifference curve to the ideal point (given as X and Y in figure 4.2a) depict the relative amount of each dimension that an individual is willing to forgo as she moves away from her ideal point. In figure 4.2a, these amounts are equal, since both dimensions are of equal importance in determining her policy preference. In figure 4.2b, the individual is willing to compromise far more on her ideas than she is on her interests, since she values her interests more. Similarly, in figure 4.2c, she is willing to compromise more on interests than ideas, since the latter are more important to her.

Changing Preferences through Nationalizing the Interest Traditional rational-choice theory suggests that once economic interests are correctly specified, the preferences of individuals or groups should become self-evident. Beyond this, the genesis of preferences is generally not disputed. Interests are considered exogenous to policy outcomes, and individuals or groups can determine self-evidently whether a particular outcome benefits or harms their interests. Yet interests are not as unproblematic in accounting for preferences as rational-choice theory maintains. Increasingly, scholars are coming to accept that ideas help to shape interests (Blyth 2002, 2003).

In the extreme, nationalizing the interest suggests that interest groups use ideas or ideology to shape nongroup members' perceptions of their own self-interest. The main point is that the group engages in nationalizing the interest when, by employing an idea or ideology, it *persuades* nongroup members to acquiesce to or even support the policy objective of the group.

A reasonable assumption (given the resources available to groups versus individuals) is that groups enjoy a greater understanding of the arguments (often conveyed in the form of ideas) about policy effects than do individuals and thus enjoy an opportunity to exploit this asymmetry of knowledge. The use or misuse of such knowledge per se does not, however, constitute nationalizing the interest, since at the heart of this strategy is the use of arguments or ideas to counter perceptions of conflicting interests (between the group and the individual).

Groups therefore use arguments and ideas both to *reinforce* a common interest and to *counter* an opposing interest. In both strategies, groups use arguments and ideas to persuade individuals, but this persuasion may be moderate or extreme, with the former meaning persuasion to support policy X once it is seen to coincide with one's self-interest, and the latter meaning persuasion to support policy X, even when it is contrary to one's self-interest. The ultimate form of persuasion is therefore when individuals are induced either to reinterpret their own interests or to disregard them.

A further complication is that groups can use arguments deliberately to mislead. The effectiveness of such a strategy depends on how well informed nongroup members are and how many other arguments they consider. As will be discussed later, the further choice between using honest and misleading arguments depends on whether the interests of the group and individual coincide or conflict. When the group's and the individual's interests coincide (see figure 4.3), the group merely needs to inform the individual of this shared interest, thereby expanding the "group" from a collectivity of actual fee-paying members to one consisting of all individuals who share the interest. In this case, any recourse to ideas as persuasion is wasted effort. When the group's and the individual's interests conflict, however, misleading arguments can compete with honest ones as mechanisms of persuasion.

Table 4.1 presents the interplay between (1) individual and group interests and (2) an individual's knowledge of her own self-interest. The objective relation between the interests of the individual and the group is simplified as a dichotomy: either they coincide, or they conflict. The three rows in table 4.1 depict the knowledge of the individual about her own economic interests. She may be clear about what her interests are, and these may either coincide or conflict with those of the group. If her (immediate) interests coincide with the group's interest (cell A), the group merely confirms this mutuality of interests: it does not invoke anything other than common interests to garner her support. To the extent that the group employs ideas, these are used merely as arguments to reinforce interests. If, on the other hand, her interests conflict with the group's interest, the group may use positive externalities to persuade her both of the multidimensionality of the relevant commodity and of the value of its added dimensions (cell B). Graphed in figure 4.4 (where *IT* signifies interests, *ID* ideas, and subscripts *I* and *G* signify individual and group, respectively), this scenario constitutes a powerful use of nationalizing the interest, since it

a. Uninformed individuals

Interests

Group

Individual

Ideas or Ideology

b. Informed individuals

Interests

Group and Individual

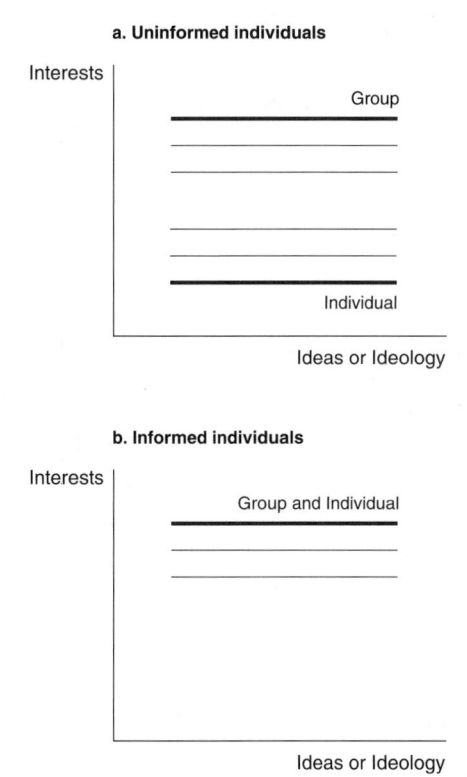

Ideas or Ideology

Figure 4.3
The group's and the individual's interests coincide

entails a change in the individual's preference from one motivated predominantly by self-interest to one also motivated by an idea or ideology. The group therefore heads off potential opposition by persuading the individual of at least a tangency of mutual interest (the two indifference curves touch at IT_{I*G}, ID_{I*G}). At this point, both the group and the individual move outward from their ideal positions on both dimensions and toward the ideal positions of the other actor. Note that the ideal point of each actor remains fixed. The individual is persuaded to value the commodity for its private consumption purposes and also for its other dimensions. The group may attempt to use misleading arguments to persuade the individual in cell B to support the group's policy objective, but since she already knows her interest, such arguments would fall on deaf ears. Hence, this is not included in cell B as a realistic form of persuasion by the group.

The Demand Side

Table 4.1
The interplay between the mutuality of individuals' and groups' interests, and individuals' knowledge of self-interest

	Individual's and Group's Interests Coincide	Individual's and Group's Interest Conflict
Individual knows her interests	A. Group uses ideas as reinforcing arguments ("You really are one of us.")	B. Group uses ideas as persuasion ("Okay, we know you are not one of us, but X [the positive externality that our goal creates or enhances] benefits the broader societal welfare.")
Individual does not know her interests	C. Group uses ideas as reinforcing arguments ("You actually are one of us: you just didn't realize it.")	D. Group uses ideas as persuasion (using the argument in cell B) or provides misleading arguments ("You actually are one of us—and here is the selective evidence.")
Individual is mistaken about her interests	E. Group uses ideas as reinforcing arguments ("You were misinformed: the evidence shows that you are one of us.")	F. Group ignores (because the individual mistakenly believes her interests coincide with those of the group) or provides misleading or reinforcing arguments

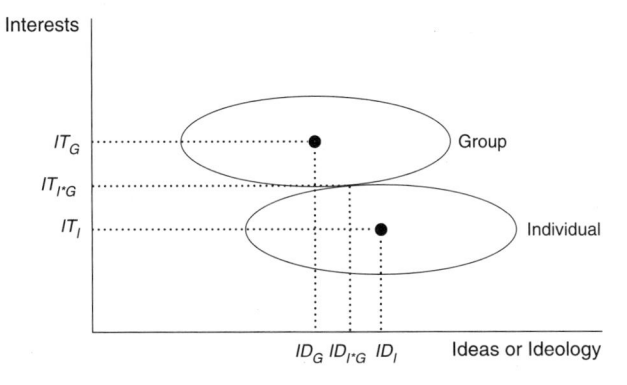

Figure 4.4
The group's and the individual's interests conflict (and the group invokes ideas)

a. Uncertain individual

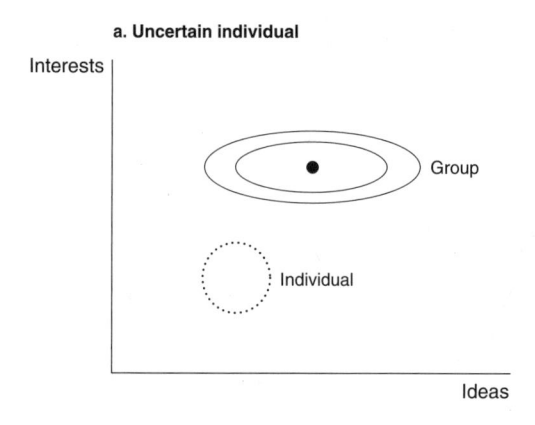

[Graph with axes "Interests" (vertical) and "Ideas" (horizontal). A solid ellipse labeled "Group" with a point inside is positioned upper-middle. A dotted circle labeled "Individual" is positioned below-left of the group.]

b. Group positions individual's ideal point

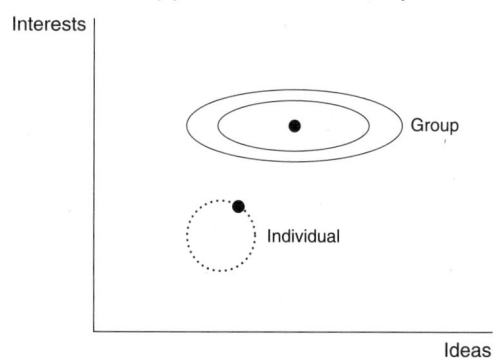

[Graph with axes "Interests" (vertical) and "Ideas" (horizontal). A solid ellipse labeled "Group" with a point inside is positioned upper-middle. A dotted circle labeled "Individual" with a point on its upper-left edge is positioned below the group.]

Figure 4.5
The group's and the individual's interests conflict (and the group exploits asymmetry of information)

Individuals in the second row are uncertain as to where their economic interests lie, a frequent occurrence in times of policy reform. For individuals where the group knows that their (immediate) economic interests coincide with the group's interest, the group simply informs them of this fact (cell C). (As in cell A, the group may employ ideas as reinforcing arguments.) In figure 4.3, this is shown as a movement from cell A to cell B. The group does not invoke ideas to counter interests and thereby does not engage in nationalizing the interest.

A more interesting case is the individual in cell D who is uncertain of her interests, and the group knows that her interests are in conflict with its own. Here, the asymmetry of information between group and individual allows the group actually to position the individual's ideal

The Demand Side

c. Group expands use of ideas to position ideal points

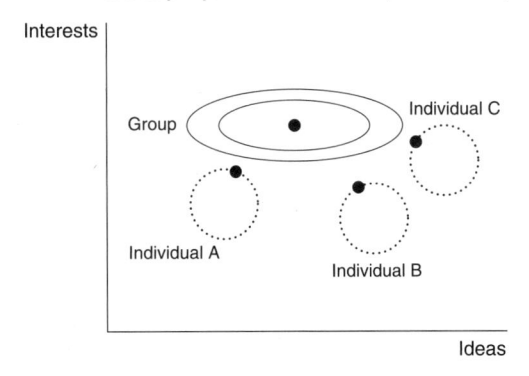

[Figure: Interests vs. Ideas axes showing Group (horizontal ellipse) with Individual A, Individual B, and Individual C as dotted circles]

d. Individuals shift group's indifference curves

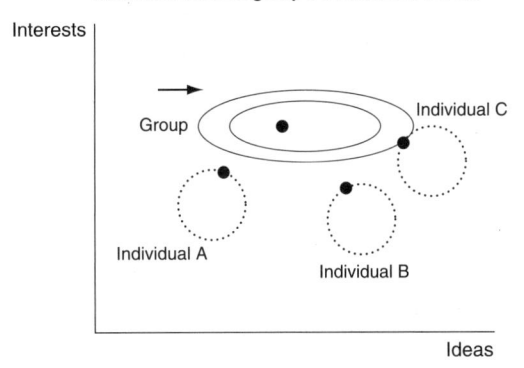

[Figure: Interests vs. Ideas axes showing Group (horizontal ellipse with arrow indicating shift) with Individual A, Individual B, and Individual C as dotted circles]

Figure 4.5
(continued)

point as near to its own as possible. In figure 4.5a, the group's ideal point is situated in a horizontal ellipse, meaning that the group is predominantly motivated by economic interest but that ideas receive some expression as well. The ideas dimension may reflect heterogeneity of preferences among individual members of the group, with some members feeling more strongly about the ideas dimension than others, or the preferences of all members may be driven by interests (as in figure 4.1a), but the image portrayed to the outside world is softened and massaged with ideas (Shepsle's "hook"). The dotted circle for the individual represents the feasible set of ideal points. (This is given as a circle, since no a priori reason exists to assume a particular elliptical shape.) She is uncertain where to locate her ideal point within this set and so cannot identify a policy preference. By nationalizing the interest, the group is able to position the individual's ideal point on the perimeter of her uncertainty, nearest to the group's own ideal point (figure 4.5b). If the group were to expand its nationalizing the interest strategy, it might influence the interests of even more individuals who face this same uncertainty—as shown in figure 4.5c. It should be noted that unlike those in cell B, these individuals may be susceptible to persuasion by misleading arguments. A strategy based on misleading arguments alone would risk exposure in public debate. Yet one based solely on a nationalizing the interest strategy would hinge on the attractiveness of the idea and how credibly it could be linked with a positive externality.

Individuals in cells B and D are of key importance in nationalizing the interest strategy. Thus far, we have seen that by using ideas, an interest group is able to "hook" these individuals either by altering the shape of their indifference curves or by positioning their ideal points within areas of uncertainty. That is, the group exaggerates its commitment to the east-west dimension (ideas and ideology) to encourage movement of individuals on the north-south dimension (interests). By portraying its policy preference as one that yields economic benefits to its members and also generates more general benefits (say, a clean environment, national security, rural values, and so on), the group captures the attention of nongroup members who care about these factors as well. The image and the argumentation of the group acquire an ideas dimension that attracts nongroup members—but this is not to say that such individuals naively accept the group's message. The "hook" of ideas has two ends. Because individuals care about the east-west dimension, they can play hard to get with the interest group. They can demand some evidence of the group's stated commitment to ideas (environment, national security, rural values) in return for support for the group's policy objective. These may be in the form of side agreements or concessions of various sorts. The group, in turn, is willing to concede on the east-west dimension, since it cares relatively less about it. (Taking figure 4.2b as the group's preference function, it would be willing to concede far more of X than Y to move closer to the individual's ideal point.) Figure 4.5d illustrates the east-west movement of the group's preference function, bringing it nearer to the ideal points of individuals B and C. Note, however, that a commitment on ideas made to B and C distances the group further from individual A. Assuming a single ideas dimension (as we have thus far), the group may simply accommodate the majority and cut its losses with A.

The Demand Side 93

```
Interests │
         │
         │        ┌─────────────────┐
     ───→│        │  •      Group   │
         │        └─────────────────┘
         │           ┌──────────────────┐
         │           │   •    Individual│
         │           └──────────────────┘
         │
         └────────────────────────────────
                         Ideas or Ideology
```

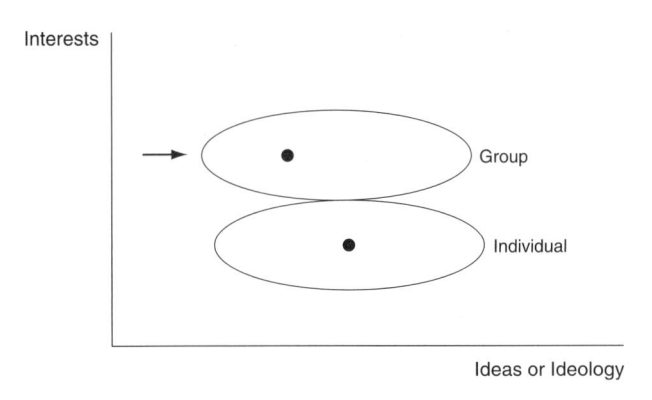

Figure 4.6
Group gains support for interests but concedes on ideas

However, it is more likely that multiple dimensions of ideas exist. For example, a belief in family values and environmentalism might be *two* dimensions of ideas, so that one's position on the former would not determine one's position on the latter. With multiple dimensions to ideas, a group could appeal to different segments of the population by tailoring its position across the various dimensions. Thus, environmentalism might resonate with some individuals and preservation of family values with others. The east-west dimension would be replaced by an N-dimensional space to allow the group to move toward B and C on, say, the dimension of environmentalism but toward A on the dimension of family values. But as N-dimensions are difficult to graph, figure 4.6 illustrates the same east-west movement as in figure 4.5d but in response to individuals who know that their interests conflict with the group (individuals in table 4.1, cell B—previously graphed in figure 4.4).

An individual in cell E mistakenly thinks that her economic interests conflict with those of the group, so the group provides her with information on their commonality of interests (using ideas as reinforcing arguments, as in cells A and C). Finally, the group's strategy with regard to an individual in cell F is ambiguous. It may choose to leave her alone, since she already (mistakenly) believes that her interests coincide with those of the group. Or the group may attempt to provide this individual with misleading arguments that confirm her mistaken understanding of her interests.

Table 4.1 demonstrates that of the six possible types of individuals, only two provide the group with the opportunity to nationalize its

Table 4.2
The case of repeal and the Anti-Corn Law League

	Individual's and League's Interests Coincide	Individual's and League's Interest Conflict
Individual knows her interests	A. League uses ideas as reinforcing arguments to export-sector interests ("Repeal will increase British exports.")	B. League uses ideas to persuade landowners ("As Christians, you have a moral obligation to support free trade." "Free trade will bring peace and prosperity.")
Individual does not know her interests	C. League uses ideas as reinforcing arguments to uncertain workers and urbanites ("Repeal will not lower your wages." "Landowners are monopolists who benefit at your expense.)	D. League uses ideas to persuade diversified landowners (using the arguments in cell B) or provides misleading arguments.
Individual is mistaken about her interests	E. League uses ideas as reinforcing arguments to workers ("The Malthusian argument is wrong; repeal will not lower your wages.") and to tenant farmers ("It is the landlord, not the farmer, who benefits from protection.")	F. Not applicable to repeal

interest (cells B and D). This would entail persuading people to support (or acquiesce to) a policy that they know is not in their personal interest or a policy that they are uncertain is in their interest (but in fact it is *not* in their interest). Here, ideas are used to *counter* interests. The defining feature of cells C and E is the uncertainty surrounding individuals' interests. Because these two cells reflect uncertainty as to the likely effect of policy on interests, the group will craft arguments that seek to *reveal* the obscured interests of individuals in cells C and E.

Table 4.2 applies table 4.1 to repeal and the strategy of the Anti-Corn Law League. In cell A, the League appealed to individuals whose interests closely matched those of the League—namely, exporters. Here, the League's activities were those of a normal interest group attempting to increase its membership and financial backing. In chapter 3, I explain how the League was able to organize British export interests into an effective lobbying group. In cells B and D, the League invoked positive externalities in its appeals to landowners. The portfolios of landowners in cell B were undiversified, whereas those in cell D were diversified (as is discussed in chapter 5). To the undiversified landowners in cell B, the League linked free trade with morality, peace, and prosperity to persuade landowners to accept a policy that, to a greater or lesser extent, was damaging to their economic interests. (This is not to say that the League did not use these same images in appeals to other audiences but that the appeals to landowners demonstrates their nationalizing the interest strategy most effectively.) The interests of diversified landowners (cell D) are less straightforward. As their asset portfolios began to acquire more industrial investments, some may have recognized a shift in their interests from protection to free trade (thus reflecting a movement toward cell A). To these landowners, the League needed to provide evidence that repeal would enhance British manufacturing exports. Yet other diversified landowners may not have come to recognize a shift in their interests (or perhaps their assets were only marginally diversified), and so the appeal to these landowners would be the same as to the undiversified ones in cell B. The League may have used misleading arguments, but evidence of this is negligible. In cells C and E, the League targeted workers and tenant farmers with arguments relating to theories of political economy (such as the theory of rent and the relationship between wages and prices) and class conflict. Here the League used the ideas of the political economists to *reveal* and to some extent *shape* the interests of workers and farmers (crafting different arguments, or "multiple dimensions of ideas," as discussed above). While this use of ideas runs parallel to the strategic use of ideas that underpins a nationalizing the interest strategy, the key difference is that the theories and argumentation that the League applied to workers and farmers were meant to uncover a latent commonality of interests among industrialists, workers, and farmers, whereas the positive externalities used to appeal to landowners were meant to persuade them to support a policy that ran counter to their perceived interests. The following section explores how the League nationalized its interest in free trade, with reference especially to cells B, C, and E in table 4.2.

The Anti-Corn Law League: Nationalizing the Interest in Free Trade

The following analysis of the lobbying of the Anti-Corn Law League focuses predominantly on the extent to which the League invoked the use of positive externalities in its appeal to the British public. Chapters 1 and 2 describe the Anti-Corn Law League's electoral strategy (namely, its registration campaign), and chapter 3 examines how interests gave rise to its organizational success, but thus far less attention has been given to its campaign of persuasion. While the League embodied the economic interests of the Lancashire cotton industrialists, it appealed to the electorate with images of morality and ethics. Repeal would not have succeeded without the efforts of the Anti-Corn Law League, organized and led by the free-trade apostles Richard Cobden and John Bright. This well-organized, well-led lobby effectively nationalized the manufacturers' interest in *immediate* repeal of the Corn Laws.[10] All three conditions favorable to nationalizing the interest were in place for the League:[11] (1) the existence of positive externalities, made even more persuasive by a well-developed body of theory on free trade; (2) excellent organization and leadership; and (3) a conducive institutional environment—in the form of legislation from the 1832 Reform Act, a partial ideological vacuum created by the Conservative and Liberal parties (as neither had integrated their loose ideological framework into a cohesive party organization), and support for free trade within the Board of Trade. Previous chapters have covered the organization and leadership of the League; the following section addresses its use of ideas and the institutional environment.

Positive Externalities

The League functioned both as an "ordinary" interest group (in gaining the support of like-interested individuals) and as an "extraordinary" group (in nationalizing its interest). In its capacity as an ordinary interest group, the League acquired the support of export-oriented interests that had multiplied across the country in the 1830s and early 1840s, as shown in chapter 3. But the League also targeted its appeal to the general public by linking free trade to three compelling ideas: national prosperity, morality and Christianity, and the injustice of an aristocratic monopoly (in the first instance, of economic resources but, by implication, of political resources).

National Prosperity The League sought to make repeal synonymous with British national prosperity by first, transforming the political economists' qualified support for free trade into an argument for immediate repeal of the Corn Laws. Having done so, it could then draw on the arguments of the political economists to strengthen its case for the welfare-enhancing effects of free trade, including the argument that repeal would not result in lower real wages.

Political economists were concerned with the effect of free trade on the overall fiscal position. Although Peel instituted the first peacetime income tax in 1842, the government still relied on customs duties for a large share of its revenue in 1846. Sensitive to this reliance, Nassau Senior advocated levying duties only for the purposes of revenue, while J. R. McCulloch argued for a moderate, fixed duty to replace the sliding scale. A fixed duty would remedy the problem of speculation and would protect agriculture as a business while also bolstering the government's revenue. The League rejected the revenue defense for maintaining even moderate duties on agriculture. Charles Villiers, League activist and Member of Parliament for Wolverhampton, argued that the Corn Laws actually reduced revenue from customs by increasing the domestic cost of production of exportables (by inference through increasing wage costs) and thereby limited foreign trade, including the volume of taxable imports.[12] The Corn Laws also reduced the government's revenue from excise duties by limiting domestic consumption. Although customs and excise provided 75 percent of government revenue, Villiers maintained that repeal would not lead to a loss of revenue.

Having set aside the issue of revenue loss, the League could then argue that repeal would benefit not only British manufacturing exporters, but because the country's wealth depended on industry (and not on agriculture), repeal would also enhance the larger British economy. James Deacon Hume (who served for thirty-eight years in the Customs Department and eleven years in the Board of Trade) testified before the House of Commons Committee on the Import Duties (1839). In response to the question "Do you consider the wealth of England to be caused and maintained by her commercial and manufacturing industry?," he replied, "Certainly: if meant as in contradistinction from the produce of the soil.... [H]aving always had the land, but not the trade, I must conceive that the increase of our riches arise from the trade and not from the land." Hume's testimony was printed as a League pamphlet (Hume 1996, 30) and distributed widely among the British electorate, as it effectively made the case that what was good for British industry was also good for Britain. Cobden broadened this argument by promising cumulative prosperity from repeal, based on the following formula (Read 1967, 32):

(1) Repeal would benefit British manufacturers by opening wider markets for goods sent out in exchange for the much increased volume of foreign corn which would be imported after repeal.

(2) This in turn would benefit British workmen by creating a much greater and steadier demand for labour, and therefore higher and more regular [nominal] wages, at the same time as it produced cheaper and more plentiful food [raising real wages].

(3) This greatly increased volume of international trade, by bringing peoples and Governments into closer relationship and interdependence, would encourage the opening of a new era of international fellowship and peace. Economic self-interest would discourage the outbreak of wars which disturbed this network of international trade.

Cobden thus sought to link free trade both to national prosperity and international peace, a classic nationalizing of the interest strategy that sought to portray free trade in multiple dimensions. Yet in making this case, Cobden had to confront the belief of many manufactures and the argument of the protectionist Anti-League that free trade would result in cheap labor (lower nominal and real wages). Manufacturers (in cell A, table 4.2) supported repeal because it offered more trade, higher profits, and, contrary to Cobden's case, they believed it meant lower wage costs. Protectionists, meanwhile, latched onto the cheap labor motive to portray industrialists as the villains in the class struggle. Cobden and the League thus embarked on a campaign to persuade workers that repeal would not result in cheap labor (table 4.2, cells C and E), while at the same time assuring manufacturers that repeal meant more trade and cumulative prosperity.

The nub of the cheap-labor issue was the relationship between bread prices and wages. This was one of the key points of controversy between protectionists and free traders, and it dated back several decades.[13] The aim of the League was to disabuse workers of the popular Mathusian argument that repeal would mean higher profits for industrialists but lower wages for workers (table 4.2, cell E). Cobden maintained that wage rates were set by the demand for labor and that the increased trade resulting from repeal would result in a higher demand for labor, which in turn would raise wages. In 1841, Cobden attempted to persuade Manchester workers that repeal would raise their wages (Read 1967, 34):

Why should an increased trade in food lower wages? ... Did any working man come there so ignorant as to suppose that his master had the power of reducing his wages as he chose? ("He has.") Then if he had, would any working man tell him why his master should be so good-natured as to be giving 18s. per week, when in Ireland they were giving only 4s. per week? (Great uproar.) He believed there was no one in that room who would not agree with him in saying that if the masters had the power of regulating wages, the working men would be put upon a much shorter allowance than they were. The price of labour was regulated, like the price of apples in the market, by the quantity there was, and the demand there was for it; and as the population of this country was increasing to the amount of a thousand a day, we must try to get an increased market for our own labour; and how was this to be done, if we refused permission to foreign countries to trade with us?

It is difficult to judge the extent to which Cobden and the League persuaded workers that repeal would not mean lower wages. One should not, however, underestimate the persuasiveness of the League. Howe (1997, 32) notes that "The League's impact through speechmaking and in print was unprecedented for its range and ability to create an audience for economic, social, and political issues." He goes on to quote Bagehot, who was "strongly influenced" by the Leaguer's speeches on political economy, as commenting that "There has never, perhaps, been another time in the history of the world when excited masses of men and women hung on the words of one talking political economy" (Howe 1997, 32). Moreover, the very same political economy arguments used by the League (particularly the relationship between wages and prices) featured prominently in both the Commons and Lords' debates on repeal in 1846 (see chapters 7 and 9). Hence, even if workers were not persuaded, sufficient numbers of MPs and peers responded to the League's appeal to make it an important issue of controversy in the repeal debates.

The Morality of Free Trade A further example of Leaguers nationalizing the interest is their frequent appeals to a higher order. Morality and ethics were often woven into their economic arguments in an effort to pitch the battle in terms of good versus evil and thus featured prominently in their exchanges with landowners (table 4.2, cells B and D). Free traders clearly had the advantage over the protectionists in this form of argumentation. In his lecture on "The Economics and Morals of Free Trade," Philip Harwood reasoned that free trade constituted (1) a "civil liberty," as it ensured the right to buy in the cheapest market and sell in the dearest; (2) "political justice," or a justice that shows no favoritism or partisanship; (3) "peace" in bringing peace between nations and peace between classes; and (4) "civilization," or the bringing of man near man, for mutual help and solace (Schonhardt-Bailey 1997, 2: no. 31). One historian argues that Cobden's contribution "consisted in clothing free trade with a moral cloak, not in elaborating a 'philosophy of history'" (Biagini 1992, 14). Biagini (1992, 14, 38) continues:

> The alliance between Christianity and Liberalism was one of the reasons for the latter's success.... It was difficult to start any radical popular movement without arguments involving a political interpretation of the Bible: when [free-trade agitator] John Buckmaster began his campaign to convert the agricultural labourers and artisans of country villages to the cause of free trade, he focussed on "the anti-Scriptural character of the Corn-Laws," maintaining that "if the Corn-Laws had been in existence when Jesus Christ was on earth He would have preached against them."

Yet the League's emphasis on morality was challenged by the Chartists who sought to persuade ministers and clergy to endorse a more sweeping campaign for parliamentary reform. Chartists countered the free-trade and morality link with their own argument for the morality of parliamentary reform. They maintained that a Parliament constituted of the landed interest was highly unlikely to repeal the Corn Laws and that a truly moral stance would endorse universal suffrage as the first step to a democratization that would then give rise to repeal. Thomas Blackie (secretary to the Edinburgh Chartist Association) thus appealed to Corn Law Convention delegates (Schonhardt-Bailey 1997, 2: no. 23):

> If, therefore, Gentlemen, you are desirous to succeed in obtaining a free trade in corn, your only way of doing so is by employing every constitutional means to obtain a Reform of the Commons House of Parliament. Some may allege that, although the Corn Laws are a moral and religious question, or a question connected with morals and religion, that Reform of Parliament is not, and that you have only to do with moral and religious questions. To this we answer, as the Corn Laws can only be repealed by first obtaining a Reform of Parliament, that such reasoning and notions of morality and religion would limit your [Corn Law] conference to a consideration of the evils of the Corn Laws, and would prevent you entering on the consideration of the only remedy which can be procured for these evils. But we submit, that morality and religion have as much to do with the Reform of Parliament as with the Corn Laws.

The clash between the League and the Chartists over the idea of morality illustrates an attempt by workers (or more specifically, their Chartist leaders) to force the League to demonstrate its commitment to morality (that is, the Chartists were attempting to move the League along the east-west dimension of figures 4.5d and 4.6). In the case of repeal, the League refused to move in the direction of the Chartists; it refused to refashion its free-trade and morality link to make universal suffrage a prerequisite. It is conceivable that civil strife by workers might have forced the League to endorse the "morality of universal suffrage" and indeed, the Plug Strikes of August 1842 were an attempt by workers to force industrialists to support the Charter. Yet the League remained firmly behind its single objective of repeal and tried to persuade workers that the time was not yet ripe for universal suffrage and that in the future the middle classes would bring about universal suffrage. John Bright's appeal "To the Working Men of Rochdale" to return to work illustrates the struggle between the Chartist leaders and the League for the support of workers (Prentice 1968, 2: 377–378):

> Your [Chartist] speakers talk loudly. They tell you of your numbers and your power, and they promise marvelous results *if you will but be firm*. They deceive you; perhaps they are themselves deceived. Some of them contrive to live on this deception, and some are content with the glory of their leadership. They flatter you grossly, and they as grossly calumniate your employers. They pretend to be working out your political freedom; they know that *that* freedom can only be obtained through the electoral body and the middle classes, and yet they incessantly abuse the parties whom it is your interest to conciliate and convince. For four years past they have held before your eyes an object *at present* unattainable, and they have urged you to pursue it; they have laboured incessantly to prevent you from following any practical object.... They have striven continually to exasperate you against those who alone will or can aid you to overturn the usurpations of the aristocracy.... Your first step to entire freedom must be *commercial* freedom—freedom of industry. We must put an end to the partial famine which is destroying trade, the demand for your labour, your wages, your comforts, and your independence. The aristocracy regard the Anti-Corn Law League as their greatest enemy. That which is the greatest enemy of the remorseless aristocracy of Britain must almost of necessity be your firmest friend. Every man who tells you to support the Corn Law is your enemy.... Whilst that inhuman law exists your wages must decline. When it is abolished, and not till then, they will rise.... You may not thank me for thus addressing you, but, nevertheless, I am your friend. Your own class does not include a man more sincerely anxious than I am to obtain for you both industrial and political freedom.

Thus Bright sought to block the Chartist appeal to workers with an implicit promise of universal suffrage in the future beyond repeal. He sought to characterize repeal as "industrial freedom," which industrialists and workers would both enjoy from free trade. Hence, the League probably recognized that its appeal to a higher order would not persuade workers to support repeal, and so it sought to shape the interests of workers in universal suffrage in such way as to demonstrate that repeal was the precursor to universal suffrage, not the other way around.

While the League's emphasis on morality was unlikely to gain many supporters among the working class, it nevertheless enjoyed considerable success in obtaining the backing of the religious community[14] (and thereby, a notable section of both the middle class and the aristocracy).[15] In 1841, the League organized a conference of over six hundred ministers in Manchester "in an attempt to prove the link between Christianity and repeal of the Corn Laws": "The clergymen who assembled in Manchester quickly agreed on the sinfulness of the Corn Laws, 'which violate the paramount law of God, and restrict the bounty of his Providence'" (Read 1967, 32). Finally, in 1846, when repeal had passed and the Anti-Corn Law League met to dissolve its existence, Cobden explained "why he believed repeal to be the most important event in history since the coming of Christ" (quoted in Read 1967, 65):

There is no human event that has happened in the world more calculated to promote the enduring interests of humanity than the establishment of the principle of free trade,—I don't mean in a pecuniary point of view, or as a principle applied to England, but we have a principle established now which is eternal in its truth and universal in its applications... it is a world's revolution and nothing else.

Anti-Aristocracy, Anti-Monopoly For some historians, at the heart of repeal was class conflict between the industrial middle class and the landed aristocracy. In spite of the 1832 Reform Act, 80 percent of MPs were still landowners, and in the eyes of industrialists, most of them enjoyed unfair rents from the Corn Laws. Simply put, industrialists perceived the Corn Laws not only as ensuring an economic monopoly for landowners but also as representing their near political monopoly. Landowners maintained that they suffered a heavy tax burden and therefore they were entitled to protection as compensation for their tax burden (Schonhardt-Bailey 1997, 1: no. 4 and 2: no. 22). Leaguers replied with evidence to show the land tax had not increased since 1692, while land values (and therefore, rents) had increased sevenfold (Schonhardt-Bailey 1997, 2: nos. 13, 15, 27).

The League's anti-landed-interest theme had a number of goals. First, it sought to rally the middle class around repeal (table 4.2, cell C).[16] Perhaps one of the clearest statements of the class conflict between the industrialists and the aristocracy was in a speech by Bright

The Demand Side

in Covent Garden. According to *The Times*, the theater was filled to overflowing and the popular speaker was received "with deafening cheers" (Hirst 1903, 208). Bright's incendiary speech spoke of the free-trade struggle as "a struggle between the numbers, wealth, comforts, the all in fact, of the middle and industrious classes, and the wealth, the union, and the sordidness of a large section of the aristocracy of this empire" (Schonhardt-Bailey 1997, 2: no. 19).

Second, Leaguers sought to isolate landowners from tenant farmers and thereby undermine the landowners' claim to represent the common interest of all agriculturalists in protection. The League built its case to tenant farmers on the theory of rent developed by Malthus, Torrens, Ricardo, Mill, and others. This theory—though often contested[17]—generally argued that the interests of landowners and farmers were, at their very core, diametrically opposed. This allowed the League with the opportunity to drive a wedge between landowners and tenant farmers (Schonhardt-Bailey 1997, 2: no. 4), and with respect to the concept of nationalizing the interest, it allowed the League to shape the interests of tenant farmers (table 4.2, cell E). The argument put to tenant farmers was that it was the landlord, not the farmer, who benefited from high food prices. As food prices rose, so too would the value of land. Thus, while in the short-term, tenant farmers may enjoy the benefits of higher prices for their produce, in the longer term, as they renewed their leases, these benefits would evaporate with higher rental charges (Schonhardt-Bailey 1997, 2: nos. 15, 26, and 2: nos. 13, 16, 25, 34).[18] Only when tenant farmers possessed long leases would their interests resemble those of landowners. Landowners retorted that the League could not tell manufacturers about the high prices they paid as a result of food tariffs and at the same time persuade farmers that they did not benefit from the high prices associated with the Corn Laws (Schonhardt-Bailey 1997, 2: no. 21). They also challenged the rent argument directly, claiming that landowners received only 3 percent return (rent) while capitalists received from 20 percent to 50 percent interest on their investments (Schonhardt-Bailey 1997, 2: no. 22).

A third goal behind playing the class-conflict card is that by vilifying the landed aristocracy, the League forced MPs and peers into a defensive position. While ostensibly unrelated to nationalizing the interest, this tactic was particularly effective on peers as they considered repeal in June 1846 (see chapter 9). By forging a momentum of public opinion in favor of free trade, landowners in Parliament who continued to defend protection came under greater pressure to explain and justify their own motives as representatives of the British public and as "disinterested" public officials (trustees).

In sum, the positive externalities of national prosperity, morality, and anti–landed interest all served to garner support for repeal among the working and middle classes and to weaken the resolve of protectionist landowners. As Howe (1997, 33) has aptly characterized it,

> Through its secular and religious language, the League thus successfully combined the "moral cravings of the middle class" with a universalist rather than sectarian or class-based rhetoric, which underpinned its claim to speak for the people, or even the nation. By so doing it won over to the cause of Repeal large sections of national opinion.

Institutional Environment

Three institutional features were conducive to a nationalizing the interest strategy: the 1832 Reform Act, an ideological vacuum created by the Conservative and Liberal parties, and support for free trade in the Board of Trade.

A key feature of the League's operational strategy was its nationwide propaganda and electoral registration campaign, as is discussed in chapters 1, 2 and 3. After electoral losses in 1841 and 1842, the League focused on returning a pro-free-trade majority in the anticipated parliamentary general election of 1848. Its strategy included manipulating the voter registers, by adding as many free traders and deleting as many protectionists as possible. In fourteen heavily targeted counties, through objections at the annual revisions of the registers, the League achieved a success rate in terms of electors struck off of 50 percent (see table 2.1). Moreover, as table 2.1 indicates, between 1841 and 1845 the growth of the electorate in the county constituencies in Lancashire and Cheshire was particularly marked, providing evidence of the success of the League's registration campaign. The League exploited the 40 shilling county property qualification for voting, a feature of 1430 that was left intact in the 1832 Reform Act. In comparison with the act's new property qualifications that required yearly values of £10 and £50 for copyholders and leaseholders, respectively, and £50 annual rentals for tenants, the 40 shilling qualification was a conspicuous anomaly. The League used the 40 shilling franchise to create several thousand new free-trade voters in county constituencies with large urban electorates, constituencies whose number was increased from 188 to 253 (an increase from roughly 29 percent to 38 percent of the total parliamentary seats). The 1832 Reform Act thus provided the League with the means either to purchase directly or encourage others to purchase voting rights for free traders in county constituencies. (And the growth in annual League subscriptions from £5,000 in 1839 to £250,000 in 1845 suggests that the League possessed the finances to assist in the purchase of ever-increasing numbers of new free-trade voters.) Hence, the importance of these voting rights was magnified by the increase in the number of county seats. This League strategy was targeted at individuals with explicit free-trade interests (table 4.2, cell A) and those whose free-trade interests needed uncovering by the League (table 4.2, cell C). The League thus sought to enlarge the free-trade lobby by making politically active both industrialists and urban residents whose interests most likely would have coincided with the League.

A weak party system is a second institutional feature that bolstered the efforts of the League to nationalize the interest of its members. According to party theorists, the Conservative and Liberal parties of the 1830s and 1840s were cadre parties, or groupings of notables, and the real impetus for modern parties arose only with the extension of the suffrage in 1867 and 1884 (Duverger 1961; LaPalombara and Weiner 1990). Thus, in 1846, the parties were internally created and faced no new (mass) parties in what approximated to a two-party system. Both exhibited weak organization and cohesiveness, and in particular, neither had yet molded its loose ideological orientation into a cohesive party organization.[19] (While chapter 6 finds some ideological cohesion within the Conservative party, that this cohesion evaporated so easily in 1846 is further evidence of the internal weakness of this party.) In this context, the overriding ideological debate—namely, over free trade—originated from outside Parliament, with the League easily trouncing its poorly funded and poorly organized opponent, the Anti-League.

A third role for institutions is that played by the Board of Trade and the Treasury. Both of these government departments are prime examples of how institutions filter the ideas or ideologies that gain political access and how ideologies acquire added permanency by virtue of becoming the established wisdom of authoritative institutions. Certainly, James Deacon Hume's (joint secretary to the Board of Trade) testimony before the House of Commons Committee on the Import Duties in 1840 (Schonhardt-Bailey 1997, 2: art. 2) was a brilliant argument for repeal and was referred to frequently in the parliamentary debates leading up to repeal.

Conclusion

Traditional interest-group theorists like Schattschneider saw interest groups as falling into two types: they pursued either economic objectives or ideological objectives. Rational-choice theorists like Olson shifted the analysis of interest-group activity toward a more precise specification of the motivations of individuals to join a group (or not), and these motivations were almost always seen in terms of economic self-interest. Both interest-group theory and the logic of collective action have provided a firm basis for understanding how and why groups organize. The assumption of these two literatures is that the relevant dialogue is between group leaders and group members. Less widely discussed, however, is how groups appeal to *nonmembers*— how they gain the acquiescence if not the support of these individuals for their policy objective. The concept of nationalizing the interest offers a contribution toward understanding the relationship between groups and nonmembers, and at the heart of that relationship is the persuasive use of ideas.

The Anti-Corn Law League provides an excellent example of this strategy, as the evidence in this chapter has illustrated. To end this chapter on a lighter note, even political parodies published in the wake of repeal appreciated the importance of the League in persuading "the people" (*A Polical Parody on Tubal Cain* 1846):

For the League arose, and with voice of might,
Had opened the peoples mind;
And the land was rife with the words of strife,
For men were no longer blind.
And [Peel] said, Alas! that I should aid,
Or that skill of mine should plan,
Protective laws to tax the bread,
Which God gave free to man.

And for many a day did Robert Peel,
Sit brooding o'er his woe,
And he spoke no more for protective law,
And his strength seemed waxing low;
But at length he rose with cheerful face,
And bold courageous eye,
And took his stand with a sturdy band,
And joined the Leaguers cry.

5

The Waning Demand for Protection: Portfolio Diversification of Landowners

Introduction

Two strands of thought relating to Britain's historic move to free trade in 1846 offer contradictory interpretations of the underlying domestic economic and political forces at work. On the one hand, the Ricardo-Viner specific factors model implies that owners of two factors—land and capital—stood diametrically opposed to one another on the issue of free trade. In the end, according to this view, capital gained the upper hand as exemplified by the repeal of the Corn Laws. On the other hand, studies in the economic-history literature posit that the economic interests of these two groups of factor owners were not mutually exclusive. Rather, their interests overlapped as a result of rapid economic changes in the 1830s that intensified landowner diversification into nonagricultural ventures. The implication of the latter version is that landowners as a group became divided between undiversified landowners, whose economic interests remained closely tied to agriculture, and diversified landowners, whose interests in agriculture had lessened while their interests in nonagricultural sectors had increased. Hence, the undiversified group continued to perceive themselves as true "losers" from free trade in grain, while members of the diversified group stood to gain or simply became indifferent to free trade.

This chapter examines the inadequacies of the specific factors model as it relates to nineteenth-century Britain and introduces two modifications that allow the model to account for the anomalies observed in the case of repeal. Altering two key assumptions of the specific-factors model, this chapter introduces the concepts of portfolio diversification and investment capital flows into the framework of factor specificity (thus developing a version of the model that is stock-flow consistent). The predicted political consequence of this modified version of the model is that diversification lessened widespread protectionist sentiment among the landed elite. Most important, this diversification was more pronounced in Peelite than in Non-Peelite Conservative constituencies and thus contributed to the intra-Conservative party cleavage discussed in chapter 2.

Second, this chapter extends the concept of portfolio diversification (as presented in the economic-history literature) to the realm of policy making by examining statistically the correlation between diminishing protectionist sentiment—through diversification—and the free-trade policy outcome. This constitutes a "first cut" in estimating a demand-side model for repeal. While the findings are supportive of the diversification hypothesis, a more comprehensive demand-side model is estimated in chapter 6.

The Specific-Factors Model and the Long- and Short-Run Dimensions of Capital Formation

The Ricardo-Viner specific-factors model in neoclassical trade theory defines some factor inputs as industry-specific and others as intersectorally mobile. Industry-specific factors give rise to industry-specific interests that may either favor or oppose protection, depending on the form of trade competition facing the industry. Owners of factors specific to the domestic import-competing industry gain from protection (via a relatively higher price obtained for the industry good), while owners of factors specific to the export sector lose (similarly, via the relatively lower price of the industry good). The preference of the mobile factor owner (for example, labor) is ambiguous: although he can move into the protected sector, his welfare remains contingent on his unique consumption preferences. It follows that owners of factors specific to a particular industry will tend to seek protection for their industry and oppose protection for any other industry, while mobile factor owners will more likely remain inactive.

Standard applications of the specific factors model to the repeal of the Corn Laws (e.g., Caves and Jones 1985) propose (1) that landowners (as owners of factors specific to the import-competing industry) and capital owners (as owners of factors specific to the export sector), deriving incomes from undiversified claims to factors, opposed each other and (2) that after 1832, industrialists had taken over the House of Commons, thereby engineering the shift toward free trade. While it is true that factors remained industry specific and that trade policy had the effect of redistributing income, thereby creating unambiguous winners and losers, neither of these propositions is correct.

Taking the second proposition first, while the 1832 Reform Act did extend the suffrage to many middle-class manufacturers, it had not by 1846 substantially altered the composition of the House of Commons (although the League was making clear progress with its registration campaign, as seen in chapter 2). The Parliament of 1841 to 1847 remained firmly under the control of landowners. By one estimate, about 80 percent of the House of Commons consisted of the landowning aristocracy and gentry (Aydelotte 1967). If landowners wished to halt the repeal legislation, as a group they possessed the votes to do so.

It is, however, the first proposition to which this chapter is directed. The specific factors model implicitly assumes (1) that undiversified holdings of factors prevail (that is, each person owns only one, or primarily only one, factor of production) and (2) that capital as a factor of production refers to the stock of fixed capital available for productive purposes. Extensions to neoclassical trade theory have at times relaxed the first assumption but have generally retained the second. Mayer, for instance, constructs an equilibrium tariff model that allows each person to own more than one factor and allows factor shares to vary among people (Mayer 1984). Each factor owner has an optimal tariff rate whose value is determined by the individual's factor ownership. The equilibrium tariff thus hinges on the underlying factor-ownership distribution, and it is the median factor owner's optimal tariff that determines the actual tariff rate. Mayer applies the idea of diversified holdings to the long-run Heckscher-Ohlin model and its resulting Stolper-Samuelson theorem and to the short-run specific-factors model. His intent is not to bridge the two models through the mechanism of portfolio diversification but rather to explore the implications of his modified assumptions for the long-run adjustment of tariffs to changes in the distribution of factor ownership, voting costs, and voter-eligibility rules and for the short-run attempts of small minorities of factor owners—under majority voting—successfully to obtain tariff protection for their industries.

In contrast to Mayer's case of diversified holdings, we may alter the assumption of undiversified holdings in the specific-factors model by considering capital in two forms—as stocks and as the income flows from those stocks. Income accruing from the ownership of a specific factor (for example, capital originating from the productive use of land) could be invested in other sectors of the economy offering a higher marginal return on capital.[1] As a consequence, the allocation of capital flows in nineteenth-century Britain differed markedly from the allocation of capital stocks. Moreover, this "flow" of investment capital from one sector to another was facilitated by the newly emerging market in long-term capital, as evidenced by the rapid growth in British stock-market activity during the second quarter of the nineteenth century.

The beginnings of a capital market can be interpreted as the start of a transition from a state where capital is fixed to one where it becomes more mobile between sectors. In Britain, capital flows, responding to unequalized returns, shifted into higher-yielding industrial sectors of the economy, thereby altering the ownership distribution of the capital stock. In other words, the demand for a capital-market increases the more the desired allocation of flows diverges from the allocation of stocks. This new ownership distribution created economic and political incentives for a policy change that favored owners of industrial capital (for example, a move to remove protection for agriculture). The contribution of this chapter is that it introduces portfolio diversification in nineteenth-century Britain into a medium-run model with a dynamic component—capital flows that reflect divergent returns in industry and agriculture.

Portfolio diversification significantly alters the political interpretation originally posited by the specific-factors model. Protective tariffs continued to be ardently favored or opposed by the owners of factors whose income and underlying assets continued to be tied to specific industries,[2] but the policy stance of factor owners whose returns could be more easily reallocated elsewhere became ambiguous. This was so especially where these returns (in the form of investment capital) found their most profitable outlet in industries specific to other factor inputs. The interests of these individuals would have derived from each person's unique portfolio—that is, from the extent of diversified holdings or, interpreted strictly, from the discounted expected future income stream from holdings under each policy alternative (the latter clearly more difficult to gauge than the former).[3] Simply put, as some landholders diversified more extensively, their interests either began to resemble more closely those of industrialists favoring free trade or became less sharply defined, thus bordering on indifference. Only those individuals who could not diversify out of agriculture (for example, tenant farmers with long leases or landowners facing impending insolvency) would remain staunch advocates of protectionism.[4] Since the specific-factors model misses the importance of a growing British capital market, it fails to recognize that the support for protectionism was diffusing within the ranks of those who supposedly were its leading advocates. The division between owners of factors and their supposed conflict of interests, then, is much fuzzier than the model implies.

The Evidence

Evidence for the portfolio diversification hypothesis is given in two forms—empirical and statistical. The former draws from the economic-history literature and offers an account of the progression of diversification, especially its escalation during the late 1820s to 1840s, a period of rapid growth in the newly emerging stocks and shares market. The latter attempts to establish a link between growing diversification and MP voting behavior on the question of free trade in grain.

Diversification in Economic History

Diversification of portfolios by landowners was by no means a new development in the nineteenth century. Beginning in the late sixteenth and early seventeenth centuries, both the older aristocracy and rising gentry invested extensively in nonagricultural activities, including minerals and mining (coal, lead, steel, salt, alum, and so forth), urban development, shipping, and joint-stock companies. Lawrence Stone (1965) explained that even though "industry was not the road to great riches," it provided to both peers and gentry an interesting diversion and an extension of the taste for gambling. In his analysis of 158 peerage families during the period 1560 to 1639, Stone found that 25 percent of these profited by mining activities on their estates, 9 percent invested in fen drainage, 15 percent in developing London, 14 percent in shipping, and 63 percent in trading, colonial, and industrial concerns. Moreover, he found the older nobility no less willing than the newer nobility to invest in nonagricultural activities (Stone 1965, 377–383).

J. H. Plumb (1967) extended the notion of diversification to the eighteenth century. According to Plumb (1967, 5), cheap water transport (provided through canal ventures) allowed greater diversification of portfolios among the gentry. The opening of rivers and coastal traffic enhanced agricultural production by creating new metropolitan markets for agricultural goods and created new outlets for enterprises in timber sales, gravel, and minerals.

Consequently, by the early nineteenth century, some landowners were at least marginally involved in industrial activities. The obvious question then becomes this: given some degree of diversification, why did landowners support agricultural protection as long as they did? It may be (1) that landowners diversified but the returns on their nonagricultural income were inconsequential relative to their agricultural income (most likely because landowners' investment in nonagricultural sectors was small relative to their agricultural holdings) or (2) that numbers of landowners actually diversifying remained few relative to those not diversifying. A third and quite different explanation is that the type of industrialization in the eighteenth century differed from that in the nineteenth: the former was led by domestic demand for nontradables, and the latter was led by exports. Thus, landowners diversifying into industry in the eighteenth century would be more likely to retain their preference for agricultural protection, whereas landowners similarly diversifying in the nineteenth century would be less likely.

In any case, two critical economic changes in the second quarter of the nineteenth century—the expansion of exports in mining and heavy industry and the development of the capital market—marked that period as a turning point. There was an increase in the returns to diversified holdings, the size of nonagricultural holdings, and the numbers of landowners diversifying. These changes, moreover, transformed the process of investing outside agriculture—all of which dampened landowner support for agricultural protection. These changes seem to have been triggered by (or to have coincided with) the same event—the beginning of the railway boom in the mid-1830s (peaking in 1836 and 1837 and again in 1844 to 1846).

The first such sudden economic change was the expansion of exports in mining and heavy industry. While export growth and the railway booms should actually be considered a two-way causal relationship,[5] this sudden export growth nevertheless was created in the very industries (coal, iron, and steel) in which landowners had been long-time investors.[6] Although their portfolios already included such investments, the intensity and economic importance of these investments increased with the growth of these industries.[7]

The second change was the development of the capital market. Although the beginnings of a formal market in capital may be traced to long-term borrowing by the state in the late seventeenth century (Stasavage 2003), it was not until the early 1800s that the London Stock

Exchange obtained a formal constitution and its own building. The market that existed during the eighteenth century was not a national market; rather, it was concentrated in London and confined largely to the trade of government securities (Morgan and Thomas 1962; Cottrell 1980). From the beginning of the nineteenth century to the mid-1820s, very little share trading existed outside London. However, with the repeal of the Bubble Act in 1825 (which had required all companies to obtain a royal charter or act of Parliament and made it illegal for any broker to buy or sell shares in unchartered companies), share trading boomed as joint-stock companies—most notably insurance and banking companies—could now sell their shares on the stock exchange.[8] Further legislative restrictions on the privileges of incorporation were lifted in 1834, 1837, and 1844, thus contributing to the growth of trading in joint-stock companies (Morgan and Thomas 1962).

More important, after the successful opening of the Liverpool and Manchester line in 1830, confidence in railway stock surged, as evidenced by the "railway manias" of the mid-1830s and mid-1840s. After 1830, a company needed only to advertise in a railway journal that stocks were available to be flooded with applications. For example, in 1836 the New Gravesend Railway received 80,000 applications for the 30,000 available shares; the Great North of Scotland Railway, more than three times the number of its shares in 1845; the Direct Western Railway, 1,400,000 applications for its 120,000 shares; and the Direct London-Exeter, 400,000 for its 120,000 shares (Pollins 1954, 233).

Before the emergence of later technological changes (such as the telegraph and telephone), railway shares offered the single most important factor in the integration of Britain's emerging capital market—a common security that could be traded actively on more than one market. Without common securities, "localized imbalances in the supply of, or demand for, stocks and shares would continue to result in dramatic price fluctuations and an inability to meet requirements. With common securities, local price changes would generate an immediate flow from, or to, that centre so that all markets would rise and fall in line" (Michie 1985, 68).

Such common securities diminished the previously localized nature of the provincial markets as active trading between non-London markets expanded throughout the 1830s and 1840s. Elsewhere I have illustrated the rapid growth in provincial stockbroking and found that railway stocks propelled this growth (Schonhardt-Bailey 1991b).[9] Indeed, according to one estimate, railway construction "almost exclusively" accounted for the establishment of the provincial long-term capital market (Killick and Thomas 1970).[10]

Stock-market activity, however impressive its growth, must necessarily be joined to the interests of landowners to warrant the claims that landowners were indeed diversifying into nonagricultural ventures such as railway shares and that this diversification had potential political ramifications. One conservative estimate has put the average percentage of gentlemen landowners among subscribers for all railway companies floated in 1844 and 1845 at 18 percent (Broadbridge 1970, 144), while others have estimated the figure for the period 1820 to 1844 to be 28 percent (Hawke and Higgins 1981). In fact, many railway companies deliberately reserved a certain percentage of shares (say, 20 percent) for landowners. Landowners were considered valuable shareholders not only because they had substantial resources but also because a company with a considerable number of landowners as shareholders could use this as clout to prevent present or future opposition to the railway line from other landowners (Pollins 1954, 238).

Landowner interest in railways stemmed not only from the ownership of shares but also from the high prices paid to them by the railway companies for their lands. Rather than face the possibility of legal battles over the value of land—costing four times the price of land purchased unopposed—railway promoters "bought off" landowners by paying them, on average, twice the current market value for their land. In 1844, the Board of Trade estimated that the excess land costs alone made Britain's railways £1,000 more expensive per mile than railways on the continent (Irving 1984, 14–15).

The economic-history literature thus provides evidence for the increasing diversification of the landed elite into mining and heavy industry, as well as railway development. This is not to suggest, however, that such diversification directly translated into a conversion to supporting a free-trade policy stance. Coal, iron, and steel exports became increasingly more important in the 1830s and 1840s, but so too did domestic consumption of these goods (especially for domestic railway construction). Additionally, landowner interests in railway promotion could in some cases be linked to the transportation of agricultural goods to domestic markets rather than the development of export industries. Nevertheless, diversification into nonagricultural ventures allowed landowners to spread their investment risks among various sectors of the economy not directly benefiting from the expansion (or maintenance) of British agricultural production. As stated earlier, the actual interests of these individuals must be derived from each landowner's unique portfolio—that is, the diversification of holdings (as a proxy for the discounted expected future income stream from his holdings). Either, in the extreme, landowner interests began to resemble those of industrialists favoring free trade, or more moderately, their interests simply became less sharply defined, perhaps bordering on indifference.

Diversification and MP Voting Patterns on Free Trade

Previous studies that have addressed the issue of diversification in the repeal of the Corn Laws have generally focused on the *individual* interests of Members of Parliament. A primary source of motivation for voting, according to this view, stemmed from MPs' personal pecuniary interests. Indeed, it has been argued that the reason attempts by the 1841 to 1847 government to regulate railways effectively were doomed to failure was that MPs—the majority of whom were shareholders in railways and one-seventh were railways directors—rigorously defeated any "dangerously restrictive" proposals (Briggs 1959, 340). The argument continues that MPs were beginning to diversify their personal portfolios in the years prior to 1846; as they increasingly invested in business and industrial sectors of the economy,[11] they personally had less to lose and more to gain from eliminating agrarian protectionism. Timothy McKeown (1987) tests a similar hypothesis. Although he finds a systematic relationship between voting behavior and "personal pecuniary interests" of MPs, he does not cite this as the critical factor making possible the abolition of the Corn Laws (McKeown 1987, 1989).[12]

One step beyond gauging the effect of personal portfolio diversification on the behavior of Members of Parliament entails examining the effects as channeled through diversification by their constituents. It is the argument of this chapter that as individuals (and constituencies in the aggregate) invested returns from land into nonagricultural ventures such as industry and railways, political support for protectionism waned, particularly among Peelite MPs, thus contributing to the movement in their ideal point *toward* (though not *at*) free trade.

Two approaches, differentiated by data type (individual versus aggregate), are adopted for testing the relationship between diversification and MP voting behavior. Neither approach is ideal, but taken together they provide a reasonable test of the hypothesis. A better test of diversification would rely exclusively on individual-level data to capture the income flows element of the argument. That is, whereas aggregate-level data on asset stocks may capture shifts in the overall distribution of land and capital ownership (and consequently a possible diversification at the aggregate level), the underlying assumption is that all individuals have undertaken exactly the average diversification of their personal portfolios by investing returns from one factor into another factor. Some landowners may instead have moved wholly into the industrialists category; alternatively, the number of industrialists may have grown more quickly relative to landowners. As such, individual and aggregate-level data will provide different pictures of diversification. Aggregate-level diversification may indeed reflect individual-level diversification. Alternatively, diversification may occur only at the aggregate level, but with individual interests remaining industry-specific. Thus, landowners would remain tied to agricultural protection, and industrialists would remain tied to free trade, although the balance of interests would become more evenly distributed as the number of industrialists grew.

There are also drawbacks to relying solely on micro-level data: such data are rare for early nineteenth-century Britain, and the data available are incomplete and inconsistent. Consequently, I test the diversification thesis using both individual and aggregate data. Positive and consistent findings at both levels of analysis would support the hypothesis that diversification was indeed occurring at the individual level and that the more aggregate-level statistics were an accurate reflection of this diversification.

Testing the Hypothesis
Two sources of data were used to test the hypothesis that MPs who represented constituencies with greater diversification were more likely to vote in favor of free trade than those representing less diversified agricultural constituencies. The first source—death-duty registers[13]—provides data at the individual level. The years 1830 and 1850 were chosen to construct a random sample of 1 percent for each year (162 and 184 individuals, respectively).[14]

Figures 5.1 and 5.2 provide maps of both the 1830 and 1850 samples. These illustrate a fairly even geographic distribution, with the expected concentration around London. A comparison of the regional distribution with actual population figures for England in 1831 and 1851 suggests that the sample distributions appear to match the population figures relatively well. It should be noted, however, that in 1830 the South East (including London) and to a lesser extent the Midlands

The Demand Side 117

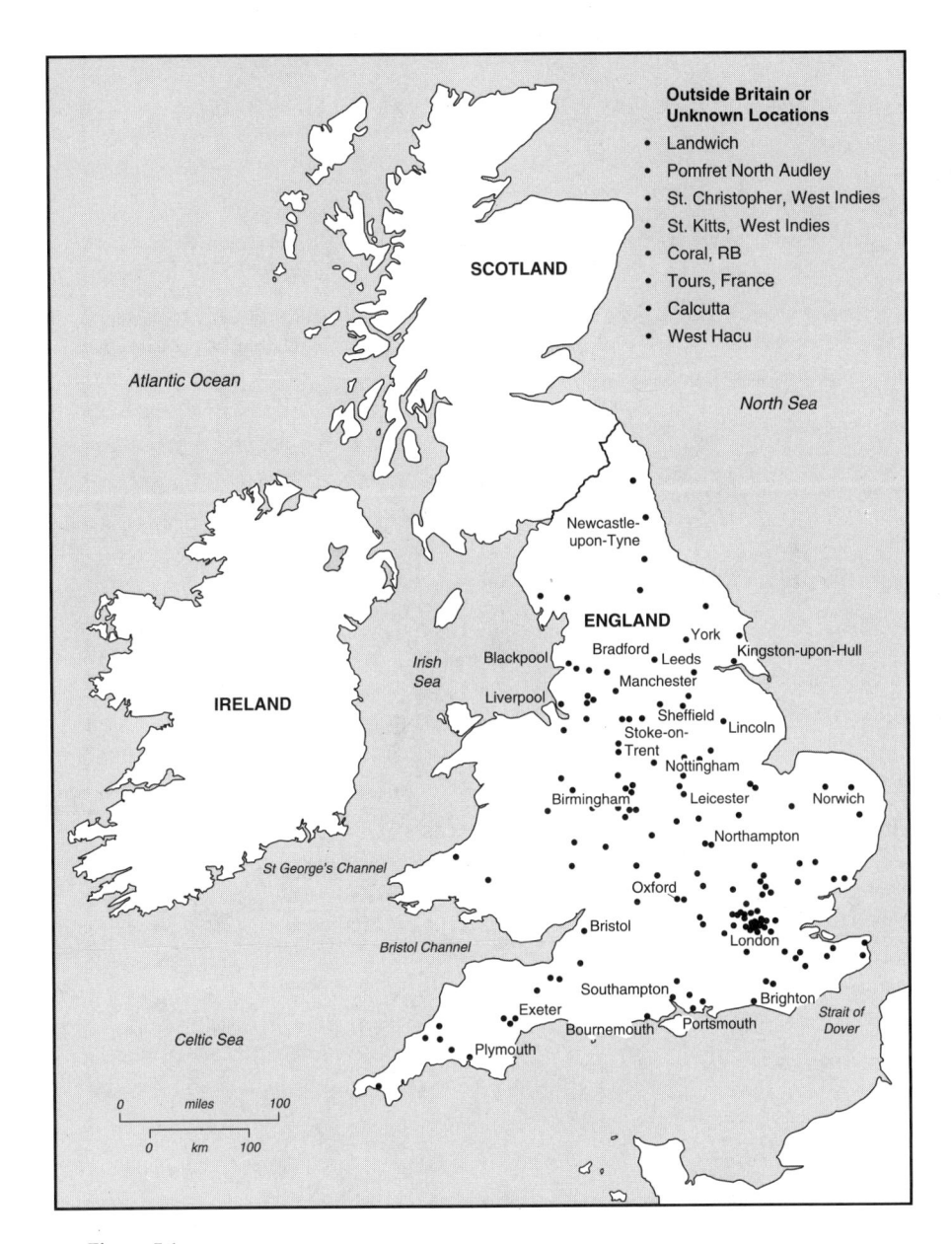

Figure 5.1
Geographical distribution of death-duty register sample, 1830

Figure 5.2
Geographical distribution of death-duty register sample, 1850

appear overrepresented, while the northern regions are underrepresented. For 1851, the regions fairly accurately correspond to the population figures.

The components derived from the registers include (1) stocks (that is, stocks or shares in railways, utility companies, canals, joint-stock companies, insurance companies; investments in a business or trade; and mining interests when listed separately from real estate); (2) government securities (consols, reduced annuities, and so on); (3) charges on real estate (including both absolute and annuity bequests charged on real estate holdings, and real estate sold whose value was then taxed); (4) cash bequests (from bank stock and monies from sources unspecified); and (5) residue (which in many cases included the value of real estate property when instructions were given for its sale, the proceeds of which were then subject to taxation). Unfortunately, real estate was not subject to death duty taxes and subsequently was not valued until the early 1850s. Variables 3 and 5 together provide the best proxy for estimates of real estate, given the clear overlap between the two.

An examination of stock holdings by region and county illustrates the spread of capital-market activity: whereas in 1830 stockholders appeared in only four counties (all concentrated in London and the South), in 1850 stockholders appeared in thirteen counties (spreading regionally from the South East and South West to include East Anglia, the Midlands, the North East and North West, and Wales). Moreover, the percentage of individuals owning stock increased from 3.7 percent in 1830 to 12.5 percent in 1850, also supporting the notion of an expanding capital market discussed earlier.

The second data source—income-tax returns—also provides data on the extent of diversification, but at the constituency level (that is, borough and county) and for the years 1814 and 1856. Although 1814 and 1856 were not "ideal" years (ideal would have been 1825 and 1845), the lack of any income tax structure between 1815 and 1842 meant that 1814 was the latest possible year of the first period (excluding the unrepresentative final wartime tax year, 1815).[15] Further, 1856 was chosen since it was the first year after reinstitution of the income tax that the Parliamentary Papers offered a complete county and borough breakdown for all the tax schedules. The two years are similar in that both were war years and both operated under a virtually identical tax structure (Hope-Jones 1939, 121).

Income-tax returns consisted of four schedules: schedule A (profits from the ownership of lands, farm buildings, houses, and tenements); schedule B (profits from the occupation of lands, houses, and tenements—in short, profits from farming); schedule D (profits from trade or manufacturing business, profession, employment, or vocation and miscellaneous items such as foreign securities and possessions); and schedule E (annuities, pensions, and stipends paid to holders of public office). An adjustment of the data (Schonhardt-Bailey 1991b) enabled me to divide schedule A into two parts, A1 and A2, with the former comprising income from rural landownership and the latter comprising income from urban landownership.

To determine whether MPs from constituencies with greater diversification were more likely to vote in favor of free trade, I constructed indices of diversification for each sample. Individual scores were averaged to obtain one score for each county in the death-duty register sample, whereas separate scores could be obtained for boroughs and counties in the income-tax-return sample. Indices used for both samples are given in table 5.1. The first term in the death-duty register diversification index (stocks/sum of all Xs) denotes the rela-

Table 5.1
Indexes of diversification

Death-Duty Registers

$$\text{Diversification index} = \frac{X1}{\text{Sum Xs}} - \frac{(X3 + X4)}{\text{Sum Xs}}$$

where

$X1$ = Stocks and shares
$X2$ = Government securities
$X3$ = Charges on real estate
$X4$ = Residue
$X5$ = Cash, bank stock, money from unspecified sources

Income Tax Returns

$$\text{Diversification index (for counties)} = \frac{D}{\text{Sum}(A1, A2, B, D, E)} - \frac{A1}{\text{Sum}(A1, A2, B, D, E)}$$

$$\text{Diversification index (for boroughs)} = \frac{(D + A2)}{\text{Sum}(A1, A2, B, D, E)} - \frac{A1}{\text{Sum}(A1, A2, B, D, E)}$$

where

$A1$ = Income from rural landownership
$A2$ = Income from urban landownership
B = Income from farming
D = Income from trade, manufacture, and so on
E = Income from public office

tive diversification into stocks and shares, whereas the second term (charges on real estate + residue/sum of all Xs)[16] is the proxy for agricultural holdings.[17] The income-tax returns diversification index follows the same approach, but it broadens the scope of the first term to include all profits from trade and manufacture and for boroughs also includes profits from urban landownership. The second term isolates rural landowners as much as is possible. The diversification indices range from -1 to $+1$; the higher the score, the greater the diversification into stocks and shares (in the case of the death-duty registers) or the greater the diversification into the broader array of nonagricultural ventures (in the case of the income-tax returns).[18]

Diversification indexes for both samples are divided into "level" variables and "difference" variables. The former are simply the diversification scores for each sample year (1830 and 1850 for the death-duty registers and 1814 and 1856 for the income-tax returns), while the latter subtract the early year from the later year to obtain the change in each diversification score over time.

Table 5.2 gives results for the "level" diversification variables in a multivariate logit model, using the first and third readings of repeal in 1846.[19] MP party identification,[20] predicted district economic orientation,[21] and the effect of the Reform Act of 1832[22] are included as control variables. (These variables are developed further in chapter 6. See book Appendix 1 for a summary list of the variables used in this and other chapters.)

In three of the four regressions, the measure for diversification is significant at the 1 percent level, which lends support to the hypothesis that MPs representing constituencies with greater diversification were more likely to vote for free trade in 1846. The more comprehensive income-tax-return sample provides more consistent results than does the death-duty sample. Nevertheless, obtaining as high as 1 percent significance for the first 1846 reading of repeal for such individual-level historical data as death duties is encouraging. Moreover, in the previous and more extensive presentation of these regressions, both samples exhibited the same trend: each began with weak significance for diversification before the 1840s and strengthened in significance in 1846, as one would expect if diversification were increasing during the 1830s and early 1840s (Schonhardt-Bailey 1991c).

Central to the argument of this book is that Non-Peelite and Peelite Conservatives represented districts with rather different economic interests. As outlined in the previous chapter and developed further in

Table 5.2
Results of logistic regression for first and third readings of repeal

	Death-Duty Register Sample		Income-Tax Returns Sample	
Variable	27 February 1846	15 May 1846	27 February 1846	15 May 1846
Constant	−4.858***	−5.084***	−10.681***	−7.908***
	(1.006)	(1.053)	(2.892)	(2.413)
Diversification	1.392***	0.818	2.563***	1.743***
	(.523)	(.516)	(.709)	(.600)
Party affiliation	1.966***	1.692***	2.183***	1.599***
	(.219)	(.207)	(.325)	(.254)
District economic orientation	0.836***	0.941***	0.330	0.511**
	(.178)	(.192)	(.251)	(.261)
Effect of the Reform Act of 1832	−0.236	−0.105	1.017	0.618
	(.213)	(.217)	(.675)	(.582)
−2 log likelihood	275.9	265.5	151.2	165.2
Percentage of correctly predicted	84	80	81	78
Errors (observed yeas)	37	44	30	32
Errors (observed nays)	21	23	15	16
Number of cases	371	334	240	221

Note: Standard error in parentheses.
*$p < .10$.
**$p < .05$.
***$p < .01$.

chapter 6, Non-Peelite Conservatives represented districts with "hardcore" protectionists interests, while Peelites represented districts with "soft-core" protectionist interests, wavering on free trade. In the context of diversification, this means that we should expect to find that Non-Peelite Conservatives tended to represent districts with less diversification into nonagricultural ventures while Peelites represented districts with more diversification. Table 5.3 and figures 5.3 and 5.4 provide empirical support for this hypothesis. Table 5.3 provides the percentages predicted by diversification for each party group, using simple multinomial logistic regression. For both the death-duty-register sample and the income-tax-return sample, we find a distinct difference between Non-Peelite and Peelite Conservatives. Most dramatic is the difference between the two using the death-duty-register sample. With this sample, diversification correctly predicts about 90 percent of Non-Peelite Conservatives but only about 14 percent of

The Demand Side

Table 5.3
Party affiliation: Percentage correctly predicted from diversification, using multinomial logistic regression

	Non-Peelite Conservatives (percentage correctly predicted)	Peelites (percentage correctly predicted)	Whig-Liberals (percentage correctly predicted)	Reformer (percentage correctly predicted)	Total Percentage Correctly Predicted
Diversification from death-duty register sample	90.5%	14.3%	16.2%	7.9%	48.6%
Diversification from income tax returns sample	81.4	59.1	50.0	76.9	72.5

Peelites (the gap is less wide for the income-tax-return sample but still notable at 81 percent to 59 percent). Further analysis of the multinomial regression results would reveal distinct differences between the two sets of constituencies, but a simpler and more intuitive presentation of this difference can be given in the form of distribution of diversification scores by party group.

Figures 5.3 and 5.4 illustrate the distributions of diversification scores by MP party affiliation. These are given in the form of box and whiskers plots (Bohrnstedt and Knoke 1994), where a narrow box (hinge spread), short whiskers (lines extending to the largest and smallest values that are not outliers), and few outliers (solid circles indicating outside values and open circles indicating far outside values) represents a tight distribution (for example, the Reformers in figure 5.4) and a wide box, long whiskers, and possibly some outliers (such as Non-Peelite Conservatives in figures 5.3b and 5.4a) represent wide distribution. The median of the distribution is represented by the dividing line inside the box. As with the regression analysis, the aggregate data (figure 5.4) tell a clearer, more robust story of considerably greater diversification in Peelite constituencies (indeed, on par with that of Liberals and Reformers) than in Non-Peelite Conservative constituencies. At the individual level (figure 5.3a), diversification is marginally greater in Peelite than in Non-Peelite Conservative districts in 1850. Notably, however, this had increased from 1830 to 1850 (figure 5.3b). Overall, it seems reasonably certain that diversification contributed to

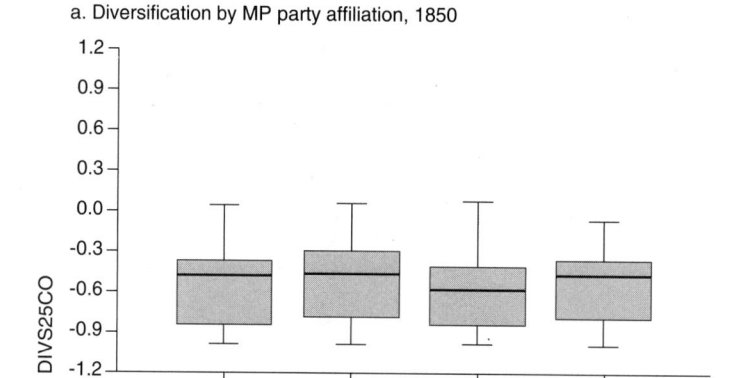

a. Diversification by MP party affiliation, 1850

b. Diversification by MP party affiliation (difference between 1830 and 1850)

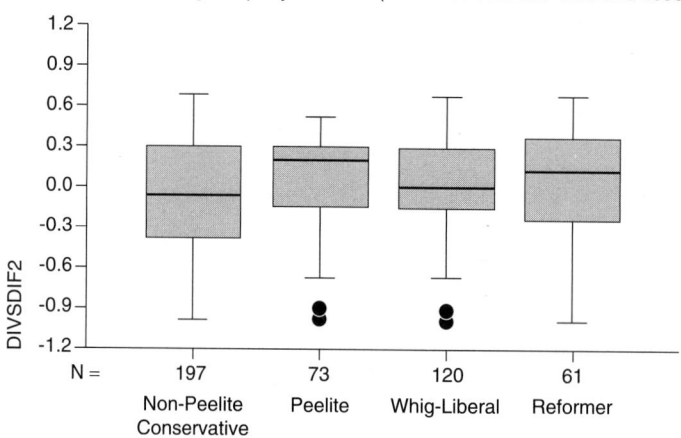

Figure 5.3
Death-duty register sample

The Demand Side

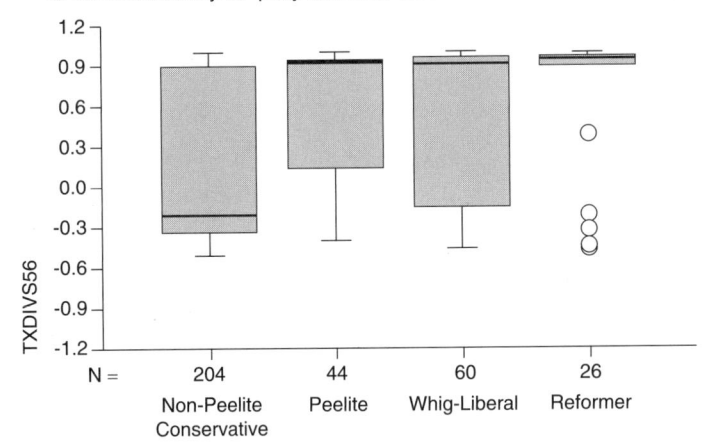

a. Diversification by MP party affiliation, 1856

b. Diversification by MP party affiliation (difference between 1830 and 1850)

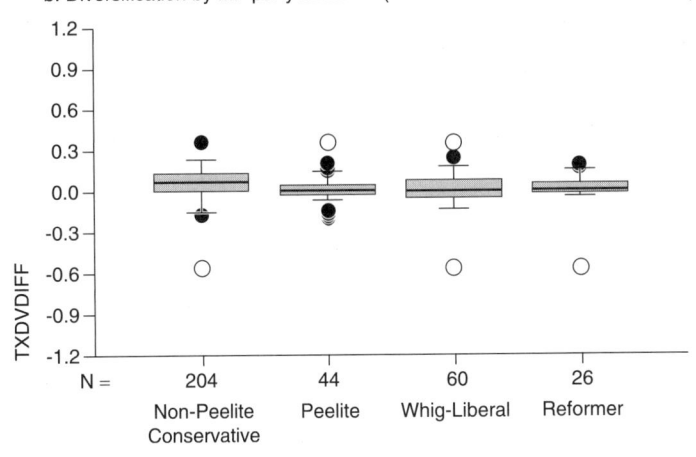

Figure 5.4
Income-tax returns sample

the cleavage in the economic composition of Peelite and Non-Peelite Conservative constituencies.

Conclusion

This chapter focuses on the application of the specific factors model to the case of Britain in the first half of the nineteenth century. First, it is very likely that the driving force behind diversification of the asset portfolios of landowners was the rapidly emerging capital market, evidenced in the 1830s by the spread of the stock-market activity throughout Britain. Second, the apparent difficulty in reconciling conventional applications of the specific-factors model with the decision of MPs to repeal the Corn Laws may well be overcome by switching from a model based on a measurement of the asset stocks of voters to one that incorporates the corollary of industrialization—namely, the diversification of factor returns from land rents into higher yield industrial capital. This makes a model based on income flows rather than on capital stocks a more meaningful tool.

The results at both the individual and the aggregate levels suggest that as landowners diversified into industry, MPs from districts that were more diversified away from agriculture were more likely (in 1846, at least) to vote in favor of free trade than were those from less diversified districts. Moreover, diversification appears to have been greater in Peelite than in Non-Peelite Conservative constituencies.

Early industrializers such as Britain and the United States mobilized capital in smaller units, since the average scale of each business was smaller than it was for later industrializers. In Britain, the combination of a large role for direct investment (in the form of ownership of industrial production by landowners) and the early development of securities markets enabled profit-maximizing landowners to switch directly into industrial investment. It is the hypothesis of this chapter that such direct ownership of industrial capital was an important factor in changing the trade preferences of some landowners.[23]

6   Votes in Parliament, Dissected into Ideology, Party, and Interests

Introduction

While the 1846 repeal of the Corn Laws was remarkable for many reasons, particularly relevant for this chapter is that it split the Conservative party for a generation. As noted in chapter 1, the Conservatives entered government in 1841 with a strong and (what appeared to be) unified commitment to protecting agriculture, and Prime Minister Peel completely reversed this stance within five years. The Peelites followed Peel, while the Non-Peelite Conservatives remained firmly committed to protecting agriculture. Immediately following repeal, the Peel government fell, and the Conservatives remained divided and for the most part out of office for decades to come. Historians have long debated why the Peelites reversed their stance on the defining issue of this Parliament and to what extent the Conservative party was divided *prior* to Peel's motion to repeal the Corn Laws without finding definitive answers.[1] The puzzle of the Peelites is important to political scientists because it raises the fundamental question of what motivates legislators—and especially, what motivates them to reverse their position on a crucial policy issue. At least three literatures lend insights into this question.

Modes of Representation
Studies of political representation have for many years contrasted the "delegate" and "trustee" roles of legislators. As noted in chapter 1, delegates are said to represent the interests (normally economic) of their constituents, whereas trustees represent what they deem to be the national or wider public interest. Painted in stark contrast, delegates are motivated entirely by the interests of their constituents, while trustees are motivated entirely by their own ideological predisposition. Yet as

some empirical analyses of roll-call votes attest, the reality is not so simple. Indeed, legislative behavior is the combination of constituency preferences and legislators' ideology (Richardson and Munger 1990). The controversy rests in the methodology used to disentangle interests and ideology and in the interpretation given to legislator "ideology." Some maintain that once constituency interests have been properly measured, deviations in voting patterns reflect legislators' ideology, which can be interpreted as "shirking" (Peltzman 1984; Kalt and Zupan 1990; Irwin and Kroszner 1999). Others criticize this interpretation of ideology as synonymous with shirking (however measured), preferring to describe it as "reputational capital" or a brand name that voters use to assess and discipline their representatives (Dougan and Munger 1989; Richardson and Munger 1990; Coates and Munger 1995). A third group maintains that even if the economic interests of constituents could be perfectly measured, such models of legislative voting behavior would fail to capture accurately roll-call voting because they ignore logrolling behavior that serves to package these interests into structured (which may be deemed "ideological") patterns of voting (Poole and Rosenthal 1997).

In spite of the difficulties identified by these and other authors (such as Jackson and Kingdon 1992), this chapter attempts to gauge the relative weights of constituency preferences and MPs' personal ideology in the critical votes leading up to and including the repeal of the Corn Laws. While the findings are interpreted with caution, an abrupt change appears to have occurred in 1846: MPs—and particularly the pivotal MPs—appear to have eschewed ideology in favor more of the preferences of their constituents. The evidence suggests that repeal gained passage as some MPs switched from voting more as trustees to voting more as delegates.

Roll-Call Voting in the 1841 to 1847 Parliament

Within the vast multidisciplinary literature on repeal is a subset of researchers (Cox 1987; McKeown 1989; Schonhardt-Bailey 1991c, 1994; McLean 1995a; McLean 1995b; Verdier 1997; McLean 2001) who have attempted to dissect the respective influences of ideology and constituency interests on the votes of MPs in the 1841 to 1847 Parliament.[2] Most of these authors have drawn on Aydelotte's (n.d.) pioneering data, which sampled the roll-call votes of the 1841 to 1847 Parliament.[3] Their work has sought, in part, to resolve a dispute between proponents of ideological explanations for repeal (Kindleberger 1975;

Rohrlich 1987; Hilton 1988; McLean 1995a) and proponents of interest-based explanations (Thomas 1939; Brock 1941; Anderson and Tollison 1985; Schonhardt-Bailey 1994). The former emphasize the loyalties and allegiances of MPs to the constitution, religion, and political party or their conversion to free trade as part of a liberal ideology (MPs as trustees), while the latter maintain that repeal-minded MPs acted as conduits for free-trade interests that were created from industrialization (MPs as delegates).[4]

The answers that Cox, McKeown, Schonhardt-Bailey, McLean, and Verdier provide to the question of the sudden shift to repeal in 1846 provide some of the building blocks for the present analysis. Cox's (1987, 148–165) analysis of Aydelotte's data provides ample justification for an electoral connection in 1841 to 1847, although it does not investigate repeal per se (nor is this the intent of his work). Inasmuch as he offers an explanation for repeal, it rests on the presumed "independence" of the Peelites (Cox 1987, 21). Some historians (Jones and Erickson 1972) have argued that the Peelites represented the epitome of independence from party and constituents' interests—in a nutshell, the ultimate trustees.[5] Cox's empirical support for this hypothesis is limited to the absence of a link between constituency influence and votes of Conservative MPs but the existence of one for Liberal MPs (Cox 1987, 159). His findings unfortunately do not distinguish between Peelite and non-Peelite Conservatives, and so he provides no empirical support for the independence hypothesis.

McKeown, in contrast, focuses on the repeal votes and finds that economic interests constrained the votes of MPs—though he maintains that the pace of changes in interests could not have been swift enough to cause the abrupt shift to repeal. He attributes the shift to the Irish Repealers (who sought the repeal of the union in Ireland) and the Peelites, who converted not from any change in economic circumstances, but "for their own reasons" (McKeown 1989, 378). Repeal thus becomes a peculiarity of British history. While McKeown's model also tests the effect of party affiliation on MPs' votes, he never integrates party and economic interests into a single model. Elsewhere (Schonhardt-Bailey 1994), I integrate party affiliation and constituency interests into a single model in which party affiliation is largely (though not entirely) an intervening variable between changes in constituency interests and MPs' votes. Neither McKeown nor I (in my earlier paper), however, attempt to incorporate ideological motivations into our models.

McLean is concerned primarily with Peel's pivotal role in the repeal process and maintains that the Irish potato famine sparked the abrupt shift in Peel's change of mind. He argues that by merging the issue of famine relief with that of repeal, Peel transformed the single dimension of repeal to one of multidimensionality. He tests his multidimensionality argument on the votes of MPs. He merges Aydelotte's and Schonhardt-Bailey's datasets, adding new measures for MPs' and constituency ideology (defined, for the most part, in terms of religious beliefs). He then focuses on just the Conservative votes on repeal in an attempt to dissect the respective influences of interests (both personal and constituency) and ideology (again, personal and constituency) on votes. As noted in chapter 2, his best-performing model for English Conservative MPs fails to account for the votes of fifty-five Peelites and twenty-seven Non-Peelite Conservatives on the final reading of repeal. He concludes that while both economic interests and ideology affected the votes on repeal, ideology mattered more.

Finally, Verdier focuses on why Peel chose to endorse repeal and so is less concerned with the decisions of other MPs. However, inasmuch as his "political model" characterizes the Conservative party as internally divided between front benchers (who sought party aims) and backbenchers (who were motivated more by constituency pressures), he implicitly models the voting decisions of Conservative MPs. Drawing both from Aydelotte's and McKeown's data, he finds more support for a political model than an economic one. As does the analysis in this chapter, he detects an internal divide within the Conservative party that spanned issues other than repeal and existed prior to 1846. While he chooses to characterize this divide as front bench versus backbench, he notes that the minority of Conservative backbenchers who supported Peel were generally from large, urban boroughs and faced serious contests from Liberal challengers. This coincides with this chapter's depiction of Peelites as representing more free-trade-leaning districts, with the rationale that Peelites were also more sensitive to electoral pressures than were Non-Peelites. Yet his work is limited in that he offers no measure for ideology; the empirical analysis (like McLean's) is limited to Conservative MPs; he applies an inappropriate model (ordinary least squares) to measure roll-call votes; and he obtains results that compare unfavorably with those obtained later in this chapter.

As this brief survey reveals, no researcher of repeal has yet attempted to analyze the combined effects of interests, party affiliation, and MPs' personal ideology in a single model for both Liberal and Conservative MPs. Hence, while most agree that all these factors contributed to repeal, theory has been limited by the empirical analysis. Moreover, no attempt has been made to place such an analysis of repeal into the broader context of roll-call votes on other issues in the 1841 to 1847 Parliament, and so any discussion of the dimensionality of this Parliament, or of repeal itself, has been constrained. Finally, the empirical success of the models of these researchers has been limited at best.

This chapter seeks to advance the understanding of parliamentary voting in the 1840s in three ways. First, Aydelotte's analysis of the underlying orientations of opinion (or dimensions) that divided MPs is improved on by applying Poole and Rosenthal's NOMINATE technique (Poole and Rosenthal 1991, 1997). Using Guttman scaling analysis, Aydelotte found that a single scale (dubbed the "Big Scale") captured voting patterns in 120 (about 65 percent) of the 186 divisions sampled. Within this subset of 120, the single scale could then classify according to their votes 95 percent of the 815 members. Using NOMINATE, one dimension classifies 89.5 percent of the votes in *all* 186 divisions, and two dimensions classify 92.04 percent of the votes.[6] (Hence Aydelotte's Guttman scale analysis proved quite effective, but at the cost of discarding sixty-six divisions. NOMINATE incorporates *all* 186 divisions, though with a slightly lower classification rate.) Thus, scaling techniques that rely on both deterministic *and* probabilistic models find a highly structured voting pattern (or low dimensionality) for this Parliament, meaning that decisions on each roll call can be linked to decisions on other roll-call votes. While this structure is an abstraction, it provides an initial representation of the ideological positions of MPs.[7] I then attempt to refine this measure of ideology by adapting a version of Kalt and Zupan's (1990) "residualization approach," thereby dividing the NOMINATE scores into three components—party, constituency interests, and a residual. The residual appears to constitute an improved measure of MPs' ideology (after extracting the influences of party and constituency interests).

Second, this chapter analyzes the votes on and leading up to repeal using party, interests, and ideology. This model accounts for 97 to 99 percent of the votes.

Third, the findings of this analysis call into question the presumed "independence" of the Peelites as they voted for repeal. Indeed, just the opposite appears to be the case: insofar as Peelites voted as trustees, they did so only up to 1846. Their conversion to repeal did not demonstrate their commitment to beliefs independent of their constituents; rather, *their conversion reflected a departure from voting more as trustees to voting more as delegates.*

When Ideology Matters Less

Political scientists in a variety of subdisciplines have sought to establish the importance of ideas and ideology as causal factors in policy making.[8] The goal of much of this literature is to specify the conditions under which ideas or ideology become relevant for policy making. Often the supposition is that interests form the core of behavioral motivation, but that ideology can sometimes interact with or override this motivation. In contrast, the results in this chapter show how ideology dissipated as a causal force and was replaced in part by constituents' interests. Rather than identifying where ideology mattered (or mattered more than other factors), we observe a case in which ideology came to matter *less* in a crucial policy shift.

Disentangling Ideology, Party, and Interests

While the Conservative party shared a distinct ideology—namely, the defense of traditional British institutions such as the monarchy and the Protestant establishment (including its property and privileges)—it was also a coalition of two interest-based alliances. One faction was the Non-Peelite Conservatives, who voted to retain protection. The vast majority of these MPs represented highly rural and agricultural districts with little or no diversification by landowners into nonagricultural ventures. The other faction was the Peelite Conservatives who voted with Peel's motion for repeal. Peelites represented districts with more of a mixture of agricultural and industry interests and with greater diversification by landowners into nonagricultural ventures. Because agricultural interests were still important in these districts, constituents tended to support continued protection, though not as stridently as constituents in Non-Peelite Conservative constituencies. Hence, the Non-Peelite Conservatives represented districts with "hardcore" protectionist interests, while the Peelites represented districts with "soft-core" protectionists interests, wavering on free trade. Yet from 1841 to 1845, the Peelites voted with their Conservative colleagues to retain protection, with the aim of preserving Conservative party unity and thereby traditional British institutions—even though this conflicted with their representation of evolving free-trade interests. For Peelites, ideology and constituency interests were more likely to conflict, whereas for Non-Peelite Conservatives, they were more likely to coincide. In 1846, Peel's introduction of the repeal bill shattered the ideology that was the glue of the Conservative party, leaving both factions to vote more according to the interests of their constituents.

Poole and Rosenthal's (1991, 1997) NOMINATE technique and Kalt and Zupan's (1990) "residualization approach" are used to disentangle ideology, party affiliation, and constituency interests. The intent is not to position ideology, party, and interests in competing roles but rather to estimate the contribution of these causal factors to the voting behavior of MPs as they approached the ultimate decision that ended Peel's government. NOMINATE scores serve as a first cut into measuring MPs' ideology, while an adapted version of the Kalt and Zupan method is used to divide this measure into three contributing components—party, constituency interests, and a residual that is argued to be a proxy measure of MPs' personal ideology.[9]

Methodological Approaches to Measuring Ideology, Party, and Interests

Ideology is notoriously difficult to measure, and it is even more so when the political actors under scrutiny are in the domain of history. Yet because ideology lies at the heart of the puzzle of the Peelites, some measurement is required. This chapter draws on two recognized approaches for measuring legislators' ideology. Neither method is faultless.

NOMINATE

Poole and Rosenthal's (1991, 1997) NOMINATE technique is said to improve on alternative methods of analyzing roll-call voting, such as factor analysis and multidimensional scaling (Poole and Rosenthal 1997, 51–57; Voeten 2000, 192–195). It has, however, received some criticism (Koford 1989; Wilcox and Clausen 1991; Jackson and Kingdon 1992; Snyder 1992; Heckman and Snyder 1997; Groseclose, Levitt, et al. 1999). While Poole and Rosenthal (1997) have addressed some of these concerns, others remain unresolved—for instance, the tendency toward low dimensionality. Hence, NOMINATE's finding of low dimensionality for the 1841 to 1847 Parliament should be treated with some caution.[10] Nonetheless, it is also fair to say that as the cruder (but more transparent) Guttman scaling technique also revealed low dimensionality, outright skepticism is probably unwarranted.[11]

An analysis of dimensionality serves two fundamental purposes here. First, the primary dimension obtained from NOMINATE provides an initial measurement for MPs' ideology, which can then be dissected using the Kalt and Zupan method. Second, by knowing the structure of the overall voting pattern, we can evaluate the extent to which the ultimate repeal vote deviated from this structure.

Kalt and Zupan Method

Kalt and Zupan (1990) developed a technique for measuring the influence of ideology, particularly as distinct from constituency interests. Using a principal-agent perspective, the authors maintain that legislators who vote according to their ideology "shirk" by failing to meet their obligations as agents of their principals (constituents and voters).

I adopt the basic Kalt and Zupan approach but adapt it in a way that attempts both to address some of the criticisms leveled against the authors for including legislators' party affiliation as a predictor (Uslaner 1999, 34–35) and produce discrete measures for interests, party, and MPs' personal ideology. Specifically, the first-dimension coordinates from NOMINATE are substituted for the Americans for Democratic Action (ADA) rating, and then four variables are included to measure constituency interests:[12]

$$\text{NOMINATE coordinate 1} = f(\text{constituents' interests}) + error_1. \quad (6.1)$$

This produces a fitted value, which I call *constituency interests*, and a residual value ($error_1$). The former can be thought of as that portion of the first-dimension coordinate that is accounted for by constituency interests, while $error_1$ retains elements of both MP ideology and party affiliation. Unlike Kalt and Zupan, I do not include the legislator's party affiliation in this first equation. Rather, an MP's party affiliation is introduced as a predictor of $error_1$ in a second regression:

$$error_1 = f(\text{MP party affiliation}) + error_2. \quad (6.2)$$

Equation (6.2) produces a fitted value for *party* and a residual value ($error_2$). *Party* can be thought of as that portion of the first dimension that is accounted for by an MP's party affiliation. At the same time, however, MP party affiliation also reflects the partisan preferences of constituents. At the parliamentary level, this variable captures MP

The Demand Side								135

party affiliation, but at the constituency level, it serves as a proxy for the partisanship of constituents.[13] *Error*$_2$ is, by definition, that portion of the first-dimension coordinate that we cannot explain by interests and party affiliation, but by interpretation, it is a measure of *MP ideology*. Having stripped the first-dimension coordinate of its interests and party components, we obtain a measure of MP ideology that is not simply a summary statistic for policy issue positions. This measure is not, however, unproblematic, as is discussed below in the section on the schism between Non-Peelites and Peelites.

Applying NOMINATE to the Parliament of 1841 to 1847

Because the focus of this chapter is on one Parliament, a static NOMINATE model is used,[14] and so legislators are assumed to have fixed coordinates. The roll-call votes used here include all of the divisions from the original Aydelotte dataset. However, as data on the economic composition of constituencies are not available for Scotland, Wales, and Ireland, only English MPs (who cast at least twenty-five votes in the 186 divisions)[15] are included in the analysis. These limitations reduce the available number of cases from 590 to 483 MPs.[16]

As one dimension classifies almost 90 percent of the votes (with a second dimension adding only marginal improvement), the analysis of this chapter focuses on the first dimension. The first-dimension coordinates obtained from NOMINATE appear to reflect well the revealed preferences of MPs on the major issue that divided the Parliament—free trade or protection.[17] The first dimension correctly classifies approximately 98 percent of the votes in motions for repeal in the years leading up to 1846, with about seven errors for each vote.[18] This success declines somewhat for the critical vote in 1846, where 95.8 percent of the votes are correctly classified, the PRE is .905, and the errors climb to 17.[19] In fact, the classification success of both dimensions falls somewhat over the course of the Parliament but particularly in 1846 and 1847.[20] It is plausible that a new policy issue (not captured by NOMINATE) began to replace trade policy. A study of voting patterns after 1847 could better resolve this uncertainty as it would provide a longer time frame for gauging the dimensionality of roll-call votes. However, given the dislocation post-1846, it is unlikely that a dimension that may have emerged during the 1841 to 1847 Parliament would have carried over into a new Parliament. Moreover, the history of British politics offers no clear view as to what might have constituted a

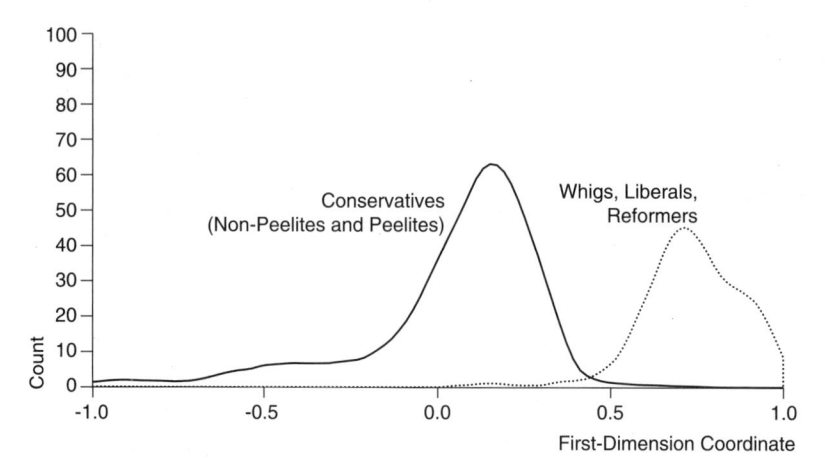

Figure 6.1
Two-party distribution within NOMINATE's first-dimension coordinate

single underlying orientation of opinion (other than trade policy) at the time of repeal and its immediate aftermath.

An analysis of the overlap of the first dimension with party affiliation reveals more. Roughly speaking, the parties split on the question of free trade, with the majority of Liberals favoring free trade and—at least until the intraparty split in 1846—the vast majority of the Conservatives favoring protection. Hence, a simple density plot of the coordinates of MPs for the first dimension should reflect a Liberal cluster and a Conservative cluster. Figure 6.1 confirms this expectation, as a clear gap separates the Conservatives from the Liberals, thereby illustrating the overlap between party affiliation, positions on trade policy (up to 1846) and the first dimension.

A more refined party breakdown lends further support to this interpretation. Figure 6.2 shows a density plot of the spatial positions of MPs across the 186 divisions,[21] but with a four-party classification—non-Peelite Conservatives, Peelite Conservatives, Whigs-Liberals, and Reformers.[22] Along the first dimension, MPs divide into these four clusters: non-Peelite Conservatives, Peelite Conservatives, Whig/Liberals, and Reformers (the mean of the first dimension for each of these, respectively, is −0.032, 0.249, 0.712, and 0.788).[23] Non-Peelite Conservatives are less tightly clustered (that is, they occupy more issue space) than any of the other three party categories. The Peelites are, in contrast, more tightly clustered with only a very slight positive skew, meaning that they occupied less issue space than the non-Peelite Con-

The Demand Side 137

[Figure: histogram showing party distributions along First-dimension coordinate, with labeled curves for Non-Peelites, Peelites, Whigs/Liberals, and Reformers]

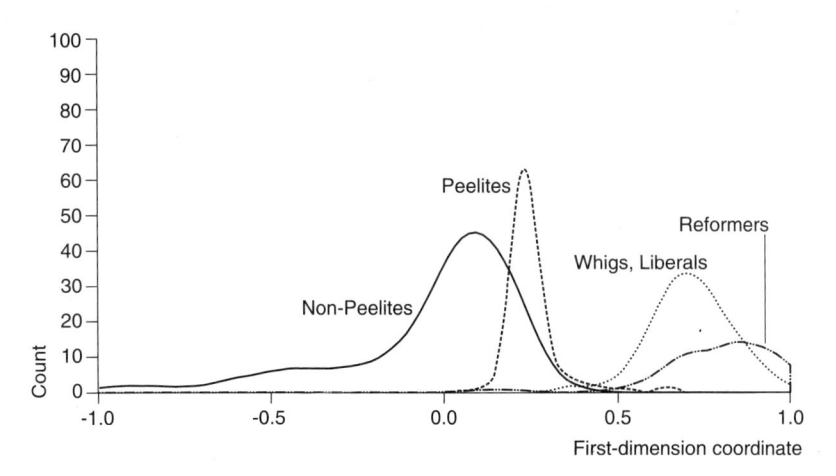

Figure 6.2
Major party groupings within NOMINATE's first-dimension coordinate

servatives. The first-dimension coordinates of Liberals and Reformers are fairly evenly distributed, but—as expected—clustered near to the free-trade end of the spectrum.

The distinct spike in the Peelite distribution supports the contention that the Peelites thought about issues differently than Non-Peelite Conservatives did—and that they did so well before 1846.[24] Yet the possibility remains that this distribution may instead be capturing a tautology. That is, the first dimension may simply be capturing MPs' votes in May 1846, and so the Peelites were distinct because they voted distinctly in 1846. Aydelotte's original Guttman scales can be used to test whether the Peelites and Non-Peelite Conservatives exhibited distinct voting patterns on roll calls that were *unrelated to repeal*. A two-tailed simple *t*-test for equality of means reveals that the scores of Peelites were indeed significantly different from those of Non-Peelite Conservatives on sixteen out of the nineteen scales that were unrelated to repeal.[25] Moreover, the same test applied to McLean's revised version of seven of these scales (McLean 1995a) shows that the differences between the two groups are again statistically significant.[26]

Figure 6.2 can be supplemented with contingency tables of constituency types and party affiliation to lend further evidence of the Conservative party as a coalition of interest-based alliances. Tables 6.1 and 6.2 illustrate that the Conservative party was forged from two alliances of economic interests.[27] The strident protectionists (Non-Peelite Conservatives) represented mostly agricultural districts with protectionist

Table 6.1
Association between MP party affiliation and district type

District Type	Non-Peelite Conservatives	Peelites	Whigs-Liberals	Reformers	Total
County	140 (50.9%)	14 (15.4%)	21 (14.0%)	5 (6.8%)	180 (30.5%)
Borough	135 (49.1%)	77 (84.6%)	129 (86.0%)	69 (93.2%)	410 (69.5%)
Total	275 (100%)	91 (100%)	150 (100%)	74 (100%)	590 (100%)

Table 6.2
Association between MP party affiliation and district economic orientation

District Economic Orientation	Non-Peelite Conservatives	Peelites	Whigs-Liberals	Reformers	Total
Most protectionist	106 (38.5%)	11 (12.1%)	18 (12.0%)	6 (8.1%)	141 (23.9%)
Protectionist oriented	116 (42.2%)	50 (54.9%)	67 (44.7%)	30 (40.5%)	263 (44.6%)
Neutral or mixed	33 (12.0%)	20 (22.0%)	32 (21.3%)	19 (25.7%)	104 (17.6%)
Free-trade oriented	14 (5.1%)	8 (8.8%)	20 (13.3%)	12 (16.2%)	54 (9.2%)
Most free trade	6 (2.2%)	2 (2.2%)	13 (8.7%)	7 (9.5%)	28 (4.7%)
Total	275 (100%)	91 (100%)	150 (100%)	74 (100%)	590 (100%)

interests, while the moderate protectionists (Peelites) represented a mixture of agricultural and industry-oriented districts. From table 6.1, we can see that the Peelites, Whigs-Liberals, and Reformers were all predominantly from boroughs, while the Non-Peelite Conservatives were evenly split between county and borough districts. As this split depicts a rural/urban divide, Peelites were more likely to represent free-trade-leaning interests than were Non-Peelite Conservatives (a finding that fits nicely with the constituency-based cleavage identified in chapter 5). Table 6.2 lists districts according to their economic orientation, from "most protectionist" to "most free trade." Once again, the vast majority of Peelites represented "protectionist oriented" or "neutral" districts (very similar to those represented by the free-trading

The Demand Side

Liberals and Reformers), while the vast majority of Non-Peelites represented the "most protectionist" and "protectionist-oriented" districts.

This configuration is consistent with the argument that the Peelites supported their fellow Conservatives as long as what was at stake was the long-term interest of party unity.[28] Protection, therefore, was subsumed within the broader Conservative party defense of traditional British institutions, even though increasingly it squared less well with the preferences of some of the Peelites' constituents. But once voting for protection no longer served the Peelites' desire for party unity—as Peel's support for repeal in 1846 foreclosed this outcome—their voting behavior appears to reflect their interest in more closely representing their constituents' preferences. For Peelites, this meant that protection ceased to form part of the bundle of traditional British institutions. In brief, the Conservative party was an ideological coalition that cut across two distinct interest-based alliances and so was inherently unstable.

Interests in an Ideological Parliament

In spite of a seemingly impressive ability to classify MPs' votes, the NOMINATE technique suffers from a number of problems in this context. First, while spatial positions revealed by NOMINATE are the product of votes by MPs on all divisions over the duration of the Parliament, they provide no information on *why* MPs voted as they did. We know that their votes reveal a pattern, but we do not know what explains the pattern of the first dimension. It is tempting to suggest that it must reflect the major conflict of the Parliament—namely, trade policy. But that is not enough: the aim here is to identify separately the contributions to explaining that pattern from MPs' ideology, party affiliation, and constituency interests. To do this requires more detailed analysis to sort out the appropriate weights for these three influences.

Dissecting Interests, Party, and MP Ideology: The "Errors"

A very simple way to begin to identify the role for constituency interests in the critical repeal division of 1846 is to study those seventeen MPs whose votes could not be correctly classified (by a one-dimensional NOMINATE model). Table 6.3 lists the seventeen MPs, along with their constituency, party affiliation, first-dimension coordinate, and four indicators of constituency economic composition.

Table 6.3
Third reading of repeal: Errors in a one-dimensional spatial model

Name	Constituency	Party	Coordinate 1 score	Diversification (death duty)	Diversification (income tax)	District Type	District Economic Orientation
Voted no, predicted yes (10):							
Sir R. Vyvyan	Helstone	Conservative	0.019	−1.0	—	1	2
Lord J. Manners	Newark on Trent	Conservative	0.046	−1.0	0.9596	1	2
W. B. Ferrand	Knaresborough	Conservative	0.063	−0.49	—	1	2
R. B. Sheridan	Shaftesbury	Conservative	0.108	−1.0	—	1	2
E. S. Cayley	Yorkshire County	Liberal	0.148	−0.49	−0.2492	0	2
Lord Worsley	Lincoln County	Liberal	0.223	−1.0	−0.4720	0	1
E. Heneage	Great Grimsby	Liberal	0.230	−1.0	0.8768	1	2
W. J. Denison	Surrey County	Conservative	0.249	−0.37	0.2034	0	1
J. S. W. Drax	Wareham	Conservative	0.289	−1.0	—	1	2
J. Bell	Thirsk	Liberal	**0.305**	**−0.49**	—	**1**	**2**
Mean			**0.168**	**−0.784**	**0.2637**	**0.7**	**1.8**
Voted yes, predicted no (7):							
Sir Frederick Thesiger	Abingdon	Conservative	−0.059	—	0.9293	1	2
H. Stuart	Bedford	Conservative	0.008	−0.75	—	1	2
W. S. Dugdale	Warwick County	Conservative	0.009	−0.27	−0.1795	0	1
T. G. B. Estcourt	Oxford University	Conservative	0.009	−0.23	0.9417	1	2
J. Masterman	London City	Conservative	0.009	−0.54	—	1	3
W. T. Egerton	Cheshire County	Conservative	0.013	−0.65	−0.1146	0	1
W. Beckett	Leeds	Conservative	0.015	−0.49	0.9729	1	5
Mean			**0.0006**	**−0.488**	**0.510**	**0.714**	**2.29**

The first two indicators are measures of portfolio diversification by landowners, based on death-duty registers and income-tax-return schedules. From chapter 5, we know that the greater the diversification, the more likely the MP was to vote for repeal. The other two, district type and district economic orientation, are the same variables presented in tables 6.1 and 6.2.

The errors in the upper section of table 6.3 are protectionist MPs. According to a spatial model, they should have voted for free trade but failed to do so in 1846. Conversely, the errors in the lower section are free traders—but were designated as protectionists by their other votes in the 1841 to 1847 Parliament. Comparing the means of the first-dimension scores, we can see that the protectionist MPs averaged a considerably higher score than did the free traders—which is another way of illustrating the errors in predicting these votes. Notably, the protectionist errors are on average further from the cut point (the point that divides the yea and the nay votes) than the free-trade errors—that is, they are "bigger" errors. Yet the means of all four economic-interest variables would place each group in the correct voting camp: the average scores for the free traders are all larger than those for the protectionists, which is what an economic-interest model would predict. Because the groups are very small, we cannot say that the means are statistically significant[29]—however, as the story is consistent across all four variables, we can conclude that there is some further support for the role of constituency economic interests affecting the votes of these MPs.

Dissecting Interests, Party, and MPs' Ideology: The Schism between Non-Peelites and Peelites

The model presented above provides a more comprehensive way to assess the extent to which MPs voted as trustees and/or delegates.[30] Equations (6.1) and (6.2) dissect the first-dimension coordinate into three variables—constituency interests, party, and MPs' ideology. Figure 6.3 provides density plots of these three variables, along with the original first-dimension coordinate.

The bimodal distribution of the first-dimension coordinate reflects the two major party divisions, with Conservatives on the left and Liberals on the right (as seen in figure 6.1). Constituency interests is a more dispersed measure, but nonetheless illustrates a prominent clustering of free-trade-oriented interests toward the right side of the graph. The party variable simply illustrates the four party subgroups

a. First-dimension coordinate

b. Constituency interests

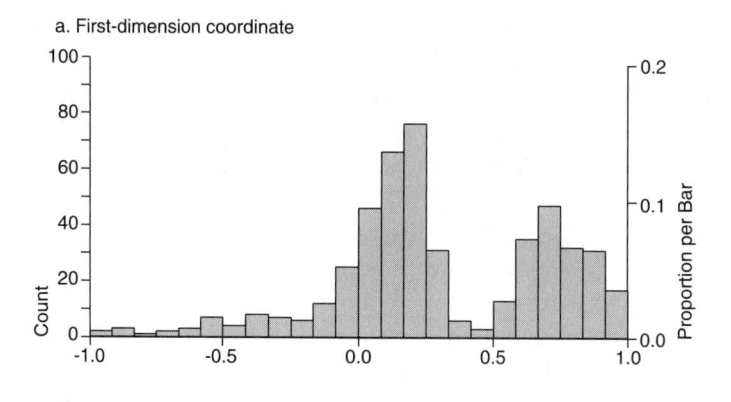

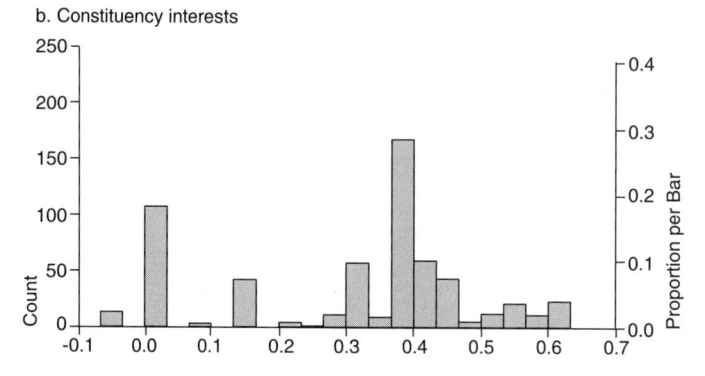

Figure 6.3
First-dimension coordinate separated into interests, party, and (new) ideology

(as components of the first-dimension coordinate). Most revealing, MPs' ideology, once stripped of interests and party, begins to resemble a normal distribution, albeit with a negative skew. While it is tempting simply to assume that this residual term provides an adequate measure of MPs' personal ideology, it remains a logical possibility that it may be a consequence rather than a determinant of votes in Parliament (and therefore cannot be considered to be exogenous in a model of voting behavior). It is also conceivable that this variable reflects the pattern of ideological consistency imposed by the national parties. While it may be impossible to say with absolute certainty that this variable is an acceptable proxy for MPs' ideology, figures 6.4, 6.5, and 6.6 help to clarify that this variable does indeed appear to measure a normal left-right ideological continuum, with left leaning toward free trade and right leaning toward protection. (Hence, MPs' ideology differs from

The Demand Side

c. Party

d. MP's ideology

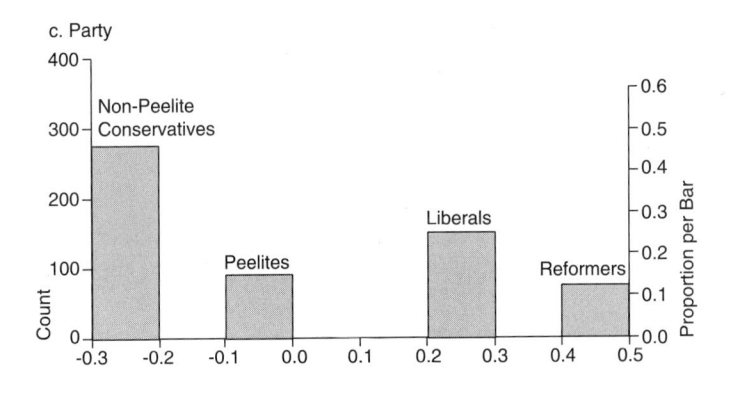

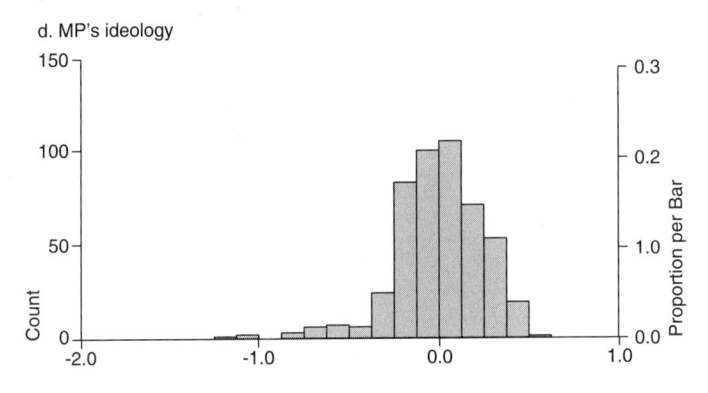

Figure 6.3
(continued)

the first-dimension coordinate in figures 6.1 and 6.2, where parties situated toward one end of the spectrum supported protection and those to the other supported free trade. This transformation of the ideological spectrum is a feature of stripping the party component from the first-dimension coordinate to arrive at a "purer" measure of MP ideology.)

Figures 6.4 and 6.5 are density plots of MPs' ideology, with groupings for district type and district economic orientation. Both plots tell the same story: MPs from rural, agricultural districts (which opposed repeal most stridently) were to the right in their ideological orientation, while MPs from districts with more urban or industrial interests (which viewed repeal more favorably) were near to the center or slightly left of center in their ideological orientation. That this measure coincides with the interests of constituents should be no surprise as others have found that constituents tended to select likeminded MPs, and MPs, in turn, tended to select constituencies in which they could

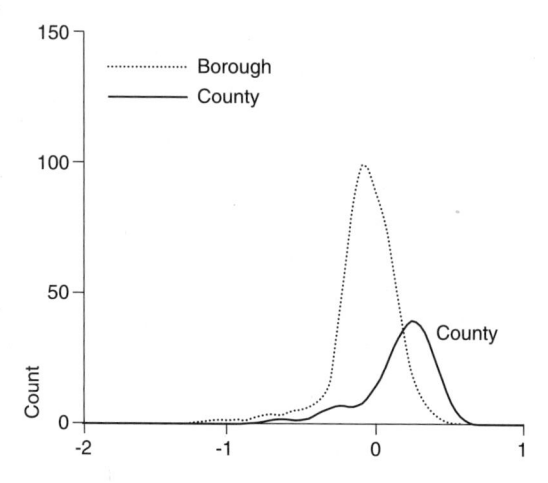

Figure 6.4
New MP ideology by district type

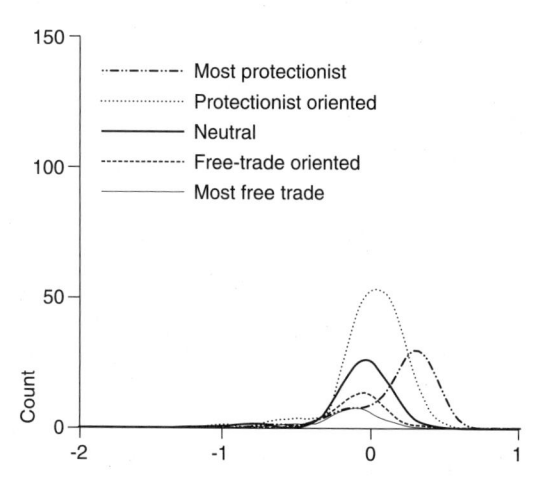

Figure 6.5
New MP ideology by district economic orientation

The Demand Side 145

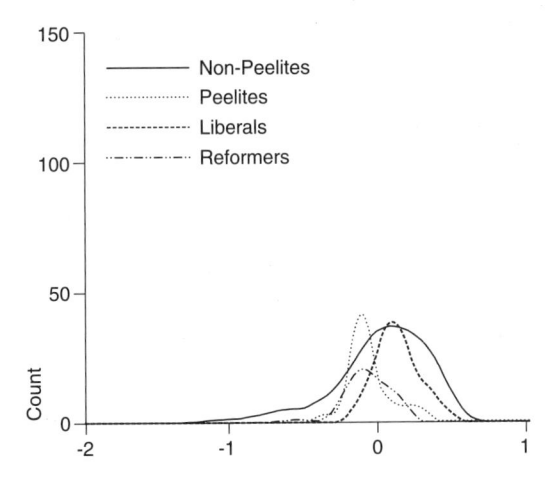

```
150 ─
         ──────── Non-Peelites
         ············ Peelites
         ─────── Liberals
100 ─    ─·─·─·─ Reformers

 50 ─

  0 ─
      -2        -1         0         1
Count
```

Figure 6.6
New MP ideology by party affiliation

win (Cox 1987, 151). Of particular interest is the distinctly right-of-center position of MPs from highly protectionist districts (figure 6.5). From table 6.2, we know that the vast majority of these MPs were also Non-Peelites. In contrast, MPs from protectionist-oriented and neutral districts—many of whom were Peelites—tended to be positioned at the center or slightly to the left of center.

Figure 6.6 is also a density plot of MPs' ideology but with party groupings. We see an ideological distinction between Non-Peelite Conservatives and Peelites, which undermines an interpretation of the residual as measuring the ideological *consistency* imposed by the Conservative party. Moreover, figure 6.6 provides an illustration of the core argument of this chapter. The Conservative party was a coalition of two distinct interest-based factions. While the Peelites shared the general ideology of the Conservative party (represented in figure 6.6 as overlapping ideological space with the Non-Peelites), they formed a distinct (left-of-center) subset, which in turn was aligned with the interests of their constituents. Prior to 1846, their protectionist votes conflicted with a personal ideology that coincided more with constituents' interests. Meanwhile, the Non-Peelite Conservatives, positioned to the right of center, faced no such conflict between personal ideology and constituents' interests. Finally, it is worth noting a comparison between figures 6.2 and 6.6.[31] In figure 6.2, ideology, partisanship, and constituency interests are intertwined, whereas in figure 6.6, the effects of partisanship and constituency interests on the first-dimension coordinate have been extracted, leaving what appears to be a purer measure of MPs' ideology. Figure 6.6 reveals, moreover, that MPs' ideology appeared to share a considerable amount of common space. Yet even in this common space, Peelites retained a distinct ideological identity.

Regression Analysis of Repeal Votes

From the model presented in this chapter, we obtain our three key predictors of the repeal vote—constituency interests, party, and MPs' ideology. To these predictors, the second-dimension coordinate from NOMINATE is added as a way to test for the robustness of the key variables. Table 6.4 presents the results of logistic regressions for annual votes on repeal leading up to and including the final vote in 1846.[32]

For the final repeal vote, the model correctly predicts all but five of the votes of the Peelites, which is no small task.[33] What is more intrigu-

Table 6.4
Motions for repeal from 1842 to 1846

Variable	11 July 1842	15 May 1843	26 June 1844	10 June 1845	15 May 1846
Constant	−23.076**	−42.030***	−22.713***	−22.272***	−3.168***
	(9.132)	(12.008)	(5.867)	(7.793)	(.997)
Constituency interests	51.302**	67.573***	48.587***	42.378***	12.636***
	(21.418)	(19.249)	(13.306)	(14.127)	(3.268)
Party	25.681***	55.620***	20.924***	32.633***	24.621***
	(7.522)	(16.222)	(5.055)	(12.054)	(4.020)
MPs' ideology	32.425**	51.153***	30.086***	32.704***	2.101
	(13.397)	(14.780)	(8.642)	(12.144)	(2.343)
Second-dimension coordinate	−1.221	−1.974	−1.983	−0.846	−7.673***
	(1.906)	(2.018)	(1.343)	(1.1459)	(1.604)
−2 log likelihood	14.12	29.52	24.74	19.60	66.29
Percentage correctly predicted	99.27	98.94	98.86	98.27	97.32
Errors (observed yeas)	1	1	1	2	5
Errors (observed nays)	1	3	3	3	6
Number of cases	274	376	350	289	411

Note: Standard error in parentheses.
*$p < .10$.
**$p < .05$.
***$p < .01$.

ing is that MPs' ideology appears to have had little or no bearing on the repeal vote, while constituency interests, party, and the second-dimension coordinate[34] are all significant at 1 percent.

The strong performance of constituency interests and party in predicting the repeal vote does not, however, suggest that MPs' ideology had no role to play in the progression to repeal. From previous divisions on repeal, we see a dramatic shift in the role of MPs' ideology in 1846. From 1842 to 1845, the ideology of MPs is highly significant (at 1 percent in 1843 to 1845 and 5 percent in 1842), as too are all the remaining variables except the second-dimension coordinate. As a model, the variables explain 98 to 99 percent of the repeal votes. This suggests that the portions of the first-dimension coordinate that can be attributed to constituency interests, party, and MPs' ideology *all* carried weight in the voting decisions of MPs *until* the actual repeal vote. In 1846, an abrupt change occurred: MPs' personal ideology appears to have had little or no influence in their decision. Rather, they were motivated more by the desire to further their constituents' interests. Repeal appears to have gained passage as (at least some) MPs switched from voting as trustees to voting as delegates.

The coefficient estimates from table 6.4 may be used to conduct simulations that allow us to estimate the *substantive* effect of changes in key variables—particularly, constituency interests and MPs' ideology—on the simulated probability of a free-trade vote. Using the parameters from the logistic regressions from table 6.4, 1,000 simulated sets of parameters are generated (King, Tomz, et al. 2000; Tomz, Wittenberg, et al. 2001). From these, two probabilities are calculated for each of the key variables, creating a set of probabilities for each faction of the Conservative party. The first is the probability of a vote in favor of free trade when MPs' ideology and the second-dimension coordinate are set to their mean values, constituency interests is set to its minimum value, and the party variable is set equal to Peelite. This simulates the probability of a Peelite from a highly rural constituency (whose ideology and second-dimension coordinate values are considered average) voting for free trade. The second simulates the change that results in the first set of probabilities when constituency interests is changed to its maximum value. This allows us to compare the probability of a free-trade vote from a Peelite representing a rural constituency with one representing an industrial, export-oriented district (all else held constant). Similarly, the probability of a free-trade vote is calculated for a Peelite whose ideology falls at the extreme left of the

Table 6.5
Estimated effects of constituency interests and MPs' ideology on Peelites and Non-Peelite Conservatives

Variable	Peelites 11 July 1842	Peelites 15 May 1846	Non-Peelite Conservatives 11 July 1842	Non-Peelite Conservatives 15 May 1846
Constituency interests:				
Probability of yes vote[a]	1.78e-06	.029	.006	4.42e-04
	(4.17e-05)	(.035)	(.071)	(.002)
Difference in probability of yes vote[b]	.997	.955	.773	.321
	(.017)	(.059)	(.334)	(.181)
MPs' ideology:				
Probability of yes vote[c]	1.84e-06	.261	.009	.019
	(4.81e-05)	(.256)	(.094)	(.076)
Difference in probability of yes vote[d]	.984	.573	.767	.033
	(.085)	(.340)	(.364)	(.118)

Note: Standard error in parentheses.
a. Pr(yes) when MPs' ideology and second-dimension coordinate are set to their mean values, constituency interests is set to its minimum value, and party is set to equal Peelite.
b. The difference in the Pr(yes) when constituency interests is changed to its maximum value.
c. Pr(yes) when constituency interests and second-dimension coordinate are set to their mean values, MPs' ideology is set to its minimum value, and party is set to equal Non-Peelite Conservative.
d. The difference in the Pr(yes) when MPs' ideology is changed to its maximum value.

spectrum, with the remaining variables (constituency interests and second-dimension coordinate) set at their mean values. As with constituency interests, a second probability then simulates the change that results when we consider a Peelite whose ideology falls at the extreme right of the spectrum (all else held constant). This same set of probabilities is replicated for the Non-Peelite faction of the Conservative party. For simplicity, probabilities from just the early division and the final division are considered, with the results given in table 6.5.[35]

From table 6.5, we can see that, over the whole of the Parliament, constituency interests and personal ideology weighed more heavily for Peelites than Non-Peelites (as the differences in all the probabilities are greater for Non-Peelites). This suggests that Non-Peelites were driven more by the broader Conservative ideology (which viewed protection as a traditional British institution) than were Peelites, which is consistent with my argument. Nonetheless, constituency interests and personal ideology also affected the votes of Non-Peelites, but more so in 1842 than in 1846. In 1842, both variables generate an increase in the probability of a free-trade vote of about .77, while in 1846, the constituency-interest variable generates an increase of just .32, and personal ideology generates a minuscule (and statistically insignificant) .03. It seems fair to say, then, that in the final 1846 vote, Non-Peelites were affected in part by constituency interests but *not* by personal ideology.

For Peelites, it appears that constituency interests had a strong effect on voting behavior for the duration of the Parliament. Changing the orientation of the district from rural to industrial increases the probability of a Peelite voting for free trade from virtually zero to almost one. In contrast, the effect of ideology is strong in 1842 (with a change from its minimum to its maximum value resulting in an increased in the probability of a free trade vote from almost zero to almost one) but weak (and statistically insignificant) in 1846. This provides evidence in support of the contention that as the influence of ideology dissipated in 1846, Peelites voted more as delegates.

MPs' Ideology: Shirking or Reputation Building?

A lively debate in the legislative-studies literature contrasts "bad" ideology with "good" ideology (Richardson and Munger 1990). For some, legislators who serve their own ideological preferences instead of the preferences of their constituents are labeled as (bad) "shirkers" (Peltzman 1984; Nelson and Silberberg 1987). For others, ideology serves a (good) reputational purpose inasmuch as legislators who vote against their established (ideologically based) reputations do themselves a disservice by devaluing that reputation (Dougan and Munger 1989; Richardson and Munger 1990). This chapter provides some insights into the strengths and limitations of both interpretations of ideology by providing a relatively simple case with which to explore the interplay between ideology and constituency interests.

The case of mid-nineteenth-century Britain is unusual in that it is one of the few examples of a political environment in which a single issue is dominant. Politics in the 1840s most definitely revolved around trade policy: the election of 1841 was characterized largely as a mandate on trade policy (with the Conservative party standing for protection); the overriding issue of the Parliament of 1841 to 1847 was the Corn Laws; and repeal caused the ultimate demise of the Peel government and the disintegration of the Conservative party. This single-issue dominance allows us to simplify the interests of constituents according to their preferences on trade policy (as shown in table 6.2). Let us further assume that the trade-policy preference of the median voter can be defined by an aggregate measure, derived from "district economic orientation" (from table 6.2).[36]

It is almost certain that the median voter in Non-Peelite Conservative constituencies favored protection. This means that Non-Peelite Conservatives were not "shirkers," as they consistently voted for protection throughout the Parliament. However, these MPs were also wedded to a Conservative ideology in which protection was considered a fundamental British institution. Moreover, the Conservative party's reputation for defending protection was critical to the 1841 election. It is therefore impossible to be certain about what motivated the protectionist votes of Non-Peelite Conservatives, as a Conservative ideology and constituency interests point in the same direction. Moreover, a concern for maintaining their reputations as true defenders of "Conservatism" may have figured in the 1846 vote, as these MPs saw their leader and the rest of their party defect to free trade. In short, these MPs may have been voting as simple delegates for the duration of the Parliament or may have been motivated by a broader Conservative ideology. What is clear is that they were *not* shirking.

The preference of the median voter in Peelite constituencies is less certain but in all likelihood was borderline protectionist, with some leanings toward free trade. As such, it is a stretch to characterize a free-trade vote in 1846 as "shirking." Indeed, the notion of shirking is virtually meaningless in a context of a median voter who is situated near (if not at) the point of indifference. But to characterize Peelite voting as reputation building is no more helpful, as an ideological reputation suggests constancy in voting—not an abrupt reversal. The most appropriate interpretation of Peelite voting behavior (subject to the limitations of econometric testing)[37] is as described earlier, that before 1846, Peelites voted according to a general Conservative ideology, but in 1846 their votes reflected a median voter who was leaning toward free trade.

Finally, this case points to two general limitations of both the shirking and reputation-building interpretations of ideology. First, neither interpretation is conducive to an understanding of why legislators abruptly *change* their votes. In the case of repeal, the source of change stemmed from the instability inherent in a Conservative party that,

The Demand Side

while sharing a general Conservative ideology, was the marriage of two distinct interest-based alliances. That is, Peelite conversion to free trade came from a conflict between a Conservative ideology and constituents' interests, which eventually erupted when their leader moved for repeal. Without examining how interests interact with ideology, it is impossible to understand an abrupt reversal such as repeal. Hence, where the task is to explain shifts in voting patterns (particularly for issues such as trade policy where interests are highly charged), a focus strictly on ideology (defined either as shirking or reputation-building) has severe limitations.

Second, the quantity measure of shirking suggested by Kalt and Zupan (1990, 116)—namely, the absolute value of the ideology residual—can result in misleading findings where the direction of interests is of fundamental importance. Comparing this measure across party groups, it appears that Non-Peelite Conservatives demonstrated far more shirking than Peelites, Whigs/Liberals, and Reformers, as we obtain measures of shirking for each party group of 0.235, 0.144, 0.141, and 0.139, respectively. This would suggest that Non-Peelite Conservatives were even more protectionist than their constituents desired, while the rest were more closely aligned with the interests of their constituents. In Kalt and Zupan's view, Non-Peelites should therefore have lost electoral support as a consequence of their shirking. But in fact, Non-Peelite Conservatives were marginally more successful than Peelites in the general election of 1847,[38] which suggests that Non-Peelites may even have gained support from maintaining their protectionist *reputation*. Hence, in cases where extreme views are likely to generate support, such a simple quantitative measure of shirking can mislead. Thus, if we accept that Non-Peelite Conservativs *were* shirking, the presumption that shirking is an electoral liability would require reconsideration.

Conclusion

This chapter has sought to answer the puzzle of the Peelites by characterizing the Conservative party as a coalition between two interest-based alliances with a shared concern for retaining traditional British institutions. Non-Peelite Conservatives, who represented mostly agricultural districts, had no motivation to follow Prime Minister Peel as he moved for repeal: both their Conservatism and representation of rural constituencies pointed toward retaining a firm commitment to protection. Peelites, who represented districts with comparatively more free-trade-leaning interests, faced a conflict between their concern for Conservatism and their representation of constituents who were either borderline protectionists or leaning toward free trade. Prior to 1846, they voted in accordance with Conservatism. But in 1846, when their leader foreclosed the option of retaining party unity, Peelites shifted from voting as trustees to voting more as delegates.

More broadly, this chapter has sought to develop a methodological framework for disentangling the influences of constituency interests, party, and personal ideology on the roll-call votes of legislators. It applies widely recognized (though not necessarily universally accepted) methodologies—such as the NOMINATE technique and the Kalt and Zupan residualization approach—in a way that allows us to gauge the relative influences of interests, party, and ideology on MPs in the votes leading up to and including the final third reading of repeal. Yet as the British case and its data are obviously historical, one might question whether the analysis presented here is generalizable to other, more contemporary legislative settings. Certainly, nineteenth-century British parties were less cohesive and constituency interests were less complex than in contemporary Britain—but these are differences of degrees. The historical setting made the ideological climate in 1846 unique—but not so much as to prevent present-day observers from drawing parallels between intra-Conservative party cleavages on repeal with those on the European Union. Moreover, this chapter has shown that the ideological makeup of the Parliament of 1841 to 1847 can be largely understood within a left/right continuum (though with adaptation to the terms *left* and *right*). Hence, just as other non-American applications of the NOMINATE method have demonstrated (Hix 2000; Noury 2000; Voeten 2000), while legislative settings may differ considerably, the methodologies applied to study them have much in common.

What remains certain is that the findings of this chapter call into question some of the historiography of nineteenth-century trade policy that tends to view the conversion to repeal by Peelites as a statement of independence from party and constituents. Rather, the message here is that Peelites shifted their votes to more closely match the free-trade-leaning preferences of their constituents. The findings also point to the need to understand the interplay between ideology, party, *and* interests as motivations for roll-call voting behavior. The progression to repeal,

The Demand Side

and indeed repeal itself, cannot be understood without reference to all three influences.

As this chapter concludes part 1 of the book, it is worth reviewing the demand-side pressures for free trade. Chapter 3 finds evidence to suggest that significant changes in the British export sector between the mid-1820s and mid-1840s helped to intensify and spread more widely its free-trade interests, thereby contributing to the rise of the Anti-Corn Law League. Chapter 5 presents evidence suggesting that the demand for protection declined by the early 1840s, owing to the portfolio diversification of (some) landowners into nonagricultural ventures. This diversification was, moreover, greater in Peelite than in Non-Peelite Conservative constituencies. In short, at about the same time as manufacturers were clamoring more loudly and effectively for free trade, landowners were becoming less wedded to protectionism. Chapter 4 examines how the Anti-Corn Law League engaged in a strategy of "nationalizing the interest." That is, by linking repeal to unifying themes such as morality and antiaristocracy, it appealed to the general British public to support free trade. Finally, building on the analysis in chapter 5, the present chapter provides a more complete empirical test of the effect of demand-side pressures on the votes of MPs in the lead-up to repeal and on repeal itself. This chapter presents evidence to suggest that in 1846, the pivotal MPs—the Peelites—abruptly shifted from voting as trustees to voting as delegates. In other words, they (like their Liberal counterparts) shifted their voting behavior to reflect the net increase in constituency demand for free trade. The role of economic interests has been prominent in these chapters, although ideas were found to be critical to the lobbying of the League, and Conservative ideology severely constrained the voting behavior of Peelites before 1846. The key defining institution in the demand-side story has been the 1832 Reform Act, which gave rise to the politicization of middle-class interests and shaped the lobbying strategies of the League.

The demand-side provides ample evidence for how and why constituency interests shifted toward free trade, how these interests became mobilized, and how various segments of the British public were persuaded by the arguments of the Anti-Corn Law League. The present chapter details how MPs voted on repeal and particularly how the Peelites abruptly shifted from voting as trustees to voting as delegates. The demand side has thus provided important insights into how repeal came about. But the fundamentally important questions left unanswered by the demand-side are why the Peelites shifted their position so abruptly and, following their abrupt reversal, why the Lords reversed their steadfast support for protection. As outlined in chapters 1 and 2, part 2 of this book explores the motivations of MPs and peers by analyzing their speeches in Parliament. This analysis is intended to tease out the supply-side story behind repeal. Chapter 7 reveals that a reinterpretation of repeal allowed Peelites to vote as delegates but to justify their betrayal of a protectionist Conservative ideology in the language of disinterested and moral trustees whose only motive was to promote the nation's well-being. Chapter 8 tests the robustness of the findings in chapter 7 by asking whether Peel's reinterpretation of repeal as a policy that would preserve the territorial constitution was indeed unique to 1846. This rationale was not articulated as a theme in any of the debates on trade policy in the thirty years prior to 1846, which lends significant weight to my argument that while demand-side pressures were necessary for repeal, the final explanation for repeal must hinge on the introduction of a second dimension of argumentation, thereby splitting the Non-Peelite Conservatives from the Peelites. Chapter 9 explores the institutional conflict between a legislative chamber (the Commons) that was perceived as caving in to popular demand and one (the Lords) that perceived itself as immune to pressure from "out-of-doors." The chapter further examines how demand-side pressures for parliamentary reform ultimately persuaded peers to accept the lesser of two evils—repeal over democratic reform. Finally, chapter 10 asks whether it might have been the ideas and arguments of the League that persuaded Peelites to change their position and not changes in the economic makeup of their constituencies. While the results of this analysis of newspaper coverage in local constituencies clearly illustrate the increased intensity in lobbying by the League form 1841 to 1846 (thereby increasing the demand for repeal), they also find very little effect of free-trade ideas on the voting behavior of Peelites.

II The Supply Side

7 Conservatives Who Sounded Like Trustees but Voted Like Delegates

Introduction

Part 1 of this book demonstrates that industrialization created a swathe of free-trade interests that could have pushed some Members of Parliament to support free trade. Yet up to the end of 1845, backbench Conservative MPs remained firmly committed to protection, and without their support, repeal would have failed. Thus a shift in constituency demands was a necessary condition for repeal but was not sufficient to convert a majority of MPs to vote for free trade. As noted in chapter 2, unanimous Liberal support was not sufficient to gain repeal without the support of some Conservative MPs. To push the wavering Conservatives to free trade, the definition of repeal required reinterpretation so that it could be seen to be compatible with Conservative ideology. Peel provided this reinterpretation when he introduced the repeal legislation, and Peelites latched onto this reinterpretation as political and ideological cover for their free-trade votes. By trumpeting themselves as loyal to the longer-term preservation of the territorial constitution and judging that repeal was a necessary concession to ensure this outcome, Peelites could vote as delegates without having to justify themselves as such.

To assess this argument, chapters 7, 8, and 9 rely on parliamentary speeches to understand why legislators voted as they did on the bill. To further test the demand- and supply-side argument presented in chapter 2, I use computer-assisted content analysis to analyze parliamentary speeches on repeal, spanning from the introduction of the legislation in January 1846 to its final passage four months later. Parliamentary speeches, like any other data, must not be taken at face value.[1] However, inasmuch as Peel himself endorsed the integrity and reliability of these speeches,[2] it seems appropriate to assume that MPs articulated the reasons for their votes relatively accurately in these speeches. Moreover, as this study analyzes *all* the 587 speeches of the 205 MPs who spoke on repeal, it is unlikely that any important themes or issues surrounding repeal are missed.

Methodology

Findings Expected by the Argument

If the argument presented in chapter 2 carries weight, the speeches should reflect at least three features. First, MPs should express a concern for how repeal impinged on their perceived roles as representatives of the British public. For their part, Peelites should have characterized themselves as trustees seeking to protect the larger societal interest and welfare and, in particular, the traditional institutions of government on which these rested. In this way, Peelites would have reverberated Peel's characterization of repeal as the means to defend the traditional institutions of British government and, in particular, the territorial constitution. Non-Peelite Conservatives, on the other hand, should be expected to invoke a defensive line of argument on the territorial constitution. In a nutshell, we should expect to see a clash between Peelites and NPCs on the appropriate means to defend the landed basis of Parliament and, more broadly, on the question of whose interests MPs should serve.

Second, if Peelites latched onto Peel's reinterpretation of repeal as cover for their free-trade votes, they should have sought to do so with immediate effect. That is, Peelites' speeches leading up to the first reading division[3] on repeal should clearly justify their votes in terms of their desire to defend the integrity of the territorial constitution. If justifications unrelated to the territorial constitution or MPs' mode of representation prevail in these early speeches, this finding would undermine the argument.

Third, inasmuch as demand-side pressures (such as the growing export-oriented interests of industrialists and political leverage by the lobbying efforts of the Anti-Corn Law League) influenced the opinions of free-trade-leaning MPs, this should be evident somewhere in the debates. If demand-side issues fail to emerge as prominent themes in the repeal debates, this too would undermine the strength of the argument.

Computer-Assisted Content Analysis

Computer-Assisted Content Analysis in Political Science Many researchers in political science have used classical content analysis to describe textual data.[4] This form of analysis provides a systematic and transparent way of managing large amounts of text. It also relies on mainly "naturally occurring raw data" (such as newspapers, speeches, letters, and public documents), which avoids problems of reactivity of the respondent that may occur in interviews. Finally, content analysis provides researchers with well-documented procedures (Bauer 2000, 147). But content analysis can also suffer from problems of sampling and coding. The former raises familiar issues of representativeness, sample size, and the unit of sampling, while the latter involves issues of the nature of the categories, the organization of the coding scheme, and the adequacy of the coding process and coders (Bauer 2000, 136, 139). In particular, interpretation of the material must be reliable (that is, coding must be consistent between and among coders), and it must be valid (that is, the codes must relate to the words used in the text, and the sample must represent the whole text) (Bauer 2000, 143–144). Researchers often incorporate tests for reliability and validity into their research design, generally at the cost of duplication and repetition.

Computer-assisted content analysis—such as Alceste—offers a way to surmount the difficulties of traditional content analysis, while at the same time producing results that are entirely consistent with it (Allum 1998). Alceste stands in stark contrast to classical content analysis in four ways. First, it is insensitive to meaning and context. This may result in missed nuances, but it also guards against allowing researchers and coders to infuse their own biases into the coding and analysis. Second, it can provide an impression of a voluminous data corpus within a short space of time. Third, and following from that, the issue of reliability that arises with human coding is no longer relevant. Fourth, because large amounts of text can be analyzed quickly—which means that sampling may not be required—problems of sampling may also disappear. (In this chapter, for example, the *whole* of the 1846 Commons debates on repeal of the Corn Laws is analyzed.)

Computer-assisted analysis of political texts has, moreover, recently captured the attention and imagination of some political scientists (Gabel and Huber 2000; Laver and Garry 2000; Laver and Benoit 2002;

Laver, Benoit, et al. 2002) and has received well-deserved praise: "The ability to analyze vast amounts of text quickly and cheaply has the potential to revolutionize the study of politics" (Laver, Benoit, et al. 2002, 3). While the methods used elsewhere are useful for some purposes, Alceste is better suited to test my argument for three reasons. First, following minimal editing, the text is ready for analysis (for example, no reference text is required, as with Laver, Benoit, and Garry's 2003 Wordscore technique). Second, Alceste generates word lists and sentences that typify the classes (or themes) that are identified in the text. These can then be traced back to the original text so that the researcher may evaluate the context of the statements. Both key words and sentences are, moreover, ranked in terms of their statistical significance (of which more is said below). Third, the technique generates correspondence analysis so that the party affiliation, constituency type, or other characteristics of legislators may be mapped onto the same policy space as the identified classes or themes. In this way, one can evaluate the sorts of issues that parties or legislators from specific types of districts (rural, industrial) tended to highlight as justifications for their votes. The value of Alceste will be illustrated more clearly in the reporting of the results.

Alceste Alceste relies on cooccurrence analysis, which is the statistical analysis of frequent word pairs in a text corpus. Alceste was developed by Max Reinert (1983, 1998) and was originally used in the humanities (Reinert 1993), although its use has recently spread to the social sciences (Noel-Jorand, Reinert, et al. 1995; Lahlou 1996, 1998; Allum 1998) and to political science (Brugidou 1998, 2000; Bailey and Schonhardt-Bailey 2005; Schonhardt-Bailey 2005). It has been described as a methodology insofar as it "integrates a multitude of highly sophisticated statistical methods into an organic whole that perfectly suits its aim of discourse analysis" (Kronberger and Wagner 2000, 306).[5]

There are two preconditions for good results with Alceste: (1) the textual data must be coherent (that is, it must focus on one topic), and (2) the text must be large enough for the statistical output to be relevant, with a minimum of 10,000 words. Parliamentary debates on repeal of the Corn Laws fit these preconditions precisely: the speeches all relate to British trade policy, and the word count is 922,240.

Alceste determines word-distribution patterns within a text, with the objective being to obtain a primary statistical classification of simple statements (or *contextual units*)[6] to reveal the most characteristic words, which in turn can be distinguished as word classes that represent different forms of discourse concerning the topic of the text.[7]

The program creates a data matrix (an *indicator matrix*) that allows an analysis of statistical similarities and dissimilarities of words to identify repetitive language patterns. This matrix relates relevant words in columns and contextual units in rows, so that if a given word is present, a 1 is entered in the cell; otherwise, the entry is 0. Then, using descending hierarchical-classification analysis, the program identifies word classes.[8] The first class comprises the total set of contextual units in the initial indicator matrix. The program then attempts to partition that class into two further classes that contain different vocabulary and ideally do not contain any overlapping words. The methods used for this are optimal scaling and the adoption of a maximum chi-squared (χ^2) criterion for cutting the ordered set of words (see the appendix to this chapter for details of the χ^2 criterion). Alceste compares the distribution of words in each of the two new classes with the average distribution of words. Different forms of discourse that use different vocabulary will result in an observed word distribution that deviates systematically from one where the words are independent of each other. The procedure searches for maximally separate patterns of cooccurrence between the word classes. The χ^2 criterion is thus used as a measure of the relationship that exists between words rather than as a test.

Following an iterative process, the descending hierarchical classification method decomposes the classes until a predetermined number of iterations fails to result in further divisions. The result is a hierarchy of classes, which may be schematized as a tree diagram (such as figure 7.1, discussed below).

Results of an Analysis of the 1846 Parliamentary Debates

Identifying the Themes in the Debates

The text file of the Commons debates begins on 22 January 1846 with the opening of the parliamentary session[9] and continues through the debates on the third reading of repeal, which culminate in the final vote on 15 May 1846.[10] Table 7.1 provides a summary of the basic statistics from Alceste.[11] The total word count for the text file is 922,240, and of these, 339,713 were unique words that were analyzed by the program.[12] The passive variables[13] (or tagged indicators) refer to units of the text that the researcher identifies according to certain

Table 7.1
Alceste analysis: Basic statistics for the 1846 debates

Total word count	922,240
Unique words analyzed	339,713
Passive variables (tagged indicators)	238
ICUs (= number of speeches)	587
Classified ECUs	7,093 (= 80% of the retained ECU)
Lexical classes	6
Distribution of classes (%)	1: 19.44
	2: 10.36
	3: 9.49
	4: 10.77
	5: 30.99
	6: 18.95

characteristics. For this study, each speech is considered a *case* or a textual unit. I then *tag* each speech according to certain characteristics—the name of the speaking MP, his party affiliation, his constituency type (such as borough or county and the general economic composition of the constituency), and the timing of the speech.[14] The timing of the speech is identified as occurring during the first reading, second reading, or third reading of Peel's repeal motion or during Charles Villiers's motion for total and immediate repeal. Whereas Peel's (successful) motion proposed to abolish grain protection in 1849, Villiers's (unsuccessful) motion called for immediate repeal of protection and thus was considered more radical in its push for free trade.[15]

The *initial context unit* (ICU) is a preexisting division of the text and is specified by the user. Here, each speech constitutes an ICU, and so table 7.1 notes that there were 587 speeches on trade policy that occurred between 22 January and 15 May 1846.[16] The *elementary context unit* (ECU) is a "gauged sentence," which the program automatically constructs based on word length and punctuation in the text. Using the presence or absence of words in each ECU, the program calculates matrices on which to build the classification process. (Table 7.3 provides examples of ECUs, with each three- or four-digit reference designating a given ECU in the text.)[17] The program conducts two preliminary analyses, each using slightly different lengths for the contextual unit.[18] It then opts for the length that allows the greater proportion of ECUs to be successfully classified, relative to the total available. From table 7.1, we can see that 7,093 ECUs were classified, equating to 80 percent of the ECUs[19] retained for analysis.[20]

The Supply Side

Six lexical classes are identified in the debates. Class 5 is the largest class, with 31 percent of the ECUs. Classes 1 and 6 are the next two largest classes, with each accounting for about 19 percent of the ECUs.

Table 7.2 lists the most characteristic function words of each class, in order of statistical significance.[21] The most characteristic words are those with high χ^2 values. Words ending with "+" indicate that these are reduced forms (for example, *trade+* may refer to *trade, trading, traded,* and so on). Table 7.3 provides examples of two of the top four most representative ECUs for each class, in which the context is given for the characteristic words, and where these words are indicated with a "#" sign.[22] These examples help the researcher to describe better the classes. From tables 7.2 and 7.3 (and the much longer printouts, from which these tables are constructed), we can analyze the characteristic words and phrases in each class to arrive at conceptual headings for the classes.

Wages and Prices; and High Farming In class 1, the single most characteristic word by a fair margin is *labour+* (with the "+" signifying derivatives such as *labouring* and *labourers*), while the second is *wage+*. These, along with *price*, suggest that MPs were concerned with the relationship between wages and prices. The second quote for class 1 in table 7.3 confirms this theme.[23] At issue was whether free trade led to *higher* or *lower* wages. As discussed in chapter 4, the Anti-Corn Law League sought to persuade electors (and thereby, indirectly, MPs) that repeal would raise wages, not lower them. Whether MPs heard these arguments via their electors, from League pamphlets, or from Leaguers cum MPs (Villiers, Cobden, and Bright) is uncertain. What *is* certain, however, is that the theoretical debates of the political economists—popularized by the League—were embraced by MPs in the debates on repeal. Following Malthus and Spence, some MPs argued that lower food prices, resulting from *free trade*, would lower wages for agricultural labor. Displaced agricultural laborers would then seek employment in industry, thus lowering wages for industrial laborers and potentially raising unemployment in industrial areas. Others, following Ricardo and Torrens, maintained that *protection* resulted in lower, not higher, wages since it lowered the returns to manufacturers and farmers and thereby led them to cut production costs by reducing wages.[24]

Unusually, this class contains a second, but related, theme. Words such as *farm+, land+, capital+, rent,* and *price*, along with the first quote

Table 7.2
Characteristic words of each class by strength of association

Class 1		Class 2		Class 3		Class 4		Class 5		Class 6	
χ^2	Word	χ^2	Word	χ^2	Word	χ^2	Word	χ^2	Word	χ^2	Word
908	labour+	268	aristocrac+	288	leader+	968	potatoes	372	majesty+	866	foreign+
675	wage+	233	polic+	275	league+	722	wheat+	331	question+	748	article+
586	farm+	207	interest+	250	men+	613	quarter+	324	noble+	738	manufacture+
524	land+	177	institut+	246	elect+	518	oat+	322	measure+	580	duty
478	capital+	167	maintain+	176	constituenc+	437	price+	319	member+	562	trade+
397	rent+	139	peace+	155	candid+	415	average+	284	govern+	548	silk+
390	price+	123	commercial	153	talent+	374	disease+	255	house+	537	duties
382	cultiv+	121	legislat+	151	anti	365	crop+	207	opinion+	490	reduction+
376	employ+	120	maintenance	135	majorit+	310	supply+	206	propose+	479	timber+
273	population+	117	wisdom	133	polit+	302	potato	194	debate+	435	british
259	district+	117	power+	131	conservat+	300	grain+	181	amend+	309	raw
246	low	114	territor+	128	reform+	269	market+	169	friend+	270	export+
239	improve+	113	principle+	114	betray+	241	flour	157	express+	268	competition
237	rate+	108	polit+	114	honour+	240	rye	156	speech	259	consum+
236	agricultural+	101	public+	111	represent+	229	barley	156	repeal+	257	reduce+
235	manufacturing	98	justice+	108	whig+	225	bushel+	153	proposition+	255	cotton+
220	tenant+	98	welfare	106	confid+	224	stone+	148	law+	254	colon+
215	condition+	98	national+	105	honest+	203	quantit+	148	motion+	251	revenue+
197	acre+	96	communit+	104	man+	193	food	147	wolverhampton	246	goods
177	landlord+	81	base+	101	elector+	191	harvest+	145	immediate+	242	ship+
171	poor+	78	convict+	97	triumph+	186	dantzic	138	baronet+	239	cent+

The Supply Side

155	agriculture	77	empire+	93	parliament+	184	meal+	135	course+	235	import+
138	work+	75	long+	89	minister+	177	qualit+	127	vote+	234	shipp+
135	soil+	73	privilege+	86	public+	161	april	124	settle+	209	countries
132	increase+	72	happiness	86	borough+	161	year+	121	russell+	200	amount+
131	money+	70	restrict+	85	principle+	161	month+	119	suspension+	195	compete+
130	drain+	69	defence+	85	seat+	153	deficienc+	108	ireland+	192	tonnage+
99	children+	68	ancient	82	meetings	144	supplie+	104	address+	188	increase+
99	farmers+	68	hitherto	82	pledge+	144	famine+	102	subject+	170	tariff+
96	families	67	self+	82	rank+	123	freight+	93	gentleman+	164	baltic
92	count+	66	class+	81	baronet+	123	barrel+	93	adjust+	154	ton+
91	food	64	prejudice+	81	gentlemen+	117	date+	86	discuss+	149	taxation
86	wheat+	64	constitut+	80	protection+	113	store+	84	night+	147	excise

Table 7.3
Examples of most typical ECUs in each corpus (1846 debates)

Class	Original ECU (traceable to the original text)	Chi Squared Association (rank)	Selection of ECUs Representative of Each Class (where # designates words that have been tagged with that class)
1 Wages/prices; high farming	2,249	80 (1)	sir, the #large #farmer, with abundant #capital, and acquainted with the best methods of #agriculture, can #produce more #cheaply, can afford to #pay a #higher #rent, and, at the same time, can obtain a #better #profit, than the #small #farmer without #capital. the former can and does undersell the #latter in the market. he can and does outbid him with the #landlord; and he #prospers, whilst, the #condition of the other #daily, #becomes #worse and #worse. in #proportion, therefore, as #agriculture #improves, in #proportion as more #capital arid more #skill are #employed in the #cultivation of the #soil, the doom of the #small #farmers, who have neither #capital nor #skill,
1	2,237	56 (3)	there is, therefore, a #diminution in the #demand for those articles; stores of them accumulate in the #hands of the dealers; trade #becomes stagnant; the manufacturers #employ fewer #workmen; and, as a #necessary #consequence, the #wages of #labour, especially of #manufacturing and #skilled #labour, #tend to #fall. thus reason and experience #show, not only that there is no #connexion between #high prices and #high #wages, and #low prices and #low #wages, but that, generally #speaking, the #wages of #labour are #higher when food is #cheap, than when it is #dear. in #fact, the amount of the #wages of #labour #depends upon the relation which exists between the supply of #labour and the #means of #employing it.
2 MPs as trustees	6,615	81 (1)	and where there was dissatisfaction I see: #contentment, where there was turbulence I see there is #peace; where

Table 7.3
(continued)

Class	Original ECU (traceable to the original text)	Chi Squared Association (rank)	Selection of ECUs Representative of Each Class (where # designates words that have been tagged with that class)
			there was disloyalty I see there is loyalty; I see a disposition to confide in you, and not to agitate questions that are at the #foundations of your #institutions. deprive me of #power tomorrow, you can never deprive me of the consciousness that I have #exercised the #powers committed to me from no corrupt or #interested #motives from no #desire to gratify ambition, or #attain any personal object; that I have laboured to #maintain #peace abroad #consistently with the #national honour, and #defending every #public right to increase the confidence of the great #body of the people in the #justice of your decisions,
2	179	67 (2)	it is no #easy task to ensure the united action of an #ancient monarchy, a proud #aristocracy, and a reformed constituency. I have done everything I could do, and have thought it #consistent with #true conservative #policy, to reconcile these three #branches of the state. I have thought it #consistent with #true conservative #policy to #promote so much of #happiness and #contentment: among the people that the #voice of disaffection should be no #longer heard, and that thoughts of the dissolution of our #institutions should be #forgotten in the midst of physical #enjoyment.
3 Electoral connection	1,513	47 (2)	but had he #yielded to the pressure had he #yielded his #seat then the #cry on the other #side would have been, you are no longer a #representative, but a delegate. he had #seen some strange departures from that house of late and still more strange #fillings #up. in #plain simple #language, he had #seen that #gentlemen had resigned, not, at the command of what was properly #called

Table 7.3 (continued)

Class	Original ECU (traceable to the original text)	Chi Squared Association (rank)	Selection of ECUs Representative of Each Class (where # designates words that have been tagged with that class)
			a #constituency, but in conformity with what used to be the practice under the close #borough system. name! he hoped hon. #gentlemen would not compel him to name names; for it did so #happen, that he could name not only the #constituencies, but the #constituents.
3	3,119	47 (4)	he said the other night that he thought he was #wrong, on the occasion of his violating his #pledges to the university of oxford, in resigning his #seat; but, sir, I will prove to him now, that he is bound to resign his #seat, and #go #down to tamworth, and #place himself in the hands of his #constituents there. after the last #election the right hon. baronet #told them that they had #placed him in the #proud #position of #representing them in #parliament, and they might depend upon it that he would be faithful to the #professions he had made;
4 Agricultural market and Ireland	5,040	69 (1)	A fifth in #january could not have been more than a tenth, #instead of a half, in november; and was he to be blamed for calling that #exaggeration? then, as to the #market #prices, his hon. friend, mr. #miles, had #obtained a #return of the highest #price of #potatoes in the #various #market #towns of #ireland, in the week #ending the 24th #january, for the #last #seven #years. the #previous six #years had been very low ones; but that #document showed that on the 24th of #january #last the #average #price throughout #ireland was about 4d the #stone, or less than 3s the cwt;
4	6,977	62 (4)	it is, I say, her majesty_s ministers, who by concocting a false #alarm who by #exaggerating local #appearances of #scarcity into a #general #famine it is

Table 7.3
(continued)

Class	Original ECU (traceable to the original text)	Chi Squared Association (rank)	Selection of ECUs Representative of Each Class (where # designates words that have been tagged with that class)
			they who have caused an unnatural elevation of the #price of #food, by raising a hope that those who bought it up for gain, would be able to #sell it again at #famine #price. if the #price of #food in #ireland was at one #period unnaturally high, it was in a great measure caused by the #alarm wickedly and unfoundedly raised by the government. the #letter goes onto say but the two #last #market #prices of #potatoes and #meal have #returned to the most #moderate rates, with #supplies, which, both in #quantity and #quality, have never been #exceeded at this #season of the #year indeed,
5 Parliamentary rhetoric and timing	3,713	37 (1)	#baronet, in #preference to the #amendment of the hon. #member for #wolverhampton. if he was to look at the hon. #member_s #proposition as a mere abstract #question, he could undoubtedly #give his #vote in #favour of an #immediate #repeal; but when he had to #take into #consideration what the consequences might be in base of its #adoption by that #house, and its #rejection by the #house of #lords, he #felt himself bound to #agree with the #opinions #expressed by the #noble lord, lord J_ #russell, the #member for the #city of #london, on the previous #night, and #give his #vote in #favour of the #motion of the right hon. #baronet.
5	5,374	36 (3)	of #course the #noble lord was entitled to #ask, what are my prospects, I do not say of #carrying on the #government #permanently, but of #adjusting the corn #law? #nothing could #induce me to #undertake it excepting the prospect of success; what is the #support I may #expect? I #anticipated any such

Table 7.3 (continued)

Class	Original ECU (traceable to the original text)	Chi Squared Association (rank)	Selection of ECUs Representative of Each Class (where # designates words that have been tagged with that class)
			#question, by enabling her #majesty to reform the #noble lord of the #course I had myself #taken; and as #others were not #prepared to #form a #government, I #felt it my duty to #intimate to her #majesty that I would #cordially #support the #measures I had #advised in office.
6 International trade	4,389	58 (1)	as we #decreased the price of the #raw #material in #cotton, so it is with #silk; the declared #value may be less, but there is no less quantity #exported. now, I can readily account for the #increased quantity of the #raw #material #consumed. there is a growing taste for #silk #manufactures: it is a taste which we cannot do better than #encourage. #cotton and #wool have heretofore been formidable #rivals to #silk; and #cotton and woollen #goods have #entered #into general #competition with #silk #goods. but there is a growing desire in this country for #silk;
6	4,352	56 (3)	did hon. gentlemen remember the statements that had been made with #respect to the probable #amount of #injury that would be #inflicted upon the #silk #trade when mr. #huskisson #reduced his #tariff? upon that occasion it was said that everything would be in favour of the #foreigner, and that the #english #manufacturer would have no chance in competing; for the moment that the #relaxed #duties came #into #operation the #french would take #possession of the market, and the #english #manufacturer would be ruined. but what had been the case? the #imports had not #decreased, neither had the #exports #decreased.

on table 7.3, suggest that MPs linked the issue of wages and prices with the cost of farming. As it was anticipated that landowners would suffer an income loss from repeal, the repeal package offered some incentives to agriculturalists—a consolidation of the highways system, relief to rural districts from pauperism, a number of expenses shifted from the counties to the Consolidated Fund, and finally loans for agricultural improvements at moderate interest rates. This last incentive was part of a larger push for "high farming," which encapsulated a set of prescriptions to improve the efficiency of British farms. These prescriptions alarmed and annoyed some less efficient (and often small) farmers who anticipated financial ruin from free trade in agriculture. Hence, in discussing the effect of repeal on prices and wages of laborers, MPs tended to broaden the discussion to include its effect on the income of agriculturalists more generally. This class can thus be titled *Wages and prices; and high farming*.

MPs as Trustees   Class 2, labeled *MPs as trustees*, illustrates MPs' preoccupation with defending the landed basis of Parliament. Words such as *aristocrac+*, *polic+*, *interest+*, *institut+*, *maintain+*, *peace*, *commercial*, *legislat+*, and *territor+* are all characteristic of a concern for a policy (or form of legislation) that would restore peace between the aristocratic and commercial classes and thereby protect the landed aristocracy in Parliament. As anticipated, MPs frequently invoked the term "territorial constitution" to justify a government comprised, and acting at the behest of a landed aristocracy. The two quotes in table 7.3 also make transparent the tension between "an ancient monarchy, a proud aristocracy, and a reformed constituency" and the responsibility of Conservatives to lessen or alleviate this tension.

As I elaborate later, this is the theme that ultimately converted the Peelites to repeal, and so closer scrutiny of it is warranted. An examination of *all* the ECUs classified in this class reveals three important features. First, Peel's references to the territorial constitution were far more striking and elaborate in May than they were in early late January and early February. Table 7.3 provides the clearest statement on this theme by Peel during the first reading debates, as he noted the difficulty in unifying "an ancient monarchy, a proud aristocracy, and a reformed constituency." Yet following months of debate, Peel returned to this theme with greater clarity, as evidenced by the following quotes (chi-squared values are in parentheses):

(50) but what I doubt is, whether it be the real interest of a territorial aristocracy to attempt to maintain its authority by continuing the restriction on corn. There are certain periods in history when this can be done. The question is at present, will the just legitimate influence of the landed aristocracy be better maintained by consenting to forgo this protection, or insisting upon the maintenance of it? My firm belief is that you will more increase the just influence and authority of that body by now forgoing this protection than by continuing it.

(29) I infer, that the privileges of the territorial aristocracy will not be diminished or its influence destroyed by consenting to a free trade in corn, because I firmly believe, speaking generally, that the aristocracy will sustain no injury from it whatever. I do not believe, as I said before, speaking generally, that the value of land, or the privileges of land, or the influence of land, will be diminished. Of this I am sure, that if it will not, you are establishing for the aristocracy a new claim upon the affection and sympathies of the people by making a sacrifice of your prejudices.

Peel then invoked the lessons of 1832 to suggest that timely concessions by the aristocracy were required for democratic reform:

(20) There are many privileges which the aristocracy had possession of, voluntarily abandoned, and with no loss whatever. Formerly it was one of the privileges of the aristocracy that the land alone should constitute a qualification for a seat in this House? That was an ancient privilege of the aristocracy. You might have urged that the abandonment of that was destructive of a territorial aristocracy that the constitution and long prescription required that the sole means of entering this House was by a piece of land. You found your law evaded; you found it inefficient for its purpose, and you willingly relinquished it.

And presaging his remarks in 1848 (cited in chapter 1) are these on the French revolution:

(16) it [this House] has never pertinaciously insisted on the maintenance of a privilege when the time for forgoing that privilege had arrived. He [Peel] draws the contrast between the aristocracy of England, wisely consulting public opinion, relinquishing privilege when the time for the exercise of privilege had gone, and the territorial aristocracy of France, insisting upon the maintenance of privilege long after that period. On a former debate, my Hon. Friend the Member for Dorset compared me and he thought he was passing a severe sarcasm, I though it a compliment he likened me to M. Turgot.[25]

Second, the Peelites appear to have heightened and refined the theme of the territorial constitution *well before* Peel's statements in the third reading debates. For instance, in the first reading debates, Barkly and Clerk (MPs for Leominster and Stamford, respectively) remarked:

The Supply Side

[Barkly:] (16) ...the importance of an ancient territorial aristocracy, as contributing to maintain the balance of power in our mixed constitution, is, I believe, undervalued by political writers, and they are too apt to treat the transfer of property from this class to those beneath as a mere matter of debtor and creditor. I concur in no such view; I entertain no other feelings than those of respect and regard for the landed gentry of this country; and I should look with aversion to the repeal of the Corn Laws, if I thought there were any risk of their ancestral mansions and venerable trees falling a prey to the money lender, or even being transferred by any unnatural revolution....

[Clerk:] (16) ...he [Clerk] was as anxious as any one that the proper influence of the landlords and the landed interest should be upheld; but if the Hon. Member meant by this, that it was to depend on the maintenance and continuance of the present Corn Laws, he would only say, that he could not agree to such a principle; and he did not believe that such an argument was for the advantage of the landed interest. He believed that it would be a most dangerous argument to put forward, that the Corn Laws must be kept up for the purpose of keeping up the influence of the landed interest.

And in the second reading debates, Graham (Home Secretary and MP for Dorchester) remarked:

(56) ...and now, Sir, I come to the consideration which I own operates most powerfully on my judgment. I cannot overlook the fact, that the government of this country is, in practice, vested mainly in the landowners. The other House of Parliament is composed almost exclusively of landowners; and there is in this House a great preponderance of the landed interest. A government so based and so conducted cannot long maintain its influence in opposition to the great body of public opinion; such a government to be safe, must make it evident to all that its rule is impartial legislation....

These and other statements by the Peelites support the claim made earlier that it was not Peel who steered the Peelites to argue for repeal as a means to defend the landed aristocracy, but rather it was the Peelites who spotted the opportunity to link this theme with their Conservative ideology (which Peel then took up in the third reading).

Third, Non-Peelite Conservatives clashed with their colleagues over the interpretation of the territorial constitution, maintaining that repeal would undermine—and even destroy—the landed basis of Parliament. As Tyrrell and Gaskell (MPs for Essex and Much Wenlock, respectively) argued in the first reading debates, and Disraeli (MP for Shrewsbury and Prime Minister in 1868 and again in 1874) in the third reading debates:

[Tyrrell:] (20) ...the ties between the lower, the middle, and the higher classes would be broken, and not that alone, but throughout that great portion of the British community, which had hitherto spread traditional barriers between democratic lawlessness and affectionate loyalty, would spread a fear for coronets; for aristocracies and hierarchies, which the steadiest trade in corn, and the happiest commercial relations between this country and America, would not be able to dispel.

[Gaskell:] (35) ... if they showed a disposition to surrender at the first summons that was made to them a disposition to barter the sound blessings of which they had formerly heard so much, for considerations of political convenience, he, Mr. Gaskell, ventured to predict that the agricultural body would soon be called upon to struggle against other changes—changes more fatal to the constitution, though less injurious to themselves.

[Disraeli:] (35) I have on more than one occasion risen in this House to uphold the cause of what I call our territorial constitution, not imagining by such a word I was maintaining the mere interests of peers and esquires. I certainly should not have risen had I thought I was pleading only their cause. But this territorial constitution which I have defended, has given to this country public liberty and the blessings of local and self government. It appeals to all; it has immense ramifications; it touches every class of the community.

In sum, both Peelites and Non-Peelite Conservatives sought to defend the territorial basis of Parliament, and both sought to portray themselves as trustees of the nation's welfare. Yet for Peelites the means to this common end was repeal, and for NPCs it was protection. Moreover, this heated clash between Peelites and NPCs appears to have sharpened Peel's focus on this theme so that while he initially raised the theme, he does not appear to have appreciated its importance for the conversion of some Conservatives until late in the repeal debates. Once again, in contrast with McLean's portrayal of Peel as cunning and foresighted, the debates suggest that he followed rather than led his Peelite colleagues in articulating a "Conservative-friendly" justification for repeal.

Electoral Connection   Class 3 can be seen as the counterargument to the theme of MPs as trustees. Characteristic words such as *leader+*, *league+*, *anti*, *elect+*, *constituenc+*, *represent+*, and *candid+* allude to the lobbying efforts of the Anti-Corn Law League and its numerous tactics to convert electors and MPs to free trade (McCord 1958; Schonhardt-Bailey 1991a). In this context, Peel is often characterized as caving in to the pressures of the Anti-Corn Law League.

Yet the theme of this class, *Electoral connection*, has a significance wider than that simply of pressure-group politics. As seen in the two ECUs in table 7.3, Conservative MPs struggled to reconcile the protectionist mandate under which they were elected in 1841 with a policy shift that would blatantly violate that mandate. Hence, some MPs resigned their seats so as not to face this conundrum. While most Conservatives prided themselves on adhering to a trustee mode of representation, it did not seem hypocritical to some NPCs to invoke the delegate mode of representation in attacking Peel and the Peelites. Non-Peelite Conservatives challenged them to resign their seats rather than to violate their protectionist pledges to their constituents.[26] Characteristic words such as *betray+*, *honour+*, *confid+*, and *honest* allude to the tension surrounding whose interests MPs should serve and how one could justify reneging on an electoral mandate for protection. Liberal (free-trade-oriented) MPs, however, had no trouble in pointing to the change in public opinion as the rationale for a change in Parliament's position on trade:

[Layard, MP for Carlow:] (32) ... the judicious choice made the other day by the [MP from the] West Riding of Yorkshire; a choice, in his mind, equally honourable to the electors and the elected. What could be a more ample proof of the alteration which had come over the feelings of the people, than that a few years ago the noble lord was beaten because he was not a sufficient protectionist, and now he stood in the proud position of their representative as a free trader; ... He alluded to the Noble Lord, Viscount Sandon, the Member for Liverpool, and the Noble Lord the Member for Newark.

Others defended Peel's decision to resign his position in late 1845 and then resume it with a reformed pro-free-trade Cabinet. This is interpreted as Peel discarding his link to the landowning aristocracy in favor of the British public, as John Bright (MP for Durham and Anti-Corn Law League leader) argued:

(36) The Right Hon. Baronet took the only honourable course. He resigned. He told you by that act, I can't any longer do what you want, I can't defend your cause. The Right Hon. Baronet, no longer your minister, came back the minister of the sovereign and of the people, and not the advocate of a class who placed him at their head for their own special and private objects.

Agricultural Market and Ireland Class 4, *Agricultural market and Ireland*, contains the characteristic words *potatoes*, *wheat+*, *quarter*, *oat+*, *price+*, *crop*, *supply*, and *market+*, thereby suggesting a concern for the home agricultural market. MPs sought to establish whether the world market would provide a sufficient supply of produce for the British market—and at a reasonable price. Hence, many ECUs provide statistics on the prices of grains and the productive capacities of various agricultural exporters (Russia and the United States). Linked to this theme, however, was the issue of Ireland. Very simply, one alternative to full repeal of the Corn Laws was a temporary suspension of protection in grain to alleviate the suffering said to be caused by the potato failure in Ireland. Whether the Irish famine was an actual concern of MPs or a fig leaf for repeal has long interested historians (Kinealy 1998; Gray 1999), but the "well-established consensus" is now "that the famine was no more than an occasion for repeal" (Hilton 1998, 85).

This conclusion is born out by the evidence here. From the second ECU in table 7.3, we can see that MPs did not accept the government's characterization that the famine was severe and, moreover, that repeal would alleviate the problem. About half the top-ranking ECUs allude to Ireland, and virtually all of these express disbelief in the severity of the Irish famine or that repeal would be the appropriate policy tool for addressing the problem:

[Shaw, MP for Dublin University:] (49) ...but that the market price was rather falling than rising. The next document was the Report of the Commissioners of Inquiry, sitting at Dublin Castle, and dated the 20th of January. Did they attempt to say that, even at that period, two months further advanced, half the potato crop was then gone? No such thing. They did not give any estimate of the loss. It was a difficult calculation to make with anything approaching accuracy; but he had reason to know that so far as they had made it, their opinion was that at the end of January there might have been about one fifth deficiency in the stock of potatoes.

[Verner, MP for Armagh Co.:] (49) ...divested of the diseased portion, was still an average crop; and that there was more grain of every description in the country at that season of the year, the month of March, than had been for several years previous. In confirmation of this assertion, he would ask leave of the House to read an extract from a letter he had received from a gentleman in the county of Armagh a few days after he had made his statement to the House. The letter was to this effect: you are perfectly correct in your statement to the House relating to the large stock of provisions in this country at present....

To the extent that Peel or his ministers sought to use the Irish famine as a fig leaf to gain support for repeal, they most definitely failed. MPs were not persuaded by this argument. In sum, this theme reflects the arguments of protectionists who sought to dispute the sufficiency of food imports to satisfy the British home market and to characterize the Irish famine as an opportunistic and erroneous justification for repeal.

Parliamentary Rhetoric and Timing of Repeal The content of class 5 demonstrates a rather odd feature of the importance of institutions—

namely, the amount of time[27] that is given to an adhering to the protocol of an institutional setting. Its characteristic words—*majesty+, question+, noble+, measure+, member+, govern+,* and *debate+*—are illustrative of the language that accompanies parliamentary debates. Both ECUs from table 7.3 are illustrative of the style of discourse that gives rise to this class.

Yet the characteristic words from table 7.2 and the first ECU in table 7.3 suggest that MPs were also discussing the timing and the form of repeal. Charles Villiers (MP for Wolverhampton and leading figure in the Anti-Corn Law League) moved to amend Peel's legislation (which delayed repeal for three years and retained a nominal duty thereafter)[28] to call for total and immediate repeal. As Villiers's motion sought a more radical policy shift to free trade, it served to differentiate the hard-core free traders from the moderates. (Indeed, the failure of this motion (265 to 78 votes) demonstrates the limitations of a demand-side model of repeal. If demand-side pressures alone accounted for repeal, Villiers's motion would have carried.) MPs also considered the possibility of a temporary suspension rather than an outright repeal of the Corn Laws (which, it was argued, would provide temporary relief for Ireland). Hence, characteristic words such as *motion+, wolverhampton+, immediate+, suspension+, Ireland+,* and *adjust+* become meaningful. This class is labeled *Parliamentary rhetoric and timing of repeal.*

International Trade Finally, the five most characteristic words of class 6 are *foreign+, article+, manufacture+, duty,* and *trade+*. A scan further down this word list as well as the representative ECUs from table 7.3 suggests that *International trade* is the theme of this class. Indeed, every word listed in table 7.2 for this class refers to some aspect of international trade. A number of issues are discussed under this general theme. First, as seen from the excerpts in table 7.3, comparisons (virtually all favorable) were made between free trade in grain and previous experiences with liberalization of other commodities. The second excerpt in table 7.3 illustrates the form of argumentation drawn from Huskisson's reforms in the 1820s. Peel himself pointed to his 1842 reforms as reassurance for repeal:

(45) ...not only in the year 1842, but at a subsequent period, the House adopted the principle upon which it acted in that year. Notwithstanding the apprehensions of a failing revenue, we selected some great articles, being raw materials, for the remission of taxation. In 1844, we reduced altogether the duty on wool. In 1845, we reduced altogether the duty on cotton; and there

hardly remains any raw material imported from other countries, on which the duty has not been reduced. The manufacturers of this country have now, therefore, an advantage which they have not hitherto possessed. They have free access to the raw materials which constitute the immediate fabric of their manufactures.

Second, MPs displayed some appreciation of the broader welfare-enhancing effects of free trade (and the effects of reciprocity), perhaps from firsthand exposure to the arguments of the economists and from the nationalizing the interest strategy of the Anti-Corn Law League:

[Lord Palmerston, MP for Tiverton:] (52) ...for what is the effect of mutually hostile tariffs between ourselves and other countries? Take any foreign country—take France, for instance. The high tariffs of France and of England are alike injurious to both countries. Our high tariff against French commodities, is an injury to ourselves as consumers, and to the French as producers; while the high tariff of France against British commodities is an injury to the French consumers as well as to the English producers. Here, then, is an inconvenience on each side of the water. We cannot, however, persuade the French to reduce their tariff, but we have the power of reducing, our own; but we are told that, we ought not to do so unless the French agree to a simultaneous reduction on their side.

[Gregory, MP for Dublin:] (24) ...such a system as this was wrong, and opposed to the first principles of political economy. Let them look at France, and the wine trade of that country, for an example of the injurious effects of such a system of unnaturally diverting capital. Look at the enormous tax that country annually paid for her restrictive duties on hardware, iron, cotton, yarn, etc. Were she disposed to receive these articles from foreign countries, instead of unnaturally, stimulating a dear and inferior home production, what a market would she at once open for her unrivalled wines....

Third, links were made to various aspects of British international trade, including concerns for the timber, hop, coal, and iron industries, for trade with the colonies, and for the continued protection of the British shipping industry.

Overall, the ECUs from this class offer statements in favor of free trade. Protectionist claims are limited to arguments concerning particular industries or disputing the subsequent benefits accruing from past liberalizations.

Linkages between the Themes
Identification of the word classes enables us to describe the *discourse* of the debates as revolving around six distinct themes. Figures 7.1, 7.2, and 7.3 help us to understand the *relationships* between those themes.

The Supply Side   179

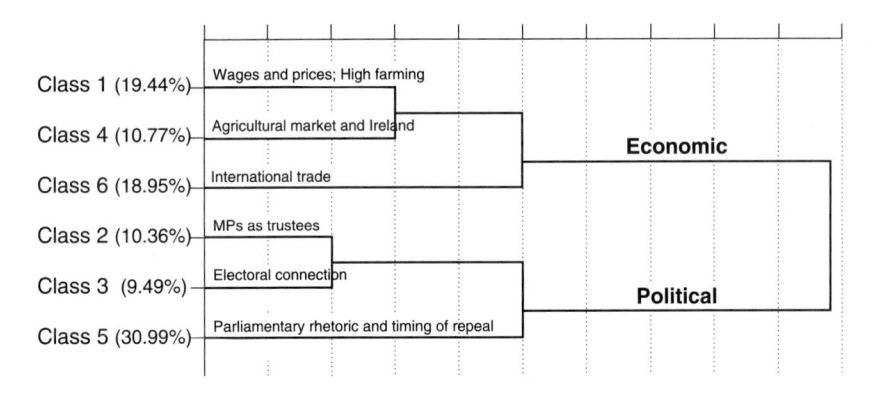

```
Class 1 (19.44%) ─┤ Wages and prices; High farming    │
                                                       ├─────┐
Class 4 (10.77%) ─┤ Agricultural market and Ireland   │     │
                                                             ├── Economic
Class 6 (18.95%) ─┤ International trade                     │         │
                                                                      │
Class 2 (10.36%) ─┤ MPs as trustees    │                              │
                                        ├─────┐                       │
Class 3  (9.49%) ─┤ Electoral connection│     │                       │
                                              ├── Political
Class 5 (30.99%) ─┤ Parliamentary rhetoric and timing of repeal │
```

Figure 7.1
Descending hierarchical classification: Tree graph of the stable classes

Tree Graph Figure 7.1 is a tree graph of the six classes, schematized according to Alcestes's descending hierarchical classification procedure. The tree structure reveals that two sets of classes are most closely linked in terms of word cooccurrences. Class 1 (wages and prices; high farming) is quite closely linked to class 4 (agricultural market and Ireland). As the two themes address the welfare of the agricultural community and, more broadly, the economic relationships between landowners, farmers, workers, and capitalists, their linkage makes sense. Similarly, class 2 (MPs as trustees) and class 3 (electoral connection) are closely linked. These themes both speak to the question: "Whose interests should MPs serve—the nation's or the particular constituency that each MP represents?" Hence, the close proximity of these classes is intuitively appealing.

Perhaps the most interesting feature of figure 7.1 is the primary bifurcation between classes with *economic* themes and classes with *political/democratic process* themes. The first group finds linkages among wages and prices; high farming, agricultural market and Ireland, and international trade, which in turn, illustrates a broader concern for how free trade might affect the British economy and, in particular, the interests of landowners, farmers, laborers, and capitalists. A second group finds linkages among MPs as trustees, electoral connection, and parliamentary rhetoric and timing of repeal. Here the focus is on the mode of representation, the legislative process underpinning the motion, the timing of repeal, and specific policy alternatives to repeal (such as suspension).

Correspondence Analysis The results from Alceste's classification can also be represented graphically in a correspondence space. The program cross-tabulates classes and words in their root form to create a matrix that can then be subjected to factor correspondence analysis (Greenacre 1993).[29] In this way, we obtain a spatial representation of the relations between the classes, where distance reflects the degree of association.[30] Correspondence analysis aims to account for a maximum amount of association[31] along the first (horizontal) axis. The second (vertical) axis seeks to account for a maximum of the remaining association, and so on. Hence, the total association is divided into components along principal axes. The resulting map provides a means for transforming numerical information into pictorial form. It provides a framework for the user to formulate her own interpretations, rather than providing clear-cut conclusions.[32]

Figure 7.2 presents a map of the correspondence analysis of the six classes, along with selected tagged indicators. Below the map, we can see that the first two factors together account for about 61 percent of the total association, with the first factor accounting for about 40 percent. A further three factors are required to account for the total association.[33] (As the number of classes is six, the "dimensionality" of the coordinate system is five, or one less than the number of classes.)[34]

One should, however, be cautious about interpreting the dimensionality of the debates from correspondence analysis. One should be even more cautious about linking the dimensionality of roll-call voting in the 1841 to 1847 Parliament (found in chapter 6 to be largely unidimensional) with the analysis of this chapter. One fundamental problem is that correspondence analysis *may* produce estimates of higher dimensionality than the method used to analyze roll-call votes (NOMINATE) (Brazill and Grofman 2002), and thus differences in dimensionality between roll-call voting and textual analysis of debates may be an artifact of the methodologies. Second, differences may be attributed to the data, with numeric data from roll-call votes producing different results than textual data from debates. Third, dimensionality may differ because voting and speaking are substantively different forms of expression. That is, MPs were concerned with a number of issues surrounding repeal. But in the end, their votes could reflect only a yea or a nay—not the multitude of issues on which they spoke. Consequently, we might expect lower dimensionality in analyses of roll-call votes, as the process of voting itself reduces dimensionality.

Figure 7.2

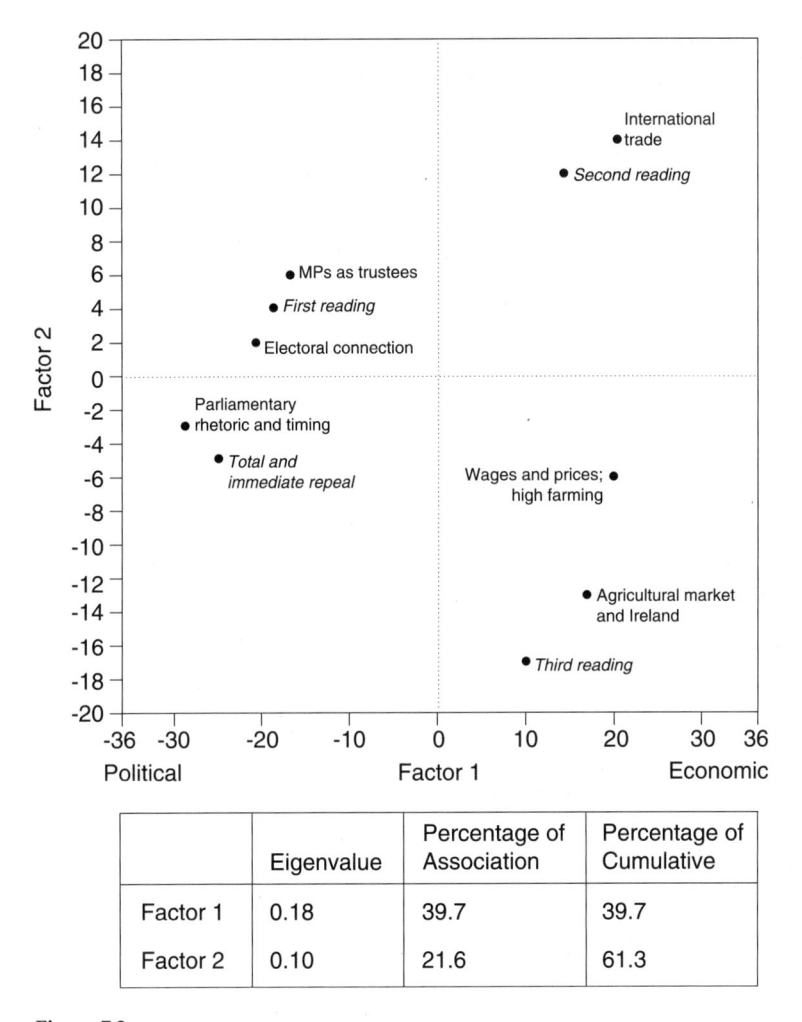

```
Factor 2
 20 |
 18 |
 16 |
 14 |                                           • International trade
 12 |                                           • Second reading
 10 |
  8 |
  6 |            • MPs as trustees
  4 |            • First reading
  2 |           • Electoral connection
  0 |- - - - - - - - - - - - - - - - - - - - - - - - - - - - -
 -2 |     Parliamentary
    |     • rhetoric and timing
 -4 |
 -6 |       • Total and              Wages and prices; •
    |         immediate repeal       high farming
 -8 |
-10 |
-12 |
-14 |                                         • Agricultural market
                                                and Ireland
-16 |
-18 |                                       • Third reading
-20 |
    -36 -30   -20   -10    0    10    20    30  36
    Political           Factor 1              Economic
```

	Eigenvalue	Percentage of Association	Percentage of Cumulative
Factor 1	0.18	39.7	39.7
Factor 2	0.10	21.6	61.3

Figure 7.2
Correspondence analysis of classes and time frame of debates

Given these difficulties, it is prudent to report the "dimensionality" of the correspondence analysis with caution and to bear in mind that speaking is not voting, even though the two are intimately connected. One obvious feature of the first (horizontal) dimension in figure 7.2 is that the variation from left to right separates the political classes from the economic classes, and so we appear to have a spatial representation of the bifurcation between politics and economics identified in the tree diagram (figure 7.1).

A more intriguing result from figure 7.2 is the location of selected tagged indicators—namely, the timing of the repeal debates.[35] The first reading debates and those on total and immediate repeal are both situated in the left-hand quadrants, suggesting that the content of these initial debates was more *political*. In particular, we find that the first reading debates are sandwiched between the two classes that addressed the trustee versus delegate roles of MPs. This suggests that, on hearing Peel's motion for repeal, MPs' first response was to question whose interests they served—that of the nation as a whole or that of their constituents. Then, during the debates on total and immediate repeal, MPs were—almost by definition—concerned with the timing of repeal and various aspects of the legislative process. The second and third reading debates, by contrast, appear to have focused on economic themes. The second reading debates are situated near the international trade theme, while the third reading debates are located near the agricultural market and wages and prices themes. This suggests that the parliamentary debates began with discussions of how a Conservative government could reconcile a reversal of its electoral mandate and how repeal would resonate with constituents. It would appear that as MPs voted on the first reading, foremost in their minds was how they reconciled a free-trade policy with an electoral mandate for protection as well as with significant and mounting pressures from constituents and lobbyists for free trade. It was not until months later that MPs shifted their focus to the *economic* dimensions of repeal. The first phase of this shift entailed discussions of the implications for British international trade. Most MPs who spoke on this theme argued that free trade would yield significant benefits to British industry and the economy more generally (which, not coincidentally, mirrored the arguments of the Anti-Corn Law League, as seen in chapter 4). But a final push by the protectionist camp in the third reading debates demonstrates a last-minute attempt to capture votes against repeal. Protectionists sought to narrow the economic discussion to focusing on the (negative) effect of repeal on Britain's agricultural market (thereby invoking elements of both the wages and prices; high farming theme and the agricultural market and Ireland theme).

Figure 7.3 shows the same correspondence space as figure 7.2, but with tags for party affiliation and measures for the economic composition of MPs' constituencies. "Borough MPs" and "County MPs" provide a rough indication of whether the MP represented an urban or rural constituency.[36] The tags "Most free trade," "Free-trade oriented,"

The Supply Side 183

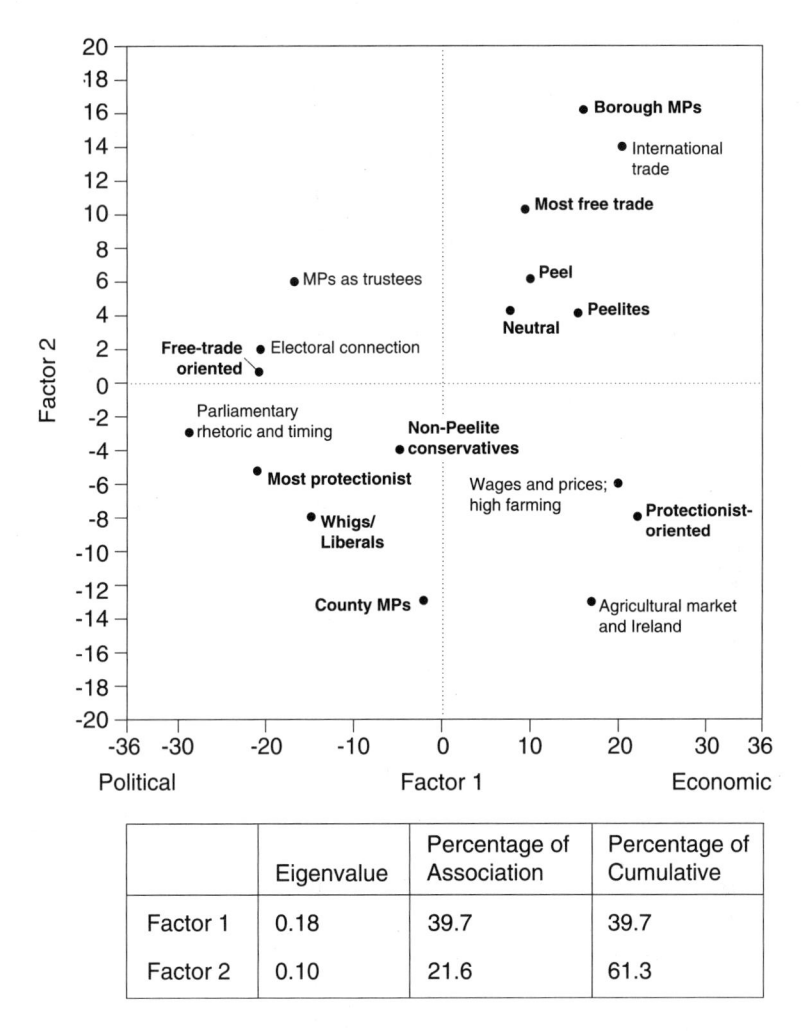

[Scatter plot showing correspondence analysis with Factor 1 (Political to Economic) on x-axis ranging from -36 to 36, and Factor 2 on y-axis ranging from -20 to 20. Points plotted include:
- Borough MPs (~18, 16)
- International trade (~25, 14)
- Most free trade (~13, 10)
- Peel (~13, 6)
- MPs as trustees (~-10, 6)
- Peelites (~20, 4)
- Neutral (~10, 4)
- Free-trade oriented (~-22, 2)
- Electoral connection (~-15, 2)
- Parliamentary rhetoric and timing (~-20, -3)
- Non-Peelite conservatives (~5, -3)
- Most protectionist (~-15, -6)
- Wages and prices; high farming (~15, -7)
- Protectionist-oriented (~27, -8)
- Whigs/Liberals (~-12, -8)
- County MPs (~-5, -13)
- Agricultural market and Ireland (~20, -13)]

	Eigenvalue	Percentage of Association	Percentage of Cumulative
Factor 1	0.18	39.7	39.7
Factor 2	0.10	21.6	61.3

Figure 7.3
Correspondence analysis of classes, MPs' party affiliation, and constituency characteristics

"neutral," "Protectionist oriented," and "Most protectionist" are the same measures for the economic orientation of the district that were used in chapter 6 (Schonhardt-Bailey 1994, 2003).[37] While the picture is not as stark as with the first dimension, a second, vertical dimension appears to capture the supply-side portion of my argument. As the argument from chapter 2 anticipates (and as highlighted earlier in this chapter), Peel and the Peelites (along with MPs from "neutral" districts—that is, leaning toward neither free trade nor protection) are all situated almost on par with the "MPs as trustees" theme. By appealing to the traditional Conservative portrayal of MPs as trustees and arguing that repeal was now the means to preserve the landed basis of Parliament, Peelites reconciled Conservatism with free trade. A second feature anticipated by the argument from chapter 2 is that both the Non-Peelite Conservatives and the Liberals are situated in the lower quadrants, suggesting that they were unaffected by the second dimension. Yet the NPCs are located nearer the quadrant divide than expected. In light of the brief survey of ECUs from this theme, it is understandable that the verbal jousting between Peelites and NPCs on the appropriate means to preserve the territorial constitution would push NPCs toward this theme.

At the extremes of the vertical dimension are the borough (urban) MPs and the county (rural) MPs. It seems apparent that some of the remaining themes—namely, international trade and agricultural market—reflected a free trade/protectionist cleavage between urban and county MPs (for example, the vertical dimension appears to capture the indirect link between constituency interests and the arguments used by their MPs on the subject of repeal and so is suggestive of the way in which constituency interests affected the thinking of MPs). In sum, while this second dimension is more ambiguous than the first, it does appear to capture the supply-side shift of the Peelites, along with the underlying conflicting demand-side pressures faced by MPs from manufacturing and agricultural districts.

Linking Themes to Characteristics of MPs
Beyond the tags indicated in figures 7.2 and 7.3, I tagged the names of each MP who spoke. These tags can be linked to specific classes, thereby giving us a clear indication of the types of themes that MPs from certain types of districts or with particular party affiliations were likely to emphasize. Given the large number of tags and classes, a simple two-dimensional space is not the most appropriate method for describ-

ing these links. Rather, Alceste assigns χ^2 values[38] to tagged indicators that are found to be characteristic of particular classes. These values (which can be interpreted using a standard χ^2 table with one degree of freedom) provide a clearer understanding of the linkages between characteristics of MPs and the themes on which they spoke. From these, five intriguing findings emerge.

First, Peelites and the first reading debates are very closely associated with class 2, MPs as trustees. This provides strong evidence in support of the first two expectations that derive from the spatial model: (1) Peelites did indeed characterize themselves as trustees and, as such, were shifting the stance on which they defended the landed basis of Parliament, and (2) they did so immediately following the introduction of the legislation (that is, before the first vote on repeal).[39]

Second, a number of tags have high chi-squared values for class 3, the Electoral connection: "first reading" ($\chi^2 = 62$), "free-trade oriented" ($\chi^2 = 26$), "most protectionist" ($\chi^2 = 16$), "Non-Peelite Conservatives" ($\chi^2 = 101$), "Cobden" ($\chi^2 = 96$), and "Disraeli" ($\chi^2 = 98$). These tags point to a heated clash between free traders ("free-trade oriented"; "Cobden") and protectionists ("most protectionist"; "Non-Peelite Conservatives"; "Disraeli") during the first reading debates over the mode of representation. Free traders, led by Richard Cobden (MP and leader of the industrialists' lobby, the Anti-Corn Law League) argued vociferously that Parliament must heed the shift in public opinion toward repeal. They maintained that MPs served the constituents that elected them; MPs were delegates and so beholden to vote for a policy that reflected the underlying shift in public sentiment. The shift in public sentiment was very much class-based, with the industrial middle class favoring free trade and most of the landowning aristocracy defending protection.[40] As such, repeal conferred not only an economic advantage to industrialists; it signified political leverage of the middle classes over the aristocracy, as the discussion of the voter-registration campaign in chapter 2 demonstrated. The protectionists were thus defending not only an agricultural monopoly but also a political monopoly of the landowning aristocracy. This camp, led by Benjamin Disraeli, despised Peel's betrayal of his party and criticized Peel's apparent disregard for the protectionist electoral mandate of 1841. Free traders and NPCs engaged in heated battle over the nature of the electoral connection, while Peelites chose to distance themselves from this theme (not wishing to defend what Conservatives disdainfully labeled as the *delegate* mode of representation).

Third, "Bentinck" registers a very high value ($\chi^2 = 198$) for class 4, agricultural market and Ireland. "Third reading" also obtains a high value ($\chi^2 = 77$) for this class. George Bentinck, a leading protectionist, sought to undercut support for repeal by launching a Protectionist party in Parliament. Belatedly (in April), he took up the leadership of this assault on the government. His strategy was to delay repeal as long as possible to prevent it from becoming law before the next general election. As Stewart explains: "The House of Commons was in its fifth year, so that if the bill could be defeated in the Lords, or sent back to the Commons with too many amendments to get through in the remainder of the session, a dissolution would probably take place before the bill could be introduced again. The Protectionists' only hope lay in an election" (Stewart 1971, 65; Disraeli 1905). Part of this strategy entailed decoupling the Irish famine and repeal by arguing that food scarcity was not a problem; that poverty, not famine, was the cause of suffering in Ireland; and that a new poor law, *not* repeal was required (Disraeli 1905, 124–128). The high χ^2 word associations that link "Bentinck" and "Third reading" with agricultural market capture this last-ditch strategy by Bentinck and his Protectionist party remarkably well.

A fourth finding shows that the third reading debates were not entirely dominated by discussions of the home agricultural market. Rather, these discussions were fused with a focus on wages and prices; and high farming. Aside from named MPs, two tags are highly associated with this theme: "Third reading" ($\chi^2 = 69$); and "Whigs/Liberals" ($\chi^2 = 30$). As indicated by the tree graph (figure 7.1) and the correspondence analysis (figure 7.3), the overlap in discourse between the agricultural market theme and that of wages, prices, and high farming is intuitively appealing. From the tags, however, we can see that in this overlapping discussion, hard-core protectionists were more concerned with issues of food self-sufficiency and debunking the link to the Irish famine, while more free-trade-oriented MPs spoke on the effect of free trade on wages and prices and on improving agricultural efficiency.

Finally, the χ^2 values confirm that the second reading debates were indeed dominated by the international-trade theme ("Second reading" χ^2 is 218 for this class). But a number of significant tags pinpoint which MPs emphasized this theme: "Peel" ($\chi^2 = 25$), "Peelites" ($\chi^2 = 39$), "borough" MPs ($\chi^2 = 38$), and MPs with a "neutral" economic orientation ($\chi^2 = 36$). Thus, as discussion moved from the political themes to the economic ones, free-trade-leaning MPs—namely, Peelites and representatives from "neutral" districts—tended to stress the national welfare-enhancing effects of free trade. To the extent that Peelites and wavering MPs employed the international-trade arguments for free trade, then theories of the classical economists and the arguments of the Anti-Corn Law League can be said to have had at least some bearing on the thinking of these pivotal MPs. Yet it would appear that the economic logic of free trade was *secondary* to the politics (namely, the issue of representation) that drove the important first reading votes. Though League pamphlets and speeches may have found inspiration in the liberal theories of the classical economists, the votes of the pivotal MPs of 1846 were not initially moved by these theories to shift their votes.

Conclusion

In part 1 of this book, we saw that in the years preceding 1846, swelling momentum for free trade (which the Anti-Corn Law League assisted but did not create) placed constituency demands on MPs to repeal the Corn Laws. Many Liberal MPs who had not already shifted to free trade by 1841 acceded to these demands in the few years that followed. Peelites (who, on average, represented either neutral or slightly free-trade-leaning districts) were susceptible to these pressures but were not willing to desert their party for free trade. Rather, to push these wavering Conservatives over the brink, a supply-side reinterpretation of repeal itself was required. Peel offered a somewhat vague reinterpretation when he introduced the repeal legislation, characterizing repeal as a means to preserve the landed basis of Parliament. Peelites immediately latched onto this reinterpretation as it offered them a way to represent more faithfully their constituents' interests *and* appear to remain faithful to Conservatism. This reinterpretation of repeal allowed Peelites to vote as delegates (representing the increasing free-trade orientation of their constituencies) but to justify their betrayal of a protectionist Conservative ideology in the language of disinterested and moral trustees whose motive was only to promote the nation's economic and social well-being. In spatial terms, this reinterpretation of repeal constituted a second dimension that split the Conservatives on the question of how best to preserve the landed basis of Parliament.

Part 2 of this book provides evidence to support the supply-side portion of the argument by making extensive use of parliamentary speeches. Three key findings are evident from this chapter. First, Peelites did indeed characterize themselves as trustees seeking to protect the larger societal interest and welfare—and, in particular, the "territorial constitution." Second, Peelites did so as an immediate response to Peel's introduction of repeal. No other justification for repeal appears to have resonated as much with most Peelites as they considered that initial leap over the divide. Third, MPs articulated other demand-side issues surrounding repeal—but they did so only after a majority coalition for repeal was in place (that is, after the first reading division). Issues relating to the effect of free trade on wages and prices, on agricultural efficiency, and on British exports and manufacturing industry more generally arose in the speeches of strong free traders and of new converts to free trade. Hence, once victory seemed probable, it is clear that MPs were keen to go on record advocating free trade for reasons that secured the interests of their constituents. One might even conjecture that once repeal had gained sufficient support in the Commons, free-trading MPs were more at liberty to embellish some of the arguments of the League, possibly in an attempt to share in its perceived popularity.

Appendix

Kronberger and Wagner (2000, 309) provide the following example of a decomposition of the original matrix into two classes:

	Specific Vocabulary of Class 2		Overlapping Vocabulary		Specific Vocabulary of Class 3		
	Food	Fruit	Say	Word j	Cure	Cancer	
Class 2	45	12	20	k_{2j}	0	0	k_2
Class 3	0	0	21	k_{3j}	33	20	k_3
	45	12	41	k_j	33	20	k

Classes 2 and 3 are optimally separate in that they have as little overlap in words as possible: "The numbers in the table (k_{2j}, k_{3j}) indicate the frequency of contextual units for each class containing a specific word j. In our example, class 2 consists of statements containing words like 'food' and 'fruit', while words like 'cancer' and 'cure' are typical for class 3. Of course, it will rarely be possible to separate statements such that words occurring in one class do not appear in the other. There will always be some overlapping vocabulary like the word 'say' in the example" (Kronberger and Wagner 2000, 309).

The Supply Side

The chi-square procedure then establishes "out of all possible procedures" two classes that maximize the following criterion:

$$\chi^2 = k_2 k_3 \sum_{j \in J} \left[\left(\frac{k_{2j}}{k_2} - \frac{k_{3j}}{k_3} \right)^2 \div k_j \right],$$

where

$$k_{2j} = \sum_{i \in I_2} k_{ij}; \quad k_2 = \sum_{i \in I_1} k_{2j}; \quad k_j = k_{2j} + k_{3j}.$$

8 Repeal in Historical Context: Key Parliamentary Debates on the Corn Laws before 1846

Introduction

In the years before 1846, the Anti-Corn Law League generated considerable pressure on MPs to embrace free trade as evidenced by its registration campaign, widespread propaganda, and speaking tours (chapters 1, 2, and 4). The League helped to create a momentum for free trade, which achieved some success in converting more Liberals and in moving Peelites nearer to the brink of free trade. The 1846 debates (analyzed in chapter 7) illustrate that MPs were highly conscious of League pressure, but these debates do not trace the demand-side momentum for repeal—that is, they do not capture how MPs perceived the League's campaign prior to the government's introduction of the repeal legislation. Hence, to gauge better the effect of demand-side pressures for repeal independent of the supply-side shift,[1] we must examine MPs' speeches on repeal before 1846.

Recall, moreover, that in chapter 7, we saw that a supply-side shift (the reinterpretation of repeal) explains why the Peelites converted to repeal. This reinterpretation of repeal is argued to have been unique to 1846, but to gauge its novelty, we must examine the statements of MPs earlier in the 1841 to 1847 Parliament. If the reinterpretation of repeal is indeed unique to 1846, we should not find MPs discussing free trade in terms of the "territorial constitution" or related concepts in the years preceding 1846.

Two further considerations also arise on the broader demand-side/supply-side interpretation of repeal. First, how did the delegate and trustee theme evolve in the thinking of early nineteenth-century MPs as they considered trade policy? The clash between Liberal delegates and Conservative trustees shaped how Peelites came to redefine repeal, and so it is worth questioning how this theme developed over time in the context of British trade policy.

Second, through textual analysis of parliamentary debates, we can gauge the influences of institutions, interests, and ideas on the thinking of MPs, and so it is worth questioning the extent to which key changes in these factors influenced MPs. In particular, (1) did the 1832 Reform Act shape how MPs viewed constituency interests on the topics of trade and agriculture, (2) did the lobbying of the Anti-Corn Law League affect how MPs viewed their roles as representatives, and (3) to what extent did MPs absorb the ideas of the political economists as they considered British trade policy in the decades preceding repeal?

Given these motivations, I apply the same Alceste textual analysis to parliamentary debates on trade policy during three key junctures prior to 1846: 1814 to 1815, leading to the passage of the 1815 Corn Law; 1826 to 1828, leading to the 1828 Sliding Scale; and 1842 to 1844, leading to Peel's new sliding scale and the defeat of League-sponsored motions for repeal. After presenting the results of the Alceste analysis in the next section, I examine the extent to which lobbying by the Anti-Corn Law League created increased pressure on MPs to support repeal. A focus on the 1842 to 1844 debates allows us to gauge the role of the League independent of (before) the supply-side shift in early 1846. At issue is whether there is sufficient evidence to suggest that the League did indeed gather political momentum for free trade early in the 1841 to 1847 Parliament.

The 1842 to 1844 debates also allow us to evaluate the second theme of this chapter—the *novelty* of the territorial constitution argument. If a shift did occur on the supply-side, this theme should *not* feature prominently (if at all) in debates on trade policy in the early years of this Parliament. Rather, it should arise as a new theme in 1846.

Third, this chapter examines how MPs viewed their roles as representatives and in particular whether the conflict between delegates and trustees featured in the prerepeal debates. Finally, it explores how changes in institutions, interests, and ideas affected MPs' thinking on trade policy. The fundamental *institutional* change was the 1832 Reform Act, which enfranchised the middle class and improved the representation of industrial areas. The Anti-Corn Law League provided the critical shift in *interests* as it mobilized a multifaceted lobbying campaign against the Corn Laws. Over a longer period, political economists like Ricardo, Torrens, and McCulloch were creating a *liberal ideology* that embraced free trade (in various forms). Though the League popularized and propagated many of the ideas of the political economists (hence, effectively fusing interests and ideas, or "nationalizing the interest"), it is likely that (some) MPs were receptive to these ideas before the League organized in 1838.

Content Analysis of the 1814 to 1815, 1826 to 1828, and 1842 to 1844 Debates

Basic Statistics

Tables 8.1, 8.2, and 8.3 provide the basic statistics for the 1814 to 1815, 1826 to 1828, and 1842 to 1844 debates. The total word count for each period was, respectively, 184,660, 135,597, and 571,775. It should be noted that in the earlier periods, debates were often not reported verbatim but rather were written more in summary (Aspinall 1956;

Table 8.1
Alceste analysis: Basic statistics for 1814 to 1815

Total word count	184,660
Unique words analyzed	69,576
Passive variables (tagged indicators)	150
ICUs (= number of speeches)	595
Classified ECUs	3,905 (= 85% of the retained ECU)
Lexical classes	5
Distribution of classes (%)	1: 20.26
	2: 18.87
	3: 28.66
	4: 6.20
	5: 26.02

Table 8.2
Alceste analysis: Basic statistics for 1826 to 1828

Total word count	135,597
Unique words analyzed	50,967
Passive variables (tagged indicators)	116
ICUs (= number of speeches)	363
Classified ECUs	2,716 (= 82% of the retained ECU)
Lexical classes	4
Distribution of classes (%)	1: 25.85
	2: 22.50
	3: 27.03
	4: 24.63

Table 8.3
Alceste analysis: Basic statistics for 1842 to 1844

Total word count	571,775
Unique words analyzed	216,692
Passive variables (tagged indicators)	174
ICUs (= number of speeches)	408
Classified ECUs	6,057 (= 75% of the retained ECU)
Lexical classes	7
Distribution of classes (%)	7: 15.59
	8: 9.94
	9: 11.69
	10: 11.31
	11: 9.23
	12: 25.59
	13: 16.66

Gordon 1983, 232–233), and so the word count is lower on average. Nonetheless, for both the 1815 and 1828 periods, the 10,000 word minimum for successful Alceste results is well exceeded. Moreover, 595 speeches and interjections were analyzed for 1814 to 1815, 363 for 1826 to 1828, and 408 for 1842 to 1844. Between 75 to 85 percent of the retained elementary context units (ECUs) were classified. Finally, the tables report a total of five classes for 1814 to 1815, four for 1826 to 1828, and seven for 1842 to 1844. (Book appendix 3 lists all the speakers for the first two sets of debates,[2] while book appendix 4 details the parliamentary activity on the Corn Laws during these time periods. Book appendix 2 lists all the MPs who spoke during the critical repeal debates in 1846.)

Identifying the Themes in the Debates

For each set of debates, tables 8.4, 8.5, and 8.6 list the most characteristic words associated with each class. Similar to the results for 1846, the most characteristic words are those with high chi-squared and values. Words ending with "+" indicate that these are reduced forms (for example, *cultiv+* may refer to *cultivate, cultivators, cultivated*, and so on).

1814 to 1815 Debates For 1814 to 1815, an examination of the word lists and the representative ECUs for each class reveals the following themes: class 1, *Prices and rents*; class 2, *Parliamentary rhetoric*; class 3, *Food self-sufficiency*; class 4, *Grain trade*; and class 5, *Petitions and civil unrest* (table 8.4).

Prices and Rents For class 1, prices and rents, words such as *poor+*, *cultiv+*, *labour+*, *wages*, *bread*, *landlord+*, *rate+*, *tenant+*, and *price+*, suggest that MPs were concerned with the effect of falling grain prices on the farmers and landowners ("cultivators"). But at the core of this discussion was the question of how falling prices—and inflated land rents—were affecting laborers, tenants, and landlords. The logic behind this theme is that the government sought not only to protect but also to extend capital investment in agriculture, particularly by protecting marginal lands (which reinforces the interest-based explanation for the 1815 Corn Law). If falling prices forced agriculturalists to abandon inferior land (which required intensive cultivation), employment would fall, and poor rates would rise. Protection provided a means to promote investment in "high farming"—that is, advanced farming methods that would lead to higher yields. Higher yields would, in turn, allow farmers to pay landlords higher rents, thereby resolving the conflict between landlords and tenants over high rents (Hilton 1977). These sentiments are seen in the top twenty ECUs from this theme (chi-squared values are in brackets):[3]

(47) he agreed that rents must and ought to fall. Rents were the effect and not the cause of prices. The landlords had properly taken advantage of the high prices to raise their rents, and they should, now the prices were low, reduce them, and would not be worse off with the lower than they had been with the higher rents.

(33) He considered rent as one of the charges which the farmer incurred in the cultivation of his land, and he knew that rents had been raised in some instances exorbitantly high.

(28) Let me next ask if the landed gentlemen will have all the advantages from the high price of corn that are held out to them? I have already noticed the effect that would inevitably be produced on the poor rates, and the price of labour, by dearness of grain and that in many instances the increased price of bread directly raises the price of labour.

(25) The cultivator of the land at home had a very heavy tax to pay before he could bring his corn to market. It was the land that paid the poor rates, that paid the functionaries of religion; it was from the rents of the land that churches were built and roads made.

Parliamentary Rhetoric Every set of debates (including 1846) includes one class whose content is best described as *parliamentary rhetoric*. This is the case for class 2 in the 1814 to 1815 debates. Words such as *propose+*, *intention+*, *move+*, *report+*, and so on illustrate that the

Table 8.4
Characteristic words of each class by strength of association, 1814 to 1815

Class 1		Class 2		Class 3		Class 4		Class 5	
χ^2	Word	χ^2	Word	χ^2	Word	χ^2	Word	χ^2	Word
94	poor+	95	exchequer	95	france	98	ch	94	sign+
86	cultiv+	94	propose+	95	countr+	97	british	92	public+
78	labour+	93	intention+	91	great+	96	duty	90	opinion+
73	sum+	92	move+	90	industry	91	licence	87	express+
71	tax	88	day+	84	supplie+	90	export+	77	people+
69	land+	84	word+	81	wealth+	86	preced+	73	represent+
67	remuner+	79	discuss+	77	market+	83	king+	69	motive+
65	wages	75	baring	75	supply+	82	ed	68	house+
64	acre+	72	wednesday	75	britain	76	ibid	66	constitut+
57	bread	69	report+	73	foreign+	75	flour	64	parliament+
56	landlord+	66	debate+	73	depend+	71	exceed+	59	popular+
51	amount+	66	robinson+	65	commerce	70	warehouse+	59	member+
49	cent+	65	friday	64	manufacturer+	67	parl	59	clamour+
47	increase+	61	speaker+	64	produce+	67	rot	56	deliber+
45	english	58	second+	62	encourage+	65	american+	56	mind+
45	witnesses	56	proposition+	62	demand+	60	repeal+	54	pray+
44	rate+	55	huskisson+	59	independent+	59	bount+	54	present+
43	holder+	55	chair	58	food	59	scotland	51	precipit+
42	reduce+	54	intend+	52	home+	57	sect	48	door+
41	tenant+	54	division+	52	dependent	56	north	48	baronet+
40	price+	54	propriety	52	derive+	55	corn+	47	hurry+

The Supply Side

40	cheap+	53	observ+	46	agriculture	54	consumption	46	person+
39	evidence	53	bill+	45	commercial	52	rye	46	improper+
38	surveyor+	52	committee+	41	manufacture+	51	gallon+	44	bill+
38	asked	51	stage+	41	resource+	51	colon+	41	opportunit+
37	fixe+	50	postpone+	38	article+	50	restrain+	40	city
35	grower+	50	adjourn+	38	applic+	50	meal+	40	police
34	consumer+	50	alderm+	37	power+	46	regul+	38	decided+
34	double+	49	pamphlet+	36	subsist+	46	continue+	38	minister+
30	comfort+	48	order+	36	policy	46	quartern	36	conduct+
29	rent+	47	chairman	36	empire	46	stop	36	common+
28	corn+	47	print+	36	advantage+	44	prohibit+	36	judgment+
28	webb	46	agree+	34	europe	44	ships	34	mob

197

substance of this class concerns the *process* of legislation and so is not of particular relevance to our discussion here.

Food Self-Sufficiency A concern for maintaining Britain's food self-sufficiency is the theme for class 3, with characteristic words including, *countr+, supplie+, foreign+, depend+, independent+,* and *food*. This theme provides empirical grounding for the self-sufficiency explanation for the 1815 law, as noted in chapter 1. As Boyd Hilton (1977, 22) explains: "It was precisely because Europe could *not* feed England that English cultivation had to be protected and expanded. Such surplus as there was abroad would rarely suffice to fill a deficiency, but would be quite enough to drive down prices, especially since the home grower, never sure how large a foreign surplus would prove to be, was liable to rush his own corn on to losing markets in panic." It was not until later in the century, when Britain relied more on foodstuffs from regions with different climatic conditions, that autarchy lost it appeal as an argument for protection (Hilton 1977, 22). Top representative ECUs illustrate this theme:

(32) If any one branch of the wealth of nations ought to be encouraged more than another, it was agriculture. It was that on which all depended. It differed from every other source of prosperity, as it was the first necessary. Even were foreign countries able to supply us, we ought not to depend on them.

(29) Situated as this country was, equally the admiration and the envy of every other, it became their duty to watch carefully over its interests, to guard against it being dependent on any country, and least of all dependent on France.

(28) He therefore told his constituents; that it was their interest; that it was the universal interest of the nation to encourage the industry of our own countrymen, by preferring the produce of our own agriculture to that of foreigners, and thus to render ourselves independent of foreign supply.

Grain Trade Class 4, *Grain trade*, refers to a long history of previous legislation on the grain trade (Fay 1932). This class reflects less a discussion and more a report of previous restrictions on foreign trade (which had bearing on the bill currently under discussion). Words such as *British, duty, licence,* and *preced+* characterize this theme. (Legislation refers to specific chapters [c12, c4] in acts of parliament under King George III [G 3].) One ECU (which is representative of the rest) illustrates that the content is more a report than a discussion:

(114) 1802. 43 G 3, c12. Further to continue the preceding act, authorizing the King to permit importation and to stop exportation. 1803. 44 G 3, c.4 ditto.

1804. 44 G 3 c.109. Repeals the prices at which corn might be exported and imported under the 31 G 3 c30 except the warehousing duties.

Petitions and Civil Unrest Class 5, petitions and civil unrest, reflects MPs' responses to the many petitions against the 1815 Corn Bill that were submitted to Parliament. Characteristic words such as *sign+*, *public+*, *opinion+*, *express+*, *people+*, *represent+*, and *clamour*, suggest that MPs were concerned about the numerous protests (both in the form of petitions and demonstrations) against the Corn Bill. The representative ECUs reveal a disdain, bordering on contempt, for these petitions. While this theme is an early precursor to the 1846 themes of *Electoral connection* and *MPs as trustees*, it demonstrates that the concept of MPs as delegates had not yet formed in the minds of MPs. Rather, most MPs saw themselves entirely as trustees, willing to act *against* the wishes of their constituents as they saw fit:

(35) ...and if the persons concerned in the tumults out of doors thought their representatives in Parliament so lost to themselves, and so forgetful of their duty to the community, as to suffer these disgraceful riots to have any influence on their conduct...

(28) Sir John Newport opposed the Committee. It would only occasion useless delay, and give opportunity for raising a clamour against the measure. The House should never suffer clamour of this kind to have the least influence upon their decisions.

(25) He gave due weight to the petitions; but when he had once made up his mind, no quantity of petitions heaped on the table, or of clamour out of doors, should induce him to give his vote against his judgment.

These sentiments fit well with Hobsbawm's assessment of the establishment of parliamentary democracy in early nineteenth-century Britain as "unthinkable." Hobsbawm noted that in 1817, George Canning "thanked God 'that the House of Commons is not sufficiently identified with the people to catch their every nascent wish.... According to no principle of our Constitution was it ever meant to be so... it never pretended to be so, nor can ever pretend to be so without bringing ruin and misery upon the kingdom'" (Hobsbawm 1968, 125).

In spite of this overall assessment, some MPs were more wary about blatant and swift disregard for public opinion (even if they remained willing to support the highly unpopular 1815 Corn Bill):

(26) Mr Alderman C. Smith said, the amendment should have his cordial support. He expressed his concern to observe, that the Hon. Gentlemen who

were in favour of the bill seemed so very anxious to hurry it through the House, in the teeth of so many numerously signed petitions, which were pouring in every day, almost unanimously and decidedly against the measure.

In sum, the evidence supports two of the three commonly cited explanations for the 1815 law—namely, propping up the economic interests of agriculturalists and ensuring food self-sufficiency for Britain. No evidence is found, however, that MPs linked the 1815 law with the budgetary aim of repaying the wartime debt. What is evident is that both contemporary and secondary interpretations of the initial shift to protection have discounted the importance of petitions and civil unrest as MPs considered the legislation. Even though MPs expressed contempt for constituency demands (thereby defending their roles as trustees), constituents (including the unenfranchised) (Taylor 1995) nonetheless sought to exert influence on MPs and MPs, in turn, felt compelled to acknowledge this pressure by defending their independence from it. Hence, we see an early tension emerging between the delegate and trustee modes of representation, with constituents pressuring MPs to behave as delegates and MPs resisting this initial pressure.

1826 to 1828 Debates For 1826 to 1828, an examination of the word lists and the representative ECUs for each class reveal the following themes: class 1, grain trade; class 2, political economy: capital, labor, land; class 3, electoral connection and public opinion; and class 4, parliamentary rhetoric (table 8.5).

Grain Trade Similar to the 1814 to 1815 debates on the grain trade, the first theme examines the history of British trade in grain, but now the focus is more on the recent history of the 1815 Corn Bill. Characteristic words such as *import+*, *year+*, *grain+*, *corn*, *freight+*, and *duty* make evident the focus on grain imports and exports. The representative ECUs, however, are more revealing in that they depict the general dissatisfaction with the rigidity of the 1815 Corn Law and a discussion of the various permutations of a sliding scale:

(36) ...the effect of which was, that the law of 1815, sanctioning the admission of foreign corn at 80s, came into operation. The next year, however, the summer having proved exceedingly fine and favourable to the harvest, the price of corn fell as rapidly as it had before risen, the consequence was, that the farmers were frightened out of their wits, and predicted,...

Table 8.5
Characteristic words of each class by strength of association, 1826 to 1828

Class 1		Class 2		Class 3		Class 4	
χ^2	Word	χ^2	Word	χ^2	Word	χ^2	Word
93	import+	98	wages	93	interest+	82	canning+
88	home	96	manufactur+	87	parliament+	81	bill+
83	year+	86	countries	79	discuss+	77	friend+
74	harvest+	85	capital+	79	house+	76	proposition+
67	scale+	79	rate+	63	question+	75	object+
64	average+	76	product+	60	minister+	72	secret+
60	grain+	75	cultiv+	50	hope+	70	propose+
58	quantit+	74	country+	49	law+	69	motion
58	corn	68	labour+	47	connect+	64	vote+
57	thousand+	66	land+	44	feelings	61	imperial
54	open+	64	increase+	44	consider+	59	resolution+
52	freight+	64	soil+	34	currency	59	original+
52	hundred+	64	wealth+	33	occasion+	55	clause
46	scarcit+	54	classes	28	class	55	huskisson+
46	specul+	51	produce+	28	particular+	55	measure+
44	last+	51	rent+	27	body	53	night+
44	british	51	taxation	25	noble	47	duke+
43	crop+	51	manufacture+	25	attention	47	support+
41	quarter+	49	money	25	proceed+	46	president
39	duty	45	cheap+	24	conduct+	41	letter+
39	growth	44	high+	23	different+	37	board
37	exceed+	42	goods	23	delay+	37	baronet+
37	grower+	41	industry	23	enter+	36	move+
36	bond+	40	proportion+	22	majesty+	34	propos+
35	barley	40	cent	22	policy	34	chair
34	price+	40	commerce	22	gentlemen	34	grant+
33	flour	39	popul+	22	manner	33	observ+
32	fixed	39	consume+	21	liberal+	32	alter+
31	duties	39	war+	21	political+	29	divide+
31	month+	39	mill+	21	sentiment+	29	essex
31	prohibit+	37	burthen+	20	assembl+	29	amendment+
30	sufficient+	36	remuner+	20	subject+	29	carri+
30	dantzic	35	prosper+	19	pursue+	28	peel

(31) ... the result was, therefore, that the ports remained closed during three starving months from August to November 1816; and did not open until the 15th November of that year, after the price had been for about fifteen weeks, above the importing price, and when all the northern ports of Europe were shut against supply.

(28) He did not think that evils to be apprehended from fluctuation of price would be corrected by commencing the duty at 20s when the price [was] at 60s. If there was a deficiency in the supply, the price would easily rise to 65s; and if by the fall in the stock of grain here the price would rise to 70s, the foreign grower would pour a great quantity into this country at a great advantage;...

(25) Let the price of corn in England be 55s per quarter, the duty on corn imported would then be 30s; so that the price of corn bought in the Baltic for 25s per quarter, and subsequently brought to England, would be 55s, independent of the cost of freight, insurance, etc., which would be a dead loss to the importer.

Political Economy Class 2, political economy: capital, labor, land, raises more general issues of the political economy of the factors of production. Characteristic words include *wages, manufactur+, capital+, cultiv+, labour+, land+,* and *classes*. The ECUs illustrate two core issues of particular concern to MPs. First, the inflationary effects of the 1815 Corn Law suffered criticism. Some MPs focused simply on the rising food prices:

(34) ... and in proportion as the price of food rose, the greater would be the necessity of having recourse to sterile soils for the production of corn; and consequently the greater would be the expense of feeding the population. If that population was industrious and by industry was adding to the general wealth of the country, it was most desirous that they should be fed at the cheapest rate.

Others argued that protection raised labor costs in agriculture, and this fed through to labor costs in manufacturing; and, moreover, protection halted other economic benefits from industrial expansion:

(28) ... capital was the life and active principle of that commerce, and on the profits of that capital the subsistence of so many depended. In raising the price of corn here by prohibition, or by high duties equivalent to prohibition, you increase the price of labour;

(32) ... but if the trade in corn were thrown open, it would afford a vent for those manufactures; and every knife or stocking sent abroad would produce a profit, that would enable the manufacturer to pay his portion of the interest of the national debt.

Huskisson's fear that an inflationary price spiral would undermine the fixed money settlement of 1819 and thereby threaten the stability of the currency forms the backdrop to this discussion. As Huskisson noted in earlier debates: "In the present value of money a monopoly of the corn market, up to the price of 80s a quarter, and the continuance of a great paper circulation, constantly convertible into coin at a *fixed* standard, are, I will venture to say, for any considerable number of years, incompatible" (quoted in Hilton 1977, 280).

A second political economy theme transcended domestic interests by arguing that freer trade in agriculture would induce other countries to specialize in agriculture and thereby leave Britain to dominate world trade in manufactures:

(30) ...and induce them to return to the natural labour of an agricultural country the production of grain. By these means this country, possessing more capital than all others, would be able to extend her commerce to an indefinite extent, by exchanging her manufactures for the corn of America and the other nations of the world;

From their parliamentary speeches, it may be seen that MPs were increasingly aware of the practical relevance of the theories of the economists for British trade policy, particularly links between trade policy and issues of inflation, labor costs, currency stability, and British economic hegemony.

Electoral Connection and Public Opinion Class 3, electoral connection and public opinion, exhibits characteristic words such as *interest+*, *parliament+*, *discuss+*, *connect+*, *feelings*, and *consider* (table 8.5). Yet it is the ECUs that illustrate the content of this class most clearly:

(36) ...gentlemen who had already addressed the House. He saw how hopeless any effort on his part must be in the present temper of the House; but he should, nevertheless, endeavour to discharge with fidelity the duty he owed to his constituents.

(29) ...but he hoped it would not be considered too much if he said, that when any question was propounded in which the people expressed a decided voice, the House was doing itself harm, by not listening to what their representatives had to say.

(22) ...springing from the people, he was of the people, and was proud of being their champion, either in or out of that House. At the present moment this petition was of peculiar interest, as it was intimately in alliance with a subject which absorbed, more than any other, the attention of Parliament—the Corn Laws.

(21) …some prayed for a total abolition of the Corn laws; other petitioners prayed that the House would not interfere in the subject at all; while a third class of petitioners, and by far the most reasonable of the three, prayed that Parliament; in legislating on the subject, would consider the interests of all classes of the people, without reference to any particular body.

As MPs assessed the many hundreds of petitions for and against change in the Corn Law, their sentiments demonstrate a marked shift from the debates of 1814 and 1815. In the space of about a dozen years, the idea of MPs as delegates of their constituents had taken hold and gained some acceptance. While the notion of MPs serving as trustees remained strong, it was no longer the unchallenged interpretation given to their role. Increasingly, MPs espoused the importance of listening to and acting on the "feelings" of their constituents.

Parliamentary Rhetoric Finally, class 4, parliamentary rhetoric, concerns the *process* of legislation, with characteristic words as *bill+*, *proposition+*, *propose+*, *motion*, and *vote+*, and so is not of relevance to the discussion here.

In sum, the analysis of the 1826 to 1828 debates reveals some expected findings (namely, that the practical implications and difficulties of the 1815 law were central to the discussion for reform) and some unexpected findings (that MPs had begun to digest the arguments of the economists more thoroughly than perhaps has been appreciated[4] and that MPs were increasingly sensitive to the preferences of their constituents).

1842 to 1844 Debates For 1842 to 1844, the word lists and the representative ECUs reveal seven classes: class 1, parliamentary rhetoric; class 2, international grain supply; class 3, class conflict; class 4, international grain trade; class 5, anti-ACLL (opposition to the Anti-Corn Law League); class 6, wages of labor; and class 7, Peel's sliding scale. As with the previous years, class 1 (parliamentary rhetoric) will be noted but not discussed (table 8.6). For the sake of coherence, I first explore the classes with economic themes (2, 4, and 6) and then turn to those with political themes (3, 5, and 7). It is important to note that the time frame of these debates includes both Peel's revision to the sliding scale in 1842 and motions to repeal the Corn Laws in 1844 (see book appendix 4). Hence, some of the themes relate only to the sliding-scale debates, some only to the proposed repeal in 1844, and some to both the sliding scale and repeal.

The Supply Side

International Grain Supply and International Grain Trade   Classes 2 and 4—international grain supply and international grain trade—are closely related but nonetheless remain distinct. *Supply* refers to just that—the supply of grain to Britain from international grain markets and particularly the method for regulating this supply. Characteristic words are *flour, foreign+, import+, duty, season+, price+, America*, and *supply+*. Central to this theme is the continuing debate over the merits of a sliding scale versus a fixed duty. Just as Ricardo had proposed the fixed duty in the 1822 (Schonhardt-Bailey 1997, vol. 1) and thereby launched the debate, J. R. McCulloch reignited it in 1841 when he argued for a fixed duty over a sliding scale (Schonhardt-Bailey 1997, vol. 2). Representative ECUs show how MPs grappled with the operational effect of the two different schemes, as they considered Peel's revision to the sliding scale:

(39) ...the question was, not whether this country should be independent, but in what way, by what terms, and by what regulation could the foreign supply which must be brought into this country be rendered most advantageous to all classes. The question that debate was to bring to an issue was, whether that object could be best effected by a sliding scale or by a fixed duty.

(34) ...as long as the sliding scale existed, so long would exaggerations of its effects be put forth. It was argued, you have upon your scale a duty of 20s, and that duty prevents a regular trade, and a constant supply being raised in foreign countries. The great advantage of a fixed duty was, that after it had been once settled, and the price of corn should become high, there could be no exaggeration.

(32) ...the consequence was the necessity of purchasing at a disadvantage, and there was a great rise of prices in the ports on the continent, and if you pay the foreigner much more for his corn than you would do, if the trade was at all regular, a great deal of money was necessarily thrown away. If then, there was a fixed duty, it would be the means of producing a revenue to the country, instead of our being exposed to constant loss, as at present.

While some argued in favor of the sliding scale, others continued to criticize the problems with speculation:

(34) ...he said there were some advantages in this scale, and among others it would yield a larger revenue to the state. If it yielded a larger revenue to the state it necessarily must bring a larger amount of foreign corn into the market, and at a time when it was most wanted. The natural effect also of the present law was to hold out expectations to the holders of corn, that by continuing to hold it they would get it admitted at a low duty.

Table 8.6
Characteristic words of each class by strength of association, 1842 to 1844

Class 1		Class 2		Class 3		Class 4		Class 5		Class 6		Class 7	
χ^2	Word	χ^2	Word	χ^2	Word	χ^2	Word	χ^2	Word	χ^2	Word	χ^2	Word
564	motion+	416	flour	204	aristocracy	1291	quarter+	927	league+	498	labour+	614	measure+
528	member+	313	foreign+	191	class+	1090	average+	731	anti	492	wage+	341	principle+
404	house+	312	import+	189	classes	841	wheat+	291	member+	438	employ+	258	govern+
261	vote+	278	duty	170	interest+	803	price+	229	stockport	366	food	171	adopt+
209	peel+	248	season+	140	people+	435	oat+	176	sign+	272	increase+	163	fixe+
195	proposition+	219	price+	126	communit+	358	dantzic	154	meetings	252	capital+	141	settle+
193	wolverhampton+	210	america	120	suffer+	358	freight+	142	assert+	241	land+	132	propose+
179	speech	208	merchant+	85	feeling+	287	return+	136	commission+	225	manufacture+	128	opinion+
179	noble+	205	american+	82	spirit+	252	barley	134	ferrand	184	rent+	123	right+
161	friend+	202	supply+	81	law+	243	meek+	127	electors	164	product+	120	noble+
160	debate+	197	market+	70	poor+	202	quantit+	126	letter+	162	rate+	118	plan+
158	right+	179	harvest+	68	sympath+	197	year+	126	count+	157	manufacturer+	103	baronet+
154	side+	168	scale+	66	abuse+	173	consul+	116	cobden+	156	population+	99	scale+
151	baronet+	138	canada+	64	institut+	164	september	111	associat+	149	machinery	98	proposal+
143	discuss+	134	trade+	62	middle	159	add+	109	petition+	138	goods	97	concili+
141	gentleman+	124	fixe+	59	political+	132	elsinore	109	mr	126	cotton+	97	change+
137	speeches	122	grain+	58	distress+	130	august+	95	manchester	125	proportion+	96	protect+
129	russell	122	canadian+	58	countrymen	127	odessa	92	dare+	122	famil+	95	final+
125	support+	118	grower+	56	provid+	123	grain+	83	borough+	106	produce+	90	majesty+

The Supply Side

125	mr	116	consum+	54	injustice	121	rye	82	knaresborough+	106	cultiv+	83	alter+
121	committee+	111	disadvantage+	52	legislat+	118	estimate+	82	bolton	105	comfort+	80	modification+
113	amend+	110	scarc+	48	motive+	117	duty	78	honour+	105	mill+	77	present+
103	lincolnshire	108	specul+	48	destruct+	112	town+	77	visit+	101	number+	76	support+
102	voting	101	regul+	46	effort+	111	london	77	report+	101	amount+	74	interest+
102	bill+	100	cargo	46	deep+	110	market+	74	language	99	industr+	74	scheme+
96	question+	95	stead+	45	enem+	103	amount+	70	district+	98	reduce+	70	satisfactory
93	intention+	94	advantage+	45	manufacturing	91	sale+	69	publish+	95	soil+	68	law+
93	govern+	93	countries	41	self+	85	lowest	69	house+	93	work+	68	mitigat+
93	viscount+	88	holder+	40	patience	84	week+	66	chairman	90	cheap+	65	oppose+
92	opposition	87	deficienc+	38	share+	82	charge+	60	election+	89	poor+	61	ought
87	evening+	86	colon+	38	removal+	79	import+	53	work+	88	want+	60	reason+
86	night+	82	unite+	37	promote+	77	calculat+	50	appoint+	87	money	60	found+
83	move+	79	abundant+	37	repeal+	75	inform+	49	heart+	82	value	56	reject+

(34) ...it is also said to be injurious to commerce, because where the corn is grown at a distance, in America for instance, the grower is subject to this disadvantage, that before his cargo arrives in this country, the sudden pouring in of wheat at 1s duty from the countries nearer England, may have so diminished the price, and increased the duty, that this speculation may have turned out, not only a failure, but ruinous.

Class 4, international grain trade, addresses more the detailed mechanics of the grain trade rather than the regulatory process. Characteristic words such as *quarter+*, *average+*, *wheat+*, *price+*, *oat+*, and *freight* suggest that MPs who spoke on this theme were comparing average prices of grain over the previous several years, so as to evaluate the merits of the 1828 sliding scale, and Peel's revision. Just two of the ECUs serve to illustrate that this class consisted more of a catalogue than a substantive discussion of policy:

(93) ...for rye 17s to 20s per quarter; for barley 10s 9d to 15s 6d per quarter; for oats 8s 6d to 10s 6d. And in 1841 for wheat 35s; rye 23s; barley 16s. 6d; oats 11s. and he adds that the freight of grain by water from the provincial ports to Copenhagen, Kiel, or Elsinore, may be computed at from 1s 4d to 1s 8d per quarter, adding to the cost of conveyance the expense of removing, warehousing, and turning the grain,...

(78) ...gentleman then read the following table, showing the percentage amount of difference between the highest and lowest annual prices: wheat in England between 1821 and 1828: highest 66s 6d; lowest 43s 3d; percentage difference 53. Between 1829 and 1837: highest 66s 4d; lowest 39s 4d; percentage difference 68. Rye in Prussia between 1821 and 1828: highest 22s 7d; lowest 10s 9d; percentage difference 102.

Wages of Labor Class 6, wages of labor, embodies some of the concerns of earlier debates (for 1814 and 1815 in prices and rents and for 1826 to 1828 in the political-economy theme). The three most characteristic words (*labour+*, *wage+*, and *employ+*) leave little question as to the substance of this theme, but further words (such as *capital+*, *land+*, *manufacture+*, and *rent+*) illustrate that MPs continued to grapple with the political economy of the factors of production and that manufactures had acquired greater prominence in this consideration. Three issues in particular concerned MPs: high food prices, unemployment, and wage rates compared with profit levels.

First, MPs noted that land scarcity would continue to force up the price of food while wages would remain static, thereby further impoverishing workers:

(54) ...before it is divided between those by whose labour and capital it is drawn from the soil. Thus wages and profits in agriculture are kept down, while rents are raised by the limited extent of land in proportion to the numbers of the people; but as those engaged in other branches of the industry must exchange directly or indirectly a large part of the produce of their labour for food,...

(48) ...a payment in the shape of rent which has to be deducted from the gross produce of the soil before it is divided between the labourer, and the farmer or capitalist who employs him. The increasing population and consequently increasing demand for the total produce of the soil, creating a greater and greater competition for land, more and more, in proportion to the amount produced, is thus subtracted from the produce,...

This poverty was made worse by the fact that food consumed well over 50 percent of workers' wages:

(35) ...an investigation had been made in several large manufacturing establishments with a view of ascertaining what proportion of the earnings of the operatives was spent in agricultural produce. In one establishment the amount of wages paid in 1836, was £33,000, the amount expended in food was £22,000, leaving £11,000 for rent, clothing, and other necessaries of life.

Beyond high food prices, agricultural protection lowered the income of foreign producers (relative to the counterfactual where they could export to Britain at any prevailing market price) and consequently lowered their demand for manufactured exports from Britain. In the eyes of British industrialists, this reduced foreign demand for their exports (from the counterfactual) and kept the level of employment in manufactures below what it would otherwise have been. The following quote touches on this theme:

(46) ...was not compensated by a general increase of the demand for labour: and that the fact was, that the number of persons out of employment was fearfully large. The account of the effect upon wages of those still employed was not quite so unsatisfactory. In the case of some classes of workmen wages had increased; but as a counter balance, one out of every two workmen in those classes had been thrown out of employment.

While protection raised the income of the agricultural sector, industrialists argued that the demand, and hence employment, effects of this were more limited because of the impact of higher land rental charges.[5] More precisely, higher land rents would raise the income of landlords who were among the more wealthy and thus would likely have a lower marginal propensity to consume manufactured goods out of additional income from higher rents.

Third, free-trade-leaning MPs endorsed the view that the economic gains from protection were absorbed by high rental charges:

(38) ...now, he should like to know in what proportion rents of land, taken in connection with the wages of labourers employed on land, stood in comparison with the profits of manufactures taken in connection with the wages paid to artisans. Rents were the same now as in 1815 [that is, they were high]; the produce of the land was two fold, and wages remained where they were....

But protectionist MPs hotly denied the existence of exorbitant rents and instead accused manufactures of profiteering:[6]

(40) ...on the other hand, the produce of manufactures had increased beyond all imagination; the profits of manufacturers had increased in a similar proportion; but he wished to know whether wages were the same now as formerly, especially those of the handloom weavers and the framework knitters and others. There was no body of men who derived so small a profit on so large an amount of capital as the landlords, and, vice versa, there was no body of men who derived so great profits on so small capital as the manufacturers.

This class demonstrates a shift in MPs' discourse on the political economy of trade—namely, the prominence of the manufacturing interest compared with that of farmers and landowners. No doubt this heightened influence was the product of the economic influence of manufactures, but very probably the Anti-Corn Law League helped to focus and harness the manufacturing interest into a more articulate and forceful voice.

Class Conflict Turning now to the political themes—classes 3, 5, and 7—we observe a distinct heating up of the discourse. For class conflict (class 3), the most characteristic word is *aristocracy*, followed by *class+*, *interest+*, *communit+*, and *suffer+*. The evidence from outside Parliament is clear that class conflict between the industrialists and the aristocracy figured prominently in the agitation leading up to repeal. This is particularly evident in the "nationalizing the interest" strategy of the Anti-Corn Law League (chapter 4). Chartism also featured prominently in this conflict but as a broader, more sweeping threat to the power and privileges of the landed aristocracy than that of repeal. With their focus on repeal, Anti-Corn Law Leaguers viewed Chartist reforms as a harmful diversion from the primary struggle for free trade but nonetheless sought to portray the League and repeal as fundamental to the interests of the workers, the industrialists, and even the farmers *against* those of the landed aristocracy. Within Parliament, MPs were alarmed by the democratizing reforms demanded by the Chartists, but most important, they feared a working-class and middle-class alliance[7] in pursuit of such reforms. Thus, the seeds of what in 1846 became the "territorial constitution" linchpin of repeal began to take hold in the minds of MPs—that is, they recognized that repeal may be a necessary concession to avoid a working-class and middle-class alliance in favor of constitutional reform:

(36) ...until they [the Chartists] shall have first obtained the political changes for which they seek; because they believe that, if the Corn Law were first repealed, they could no longer hope for any support for their designs from the middle classes, but that, if the Corn Law cannot be otherwise got rid of, the middle classes will ultimately join them in their assaults on the present constitution of the country.

(31) ...it is a feeling of hostility to our institutions which is the true key to their [the Chartists'] conduct; but this feeling never would have become so general, or so strong, had it grown up merely from a persuasion of the theoretical injustice of their own exclusion as a class from political power. It is a sense of suffering and distress, it is what the Chartists themselves have called, a knife and fork question which is at the bottom of their desire for a change in our political institutions;

MPs are also seen to have treaded carefully on the topic of the landowners' economic (and political) monopoly (as noted earlier, 80 percent of MPs in the 1841 to 1847 Parliament were also landowners). Not wishing to appear too defensive, MPs attempted to deflect criticism of a legislative body in which the vast majority of members were direct beneficiaries of the policy of agricultural protection:

(29) ...gentleman is that the agriculturalists as a class are not entitled to any legislative protection whatever. That is a doctrine broadly and unequivocally laid down, and cannot be departed from in future. The whole defence of the Corn Law, then, is narrowed to that miserable, and shallow, and untenable doctrine of non-dependence on other countries, a doctrine so narrow and so ignorant, so replete with misery, and starvation, and self-destruction....

(28) ...he did not accuse them of wilfully or corruptly perverting their legislative powers for their own purposes—they only acted in accordance with the dictates of human nature but he did complain that they had, and that in pursuance of those dictates they exercised those powers to injure and oppress the poor for their own exclusive benefit.

(26) ...I do not wish this law to be repealed in times of excitement, nor do I wish its destruction to be achieved as a great party victory; I would rather it were for ever abolished by the unanimous verdict of the honest and intelligent

classes of the country. We should regard it as a question of great national interest, not as one affecting our own profits or property;...

Anti-*Anti-Corn Law League* Class 5, *anti*-Anti-Corn Law League, illustrates the contempt in which many MPs held the Anti-Corn Law League and its pressure tactics. By far, the two leading characteristic words are *league+* and *anti*. Further words target the leader of the League, Richard Cobden, MP for Stockport (*stockport, cobden*), as allegations of Cobden subjecting his factory workers to unreasonably long hours were debated. Other words make evident that MPs sought to discredit the core activities of the League—holding meetings where Leaguers gave free-trade speeches (*meetings*) and obtaining signatures for free-trade petitions (*sign+, count+, petition+*). Several ECUs illustrate the attack on the League and its activities:

(73) ...Dr. Bowring was only desirous of uttering a sentence or two. The Hon. Gentleman who had just sat down had brought forward a very grave charge against the Anti-Corn Law League. He had stated that they had sent forth incendiaries amongst the people to whom might be attributed the attacks upon property. In his place in the House he had requested the Hon. Member to name the parties to whom he attributed these gross misdemeanours, but the Hon....

(48) ...nobody has ventured here to deny your assertions. The Leaguers are raging at their exposure. But I should not have troubled you had not Mr. Bernal doubted your statements respecting the anti-Corn Law petitions. Why, in Leeds, on several occasions, the Leaguers have been defeated by the Chartists at public meetings. The very number of signatures of the petitions prove them to be forgeries.

(42) I will read a few passages which I have extracted from some of the speeches of the Anti-Corn Law League orators, and then leave the House to judge which has been most violent, they or I—the Right Hon. Member will perhaps permit me to call his attention to the language uttered by an individual at a meeting of the Anti-Corn Law delegates, in allusion to the Right Hon....

League leaders in Parliament (including Cobden, Bright, and Villiers) not only defended the League and the legality of its activities but also used the legislative limelight to exert further pressure on their colleagues:

(36) It gives us satisfaction now to be able to state that the result has been triumphantly successful. Thus encouraged, the [Anti-Corn Law League] Council have taken steps for immediately paying visits to Warrington, Stockport, and Macclesfield; and without relaxing any of their other modes of agitation, they

will make it their first duty to visit, in a similar manner, the electors of every borough in the manufacturing districts represented by bread taxes.

Peel's Sliding Scale Class 7, Peel's sliding scale, overlaps somewhat with the international-grain-supply theme, but whereas the latter focuses on the economic implications of Peel's revision in 1842, class 7 expounds on its political implications. In particular, MPs considered how their electors would respond to the new measure, and more generally, they evaluated the principle of protection in its various forms (sliding scale, gradual sliding scale, and fixed duty), as reflected in the characteristic words: *measure+*, *principle+*, *adopt+*, and *fixe+*. As such, this theme is less about the sliding scale per se and more about its political ramifications. The ECUs illustrate both the electoral connection dimension to Peel's revised scale *and* MPs' reconsideration of the concept of protection and thus demonstrate the *political* (as opposed to economic) content to this theme:

(36) I have no doubt that they do so: I have no doubt they feel that their long cherished Corn Law can no longer be maintained in its present shape. But will the change now proposed be satisfactory either to the agriculturalists themselves, or to any one class of the community? If it is not calculated to give immediate satisfaction, is it founded upon principles so just in themselves, so consistent with truth and sound reason, that the practical working of the measure is likely to reconcile the country to it?

(34) Did the Government, then, obtain the concurrence of the agriculturalists by arguments based on the principles which Adam Smith and Mr Huskisson had compounded? On the contrary, although those principles had been long established and relied on among commercial men, they had not yet [received], he believed the concurrence of the agriculturalists. The real argument used was, that if the farmers did not consent to this alteration, they would have a change in the administration, and a party would come into office who would treat them still worse then they were treated now.

(27) If you can make the system general, then general protection cannot be special protection, and you can do no good to anybody by its adoption. Abandon this system—it is unsound; it cannot be defended upon any principle of justice or sound policy; and therefore I ask you now to give your decision against the principle. You may say, we are strong in power, we have the constituencies with us. Yes, you have the constituencies.

(26) The more discussion I hear, the more convinced I am that if protection is to be given to agriculture, it is infinitely better to maintain the present law than to attempt to conciliate any support or favour by any slight modification whatever. I think with the Hon. Gentleman, that is, the real practical question

```
Class 1 (20.26%) — Prices and rents       ┐
Class 3 (28.66%) — Food self-sufficiency  ┤── Economic
Class 4 ( 6.20%) — Grain trade            ┘
Class 2 (18.87%) — Parliamentary rhetoric ┐── Political
Class 5 (26.02%) — Petitions and civil unrest ┘
```

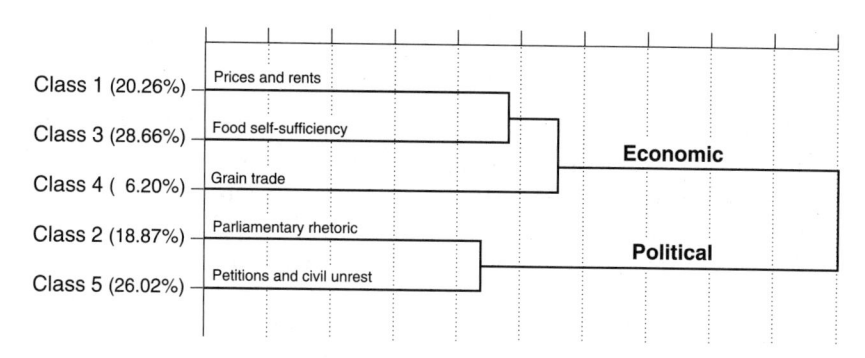

Figure 8.1
Descending hierarchical classification: Tree graph of the stable classes, 1814 to 1815

is the present law to be maintained totally and entirely without any qualification or modification of it?

Classes 3 and 5 demonstrate that two demand-side pressures weighed heavily on the minds of MPs: (1) that continued protection would facilitate an alliance of the middle and working classes in favor of sweeping parliamentary reform and (2) that the activities of the League (especially its voter registration campaign) were alarmingly effective and were forcing protectionist MPs into a defensive position. Hence, MPs were undoubtedly responsive (orally, at least) to the pressure of the League.

Linkages between the Themes

Having identified the word classes, or themes, for each set of parliamentary debates, we may now consider the relationships between those themes.

Tree Graphs Figures 8.1, 8.2, and 8.3 are tree graphs of the classes for each time period and are schematized according to Alceste's descending hierarchical classification procedure. For all three time periods (and indeed, as we also saw for the 1846 debates), there exists a primary bifurcation between classes with economic themes and classes with political themes. In figure 8.1 (1814 to 1815), prices and rents, food self-sufficiency, and grain trade are the economic themes, while parliamentary rhetoric and petitions and civil unrest comprise the political themes. Prices and rents and food self-sufficiency are closely linked, as these themes address substantive issues of political econ-

The Supply Side 215

Class 1 (25.85%)	Grain trade
Class 2 (22.50%)	Political economy: Capital, labor, land
Class 3 (27.03%)	Electoral connection and public opinion
Class 4 (24.63%)	Parliamentary rhetoric

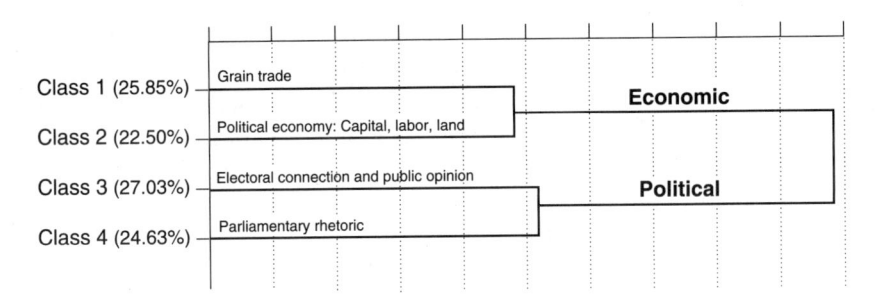

Classes 1 and 2 group as **Economic**; Classes 3 and 4 group as **Political**.

Figure 8.2
Descending hierarchical classification: Tree graph of the stable classes, 1826 to 1828

Class 1 (15.59%)	Parliamentary rhetoric
Class 7 (16.66%)	Peel's sliding scale
Class 3 (11.69%)	Class conflict
Class 5 (9.23%)	Anti-Anti-Corn Law League
Class 2 (9.94%)	International grain supply
Class 4 (11.31%)	International grain trade
Class 6 (25.59%)	Wages of labor

Classes 1 and 7 form the **Legislative** branch; Classes 3 and 5 form the **Social** branch; both group as **Political**. Classes 2, 4, and 6 group as **Economic**.

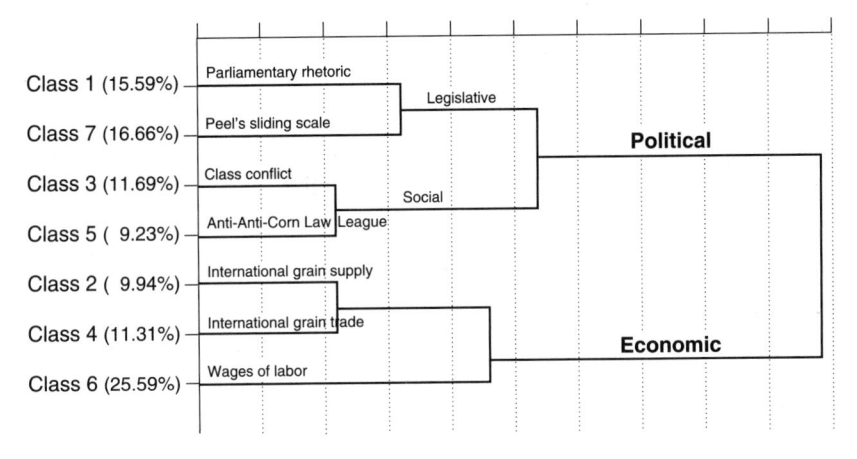

Figure 8.3
Descending hierarchical classification: Tree graph of the stable classes, 1842 to 1844

omy, while grain trade merely reports previous legislative acts. In figure 8.2 (1826 to 1828), grain trade and political economy are the economic themes, while electoral connection and parliamentary rhetoric are the political themes. Finally, in figure 8.3 (1842 to 1844), parliamentary rhetoric, Peel's sliding scale, class conflict and *anti*-Anti-Corn Law League comprise the political themes, while international grain supply, international grain trade, and wages of labor form the economic themes. The distinctive feature of the 1842 to 1844 debates is their increased complexity compared with debates of the previous years. The tree graph helps to organize this complexity by showing classes that are most closely linked in terms of word cooccurrences. Parliamentary rhetoric and Peel's sliding scale form a legislative branch of discourse within the main political group, while class conflict and *anti-Anti-Corn Law League* form a social branch within the same political group. Simply put, the legislative branch reflects discourse relating to the legislative procedure, while the social branch captures more of the sociopolitical dynamics outside Parliament. Not surprisingly, the two international grain classes are closely linked and are distinct in their use of economic discourse from the wages-of-labor class.

Correspondence Analysis Similar to 1846 (chapter 7), the results from Alceste's classification are represented graphically in a correspondence space, thus providing a spatial representation of the relations between the classes, where distance reflects the degree of association. As noted in the presentation of the 1846 results, correspondence analysis aims to account for a maximum amount of association along the first (horizontal) axis. The second (vertical) axis seeks to account for a maximum of the remaining association, and so on. The map thereby provides a way to transform numerical information into pictorial form, though interpretation remains subjective.

Figures 8.4, 8.5, and 8.6 present maps of the correspondence analysis for each set of debates, along with selected tagged indicators. (See book appendix 3 for the tagged indicators for 1814 to 1815 and 1826 to 1828. Data for the 1842 to 1844 MPs, also used in chapter 6, may be obtained from ⟨http://personal.lse.ac.uk/SCHONHAR⟩).[8] Below each map, we can see that the first two factors together account for about 65 percent of the total association for 1814 to 1815, 78 percent for 1826 to 1828, and 58 percent for 1842 to 1844.[9] Recalling that two factors accounted for 61 percent of the total association in 1846 debates, the 1826 to 1828 debates are somewhat anomalous in the large value of association explained and thus the relatively good quality of this map in representing the multidimensional space on a simple plane. Generally speaking, we can see that the first two periods (1814 to 1815 and 1826 to 1828) can be classified more simply than can the later debates (1842 to 1844 and 1846). This may suggest that over time, the discourse on trade policy became more complex as new issues (such as the activities of the Anti-Corn Law League and, in 1846, the export trade) became more salient.

Bearing in mind from the previous chapter the methodological difficulties in interpreting the dimensionality of the debates from correspondence analysis, it remains prudent to report the "dimensionality" of the correspondence analysis with caution and to note (once again)

The Supply Side 217

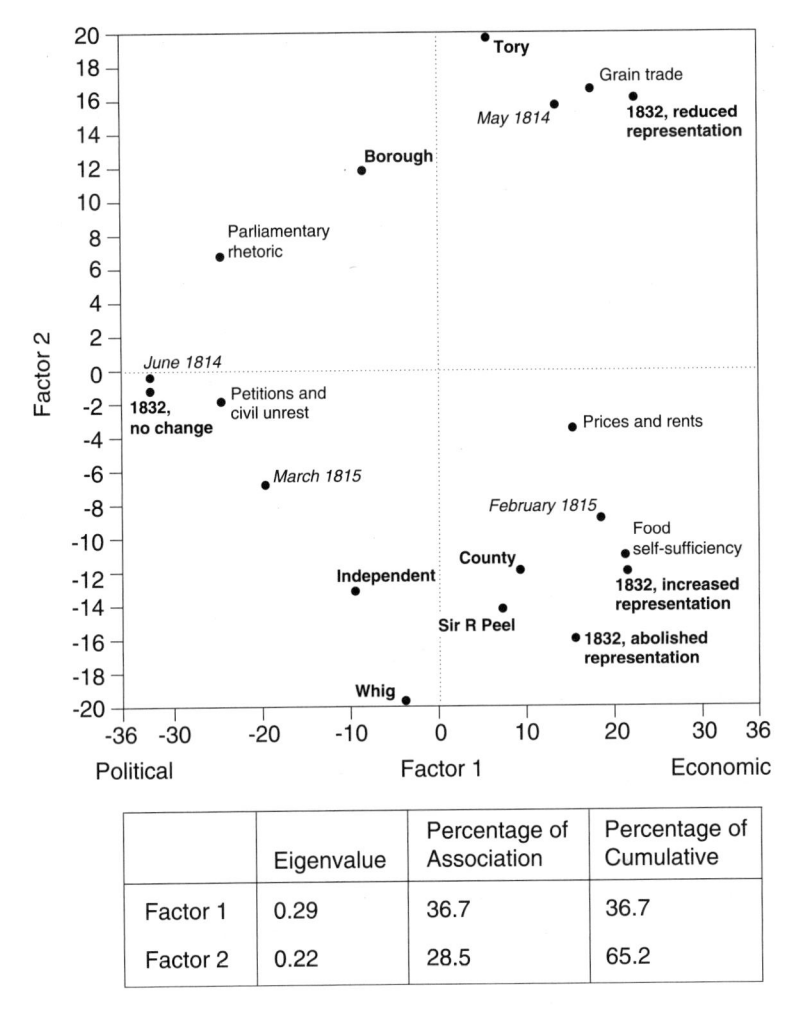

[Scatter plot showing Factor 1 (Political to Economic, x-axis from -36 to 36) vs Factor 2 (y-axis from -20 to 20) with the following labeled points: Tory, Grain trade, May 1814, 1832 reduced representation, Borough, Parliamentary rhetoric, June 1814, 1832 no change, Petitions and civil unrest, Prices and rents, March 1815, February 1815, Food self-sufficiency, County, Independent, 1832 increased representation, Sir R Peel, 1832 abolished representation, Whig]

	Eigenvalue	Percentage of Association	Percentage of Cumulative
Factor 1	0.29	36.7	36.7
Factor 2	0.22	28.5	65.2

Figure 8.4
Correspondence analysis of classes, parties, and time frame of 1814 to 1815 debates

that speaking is not voting, even though the two are intimately connected. Even so, it is remarkable that just as we saw in 1846, the first (horizontal) dimension in all three figures appears to reflect a spatial representation of the bifurcation between politics and economics, as identified in all three tree diagrams (figures 8.1, 8.2, and 8.3).

The locations of the tagged indicators tell more interesting stories. Taking each figure in turn, the tagged indicators reported in figure 8.4 are the MP's party affiliation (Tory, Whig, or Independent), the month of the speech,[10] and some MPs by name (such as Sir Robert Peel, father to the same who led repeal in 1846). Two further indicators are proxy measures for constituency economic make-up. First, county or borough is a rough measure for the rural and urban divide (which in 1815 was less prominent than in subsequent decades as most areas were still largely rural at this time). Second, the effect of the 1832 Reform Act on the MP's constituency differentiates industrial areas (which enjoyed increased representation) from rural areas (which generally experienced reductions in representation). The categories for this measure are (1) abolished representation from the constituency, (2) reduced its representation, (3) increased its representation, or (4) kept representation fixed.[11] From chapter 6 and earlier work (Schonhardt-Bailey 1994), we know that the effect of the 1832 Reform Act on MPs' votes for repeal in 1846 was both substantively and statistically significant. (While it might seem odd to apply a measure from the 1830s, this simple classification of districts might possibly be backdated to 1815, as many districts were starting to distinguish themselves as areas of industry or agriculture by this time.)

The tagged indicators reveal two features of the 1814 to 1815 debates. First, they show that during both an early month in the debates (June 1814) and the final month (March 1815), the political theme of petitions and civil unrest most closely characterized the discourse. In between these debates, the economic themes of food self-sufficiency and prices and rents were more prominent in MPs' speeches. Hence, debates on the 1815 Corn Law began and ended with MPs recognizing (but intentionally ignoring) the interests of their constituents. Very tentatively, one might conclude that while many MPs expressed disdain for representing the interests of their constituents, petitions to Parliament (which provided the unenfranchised with a means of representation, coined "virtual representation") (Taylor 1995) did indeed appear to have a bearing on the thinking of MPs because at the least they were compelled to discuss interests while denying their legitimacy. Thus, figure 8.4 provides evidence of a nascent form of electoral connection that appears to have affected MPs' speeches, if not their votes. MPs thus found themselves juggling the economics of the relationships among falling grain prices, land rents, and food self-sufficiency, with the real political pressures of constituency demands.

Second, the effects of constituency economic make-up and party affiliation are mixed. The locations of the borough and county tags suggest that the y-axis may represent an urban and rural divide, overlapping with party affiliation (Tory, Independent, and Whig). However, the locations of the 1832 Reform proxies appear more random, though it may be that 1815 was too early for these measures of industrialization to be relevant. Moreover, to the extent that the second dimension reflects early partisan sentiments and urban and rural differences, the content of the grain trade and parliamentary rhetoric classes in the upper quadrants is so weak as to blur these cleavages. One might sensibly conclude that any cleavages based on constituency economic makeup and party affiliation were only weakly evident at this time. (While this conclusion will come as no surprise to historians, it is useful to establish evidence within the parliamentary debates to substantiate this assessment.)

Turning to figure 8.5, the reported tagged indicators are party affiliation, the two proxies for constituency economic makeup, the month of the speech, and key MPs—Peel (who was the Prime Minister in 1846), Huskisson, and Torrens. Five features are evident from this figure. First, politics (namely, the electoral connection and public opinion) figure more prominently in the early months of debates on the sliding scale (November and December 1826 and March 1827), but as the legislation takes form (April 1828, first reading; May 1828, third reading), economic themes (political economy and the grain trade) prevail. A possible interpretation might be that while electoral politics sparked the momentum for reform of the 1815 Corn Law, economics ultimately determined its shape. Second, a clear divide appears between borough MPs, who tended to focus on politics, and county MPs, who were more concerned with economic themes. It may be that county MPs, with larger and more mixed constituencies, perceived a greater distance from their constituents that afforded them the luxury of more theoretical concerns. Third, as we saw in the 1815 debates, a partisan second dimension emerges between Whig and Tory MPs, with Tory MPs situated in the lower quadrant along with grain trade, and Whig MPs in the upper quadrant near the political-economy theme. Tentatively, one might infer that both in 1814 to 1815 and 1826 to 1828, Whig MPs tended to drive the discussions of economic and political economic themes, while Tory MPs focused more on the more practical and legislative implications of the grain trade. Moreover, in both sets of debates, Whigs were more closely aligned with the political themes of petitions in 1814 to 1815 and the electoral connection in 1826 to 1828, which seems to provide empirical evidence for their later advocacy of a delegate mode of representation (Hill 1929, 83–85). Fourth, and

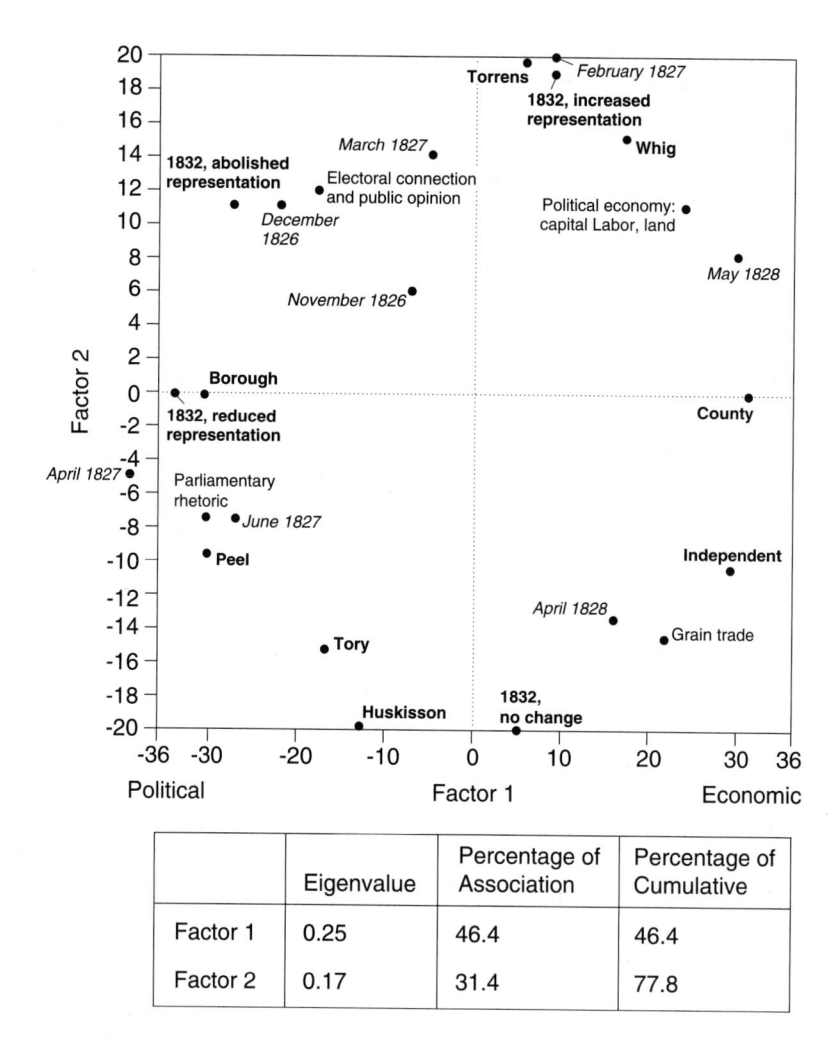

Figure 8.5
Correspondence analysis of classes, parties, and time frame of 1826 to 1828 debates

	Eigenvalue	Percentage of Association	Percentage of Cumulative
Factor 1	0.25	46.4	46.4
Factor 2	0.17	31.4	77.8

reassuringly, key party leaders such as Peel, Huskisson, and Torrens are located near their party tags. Finally, electoral connection and public opinion is located near MPs whose districts were abolished by the 1832 Reform Act and only a short distance from MPs whose districts received increased representation (with the former pulled toward the political end of the first dimension and the latter toward the economic end). It is tempting to conclude that MPs from both more rural and more industrialized areas recognized the importance of constituents'

The Supply Side   221

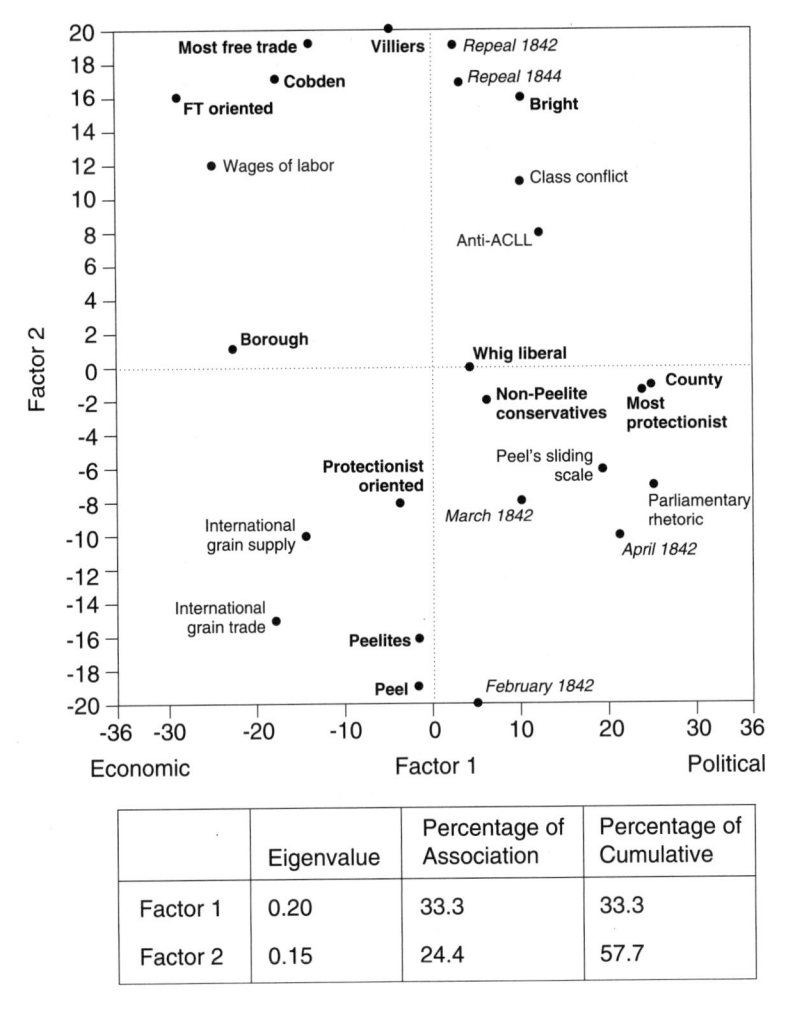

Figure 8.6

Scatter plot — Factor 2 (vertical, -20 to 20) vs Factor 1 (horizontal, -36 to 36; Economic ← → Political):

- Most free trade
- Villiers
- Repeal 1842
- Cobden
- Repeal 1844
- FT oriented
- Bright
- Wages of labor
- Class conflict
- Anti-ACLL
- Borough
- Whig liberal
- County
- Non-Peelite conservatives
- Most protectionist
- Protectionist oriented
- Peel's sliding scale
- Parliamentary rhetoric
- International grain supply
- March 1842
- April 1842
- International grain trade
- Peelites
- Peel
- February 1842

	Eigenvalue	Percentage of Association	Percentage of Cumulative
Factor 1	0.20	33.3	33.3
Factor 2	0.15	24.4	57.7

Figure 8.6
Correspondence analysis of classes, parties, and time frame of 1842 to 1844 debates

interests, though it is more likely that MPs from rotten boroughs incorporated the electoral connection discourse to defend a few landholding interests in their constituencies while those from industrializing areas (also positioned near the political-economy theme) used the same discourse to note the distress of their constituents as they faced higher grain prices from the 1815 Corn Law.

Tagged indicators for the period 1842 to 1844 (figure 8.6) include party affiliation (designated as Non-Peelite Conservative, Peelite,

Whig-Liberal); the borough or county measure for constituency economic makeup plus a more refined measure (most protectionist, protectionist oriented, neutral, free-trade oriented, and most free trade);[12] the date of the speech (thereby differentiating motions for repeal from Peel's sliding scales); and key MPs (Prime Minister Peel, Richard Cobden, Charles Villiers, and John Bright). By 1842 to 1844, socioeconomic and political cleavages are far more visible and pronounced. Figure 8.6 reveals three distinct camps: (1) the strident free traders, led by the Anti-Corn Law League leaders (the two upper quadrants); (2) the protectionists, led by the Non-Peelite Conservatives (lower right quadrant); and (3) the reforming Peelites, led by Peel (lower left quadrant). Free traders tended to represent industrializing districts (most free trade, free-trade oriented), protectionists tended to represent highly agricultural districts (most protectionist), and Peelites tended to represent agricultural districts with some degree of manufacturing interests (protectionist oriented). The proximity of each of these camps to districts with distinct economic orientations provides independent support for the argument developed in chapters 2, 5, 6, and 7, in which the cleavage between Peelites and Non-Peelite Conservatives predated 1846 and was constituency-based.

Figure 8.6 reveals three further features. First, the two themes that appear to characterize best the concerns of the reforming Peelites were international grain trade and international grain supply or, more substantively, the economic implications of Peel's revision to the sliding scale in 1842. In contrast, the Non-Peelite Conservatives were less concerned with the economic implications and more concerned with the reconsideration of the concept of protection (hence their closer proximity to the Peel's-sliding-scale theme). Peelites therefore appear to have been concerned more with the economic aspects of trade policy (thus revealing more of a reforming orientation) and less wedded to the concept of protection well before 1846, a finding that fits well with the spatial mapping of the Peelites and Non-Peelite Conservatives in chapter 2.[13]

Second, three themes best characterize the free traders in their campaign for repeal: the wages of labor, class conflict, and defending the Anti-Corn Law League against attacks by the protectionists. Notably, MPs from highly industrialized districts (including Cobden) appear to have been predominantly concerned with the economic issues surrounding the wages of labor, leaving John Bright, MP for Durham, and others to exchange barbs with the protectionists over class conflict

The Supply Side

and the Anti-Corn Law League. A final feature is the position of the Whigs and Liberals, which brings us to a possible interpretation of the second dimension. The y axis locates the free traders at one extreme, the reforming Peelites at the other, and protectionists in the middle. In the early 1840s, the Liberals endorsed neither outright repeal nor Peel's sliding-scale reform, and so in correspondence space, they are situated the furthest distance from these endpoints—that is, precisely in the middle. Hence, the second dimension appears to represent not so much a gradation as contrasting policy options at two poles, with the status quo of no change in the middle.

The Debates over Time

Table 8.7 lists the themes for 1814 to 1815, 1826 to 1828, and 1842 to 1844, along with those for 1846 (presented in chapter 7). As evidenced by both the tree diagrams and the correspondence analysis, each set of debates bifurcates into economic and political themes, and so the classes are grouped accordingly. Table 8.7 provides a quasi-time line

Table 8.7
A comparison of the themes from the 1814 to 1815, 1826 to 1828, and 1842 to 1844 debates with those from 1846 debates

Themes from 1814 to 1815	Themes from 1826 to 1828	Themes from 1842 to 1844	Themes from 1846
Economic:	*Economic:*	*Economic:*	*Economic:*
Prices and rents	Political economy: capital, labor, land	Wages of labor	Wages and prices; high farming
Food self-sufficiency			
Grain trade	Grain trade	International grain supply	Agricultural market and Ireland
		International grain trade	International trade
Political:	*Political:*	*Political:*	*Political:*
Parliamentary rhetoric	Parliamentary rhetoric	Parliamentary rhetoric	Parliamentary rhetoric and timing of repeal
Petitions and civil unrest	Electoral connection and public opinion		Electoral connection
			MPs as trustees
		Class conflict	
		Peel's sliding scale	
		Anti-Anti-Corn Law League	

for how the concepts of free trade and protection evolved in the policy debates and moreover serves as a focal point for a discussion of the questions raised in the introduction.

First, there is evidence of a demand-side momentum for repeal in the years leading up to 1846. From 1842 to 1844, we can see that the Anti-Corn Law League appears to have driven the political momentum for repeal. With its electoral registration drive and its propaganda campaign, the League blatantly antagonized the protectionists. But moreover, the League inflamed class conflict to the extent that protectionists were forced onto the defensive—that is, they were left having to defuse allegations of abusing political power to protect their economic monopoly. This mounting concern for the preservation of a governing landed aristocracy in the face of a potential League-sponsored middle-class and working-class alliance served to lay the groundwork for a concessionary strategy (repeal) that would sever this (again, potential) alliance.

Second, the supply-side shift discussed in chapters 2 and 7 appears to have been unique to 1846. That is, the analysis does not identify any theme prior to 1846 in which repeal is considered as a means to preserve the "territorial constitution." Hence, when Peel offered his reinterpretation of repeal, characterizing it as a means to preserve the landed basis of Parliament, and Peelites latched onto this reinterpretation as a way to vote as delegates but to justify their betrayal of a protectionist Conservative ideology in the language of trustees, a new dimension was created that allowed repeal to pass.

Third, and following on from above, parliamentary speeches illustrate an evolution in MPs' understanding of their representative role from that of unquestioned trustees in 1815 to a crystallization of the conflict between the delegate and trustee modes in 1846. In 1815, MPs expressed outright contempt for the sentiments expressed within petitions to Parliament, but by the late 1820s, support for the delegate mode of representation had gained momentum (for example, the "feelings" of constituents had gained more legitimacy). In the early 1840s, discussions of representation were subsumed within the clamor of the activities of the Anti-Corn Law League. Very probably it was the League's activities and the protectionists' response to these that helped to crystallize the inherent conflict between the delegate and trustee mode of representation. Thus by 1846, MPs sought to characterize their positions on repeal in terms of their roles as representatives—either as delegates adhering to an electoral connection or as trustees serving the wider public interest.

Fourth, table 8.7 helps to evaluate the influences of *institutions* (1832 Reform Act), *interests* (as mobilized by the League), and *ideas* (particularly, free-trade liberalism) on the thinking of MPs. While the absence of substantive debates on trade policy in the immediate aftermath of the 1832 Reform Act prevents us from adequately gauging the effect of this reform on repeal, previous statistical analysis suggests that this reform did indeed feature prominently in the success of repeal (Schonhardt-Bailey 1991b, 1994). Nonetheless, the evidence in this chapter suggests that the League's voter registration campaign—which exploited the property qualifications of the 1832 Reform Act—may well have forced protectionist MPs to envisage constitutional change far more devastating to their interests than repealing the Corn Laws. Thus, indirectly, these debates support the view that institutional reform in 1832 was essential to creating the conditions necessary for repeal. Next, the *interests* of industrialists, as mobilized within the "League Machine," contributed in driving the repeal momentum as MPs faced heightened class conflict and increased legitimacy for their role as delegates to an increasingly industrialized population. Finally, table 8.7 illustrates a progression in the economic understanding of (or the *ideas* underpinning) free trade and protection. In particular, the themes reflect a shift in the overall capital intensity of the economy, which is evident from the greater attention given to export interests and those of manufactures more generally. In 1815, MPs strongly endorsed self-sufficiency in foodstuffs and saw protection as the means to extend capital investment in agriculture. In the late 1820s, the growth of manufactures raised the issue of higher labor costs that resulted from protection. Industrialization also encouraged MPs to consider free trade in agriculture as a means to retain its dominance in world trade in manufactures. In the early 1840s, the political economy of trade acquired a distinct class flavor, with industrialists faulting landowners for their exorbitant rental charges and landowners accusing industrialists of profiteering. By 1846, MPs still argued about the relationship between wages and prices but by this time generally considered Britain's international trade in manufactures to be welfare-enhancing.

Conclusion

In summary, this chapter provides evidence that, first, MPs do appear to have become anxious about the lobbying activities of the Anti-Corn

Law League "machine." In particular, the debates suggest that protectionist MPs were increasingly alarmed about the prospect of a middle-class and working-class alliance in pursuit of far more radical reforms than repeal. It was this fear that in 1846 underpinned the logic for a reinterpretation of repeal that would preserve the landed basis of Parliament (the "territorial constitution") by severing any possible middle-class and working-class momentum for parliamentary reform. Second, Peel's reinterpretation of repeal as a policy that would preserve the territorial constitution was indeed *unique* to 1846. This argument was not articulated as a theme in any of the debates prior to 1846, which lends significant weight to my thesis that while demand-side pressures were necessary for repeal, the final explanation for repeal must hinge on the introduction of a second dimension of contention, thereby splitting the Non-Peelite Conservatives from the Peelites. Third, systematic analysis of parliamentary debates over time provides a unique perspective on the evolution of the delegate and trustee modes of representation in early nineteenth-century British politics. In 1815, virtually no MP defended his behavior in terms of serving the wishes of his constituents. But as early as the late 1820s (before the 1832 Reform Act), the delegate mode of representation had gained respectability, and by the 1840s, it had become commonplace if not the norm. Finally, it is perhaps not surprising that computer-assisted content analysis of parliamentary debates finds evidence of the influence of institutions, interests, *and* ideas—as most analysts of this time period would accept that all three factors had bearing on repeal. Yet the value added from this analysis is that we have located more precisely *which* institutional feature, set of interests, and range of ideas mattered and, even more, how these influences evolved during a critical period in Britain's political-economic history.

9 Free Trade's Last Hurdle: Why the Lords Acquiesced

Introduction

On 15 May 1846, Members of Parliament voted for the third and final time on Peel's motion to repeal the Corn Laws. While this vote was profoundly important for Britain, it did not signal the end of the legislative process. The peers in the House of Lords had yet to vote on repeal, and it was within their authority to reject repeal.[1] How repeal ultimately acquired the approval of the Lords on 25 June 1846 is a puzzle in itself, as it was this chamber that—virtually by definition—constituted the bulwark of protectionist landowners. While MPs may have debated the *concept* of the territorial constitution in the Commons, the right of the landed aristocracy to hold the reins of power was the *reality* in the Lords. So it is worth questioning why and how British peers came to accept repeal.

This chapter examines the role of the Lords with particular attention directed to the fundamental question: would the Lords have dared to oppose the Commons on such an important issue as repeal, knowing that to do so may have resulted in a constitutional crisis? Some analysts have concluded (either explicitly or implicitly) that such an outcome was never in the cards and thus that the real battle for repeal was in the Commons, not the Lords.[2] This chapter attempts to revise that assessment, inasmuch as it does indeed appear to have been feasible for the Lords to serve as a brake on repeal. Moreover, ample evidence exists to suggest that some peers actively pursued this route. To understand why this brake failed to materialize, however, we need to examine the political actors, the institutional context, and the ideas at play as peers considered repeal. This chapter provides the most extensive and detailed analysis of the role of the Lords in repeal to date and the first ever empirical analysis of the Lords' debates on repeal.[3] An intriguing by-product of this analysis is a comparison of the debates on repeal in the Lords with those in the Commons. This comparison reveals both striking differences and some similarities in the ways that peers and MPs viewed repeal. The comparison also highlights a particular representational and ideational convergence by the two houses of Parliament, which in turn sheds light on the progression toward democracy in nineteenth-century British politics.

Quite simply, political self-interest appears to have motivated the Lords ultimately to support repeal. The Lords were alarmed by the agitation of the Anti-Corn Law League, and they feared that by rejecting repeal, the middle-class industrialists would ally with the working-class Chartists in favor of more sweeping reforms, such as universal suffrage and reform of the House of Lords. As a landowning elite, should the Lords reject repeal, they would undoubtedly face accusations of placing economic self-interest above the well-being of the nation. Given this vulnerability, the Lords perceived repeal to be the concession necessary to appease the middle class, thereby staving off democratizing reforms even more momentous than the 1832 Reform Act (at least, until 1867). Repeal was a compromise that promised to preserve, for the time being, the territorial constitution.

This chapter further explores this interpretation within the context of previous accounts of the role of the House of Lords in the repeal legislation and presents a chronology of repeal as it made its way through the Upper House, giving special attention to the influences of leading political figures, partisanship, and the peculiar institutional makeup of the House of Lords. It presents the results of the computer-assisted content analysis of the Lords' debates, similar to previous analyses of the Commons' debates, and returns to one of the more traditional interpretations of the motivations of the Lords to assess the value of computer-assisted content analysis of the debates in resolving the puzzle of repeal's passage in the House of Lords.

The Lords as a Brake on Repeal

The debate on the Corn Bill in the House of Lords is, without a doubt, the most underresearched and perhaps as a result the least transparent part of the repeal story.[4] Interpretations of the extent to which the Lords mattered to the repeal process vary widely. There are some who see the Lords as merely "rubber stamping" the decision already made in the Commons. One of the earliest examples is Prentice's two-volume

The Supply Side

(nearly 900 pages) exhaustive history of the Anti-Corn Law League, which assigns no more than two sentences to the Lords (and he misreports the dates of the Lords' divisions) (Prentice 1968, 439). As noted in earlier chapters, more recent investigations of Britain's move to free trade have tended to ignore the Lords in favor of analyses of Peel as the pivotal actor (Hilton 1979; Irwin 1989), the agitation of the Anti-Corn Law League (McCord 1958; Anderson and Tollison 1985), the spread of free-trade ideology (Kindleberger 1975; Rohrlich 1987), or Britain's role as hegemonic leader in the international system (Stein 1984; Lake and James 1989; Pahre 1997). Some researchers have analyzed extensively the parliamentary politics surrounding repeal, but even these studies have omitted any serious study of the Lords (McKeown 1989; Schonhardt-Bailey 1991b, 1994; Verdier 1997).

Indeed, this book may have similarly eclipsed the Lords had McLean not ignited my curiosity with his unique contribution to the repeal literature (McLean 2001). McLean asks why the Lords, "a house of the landed interest," passed repeal. Arguing that "the constituency of each peer [was] his estate," McLean rejects economic-interests-based interpretations for repeal because such theories would, in McLean's view, wrongly predict that MPs and peers alike would reject repeal (McLean 2001, 35–36). For McLean, the puzzle of the Lords is solved by arguing that the Duke of Wellington, the leader of the House of Lords, endorsed repeal because he felt that it was his duty to maintain public order and support the Queen's government. Wellington perceived a threat to public order in Ireland (resulting from the potato famine) and so accepted repeal as a price worth paying both to ensure public order and to support the Queen's government (McLean 2001, 36, 54): "Once [Wellington] was convinced that the question was not corn but the Queen's government, he never wavered from the self-imposed task of getting the Queen's government's measures through the House of Lords" (McLean 2001, 40). What McLean leaves unanswered, however, is how and why his fellow peers came to accept repeal. McLean implies that Wellington's concern for public order and the Queen's government prevailed on the Lords, but he does not provide any evidence to support this.

Other assessments offer a different rationale for the peers' conversion to repeal. As early as March 1846, Richard Cobden worried that the Lords might block the legislative path to repeal: "I am afraid our friends in the country are a little too confident. The Government measure is by no means safe with the Lords yet. They will mutilate or reject it if they think the country will suffer it" (letter to G. Combe, 7 March 1846, quoted in Morley 1881, 365).

The peers, in Cobden's view, feared the agitation of the Anti-Corn Law League (letter to T. Hunter, 12 March 1846, and letter to H. Ashworth, 19 February 1846, both quoted in Morley 1881, 370, 377–378):

> In fact there are not a hundred men in the Commons, or twenty in the Lords, who at heart are anxious for total repeal. They are coerced by the out-of-doors opinion, and nothing but the dread of the League organization enables Peel to persevere. But for our forty-shilling freehold bludgeons, the aristocracy would have resisted the Government measure almost to a man.

> It is the League, and it only, that frightens the Peers. It is the League alone which enables Peel to repeal the law. But for the League the aristocracy would have hunted Peel to a premature grave, or consigned him like Lord Melbourne to a private station at the bare mention of total repeal. We must hold the same rod over the Lords until the measure is safe....

In a letter to his wife on 6 March 1846, Cobden wrote (Morley 1881, 378):

> Nobody knows to this day what the Lords will do, and I believe all depends upon their fears of the country. If there was not something behind corn which they dread even still more, I doubt if they would ever give up the key of the bread basket. They would turn out Peel with as little ceremony as they would dismiss a groom or keeper, if he had not the League at his back.

The "something behind corn" that the peers dreaded even more than repeal of the Corn Laws was *democracy*.[5] By rejecting the Commons' Corn Bill, the Lords risked sparking fierce agitation that, as McCord argues, "would dwarf that which had carried the Reform Act" (McCord 1958, 203). To be seen to be defending the institution of protection—from which most peers benefited directly—might raise serious questions as to the judgment and governing authority of the House of Lords. Smith (1992, 122) notes, "As in 1831–2, the Lords' resistance to a measure demanded by a large and powerful interest in the country backed by intense popular agitation threatened a crisis in the constitution and a revived campaign against the powers of the Upper House." Nonetheless, the Lords correctly perceived democracy to be a zero-sum game: the more power that was conceded to the masses, the less that could be retained by the landowning aristocracy. A parallel concern was that any further redistribution of political power would likely raise fears of a redistribution of economic resources (such as the landed property of the aristocracy). Hence, to challenge repeal directly would provide fodder to those seeking political reform, which might lead to a radical redistribution of economic resources. But to acquiesce to repeal would (it was thought) also redistribute economic resources by denying landowners of their valued protection. For the Lords—as well as the rest of the country—repeal unveiled the inherent tension "between democracy and property" (Turberville 1974, 415), and as the *Quarterly Review* commented in the wake of repeal, "Property is the foundation of all government, and Landed Property the foundation of all property" (quoted in Turberville 1974, 415).

In the end, peers came to accept repeal for much the same reason as did some Conservative MPs: namely, by conceding some *economic* power to the middle classes, the landed aristocracy delayed more sweeping challenges (sought by the working classes) to their *political* power. Repeal was thus perceived—by landowners and industrialists alike—as something of a compromise in the distribution of real property. While the 1832 Reform Act extended the political influence of the middle classes, the landowning aristocracy retained most of the power.[6] Repeal was the economic concession that allowed the aristocracy to retain, at least temporarily, the "territorial constitution."

Peers, Parties, and Politics

This section examines the key actors and the legislative process as it unfolded in the House of Lords. In large part, it provides the background necessary to understand the detailed analysis of the Lords' debates later in this chapter. However, it also provides the framework for understanding how influential peers sought to halt or amend repeal in the Lords and how the institutional setting of the Upper House affected this pursuit.

The Influence of a Few

Chapter 6 sought to measure the effect of interests, party affiliation, and ideas on the decisions of Members of Parliament. This sort of analysis cannot be replicated for the Lords for two reasons. First, peers did not represent geographic constituencies. They did not stand for election as did MPs, and so they were in no way delegates of any clearly identifiable constituency. On the one hand, this may have afforded them the status of the ultimate trustees. Indeed, ample evidence exists in their speeches to suggest that many peers perceived their role to be that of a trustee. On the other hand, peers were landowning aristocrats who benefited economically from agricultural protection. This tension between the nation's interest and their own personal interest weighed heavily in their consideration of repeal. But it cannot be tested directly and so will be deferred for discussion later in this chapter, where their speeches will shed some light on their intentions.

A second reason is that peers had no clearly defined party allegiance, and so party affiliation cannot be gauged. Unlike the pollbooks that recorded (however imprecisely) the party affiliation of candidates for the House of Commons at each election,[7] no similar record exists for peers. It is not that peers had no party allegiances but that these were not formally documented. From their cabinet positions in various governments, one can infer the party affiliations of selected peers,[8] but there is no systematic method for even such an inference for the larger body of peers. Hence, any attention to party affiliation in the Lords is by necessity informal and imprecise.

With these two caveats in mind, the task of gauging the influences brought to bear on peers becomes more subjective—at least, until more systematic analysis is presented later in this chapter. One influence has already been discussed—that of the Anti-Corn Law League. Beyond that external body, the personalities of two highly influential peers can be said to have influenced, in part, the decisions of their colleagues.

First, McLean has argued that the Duke of Wellington came to endorse repeal for reasons of public order and allegiance to the Queen's government. Yet McLean also notes that the reasons that Wellington gave to peers to support repeal were *constitutional*—namely, that if the Lords rejected repeal, it would be acting against the recommendations of the throne and the House of Commons (McLean 2001, 43). While there may be a link between maintaining public order and the constitution, there is a distinct logic that underpins each justification. By invoking the constitution, Wellington demonstrated that his chief concern was maintaining the constitutional balance between the two houses of Parliament, as he explained in his letter to Lord Stanley (leader of the protectionists in the Lords) in which he justified his support for repeal (Turberville 1974, 412):

Wellington in reply to Stanley gave an explanation of the principles upon which he had acted ever since 1830. He had, he said, endeavoured to manage the House of Lords upon the principle which justified the existence of the Chamber in the constitution—namely that of conservatism. He had invariably objected to all violent and extreme measures; he had, on the other hand, invariably supported Government in Parliament and used his personal influence "to prevent the mischief of anything like a difference or division between the two Houses." ...As to the measure now before Parliament, he proposed to appeal to the House not to involve the country in additional difficulties or the possibility of a quarrel between the two Chambers "on a question in the discussion of which it has been frequently asserted that their lordships have a personal interest, which assertion, however false as affecting each of them personally, could not be denied as affecting the proprietors of land in general."

Hence, what appears to have motivated Wellington's appeal to protectionist peers was his concern that if the Lords rejected repeal, it would clash with the Commons on an issue for which landowning peers had a personal stake. This, in turn, may have had serious consequences for the future of the House of Lords and for the landed aristocracy more generally. Even if Wellington personally accepted repeal as necessary for maintaining public order in Ireland and as an act of loyalty to the Queen's government (as McLean argues), the argument that he put forth to his colleagues was slightly different: he did not want the Lords to face accusations of placing their own personal interest above that of the nation.

The second influential peer was Lord Stanley, who in late 1845 had resigned from Peel's cabinet in opposition to repeal and by March 1846 had become the leader of the protectionists in the House of Lords. While Stanley presented protectionist petitions to the Lords in March, it was not until his long speech against the second reading on 25 May that Stanley passionately implored his fellow peers to oppose repeal. Historians have described this speech as "the mightiest single effort to save Protection," "one of the great speeches of the era" (Jones 1956, 118), and "the most striking in the debate" in the Lords on repeal (Holland 1980, 271). In it, Stanley invoked a number of arguments: protection was needed to ensure food self-sufficiency; Peel and his government had been duped by the agitation of the Anti-Corn Law League; the Irish potato famine was merely a pretext for repeal; the Corn Law of 1842 (Peel's sliding scale) had not failed and should therefore be retained; British manufacturing exports had not appeared to have been harmed by the Corn Laws; lower prices meant lower wages; protection was the foundation of the British empire; and so on. However, the climax of his speech came at the end when he addressed Wellington's concern that by rejecting repeal, the Lords would appear to be acting in their own personal economic interests. Stanley reversed this argument, stating that only by rejecting repeal could peers fulfill their role as trustees (*Hansard's Parliamentary Debates* 1846, 1174):

...There is another motive which is most likely to operate with highminded men; it is an unworthy fear of the suspicion that they are acting from interested or dishonourable motives.... I feel that I should... warn you against a bias in the opposite direction; against assenting to a measure injurious both to the public and to your own interests, lest you should be unjustly suspected of interested motives. My Lords, you have no right to yield to such considerations. You are the trustees for far more than your personal interests; you are the trustees for your country, you are the trustees for posterity, you are the trustees for the Constitution of the Empire.

For Stanley (and many other peers, as will be seen later), the idea of the Lords as trustees was predicated on the duty of the Upper Chamber to "check" the decisions of the House of Commons. In his view, the agitation of the Anti-Corn Law League had prevailed on the Commons, and it was the duty of the Lords to halt this agitation before it escalated into calls for political democracy (*Hansard's Parliamentary Debates* 1846, 1173):

There may be those, my Lords, who hope, by giving their consent to this measure, to put an end to agitation, and to give satisfaction to the members of the Anti-Corn-Law League. When, my Lords, was an organized agitation put down by concessions extorted from its opponents? Depend upon it, that when this body shall have once tasted the cup of political power, the draught will be too sweet to induce them to relinquish it.

Then, as evidence of the growing threat of democracy, he quoted a "free trader" as remarking that free trade (*Hansard's Parliamentary Debates* 1846, 1173–1174)

...would not only give the people more comfort, but more independence, and this was the thing [the Lords] feared. Commercial and trading liberty would promote intelligence, and give an increased impulse to those great principles of civil and religious liberty on which this country was placing its affections. After the settlement of the free-trade question, the people would then have more time to agitate for the great principle of universal suffrage. If it is good... for commerce to be free, it is good for man to be free.

Against this wave of democratic activism, Stanley argued, the Lords stood as a brake (*Hansard's Parliamentary Debates* 1846, 1175–1176):

My Lords, if I know anything of the constitutional value of this House, it is to interpose a salutary obstacle to rash and inconsiderate legislation—it is to protect the people from the consequences of their own imprudence. It never has been the course of this House to resist a continued and deliberately formed public opinion; your Lordships always have bowed, and always will bow, to the expression of such an opinion; but it is yours to check hasty legislation leading to irreparable evils; and it is yours—though the Constitution can hardly have been deemed to have provided for such a contingency—to protect the people, not against their own hasty judgments, but against the treachery of those whom they have chosen to be their representatives.... And if, by the blessing of God, your decision on this great question shall arrest the progress of this hasty and inconsiderate measure; if you shall thus give time for the intelligence of the country to act upon the public mind..., then will you justly be a "proud aristocracy"; proud of having faithfully discharged the duty vested in you by the Constitution; proud of having withstood alike the seductions of power, and the threats of popular clamour; proud of having succeeded in saving your country from this great delusion, this hazardous and fearful experiment. Your best reward, my Lords, will be the approval of your own consciences.... you will given just cause to exclaim, "Thank God, we have a House of Lords!"

And with that, after over three hours of speaking, Stanley sat. The House divided, and the vote went against Stanley. With this defeat, Stanley abandoned his active resistance to the bill (Jones 1956, 119), and without its leader, the heart of the protectionist movement in the Lords died (except for some feeble attempts at amendments to the third reading, as discussed in the next section).

While Wellington and Stanley appealed to peers from opposite directions, "Whig" peers embarked on a compromise strategy—to amend repeal by introducing a fixed duty. This plan gained the support of most of the Whigs, but both Gash and Stewart argue that it was halted abruptly on 23 May when Lord John Russell (who had persuaded Liberal MPs to support total repeal with this famous Edinburgh letter of December 1845) threatened to resign the Liberal party leadership if the Whig peers joined with the protectionist peers to oppose repeal (Stewart 1971, 71; Gash 1965, 52–53). Lord Palmerston characterized the 23 May meeting of these Whig peers as "All unanimous against the Bill, and all unanimous not to oppose it" (quoted in Stewart 1971, 71). Yet this assessment probably attributes too much weight to Russell's influence. More compelling is Cobden's conjecture that the Whig peers may have feared that if the Lords returned a fixed duty amendment to the Commons, Peel would dissolve Parliament. Such a dissolution might, in turn, return a protectionist (Conservative) majority that might "annihilate the Whig party" (Morley 1881, 385). If, instead, the Whig peers accepted Peel's repeal, they stood a fair chance of reaping the political rewards in his wake, as Morley (1881, 359) noted: "It was undoubted the interest of the Whigs to help Peel to get the Corn Law out of the way, then to turn him out. But there was the natural temptation to trip him up before the time." In any case, Whig peers did not abandon entirely the attempt either to delay consideration of repeal into the next Parliament or introduce some sort of fixed duty. But their amendments stood very little chance of success (see note 12).

Proxies, Protests, and the Political Process
Repeal's path through the House of Lords provides ample evidence of the attempts of many peers to halt its progress—attempts that began immediately. On 18 May, the Corn Bill was read for the first time in the House of Lords. Bills received from the House of Commons are "almost invariably agreed to without discussion" at the stage of the first reading in the Lords (Gordon 1983, 497). Yet repeal appears to be the only occasion in the history of the Lords where a bill from the Commons was opposed on the first reading.[9]

Nonetheless, it was on the second reading—when general principles of bills are normally considered—that the opposing peers (most important, Lord Stanley) launched their fiercest attacks. As noted earlier, opposing peers lost the second division vote on 28 May by forty-seven votes (211 to 164). Yet the details of this vote reveal a real margin of victory for repeal that was much narrower. *Hansard* divides the majority of 211 into peers who were present (138) and peers who voted by proxy (73). The 164 opposed also divide into those present (126) and those voting by proxy (38) (*Hansard's Parliamentary Debates* 1846, 1405–1406). Hence, it was the unique pre-1868 system of proxy voting[10] that ensured a safe margin of victory for repeal. Without the proxy votes, repeal would have passed but only by a narrow twelve votes.

While the proxies clearly strengthened the vote for the second reading, the real worry for Peel and his cabinet was that proxies were not allowed during the committee stage. Hence, when the bill went into committee on 11 June, Peel (and others)[11] feared that the opposition might gain considerable ground in modifying or quashing repeal entirely. Just a few days before repeal passed in the Commons, Peel circulated a memorandum to his cabinet, highlighting the damage that could be done to repeal while in committee in the Lords and, more important, querying whether any damaging decisions arrived at in committee might be overruled by the Lords out of committee (where the proxies would again count) (Peel 1857, 271–272):

There ought in my opinion to be a *private* inquiry of a confidential nature into the precedents in the Lords of overruling decisions taken in Committees of the Lords, or, speaking generally, overruling decisions of Peers present by subsequent decisions, either of Peers present without proxies, or of Peers present with the aid of proxies.

As I think one of the greatest evils that could befall the country would be the mutilation of the Corn Bill by the Lords, any constitutional remedy for such an evil ought, in my opinion, to be resorted to.

Suppose the second reading of the Corn Bill be carried in the Lords by a considerable majority, proxies having been admitted—supposing by a small majority in Committee the Bill is materially altered—if we shrink from the attempt to rescind the decision in Committee by the same constitutional means by which we carried the second reading of the Bill, shall we not distinctly imply that votes by proxy are inferior in weight and value to the votes of Peers present?...and that admission made in the case of a public measure, the principle of which is familiar to all, and which has been under discussion for the last thirty years, will not a severe blow be struck against the principle of voting by proxy?

The replies from Cabinet colleagues supported Peel's view that the Lords had the right to overrule any amendment made in committee, as Sir J. Graham's note exemplifies: "The precedents are clear and in point; they fully justify the use of proxies on the Report with the view of reversing a vote which has passed in Committee on a Bill in the House of Lords.... There never was an occasion when the use of this privilege will be more in accordance with public opinion and with the public good than in the case contemplated by Sir R. Peel" (Peel 1857, 281). As to the possibility that such an action might deem proxy votes to be "inferior in weight and value to the votes of Peers present," Lord Dalhousie cogently noted that "The reason for admitting in Committee the votes only of Peers *present*, I apprehend to be, that in the details of a measure objections may be started not readily anticipated; and it is fitting that those who determine such points of detail, should hear all reasons and arguments which may be adduced.... I cannot conceive that in the Corn Bill any such case can arise. There is not a point, not a fact, not an argument, which has not been shown and discussed fifty times" (Peel 1857, 278–279).

In the end, none of the amendments introduced in committee[12] passed, and so the issue of overruling the decisions of the committee did not materialize (no doubt to Peel's considerable relief). The failure of these amendments, moreover, persuaded Lord Stanley to abandon any attempt to divide the House on the third reading, and he urged protectionist Peers instead to register a "protest" against the bill (*The Annual Register* 1847, 97).

This brings us to the final twist in repeal's path through the Lords— the filing of the protests. Unlike MPs in the House of Commons, members of the Lords had the right to record their opposition to any vote passed in the Upper House. This written opposition, or "protest," consisted of a list of reasons for opposing the bill, to which other Lords could attach their signatures.[13] Protests were then printed in the *Journals* of the House and became a record of the reasons for dissension from the policy that had been adopted (Smith 1992, 45). In the eighteenth century, protests were used frequently as "propaganda" since their publication in newspapers was allowed, even as the reporting of parliamentary debates was prohibited. Yet as newspaper coverage of debates became legal and thus coverage of debates extensive, the use of protests diminished and finally ended around 1875 (Smith 1992, 45).

In the case of repeal, three protests were filed but the third was by far the most important. After the second and third readings, Earl Stanhope lodged two protests, but these received little support.[14] The major protest was filed after the third reading and was signed by eighty-nine Lords (the largest ever number of signatures in the history of the House of Lords).[15] This protest contained twelve points, to which all signatories appear to have agreed: (1) protection was a national security issue; (2) repeal would launch a flood of imports and fluctuations in price; (3) repeal would "throw some lands out of cultivation"; (4) it would be "unjust to withdraw protection" from landowners while they were "subject to exclusive burthens [burdens] imposed for purposes of general and not of special advantage"; (5) poor tenant farmers would suffer the most from repeal; (6) unemployment from rural labor would spread to urban areas; (6 and 7) manufacturers, tradesmen, retail dealers, and others would be harmed "from the loss of the home market, caused by the inability of [agriculturalists] to consume manufactured good to the same extent as heretofore" and from "competition with the agricultural labourers thrown out of employment"; (8) repeal would harm Ireland by lowering the value of her exports and "reducing the demand for labour"; (9) repeal would lower national revenue by reducing annual income and crippling "the resources of those classes on whom the weight of local taxation now mainly falls"; (10) deflation (the result of repeal) would "tend unduly to raise the monied interest at the expense of all others"; (11) repeal would deny the preferential treatment of Canadian corn; and (12) it would deprive

British exporters of "that which is [their] most certain market"—the colonies—and thereby "sap the foundation of that colonial system to which, commercially and politically, this country owes much of its present greatness" (*The Annual Register* 1847, 316–318).

Thus, without a division yet subject to the protest of some eighty-nine Peers, repeal passed the House of Lords on 25 June 1846. On the same night, Peel's government was defeated in the Commons by 292 to 219 on the Irish coercion bill. Holland describes the majority as "a combination of Whigs, Radicals, Irish, and Tory protectionists.... So far as concerned the protectionists, the action was inspired frankly by the motive of revenge upon the Prime Minister, the 'traitor' who, Lord George Bentinck said, had 'sold' them" (Holland 1980, 275–276). Just a few days later, on 29 June, Peel announced his resignation.

Analysis of the Debates of the Lords

Similar to the Commons' debates, the content of the parliamentary debates on repeal in the House of Lords is analyzed using Alceste. Once again, the speeches of the Lords are assumed to offer the best means of gauging their intentions. Two key issues drive this analysis.

First, to what extent do the debates demonstrate a willingness of the Lords seriously to modify, if not halt entirely, the repeal bill? While much of the secondary literature implies that the Lords essentially "rubber stamped" repeal and so largely ignores its significance, the argument here is that many peers sought to halt repeal and indeed the government expected trouble from the Lords. The discussion thus far in this chapter provides the backdrop for this argument, but a thorough analysis of the debates provides a better understanding of the justifications employed in opposition to and in support of repeal.

This brings us to the second key issue: why did the Lords fail to stop repeal? As McLean and others have argued, repeal cut against the grain of the economic interests of the landowners in the Upper Chamber, but they nonetheless relented and allowed the legislation through. McLean implies that their "conversion" to repeal shadowed Wellington's concern for the Queen's government, but it has been suggested above that peers came to accept repeal from an overriding fear of democratic reform. Their chief concern was that by rejecting repeal, the Upper Chamber would be perceived as catering to the personal interests of the landowners in that chamber rather than serving the interests of the country. Hence, repeal sparked a crisis of identify for peers as they reflected on the appropriate role of the House of Lords. In debating repeal, the Lords pondered difficult questions: (1) Should the Lords bow to the wishes of the "majority" (the House of Commons and the clamor of public opinion), or should the Lords perform more as trustees, autonomous from the majority and acting according to what they deemed to be Britain's national interest? (2) If the Lords rejected repeal and were thus seen to be serving their own pockets, might this not accelerate the momentum of democratic reform (and with it, political and economic challenges to the powers of the landed aristocracy) as free traders explicitly threatened? (3) If the Lords returned the repeal bill to the Commons with a fixed-duty amendment, thereby possibly forcing a dissolution of Parliament, might the composition of the new Parliament work against the political ambitions of those peers who advocated the amendment?

In sum, a detailed analysis of the debates of the Lords on the repeal bill promises to lay to rest the myth of the unimportance of the Lords and to ascertain more clearly both the motivations of the opposition and the ultimate acceptance of the majority.

Identifying the Themes in the Debates

Compared with the Commons, the Lords' debates were shorter and more compact. Beginning with the first reading on 18 May, the Lords continued their debates until the division on the second reading on 28 May. All these debates are analyzed below in their entirety.[16]

Thirty peers spoke during these debates: fifteen voted for repeal, fourteen voted against, and one abstained. These peers are listed in the appendix to this chapter. Table 9.1 provides a summary of the basic

Table 9.1
Alceste analysis: Basic statistics for the House of Lords

Total word count	135,535
Unique words analyzed	49,375
Passive variables (tagged indicators)	35
ICUs (= number of speeches)	79
Classified ECUs	2,306 (= 74% of the retained ECU)
Lexical classes	5
Distribution of classes (%)	1: 25.63
	2: 32.44
	3: 21.94
	4: 11.45
	5: 8.54

statistics from the Alceste analysis. The total word count for the text file is 135,535, and of these, 49,375 were unique words that were analyzed by the program. The passive variables, or tagged indicators, were the identifying features for each speech. Here, they were the name of the peer, the timing of the speech (first or second reading), and the peer's vote in the second reading (protection, repeal, or abstained). As mentioned earlier, some of the tags (such as constituency characteristics and party affiliation) used in the analysis of the Commons debates are not relevant for the Lords. Thus, their vote in the second division is included as a tag that identifies their final stance on repeal, although it must be emphasized that many who voted for repeal were not enthusiastic free traders but rather were reluctant converts (as the earlier quote by Lord Palmerston implies).

As with the Commons' debates, the initial context unit (ICU) indicates the number of speeches, which in this case is seventy-nine. The elementary context unit (ECU) is the gauged sentence, based on punctuation and word length, which Alceste uses to calculate matrices for the classification process.[17] For the Lords debates, 2,306 ECUs, or 74 percent of the retained ECUs, were successfully classified, which is a little less than the 80 percent classified for the Commons in 1846.

Five lexical classes are identified in the debates. Of these, class 2 is the largest, with about 32 percent of the ECUs, and class 5 is the smallest, with about 9 percent of the ECUs.

Similar to the Commons debates, table 9.2 lists the most characteristic (function) words of each class, ordered by statistical significance. Recall that the most characteristic words are those with high chi-squared values and that words ending with "+" indicate that these are reduced forms, or truncated versions, of the same basic word. From table 9.2 and the top twenty ECUs for each class (not listed here, but examples of ECUs for the Commons debates in 1846 were given in chapter 7), we can construct conceptual headings for each class.

Parliamentary Rhetoric As we have found for all the debates analyzed thus far, one class constitutes the words that reflect parliamentary nomenclature—or what I have described as *parliamentary rhetoric*. These include words such as *express+*, *address+*, and *debate+*—all of which reflect a certain style of speaking. This class contains no substantive arguments and so will not be explored further.

International Trade The words in class 2 (table 9.2) all refer to various aspects of international trade, with the five most characteristic

Table 9.2
Characteristic words of each class by strength of association for the House of Lords debates

Class 1		Class 2		Class 3		Class 4		Class 5	
χ^2	Word	χ^2	Word	χ^2	Word	χ^2	Word	χ^2	Word
86.81	express+	94.23	corn+	88.54	district+	93.24	public+	75.17	exercise+
86.62	address+	78.63	market+	87.92	tenant+	93.22	right+	68.37	reject+
75.96	debate+	77.32	year+	84.53	wage+	88.97	confid+	55.43	justified
74.59	friend+	75.22	quantit+	70.82	landlord+	78.73	conscientious+	52.41	pass+
65.66	richmond	74.84	goods	69.46	improve+	73.52	character+	47.66	settle+
61.05	question+	74.05	foreign+	67.93	soil+	69.04	responsibilit+	47.61	majorit+
58.76	marquis	68.84	cotton+	66.07	agricultural	65.39	vote+	46.19	bill+
54.89	word+	67.82	home	64.36	farm+	64.19	judgment+	45.61	law+
53.10	side+	65.82	wheat+	60.39	employ+	63.46	hon	45.38	cease+
50.84	brougham+	60.73	average+	59.27	tax	60.87	opinion+	45.07	evil+
48.71	oppos+	60.27	amount+	55.68	skill+	57.39	political+	43.07	resist+
45.84	cross	57.29	manufacture+	53.38	cultiv+	54.41	interest+	38.27	sanction+
45.37	occasion+	56.05	article+	49.74	crop+	53.45	baronet+	36.02	protect+
44.22	night+	55.66	timber	45.11	profit+	52.43	position+	35.54	election+
44.14	house+	55.42	increase+	45.10	reduce+	49.99	leader+	34.07	question+
44.14	personal+	55.41	tariff+	43.94	propert+	48.06	actuate+	32.75	conflict+
41.68	observ+	53.55	shipp+	41.85	capital+	47.50	men	32.01	fixed+
40.35	speech	53.46	trade+	40.43	comfort+	47.01	circumstance+	30.45	consequence+
40.14	benches	51.91	unite+	38.32	manufacturing	45.41	office	29.94	suspend+
39.23	petition+	50.80	british	37.41	classe+	43.65	honest+	29.93	decision+
39.12	opinion+	43.11	duty	36.15	rate+	41.42	private+	29.92	ought

The Supply Side

32.07	memor+	42.36	wool	35.51	competition	40.94	affair+	27.89	measure+
32.07	normanby+	39.94	fluctuat+	33.44	class	40.94	discharge+	27.47	legislat+
31.69	assure	38.94	duties	33.44	potato	39.21	talent+	26.01	suspension
31.02	noble	38.14	produce+	32.76	bread	38.20	courage	25.56	excite+
30.81	attention	38.14	russia	30.69	income+	38.19	influence+	25.37	free+
30.16	measure+	36.42	export+	29.94	consequent+	35.11	sense+	22.88	indeed
29.85	bill+	35.67	tonnage	28.56	farth+	34.81	sacrifice+	22.88	represent+
29.58	discuss+	34.65	ship+	27.20	price+	32.56	pursue+	22.65	rash
27.60	amend+	32.41	canada+	26.84	suffer+	30.66	moral+	22.62	difficult+
27.24	subject+	31.81	consumption	26.67	population	30.66	solemn+	21.23	agitat+
27.00	present+	31.38	supplie+	26.54	disease+	30.39	view+	21.23	minorit+
26.22	inconsistenc+	30.91	supply	24.98	estate+	26.67	minister+	20.59	common−

words (*corn*, *market+*, *year+*, *quantit+*, and *goods*) illustrating their particular concern for the grain trade. While trade in manufactures is also discussed in this class, it appears to be of lesser concern. This contrasts with the same class for the Commons in 1846, where the five most characteristic words (*foreign+*, *article+*, *manufacture+*, *duty*, and *trade+*) all pointed to a concern for Britain's manufacturing export trade. The ECUs for this class lend further insight into the substantive content. Aside from their concern for the grain trade (illustrated in the first quote), Peers appeared to question the impact of repeal on (chi-squared values are in parentheses):

Britain's food security: (32) ... and has it been the case that in war foreign nations have stopped our supplies? From 1812 to 1814 they were at war with the United States, from which this country drew her supplies of cotton.

Britain's balance of payments: (28) ... it had been shown that in our trade with Russia we took more goods from her than she took in return from us, leaving the inference to be drawn that the balance was made up by the export of gold.

Price fluctuations: (27) ... observe, that in two years the total amount of our fluctuation was 30 per cent; while in that one year, the fluctuation at Dantzic was 56 per cent; at Hamburg, 86; at Restock, 78; at Stettin, 84; at Odessa, 50; and at Alexandria, 54. Perhaps you may tell me, that this is the effect of our own sliding scale and of our corn law operating upon prices abroad.

Various aspects of its manufacturing trade: (24) Since 1841, our imports of timber have increased from 351,000 loads to 642,000 loads. Now in 1843, we exported to Russia, Prussia, Denmark, and Sweden, 2,200,000 yards of plain cotton; now, we export only 2,000,000.

Preferential trade with Canada: (23) ... and if an enactment similar in principle to the duties drawback law should pass Congress, permitting Canadian produce to pass through the United States for shipment, and the English market was open to produce shipped from American ports on as favourable terms as if shipped from Canadian ports, the larger portion of the exports of upper Canada would find its way through the canals of the state of New York. . . .

On the whole, the content of this class is less focused than the international-trade class identified in the 1846 Commons debates, and the broader welfare-enhancing effects of free trade—which were discussed at length in the Commons—appear to have been ignored by the Lords.

Domestic Agricultural Production Key characteristic words for class 3 include *tenant+*, *wage+*, *landlord+*, *improve+*, *soil+*, and *agricultural—*

which, together with many of the remaining words on the list and the ECUs, indicate that peers, like their colleagues in the Commons, were concerned with Britain's agricultural production and the home market in foodstuffs. But this class cannot be linked directly with one from the Commons, as it contains ideas and arguments from two different classes identified in the Commons debates—wages and prices; high farming (class 1, Commons 1846); and agricultural market and Ireland (class 4, Commons 1846). Taking each idea in turn, the ECUs illustrate the sentiments of peers.

On wages and prices, peers described the status quo in terms of benign market mechanisms and saw the goal of repeal to be that of lowering the wages of labor and, in general, reducing the income to agriculture:

(35) I say that wages like everything else, are regulated by the proportion between the demand and supply. In proportion to the demand for labour, the working classes were ready to enter into competition for that labour, which would afford them the necessaries and comforts of life.

(33) They wish to lower the price of agricultural produce for another reason. They know that thereby they will throw the land out of cultivation that the agricultural population will be forced into their town, that competition for labour will be thus increased, and wages permanently lowered.

(20) ...whose whole sources of income were drawn from the land who lived upon their farms and cultivated them themselves they would suffer still more severely. Whatever reduction might take place in the value of agricultural produce whether 20 or 30 per cent the loss would fall upon the yeomanry most heavily.... In short, it would almost annihilate them as a body.

Peers drew a link between propping up the wages of agricultural labourers and retaining the cultivation of marginal lands. As landowners, some peers were concerned with the effect of repeal on the viability of lands in cultivation, fearing that import competition would ruin the viability of marginal lands:

(56) The effect of that competition would be to throw the lighter and indifferent descriptions of land out of cultivation, and consequently deprive a large portion of the labouring population of the means of employment.

One peer rebutted this argument, though (probably inadvertently) by doing so he illustrated the benefits that accrued to landowners from high rental charges (an argument used by the League to convert farmers to repeal):

(29) It was my fortunate lot to let a considerable portion of my estate not at a reduced rent, but at a positively an increased rent. What could be a stronger proof that the farmers in that district did not anticipate any risk of the land being thrown out of cultivation by a repeal of the existing system of corn laws?

On the Irish potato famine, peers—like MPs—discounted repeal as a means to alleviate the distress. Some peers doubted the severity of the distress, while others faulted Irish agriculture for failing to create a market for wage labor:

(42) But what was the compensation to a farmer of this class? Why, the potato crop had failed, but his oats were superabundant, bringing a very fair price; and he had in his superabundant oats the means of sustaining himself, and, in their price, of recovering in some degree the loss of his potatoes.

(51) Having no means of employment, they have no prospect of obtaining money wherewith to purchase food to replace the potato crop which has failed. That is the cause of the distress of the smaller cottiers of Ireland.

On the whole, peers discussed wages and prices differently from MPs. Peers were more concerned with the practical aspects of repeal— the extent to which farms and farm laborers would suffer. MPs noted these practical aspects but extended their discussions into the realm of political economy theory (such as exploring the relationship between prices and wages).[18] On Ireland, however, both MPs and peers remained unconvinced either that the famine was severe or that repeal was the appropriate tool for dealing with the distress.

Peel as Trustee The word list for class 4 suggests an issue relating to moral, or more specifically, public-regarding behavior, with key words such as *public+*, *confid+*, *conscientious+*, *character+*, and *responsibility+*. The ECUs make obvious that peers were questioning the motives of the prime minister, Sir Robert Peel, in leading the repeal legislation. Some accepted Peel's motives as honest but the policy as misguided, particularly in the harm caused to his party:

(45) ...gentleman who filled the office of first minister of the crown had consulted what he conscientiously believed to be the best interests of the country; he acquitted him of acting from any sordid or ungenerous motive, but he must be forgiven for saying that he did not think that he and those who had acted with him had done that which public men should do.

(41) He had misgoverned and misguided this country. But if he did not impute dishonesty to the Right Hon. Baronet [Peel], what could he say of his judge-

The Supply Side

ment and courage? What had been the effect upon his party of this conduct? Was that the minister for whom their lordships would sacrifice their conscientious convictions?

Others were more scathing in their criticism, arguing that Peel had succumbed to the agitation of the Anti-Corn Law League:

(32) But I think my Right Hon. friend [Peel] fatally and unhappily mistook the character of that emergency, that he mistook the real judgement of the country. I think he committed the error the most fatal a statesman can commit. I think he mistook the brawling torrent of agitation for the still deep current of public opinion.

And yet a few registered their support for both Peel and his policy of repeal:

(30) ...have considered that the government were entitled to the benefit of that doubt. He confessed that he had now no doubts whatever upon this subject, and was prepared to give a conscientious, willing, and hearty support to this bill.

Recalling from chapter 7 that the Peelites construed repeal as a means to stave off more radical democratic reform and noting that the Lords feared democratic reform perhaps even more than MPs, it is not surprising that mention is made of repeal offering a means to preserve the landed basis of Parliament:

(31) ...though, on the contrary, it is my opinion that the sooner such measures are done away with the better will it be for the interests of that aristocracy, and the more secure will be those institutions.

Hence, in assessing Peel's motives, *peers explicitly linked repeal to the preservation of the territorial constitution*, which lends support to the argument of this chapter.

Role of Lords This final class contains a number of more subtle arguments that are less easily captured by the word list but that all reflect a consideration of the political role of the House of Lords. Key words such as *reject+*, *justified*, *pass+*, *majorit+*, *bill+*, and *evil+* hint at a possible rejection of the repeal legislation by the Lords and the consequences of that decision. For this class in particular, the ECUs are more revealing, as they suggest that peers were reflecting on the appropriate role for the House of Lords. Was it legitimate for the Lords to act against the "majority" (namely, the House of Commons and the perceived public opinion)? On this question, one peer cogently expressed the sentiments of others:

(21) This bill had been sent up by a majority of nearly 100 from the other house of parliament, and he considered that very serious consequences might ensue from its rejection by their lordships.

Was an amendment, such as for a temporary suspension of the Corn Laws, an acceptable alternative for the Lords' consideration, or would this, as the following peer argues, merely nullify protection for agriculture:

(56) Those who advocated protection would not be disposed to object to that arrangement; but I will ask, did it ever occur to the advocates of the corn law, who proposed that temporary suspension, that such a suspension of the corn law would destroy its vitality altogether?

If the Lords rejected repeal, an action that could well lead to a dissolution of Parliament and possibly the return of more free traders,[19] would not repeal then pass in the end, thereby contributing to more democratic agitation?

(29) ...a dissolution of parliament at this exciting time—town arrayed against county the angry passions that would be excited, the suspension of industry and trade, the absolute paralyzation of all the enterprise of the country that must exist....

Finally, the Lords considered their role in maintaining the so-called national policy (or "principle") of protection for "native industry" (agriculture):

(38) He stated that he objected to this bill because he wished to sustain protection to native industry. Now, the bill which was submitted to their lordships, and in which was proposed a change of the law, was based on precisely the opposite principles;

(30) I deny that what is called protection to native industry has been the principle of national policy at all times, and under all circumstances; for when I consider what has been the law and policy of this country from time to time, I do not find that such has ever been avowed as the principle of national legislation....

While somewhat disjointed, class 5 demonstrates that the Lords were seriously considering invoking their prerogative to halt the repeal bill from the Commons and, perhaps more to the point, considering the consequences of such a rejection of repeal.

The Arguments of the Protectionists: Comparing the Twelve-Point Protest with the Thematic Classes

The twelve-point protest lodged by eighty-nine protectionist peers is a useful independent check on the accuracy and validity of the Alceste methodology. Table 9.3 lists each of the twelve points in the first column and in the second column gives the class in which the idea or argument appears. Only one of the reasons given by the protectionists could not be linked to a specific class: point 4 maintains essentially that landowners were entitled to protection so long as they endured a disproportionate tax burden. Three reasons are linked indirectly (with explanations given in the notes column), while the rest of the protest arguments have direct links to the content of the classes identified by Alceste. Bearing in mind that the twelve points were the justifications of the protectionists, it is not surprising to find two classes—Peel as trustee and the role of the Lords—with no corollaries in the first column. Had the peers who voted for repeal lodged a similar list of reasons for their votes, one could conjecture that linkages could have been drawn between these two classes and their justifications. However, this is only conjecture. What is clear, however, is that these two classes—both political rather than economic in nature—stand in isolation from the rest, which lends support to my contention that the arguments of peers who supported repeal did not hinge on economic but rather on political logic.

Linkages between the Themes

This cleavage between economic and political themes also emerges in figure 9.1, which presents the tree diagram of the classes, akin to similar diagrams for the House of Commons debates (schematized according to Alceste's descending hierarchical classification procedure). In figure 9.1, as in all the debates previously analysed, a primary bifurcation exists between the political classes and the economic classes. Here, Peel as trustee and the role of the Lords are most closely linked in terms of word cooccurrences, thereby forming a "representation" branch of the tree. International trade and domestic agricultural production are also linked, though less intimately than the two political classes.

Figure 9.2 is a graph of the correspondence analysis of the classes and selected tags for the Lords, again similar to previous graphs for the Commons debates. Recall that the program cross-tabulates classes and words to create a matrix that can then be subjected to factor

Table 9.3
Comparing the twelve-point protest with the thematic classes for the House of Lords debates

Points Given in Protest	Content of Classes	Notes
1. Protection was a national security issue.	International-trade class ("food security")	
2. Repeal would launch a flood of imports and fluctuations in price.	International-trade class ("price fluctuations")	
3. Repeal would "throw some lands out of cultivation."	Domestic-agricultural-production class	
4. It would be "unjust to withdraw protection" from landowners while they were "subject to exclusive burthens [burdens] imposed for purposes of general and not of special advantage."		
5. Poor tenant farmers would suffer the most from repeal.	Domestic-agricultural-production class	
6. Unemployment from rural labor would spread to urban areas.	Domestic-agricultural-production class	
6 & 7. Manufacturers, tradesmen, retail dealers, and others would be harmed "from the loss of the home market, caused by the inability of [agriculturalists] to consume manufactured goods to the same extent as heretofore" and from "competition with the agricultural labourers thrown out of employment."	Domestic-agricultural-production class	
8. Repeal would harm Ireland by lowering the value of her exports and "reducing the demand for labour."	Domestic-agricultural-production class	

The Supply Side

Table 9.3
(continued)

Points Given in Protest	Content of Classes	Notes
9. Repeal would lower national revenue by reducing annual income and crippling "the resources of those classes on whom the weight of local taxation now mainly falls."	International-trade class ("balance of payments")	Indirect link via a macroeconomic argument. Given a change in the relative price level of agricultural and traded manufactures (from repeal), it is argued that the tax burden would fall more on the sector that suffers the loss of income—namely, agriculture.
10. "Deflation" (the result of repeal) would "tend unduly to raise the monied interest at the expense of all others."	Domestic-agricultural-production class	Indirect link. A change in the relative price levels of agriculture and traded manufactures would affect the relative income distribution adversely for the agriculturalists.
11. Repeal would deny the preferential treatment of Canadian corn.	International-trade class ("preferential trade with Canada")	
12. It would deprive British exporters "that which is [their] most certain market"—the colonies—and thereby "sap the foundation of that colonial system to which, commercially and politically, this country owes much of its present greatness."	International-trade class ("preferential trade with Canada")	Indirect link (concerns trade with colonies)
	Peel-as-trustee class Role-of-Lords class	

```
                    Parliamentary rhetoric
Class 1 (25.63%) ──┤
                                                              Political
Class 4 (11.45%) ──┤ Peel as trustee
                                    Representation
Class 5  (8.54%) ──┤ Role of Lords

Class 2 (32.44%) ──┤ International trade
                                                              Economic
Class 3 (21.94%) ──┤ Domestic agricultural production
```

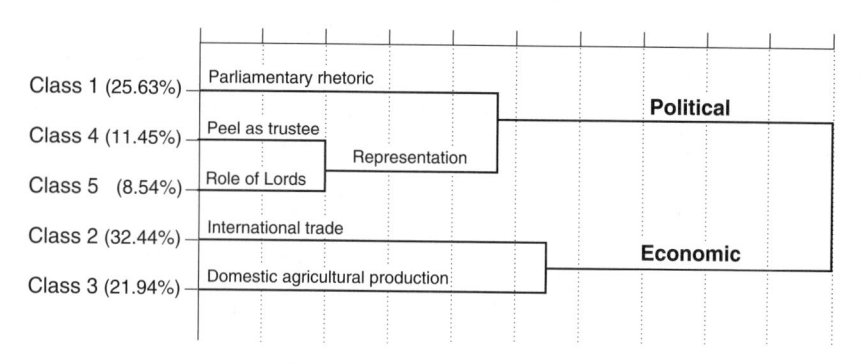

Figure 9.1
Descending hierarchical classification: Tree graph of the stable class in the Lords

correspondence analysis (Greenacre 1993). We thus obtain a spatial representation of the relations between the classes, where distance reflects the degree of association.[20] From the table below the graph, we can see that the first two factors together account for about 66 percent of the total association, with the first factor accounting for 41 percent. (These figures align quite closely with the correspondence analysis of the 1846 Commons debates, where the first two factors accounted for 61 percent of the association, and the first factor figure accounted for 40 percent.) A further two factors are required to account for the total association.[21]

Figure 9.3 illustrates the distribution of representative words from each class as shaded clouds around the focal point of each class (given as a white circle). This graph provides a fuller picture of the spread of each class, along with its proximity (and even overlap) with other classes. Below the graph are additional words that the software was unable to fit into the graph. Their coordinates are provided, and each word is represented as a point in the actual graph. While similar graphs could have been given for the previous debates, the size of the files and number of classes made these graphs very difficult to read, and so they have not been presented. Figure 9.3 is a relatively simpler graph and so is provided here as a way to help the reader grasp the spatial capacity of this form of correspondence analysis.

Bearing in mind the precautions noted in chapter 7 concerning the "dimensionality" of this correspondence analysis, it seems apparent that the first (horizontal) dimension separates the economic classes from the political classes—a feature of all the debates previously analyzed for the House of Commons. The second (vertical) dimension

The Supply Side

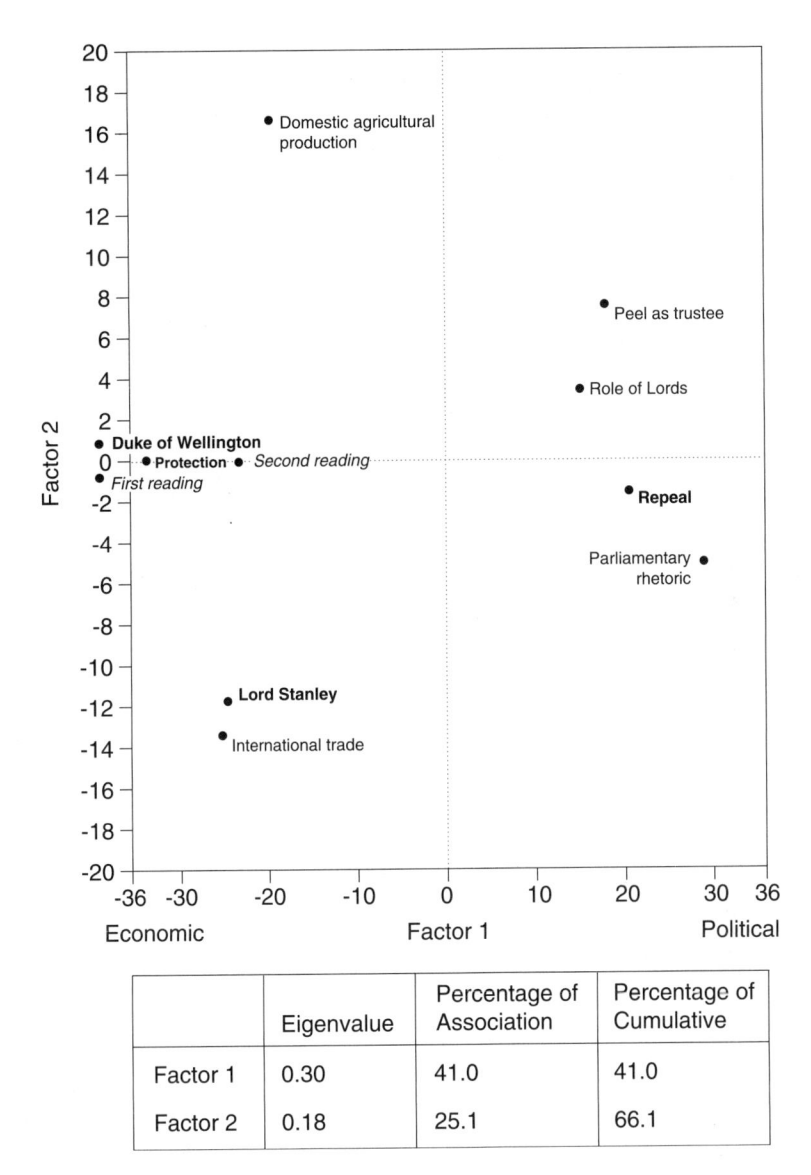

	Eigenvalue	Percentage of Association	Percentage of Cumulative
Factor 1	0.30	41.0	41.0
Factor 2	0.18	25.1	66.1

Figure 9.2
Correspondence analysis of classes for Lords' debates

254

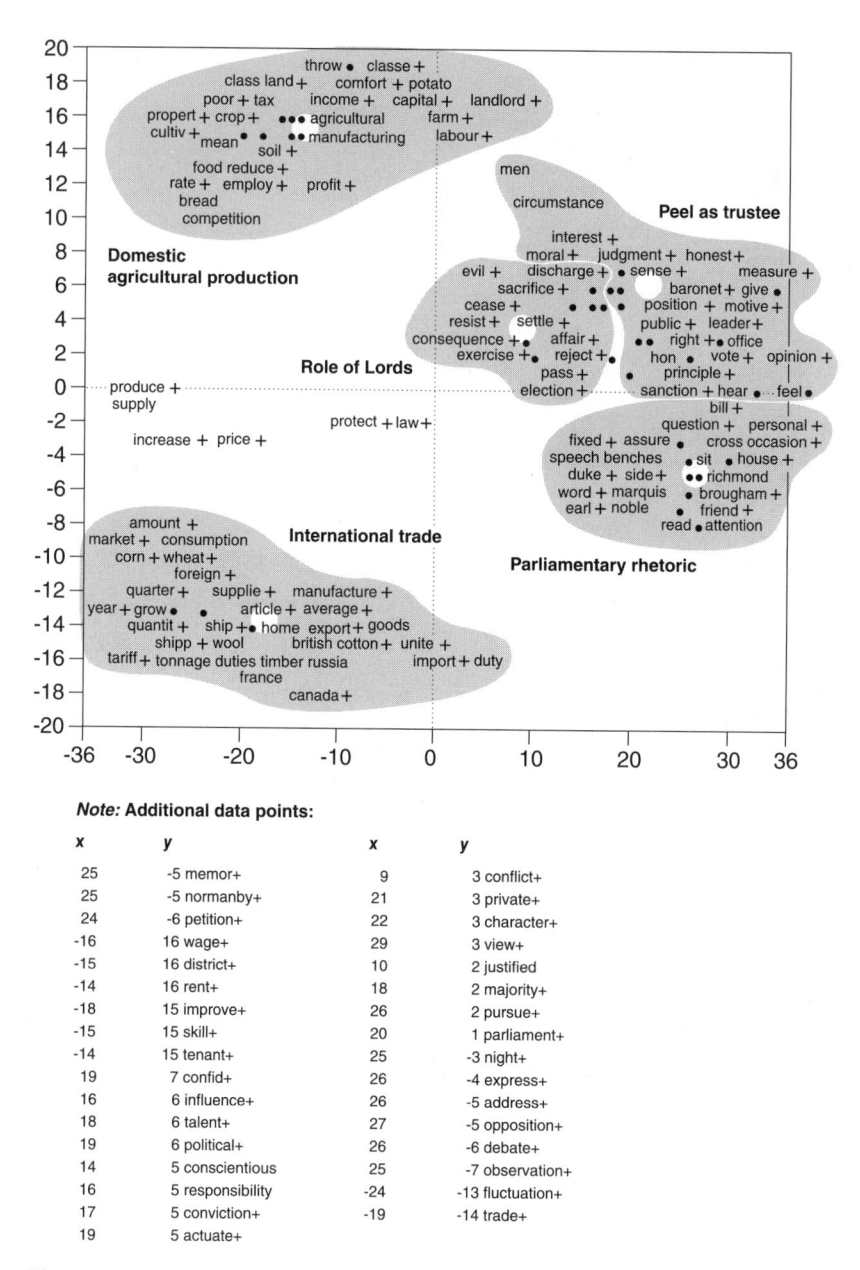

Free Trade's Last Hurdle

Note: Additional data points:

x	y	x	y
25	-5 memor+	9	3 conflict+
25	-5 normanby+	21	3 private+
24	-6 petition+	22	3 character+
-16	16 wage+	29	3 view+
-15	16 district+	10	2 justified
-14	16 rent+	18	2 majority+
-18	15 improve+	26	2 pursue+
-15	15 skill+	20	1 parliament+
-14	15 tenant+	25	-3 night+
19	7 confid+	26	-4 express+
16	6 influence+	26	-5 address+
18	6 talent+	27	-5 opposition+
19	6 political+	26	-6 debate+
14	5 conscientious	25	-7 observation+
16	5 responsibility	-24	-13 fluctuation+
17	5 conviction+	-19	-14 trade+
19	5 actuate+		

Figure 9.3
Word distribution in correspondence space: The Lords' debates, 1846

appears to dissect domestic from international economic arguments, with all the political classes falling somewhere in between. This same polarization of economic classes is evident in the 1846 Commons debates. But as the Lords' debates lack the constituency-specific tags that accompanied MPs, we cannot push the interpretation of this second dimension any further.

There are fewer tags for the Lords debates than for the Commons. These included just the names of selected peers, whether the speech occurred during the first or second reading and how the peer ultimately voted (for protection or repeal). As mentioned earlier, because peers represented no constituencies, no links or inferences can be drawn to specific interests. Nonetheless, three findings emerge. First, peers who voted for repeal are more closely associated with the political classes, while those who voted for protection are situated closer to the economic classes. This lends support to the contention that the underlying rationale for the repeal vote in the Lords was political self-interest. Protectionists focused more on the economics surrounding repeal, while peers who ultimately supported repeal spoke in terms of political representation, giving attention to Peel's political motivations and the implications of their vote for the future of the House of Lords.

Second, peers who voted for protection appear to feature more prominently during both sets of debates covered by this analysis (first and second readings), which suggests that protectionists were more outspoken in their opposition to repeal than were those who ultimately supported the repeal legislation.

Third, Lord Stanley, leader of the protectionists, is closely associated with the international-trade class. While the finale of his historic speech argued for the Lords to serve as a brake on the democratic activism that he perceived to be driving repeal, the bulk of his speech dealt with issues relating to international trade (such as food self-sufficiency, the functioning of Peel's sliding scale, the growth in manufacturing exports, and colonial trade). This preponderance of argumentation is reflected in both the high chi-squared value given to his tag for the international-trade class ($\chi^2 = 137$) and in the location of his tag in the correspondence space, very near to this same class. In contrast, the tag for the Duke of Wellington is not closely associated with any class,[22] nor is it located near any class in correspondence space. Hence, at least from the content of his speeches in the Lords, Wellington did not appear to align himself closely with one particular theme in attempting to

Table 9.4
Comparison of basic statistics for the House of Lords and the House of Commons, 1846

	House of Lords	House of Commons
Total word count	135,535	922,240
Unique words analyzed	49,375	339,713
Passive variables (tagged indicators)	35	238
ICUs (= number of speeches)	79	587
Classified ECUs	2,306 (= 74% of the retained ECU)	7,093 (= 80% of the retained ECU)
Lexical classes	5	6
Distribution of classes (%)	1: 25.63 (Parlimentary rhetoric) 2: 32.44 (International trade) 3: 21.94 (Domestic agricultural production) 4: 11.45 (Peel as trustee) 5: 8.54 (Role of Lords)	1: 19.44 (Wages and prices; high farming) 2: 10.36 (MPs as trustees) 3: 9.49 (Electoral connection) 4: 10.77 (Agricultural market and Ireland) 5: 30.99 (Parliamentary rhetoric and timing of repeal) 6: 18.95 (International trade)

gain the support of his fellow peers. Any argument that hinges on the persuasiveness of Wellington's appeal to his colleagues in the Lords cannot therefore easily be attributed to a particular rationale or theme.

Comparing the 1846 Debates in the Lords and Commons

A number of comparisons have already been made between the debates on repeal in the House of Lords and the House of Commons. Table 9.4 provides a succinct comparison of the basic statistics and class labels for both sets of debates. Most striking is the difference in the overall size—reflecting length—of the debates in the two chambers, with the Lords amounting to just 15 percent that of the Commons. MPs spent far longer debating repeal than did peers, possibly illustrating the success of Bentinck and other protectionists who sought to prolong the debates in the Commons to allow the protectionist movement time to gather momentum. Had Stanley not abandoned his protectionist lead after the second reading in the Lords, this movement may yet have gained some momentum, but it is doubtful that any success would have emerged after the definitive second reading vote in the Lords.

It is, however, the comparison of the content of the classes in the two chambers that is most intriguing. Taking each class in turn, parliamentary rhetoric is larger in the Commons, possibly because this class also includes Villiers's motion to drop the three-year delay to implementing repeal. The Lords appear to have devoted proportionately more time to discussing international trade than did MPs—but it should also be recalled that they were more concerned with the practicalities and less with the theory. It may be that this is attributable to their greater concern for the effect of repeal on colonial trade and the British empire, along with fears for food self-sufficiency. Class 3 in the Lords, domestic agricultural production, contains elements of both class 1 (wages and prices; high farming) and class 4 (agricultural market and Ireland) from the House of Commons debates, yet is smaller than the combined percentages of these two classes. It is possible that while MPs engaged in the more theoretical discussions of the relationship between wages and prices and engaged in diatribes against Peel's apparent use of the Irish famine as a fig leaf for repeal, peers either were less interested in these discussions or felt that they had been sufficiently addressed in the previous Commons debates. Class 4 in the Lords, Peel as trustee, corresponds closely to the MPs-as-trustees class in the House of Commons. While the Lords targeted Peel for an interrogation of his motives, MPs questioned the motives of *all* MPs about whether they saw their role to be mainly one of serving the nation's interest (however defined) or serving their constituents. Both the Lords and Commons spent about the same proportion of their time discussing this issue. Finally, class 5, role of the Lords, questions whether the Lords should act against the wishes of the "majority"—namely, the House of Commons and the perceived public opinion. As a measure of the interface between this chamber and British society, broadly defined, this class can be said to have an interesting parallel with the electoral-connection class in the House of Commons. In both classes, MPs and peers questioned the extent to which legislators should listen to and act on the wishes of constituents and public opinion. Seen in this way, one can begin to appreciate the extent to which *both* MPs and peers had come to understand the limitations of their powers as independent political actors. Recalling from chapter 8 the progression from a wholly trustee mode of representation in the 1815 debates to an uneasy balance between trustee and delegate modes of representation by the 1840s and now observing an appreciation of the importance of public opinion even in the House of Lords, one can see a remarkable *empirical* transformation in the interpretation of parliamentary representation in both houses during the first half of the nineteenth century.

Conclusion

Norman Gash (1965, 54), one of the leading historians on early to mid-nineteenth-century British politics, maintains that peers were persuaded to accept repeal because they respected the leadership of Peel and Wellington (an argument also made implicitly by McLean) and because the Whig peers fell into line (eventually) behind their party leader, Russell. Gash (1965, 48) rejects as "an over-simplified generalization" the notion that the Lords might have conceded repeal on economic grounds to retain their political control of Parliament (what I have construed as the "territorial constitution"). Both he and McLean agree that if economic logic had prevailed, repeal would not have been carried in the Lords, though Gash (1965, 48) acknowledges that some portfolio diversification might have reduced the attraction of protection for some peers. This phenomenon was of more importance in the Commons, as shown in chapter 5.[23] Hence, the prevailing historiography places great importance on the role of key leaders—Peel, Wellington, and Russell—in persuading the protectionists and the Whig peers to acquiesce to repeal, while it also dismisses any significant role for economics in their repeal vote. How does this chapter's analysis of the statements of the peers themselves square with this assessment?

First, the debates do not suggest that Wellington or Russell featured prominently in the Lords' consideration of repeal, but they do suggest that peers thought carefully about Peel's motives in recommending the legislation. While the analysis of this chapter does not necessarily dismiss Wellington and Russell's leadership (as it is plausible that peers used discussion of Peel's leadership to envelope leadership more generally), it does at least bring into question their importance.

A second and related point is that current historiography probably rates the influence of individuals too highly while failing to appreciate the more subtle issue of the institutional environment and the broader motivation of political self-interest. For instance, most accounts of the Lords fail to explore the weight that Peel placed on the proxy votes. Although it is true that no amendment passed in committee (where proxies did not count), had any one amendment succeeded, Peel clearly expected the Lords to overrule the decision of the committee. Had this occurred, a constitutional crisis could have erupted between the two houses of Parliament. While this scenario did not emerge, the seriousness with which the Cabinet treated the possible rejection of repeal in the Lords makes it evident that accounts of repeal that have failed to study its progress through the Lords have failed to capture the acute tension between the Commons and the Lords on the issue of repeal. The Lords acknowledged, moreover, the danger of opposing the Commons and public opinion on repeal where the Lords' own economic interests were clearly at stake. The potential backlash could raise the specter of *democratic* reform of the House of Lords. Hence, the evidence of this chapter is consistent with the argument that by conceding the economic privilege of protection, the Lords hoped to preserve their political privileges.

Third, current historiography does not capture adequately the complexity of the economic arguments used by the protectionists in the Upper Chamber. Repeal was not simply a threat to their own fortunes but was also said to threaten food security, increase price fluctuations, throw out of cultivation marginal lands, increase rates of rural and urban unemployment, harm the future of colonial trade (and thereby the future of the British empire), and so on (see table 9.3). The analysis of the debates captures these issues very well and also makes transparent the cleavage in the rationale used by the protectionists and those who supported repeal—namely, that the former focused more on the economics, while the latter were more concerned with the political issue of representation. While Gash, McLean, and others would likely agree that politics, not economics, drove repeal in the Lords, the analysis presented here provides detailed empirical evidence for this cleavage between economics and politics.

Fourth, the comparison of the themes in the Commons and the Lords reveals that both MPs and peers were increasingly receptive to the forces of democracy. While the analysis of this chapter does not provide the historical progression of this transformation within the Lords, it is nonetheless striking that peers discussed at length both their role as representatives and the motives of Peel, tussling with the concepts of trustee and delegate. MPs and peers were both coming to understand that their powers as independent political actors (namely, trustees) were becoming limited by democratic activism—made most conspicuous by the lobbying of the Anti-Corn Law League.

In sum, for the Lords, repeal was about politics—but not so much about political personalities as has been suggested. Rather, the evidence is consistent with the argument that peers acted primarily in their own political self-interest, concerning themselves with their longer term in preserving the political privileges of the landed aristocracy in Parliament.

Appendix

Peers Voting for Repeal in the Second Reading Division of the Repeal Bill

Duke of Wellington (yes)

Earl of Haddington (yes)

Earl of Dalhousie (yes)

Earl Granville (yes)

Earl Fitzwilliam (yes)

Earl of Ripon (yes)

Earl of Clarendon (yes)

Earl Grey (yes)

Earl of Essex (yes)

Lord Monteagle (yes)

Lord Brougham (yes)

Marquis of Normanby (yes)

Marquis of Londonderry (yes)

Marquis of Lansdowne (yes)

Viscount Canning (yes)

Peers Voting against Repeal in the Second Reading Division of the Repeal Bill

Duke of Richmond (no)

Duke of Cleveland (no)

Duke of Beaufort (no)

Earl of Malmesbury (no)

Earl Stanhope (no)

Earl of Hardwicke (no)

Earl of Wilton (no)

Earl of Cardigan (no)

Earl of Winchilsea (no)

Earl of Carnarvon (no)

Earl of Eglinton (no)

Lord Beaumont (no)

Lord Ashburton (no)

Lord Stanley (no)

Duke of Cambridge (abstained. In his speech, he stated that he was against repeal but would not vote as he could not bring himself to vote against the government.)

10 Feeling the Heat of the League? How Local Newspapers Affected MPs' Voting on Repeal

Introduction

Every chapter in this book has either directly or indirectly sought to explore the interplay between economic interests and ideas and, occasionally, the constraints and opportunities afforded to interests and ideas by relevant institutions. The premise of this book is that repeal cannot be understood without reference to interests, ideas, and institutions. But to say that each mattered is not sufficient; rather, the task of this book has been to dissect *when* and *under what conditions* interests, ideas, and to a lesser extent institutions gave rise to repeal. To summarize the argument thus far, three sets of actors contributed to the immediacy and, ultimately, the success of repeal. First, the Anti-Corn Law League engaged in a nationalizing the interest strategy that created support for free trade among the general public by highlighting its benefits to the wider societal welfare. This, in turn, exacerbated the demand-side pressure on MPs to repeal the protectionist Corn Laws. Second, once repeal was introduced in Parliament by Prime Minister Peel, Peelites facilitated a reinterpretation of repeal that characterized it as a means to preserve the landed basis of Parliament. This allowed the Peelites to represent the interests of the nascent free-trade-oriented interests in their constituencies more faithfully while at the same time appearing to remain faithful to the ideology of Conservatism. They ultimately voted as delegates but justified their votes in the language of disinterested trustees seeking to promote the larger national welfare. Third, peers in the House of Lords shied away from vetoing or amending the repeal bill because they feared that such a rejection—in the face of widespread public support and the support of a large majority of the Commons—would lead to more radical democratizing reforms targeted particularly at the Upper Chamber. Hence, they were not persuaded by the theories of the political economists, but rather the League convinced them that it was in their own political self-interest to support repeal. At the heart of this argument, then, lies the self-interested motivations of manufacturers, Peelites, and peers.

But to say that interests were primary is not to relegate ideas to a residual category. Interests could not have prevailed without recourse to ideas. First, for the manufacturers who drove the League machine, ideas were fundamentally important to spreading the message of free trade among the British population, and most important was the core idea that free trade would benefit the *whole* of British society, not the interests of a select few. In the words of one historian of British social history, the League argued that protection served to maintain a "privileged monopoly at the expense of the rest of the community, while the League stood for a class, and one which had the same interests as all the producers and consumers, and therefore of the whole community" (Perkin 1969, 372). And quoting Cobden, "The middle class 'have no interest opposed to the general good, whilst, on the contrary, the feudal governing class exists only by a violation of sound principles of political economy'" (Perkin 1969, 372). Second, although Peelites voted more as delegates in 1846, they were eager to characterize their votes as consistent with a revised interpretation of Conservatism—one in which repeal, not protection, served to protect the long-term interests of the landed aristocracy in Parliament, or of the territorial constitution. Had this ideological reinterpretation of repeal not emerged, it would have been far more difficult for Peelites to sell their conversion to constituents (and colleagues) to whom Conservatism as an ideology was essential. Third, while peers supported repeal largely to protect their own political privileges, it was the League's campaign that frightened the peers into acquiescence. The League's ability to persuade the general public of the broader societal merits of free trade frightened peers: such democratic activism provided an example to the more radical Chartist movement (though the relations between the League and the Chartists were tenuous at best) (Brown 1959), and it fomented class conflict against the landowning aristocracy and intraagricultural conflict between tenant farmers and landowners. Without recourse to the ideas of democracy, political economy, and even religion, the League could not have gained such prominence, and without this prominence, it is hard to conceive of the peers being frightened into accepting repeal.

Gaps in the Argument

Yet the evidence presented thus far in support of this argument contains some gaps and raises some questions that must be addressed. First, ample evidence exists that the League spread free-trade ideas to the broader population, in large part owing to its nationalizing the interest strategy. But to sustain an argument that ideas helped to push both Peelites and Liberals toward repeal, we need firm evidence that the lobbying of the Anti-Corn Law League increased in intensity in the lead-up to repeal. Adding to this the evidence of chapters 7 and 8, in which ideas propagated by the League were seen to be expressed by MPs in parliamentary debates, we can be more confident in arguing that demand-side pressures did indeed help to move some MPs toward repeal.

Second, an analysis of roll-call votes suggests that Peelites voted as delegates in 1846 to serve better the interests of their constituents but that they justified their abrupt conversion by reinterpreting Conservative ideology to accommodate repeal. However, it is conceivable that the ideas propagated by the League between 1841 and 1846 (and not the interests of MPs' constituents) accounted for their conversion—that is, it is possible that free-trade ideas in Peelite constituencies escalated to a point sufficient to convert Peelite MPs to repeal. While such an explanation lacks any rationale for the abrupt reversal in 1846, the astute critic might easily fuse this explanation with the supply-side rationale given in chapters 2 and 7 and thus propose an alternative, entirely ideas-driven explanation for the conversion of the Peelites. One might, for instance, argue that the League's democratizing scare tactics helped to facilitate the Peelites' reinterpretation of Conservatism in the early months of 1846, which in turn, led them to endorse repeal.

This would provide a fundamentally different interpretation to the one offered in this book, in which constituency interests feature prominently in accounting for the conversion of Peelites. The argument offered here is that the demand-side pressures (both interests- and ideas-based) pushed the Peelites' ideal point nearer to the brink of repeal (and further from their strongly protectionist Conservative colleagues), but it was the supply-side shift in the interpretation of Conservatism that allowed the Peelites to "jump the fence" to repeal. So to sustain the argument that Peelites were marginally, rather than fundamentally, moved by the force of ideational pressure from their constituents, any observable increase in the intensity of League lobbying should not be seen to be uniquely targeted at Peelites or their constituents. If lobbying by the League is seen to have increased markedly in Peelite constituencies, this would bring into question the importance of changes in constituency interests, such as portfolio diversification (chapter 5), growth in and geographic characteristics of the export sector (chapter 3), and the rather divergent constituency interests of Peelite and Non-Peelite Conservatives (chapter 6). The lack of intensified lobbying in Peelite constituencies would provide at least indirect support for the unique and truly novel reinterpretation of repeal (construed as the introduction of the second dimension) that split the Peelites from the Non-Peelite Conservatives.

Ideas in Local Newspapers
To fill these remaining gaps in the argument, this chapter aims to measure (albeit imprecisely) the free-trade ideas that MPs were exposed to in their constituencies from 1841 to 1846 and then link these figures to their voting records in Parliament. A crude but ostensibly valid measure of the particular set of ideas and arguments to which each MP was sensitive is the coverage of trade policy in the local newspapers for each constituency. To assess the effect of League ideas on the voting behavior of MPs (particularly of Peelites), it is essential to compare the prevalence of these ideas in the districts of Peelites with the same in the districts of Non-Peelite Conservatives, Liberals, and Reformers, and to examine the change in all these districts from 1841 to 1846.

Whether MPs read the newspapers directly or were influenced by electors who read the articles is not something that the data in this chapter can ascertain. More than likely, if influence existed, it came both directly and indirectly. This chapter does not, moreover, consider the possibility that the interests of constituents were changing so rapidly as to be the driving force for any rapid change in ideas between 1841 and 1846. In other words, rapid changes in ideas are unlikely to be epiphenomenal to underlying interests if these interests are deemed not to be changing as rapidly.

The working assumption of this chapter is that the primary direction of the influence of ideas ran from newspapers to MPs (directly or indirectly). Literature on Victorian newspapers supports this assumption, as one of the key features of these newspapers is their overtly political and partisan stance. Indeed, party politics both led to the development of new newspapers to organize voters (Brown 1985, 57) and, in part as a consequence, created a competition between newspapers "which became the norm in provincial Britain, and was organized and articulated through comment on the party struggle" (Brown 1985, 71). Yet the direction of influence between local newspapers and MPs did not flow entirely one way. Newspapers were also influenced by MPs (Koss 1981, 61):

> Although [the] political pretensions [of local newspapers] were as often exaggerated as disparaged, they struck mutually beneficial alliances with local MPs, who shared their backgrounds, favoured them with articles and informal advice, and were vaguely amenable to their influence.

Indeed, this influence of MPs on local newspaper coverage is evident in the many speeches of MPs that are reported verbatim in these newspapers. While this may raise a minor methodological issue—namely, that the assumed independence of ideas (as measured by newspaper coverage) is compromised by dual causality—this is lessened by a deliberate exclusion of MPs' speeches from the analysis (as discussed below).

The rest of this chapter describes how the sample of provincial newspapers was obtained and examines the extent to which it is representative of the larger population of local newspapers. It compares the characteristics of the sampled MPs and the content of their debates with those of the larger population of MPs in the Commons to check that the sampled MPs are indeed representative of the whole chamber, uses more traditional content analysis to analyze the provincial newspapers, and then links this to the voting behavior of the sampled MPs. It concludes by discussing remaining issues.

Sample of Newspapers and MPs

Merits and Demerits of Newspapers

Ideas are invariably difficult to measure empirically. However, provincial newspapers offer a unique tool for measuring the variation in ideas throughout England and their ultimate effect on their representatives in Parliament. Because circulations of provincial newspapers were limited geographically, they can be readily linked to the MPs who represented particular areas.[1] Moreover, provincial newspapers enjoyed relatively wide circulation because they were recirculated and read aloud in public houses (Brown 1985, 49–51). Indeed, one historian of mid-Victorian newspapers commented that "the united influence of [provincial newspapers] vastly outweighed, *within our island*, that of all the London papers put together" (Kellett 1934, 38). Provincial newspapers provided up-to-date coverage and also underpinned the cleavage between northern and southern England (Kellett 1934, 38):

> There were then few or no means by which the London papers could reach the provinces early enough to compete with [the provincial newspapers]; the northern manufacturer received his northern paper at breakfast, and read no other; and, as a result, his views were often found... to be staggeringly at variance with those of the south.

Finally, because newspapers were considered, "as if by definition, an indispensable political weapon" (Lee 1976, 150), they are particularly appropriate for measuring the influence of political ideas on politicians.

Indeed, in the early nineteenth century, newspapers could be identified readily by partisan bias and were recorded as such in directories and advertising lists. Table 10.1 provides the partisan affiliation of

Table 10.1
Sample and population of provincial newspapers, by political affiliation

	Conservative	Liberal	Neutral/ Independent	Total
Sample:				
Full newspaper sample	49.4% (77)	36.5% (57)	14.1% (22)	100% (156)
Restricted newspaper sample	47.0% (40)	38.8% (33)	14.1% (12)	100% (85)
Population:				
1842: All English provincial newspapers (Francis D. Lewis, *Advertising List*)	42.2% (89)	51.7% (109)	6.2% (13)	100% (211)
1842: All English provincial newspapers (*Hammonds Town and Country Advertising List*)	43.9% (90)	49.3% (101)	6.8% (14)	100% (205)
1846: *Newspaper Press Directory* (including England, Ireland, Scotland, and the British Isles)	35.5% (195)	38.7% (213)	25.8% (142)	100% (550)

Sources: Lee (1976, 290); *Newspaper Press Directory* (1846, 322).
Note: The full newspaper sample includes newspapers that were duplicated in cases where MPs sat for the same area or where they were subject to the same local newspapers (for instance, for MPs who sat for a borough within a county or where, as with Rutlandshire and Lincolnshire MPs, newspaper coverage was the same).

both the sampled newspapers and the larger population of newspapers. The sample is given in two forms. The "full" sample contains some double-counting of newspapers, since newspapers invariably covered the districts of more than one MP (for example, a borough MP and a county MP might share some or all newspapers, and multiple-member districts meant that MPs representing the same district would share the same set of newspapers). Hence, two or more MPs might be exposed to the same set of ideas if they represented districts that were subject to the same local newspapers. The "restricted" sample counts each newspaper just once and is reported here only for sake of transparency.

The population figures are given both for English provincial newspapers in 1842 and for the larger population of all newspapers in England, Ireland, Scotland, and the British Isles in 1846.[2] As a share of the total English provincial newspapers, the sample obtains about 40 percent. By further inspection, the sample overrepresents the Conservative newspapers for both England and the United Kingdom, though only marginally for the former. The sample underrepresents the Liberal newspapers for England but quite accurately represents them for the United Kingdom. The rather odd difference between the English and U.K. newspapers is the much larger share of neutral (or class)[3] newspapers in the United Kingdom population.[4] The sample neatly follows a middle course by overrepresenting the English newspapers and underrepresenting the U.K. ones. Overall, it seems prudent to conclude that the sample may well be biased in favor of Conservative (protectionist) views and against Liberal (free-trade) views, and so evidence of strong protectionist "ideas" that might emerge from the analysis should be treated with caution. Put another way, the sample is biased against observing a growth in reform ideas—such as repeal.

The advantages from using local newspaper coverage of trade policy as a measure of the ideas to which MPs were politically sensitive are also matched by some disadvantages or problems.

First, an examination of all the local newspapers for all the MPs of the 1841 to 1847 Parliament would be a highly time-consuming research effort. Hence, as has been indicated, a representative sample of forty-eight MPs was selected for an analysis of local newspaper coverage. These MPs are listed in book appendix 5, along with their constituency, the newspapers covering their district (along with its partisan bias), their speaking record during the 1846 repeal debates, their party affiliation, their voting record, and other information.

Second, because the focus of major London newspapers was (and still is) geared toward a national audience, these newspapers (and London MPs) were excluded from the analysis. More to the point, the intent of this analysis is to allow variation across local constituencies and their representative MPs, and so London newspapers would, by definition, blur this variation.

Third, newspapers invariably reported—sometimes verbatim—the speeches of their representative MPs. As these speeches articulated the sentiments and motivations of MPs and did not reflect what might be construed as the "exogenous" force of ideas on MPs, all speeches and statements by MPs in the newspapers have been excluded from analysis.

Fourth, it was not uncommon for MPs to live outside their constituencies, and so they might arguably have been less aware of the content of local newspapers. As can be seen from book appendix 5, about a quarter of the sample lived outside their constituencies. However, it seems reasonable to assume that even these MPs would have kept on top of the coverage of such a critical and contentious subject as repeal, even if they did so from a distance. Hence, this is not considered to be unduly problematic.

The final problem is more intractable—namely, that the so-called ideas discussed in newspapers may very well reflect underlying interests. Hence, one might critically argue that no real divide can be constructed between ideas and interests. This problem raises the broader issue of the exogeneity and endogeneity of interests and ideas. Invariably, the causal links between interests and ideas are complex and will vary from context to context. However, if ideas and interests can be understood in terms of Balentine Venn diagrams in a given explanatory space (akin to independent variables in linear regression analysis) (Kennedy 1992, 48–49, 99–100), then it is demonstrably easier to estimate their independent effects when they diverge (fail to overlap) than when they converge. In other words, if interests and ideas point to the same policy position, it would be more difficult to ascertain which matters more. However, if we assume that between 1841 and 1846 constituency interests had not suddenly and overwhelmingly shifted toward free trade (and thus remained relatively fixed) but that the climate of ideas had become highly charged with arguments for and against free trade, then a textual analysis of newspaper coverage that indicates a marked change in coverage of trade policy between 1841 and 1846 is likely to be the product of a change in ideas rather than a change in interests. (Methodologically, this is equivalent to holding interests constant while allowing ideas to vary.)

In sum, if it can be seen that free-trade ideas (propagated by the League) increased more dramatically in Peelite districts than in Non-Peelite districts, this would suggest that perhaps Peelites did not vote more as delegates in 1846 (contrary to the premise of this book) but instead voted ideologically, reflecting the enhanced free-trade ideas to which they had been exposed in their constituencies. If, however, we observe that there was little or no change in the ideas in Peelite districts or that free-trade ideas increased more in Non-Peelite Conservatives' districts than in Peelite districts, taken at face value this would suggest that the ideas of the League had little or no impact on the abrupt reversal of the Peelites (though these ideas may very well have contributed to the longer-term movement of the ideal points of both Peelites and Liberal MPs).

Details of the Sample

Two prerequisites were imposed in selecting the sample of MPs. First, MPs had to have spoken at some point during the 1846 debates on repeal. Having spoken in Parliament demonstrated a minimal level of understanding and competence on the issue of repeal. In other words, these MPs probably had read the coverage on repeal in their local newspapers and were willing to publicly express their own rationale for voting. MPs who did not speak in the debates may very well have been equally attentive to their local newspapers, but this seems less likely. Second, the MP must have had at least one newspaper (outside London) that purported to cover his constituency. In total, 240 English MPs (outside London) were found to have a newspaper published in their constituency or a newspaper that purported to cover their constituency. The indexes of *Hansard's Parliamentary Debates* were used to obtain the list of speakers for the 1846 debates,[5] and the *Newspaper Press Directory, 1846* provided information to ascertain the geographic coverage of local newspapers. According to the Hansard indexes, 205 MPs spoke in the 1846 debates on repeal, and of these, 170 represented English constituencies, 11 Scottish, 19 Irish, and 5 Welsh. Of the 170 English MPs, there were 91 MPs who both spoke on repeal and had local newspaper coverage of their constituencies. Listed alphabetically by surname, every other MP was selected, thereby giving a sample of forty-six. Yet as the goal of this analysis is to capture the impact of the ideas propagated by (and lobbying activities of) the Anti-Corn Law

Table 10.2
Comparison of constituency and party statistics for sample of forty-eight MPs and the whole of the House of Commons

Variable	Variable Categories	Sample	House of Commons[a]
Constituency type	Borough	52.1% (25)	30.5% (180)
	County	47.9% (23)	69.5% (410)
District economic orientation	Most protectionist	45.8% (22)	23.9% (141)
	Protectionist oriented	25.0% (12)	44.6% (263)
	Neutral	8.3% (4)	17.6% (104)
	Free-trade oriented	12.5% (6)	9.2% (54)
	Most free trade	8.3% (4)	4.7% (28)
Party affiliation	Non-Peelite Conservative	52.1% (25)	46.6% (275)
	Peelite	14.6% (7)	15.4% (91)
	Whig-Liberal	20.8% (10)	25.4% (150)
	Reformer	12.5% (6)	12.5% (74)
Vote on third reading of repeal	Against repeal	54.2% (26)	34.2% (202)
	For repeal	41.7% (20)	41.4% (244)
	Abstain	4.2% (2)	24.4% (144)

a. These figures include English MPs only. The totals for the votes do not tally precisely with those in the regression analysis, as some cases are omitted from missing data.

League, I supplemented the forty-six with two further MPs who represented districts in which the League was clearly active. Recall that table 2.1 reported districts in which the League challenged electors. Of the ninety-one MPs in the sampling frame, six MPs represented one of these districts. Listed alphabetically by surname (Denison, Fitzmaurice, Ingestre, Morpeth, Thompson, Worcester), the first and the last of these MPs were selected and added to the sample, giving a total number of forty-eight.

Tables 10.2 and 10.3 gauge the representativeness of the sample according to key characteristics and in terms of the content of their speeches. From table 10.2, we can see that the two most conspicuous differences between the sample and the larger population of MPs concerns the type of constituency and MPs' votes on the third reading of the repeal bill. In the sample, borough MPs are overrepresented, and county MPs are underrepresented. But given that MPs were deliberately selected on the basis of containing at least one local newspaper, this bias toward urban areas is not surprising. As borough MPs tended to be more free-trade oriented, this bias might overrate the effect of

Table 10.3
Comparison of basic statistics for sample of forty-eight MPs and the whole of the House of Commons, 1846

	Sample of 48 MPs	House of Commons
Total word count	234,390	922,240
Unique words analyzed	88,912	339,713
Passive variables (tagged indicators)	75	238
ICUs (= number of speeches)	103	587
Classified ECUs	4,060 (= 74% of the retained ECU)	7,093 (= 80% of the retained ECU)
Lexical classes	6	6
Distribution of classes (%)	1: 19.63 (Agricultural production and agricultural trade) 2: 13.03 (Trustee/delegate; class and national interests) 3: 11.97 (Wages and prices) 4: 10.71 (International trade) 5: 17.83 (Timing of repeal) 6: 26.82 (Parliamentary rhetoric)	1: 19.44 (Wages and prices; high farming) 2: 10.36 (MPs as trustees) 3: 9.49 (Electoral connection) 4: 10.77 (Agricultural market and Ireland) 5: 30.99 (Parliamentary rhetoric and timing of repeal) 6: 18.95 (International trade)

free-trade ideas on borough MPs, and so this should be considered when examining the results. The second difference between the sample and the population of MPs is that the former underrepresents the number of MPs who abstained on the third reading of the repeal bill. However, once again, this is a deliberate bias, as abstainers were less likely to have spoken in the debates and therefore were less likely to have been included in the sample. The undersampling of these MPs should be considered in the analysis of the results.

Table 10.3 presents the basic statistics from an Alceste analysis of both the sample MPs and the whole of the House of Commons in 1846 (the latter is presented in chapter 7). Predictably, the first four rows (which essentially measure the volume of text for analysis) give smaller figures for the sample than for the whole of the Commons. The percentage of classified elementary context units (ECUs) is a little less than for the whole of the Commons. More interesting, the number of classes is the same, and the content of the classes remarkably similar between the sample and the population. Each of the classes in the sample can be mapped to one from the larger population. The only class from the larger population that cannot be directly matched to the sample is electoral connection, but as this theme fits with the larger discussion of trustee and delegate, an indirect link may be made. Overall, the content of the sample MPs' debates fits reasonably well with that of the whole of the Commons.

Content Analysis of Provincial Newspapers

The primary goal in analyzing newspaper coverage of trade policy is to gauge the change in ideas from the early 1840s to 1846. Hence, all newspaper articles on or relating to trade policy were summarized for two six-month time periods: from March 1841 to August and September 1841 and from October 1845 to April and May 1846.[6] The first time period captures the period before and the general election of 1841, while the second covers the period both before and after Peel introduced the repeal bill in 1846. These offer optimal "early" and "late" time periods as both were highly politicized and focused on the prospect of a change in the Corn Laws.[7] As mentioned earlier, coverage of MPs' speeches was then deleted from the main text file.[8]

An attempt was first made to analyze the text file (of approximately 61,000 words) using the Alceste software. However, the program failed to produce stable classes, even with a number of alterations in the parameters. The size of the file precludes the possibility that the corpus was too small (as the minimum size is 10,000 words). The second precondition of Alceste—that the text be coherent in its content—is clearly not met by the variety of newspaper articles and by virtue of most of the articles having been summarized rather than entered verbatim.

I thus resorted to more traditional content analysis. Table 8.7 from chapter 8 identified the themes that emerged from the parliamentary debates of 1842 to 1844 and 1846. In slightly simplified form, these are as follows:

1. Wages of labor/wages and prices; high farming
2. International grain supply and international grain trade
3. Agricultural market (3a) and Ireland (3b)
4. International trade
5. Timing of repeal
6. Electoral connection
7. Class conflict

Feeling the Heat of the League? 275

8. MPs as trustees
9. Peel's sliding scale
10. Anti-Corn Law League and Anti-League

Beginning with these ten themes, my research assistant and I read each article summary and agreed on which themes were exhibited. Not surprisingly, other topics were prominent in some articles, and so we began an "other" set of topics, which in the end summed to nine. Thus, each article was coded according to a possible total of nineteen themes. However, no article contained anywhere close to this number, with the norm being about three or four codes.

The coded newspaper coverage for each MP was entered into a Excel spreadsheet, so that each MP was assigned an array of codes for each time period. These were then analyzed with descriptive statistics and in graphical form.[9]

Figure 10.1 provides a bar chart of the *percentage* distribution of the nineteen themes separated by time period. One topic dominated—the League and the Anti-League—and this topic increased in coverage

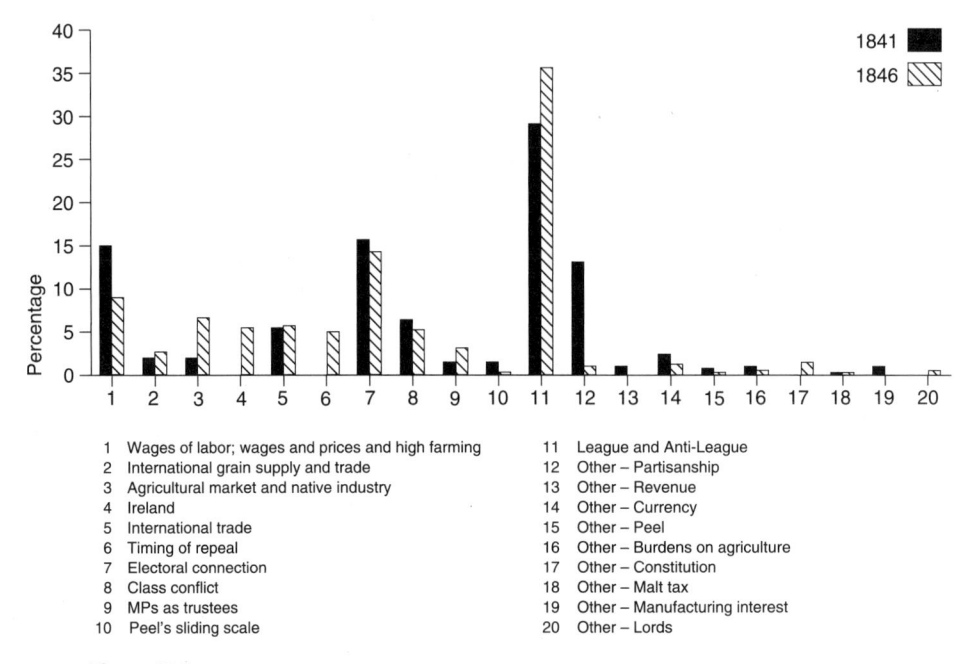

1 Wages of labor; wages and prices and high farming
2 International grain supply and trade
3 Agricultural market and native industry
4 Ireland
5 International trade
6 Timing of repeal
7 Electoral connection
8 Class conflict
9 MPs as trustees
10 Peel's sliding scale
11 League and Anti-League
12 Other – Partisanship
13 Other – Revenue
14 Other – Currency
15 Other – Peel
16 Other – Burdens on agriculture
17 Other – Constitution
18 Other – Malt tax
19 Other – Manufacturing interest
20 Other – Lords

Figure 10.1
Newspaper sample: Coverage by topic

quite markedly from 1841 to 1846. By 1846, well over a third of the newspaper articles examined mentioned the League or the Anti-League. Three other topics featured prominently—wages of labor, electoral connection, and partisanship. Each of these three topics, however, declined in coverage between 1841 to 1846—with partisanship declining sharply to its more natural level after the general election of 1841. Two topics were new to 1846—Ireland and the timing of repeal—and each received about 5 percent of the total coverage. As one would expect, newspaper coverage of the Irish potato famine linked the prospect of repeal with famine relief in Ireland. As we saw in chapter 7, however, most MPs either did not accept the government's characterization of the severity of the famine or did not believe that repeal would be the appropriate policy tool for addressing the problem. Famine was certainly covered in the newspapers, but it did not appear to drive the momentum for repeal. That the topic of timing of repeal—the question of whether repeal should be effective immediately, the Corn Laws suspended temporarily (to provided temporary relief for Ireland), or repeal adopted with a three-year delay in implementation—received a notable amount of attention is intriguing, as it suggests that the British public was reasonably well informed on the more detailed aspects of the repeal bill and its alternatives.

Inasmuch as commentary on the Anti-Corn Law League dominated provincial newspapers and this dominance increased considerably from 1841 to 1846, this provides indirect empirical support for the argument that League pressure (in the form of ideas) on MPs increased in the years leading up to repeal.

But to gauge further whether this ideational pressure pushed any MPs toward repeal, we must sort the articles according to their protectionist or free-trade bias. Figure 10.2 examines only those articles that mentioned the League or Anti-League and sorts them by orientation into protectionist, free trade, and neutral. In 1841, of the 103 articles mentioning this topic, 80 (78 percent) supported protection, 22 (21 percent) free trade or repeal, and one (1 percent) was neutral or unclear. By 1846, of the 137 articles mentioning this topic, 76 (55 percent) supported protection, 45 (33 percent) free trade or repeal, and 16 (12 percent) were neutral. Recalling that our sample overrepresents Conservative newspapers—and virtually all of these supported protection—it is not surprising that the majority of articles in both periods favored protection. But for our purposes, what is important is the *change* in coverage between 1841 and 1846, and this was toward free

Feeling the Heat of the League?

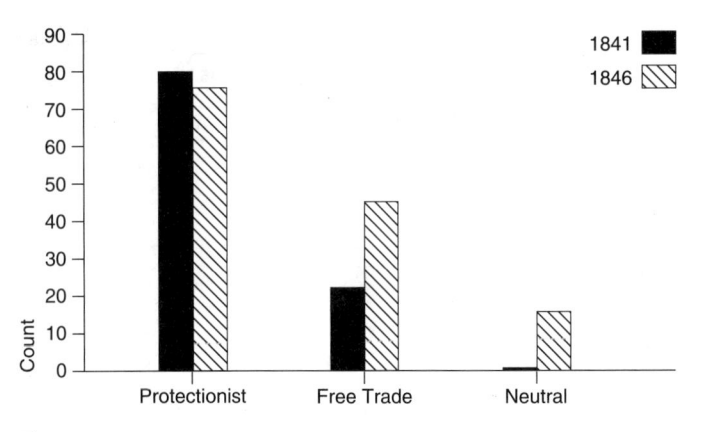

Figure 10.2
Newspaper references to the League

trade (and neutrality or indecision). The actual number of articles that supported protection, though still high, fell off marginally in 1846. Hence, the evidence thus far suggests (1) that the League/Anti-League campaigns dominated the provincial press in 1841 and increased this dominance by 1846 and (2) that protectionist commentaries dominated press coverage in both periods (though the sample likely overestimates this dominance) but that pro-free-trade coverage articles increased significantly during this period (from 21 to 33 percent), thus reducing the protectionist dominance from 78 percent to just 55 percent.

Ultimately, however, we want to know whether the protectionist and free-trade ideas discussed in the newspapers correlates with the voting behavior of MPs. In figures 10.3 and 10.4, the articles that mentioned the League/Anti-League by MPs' voting pattern on key roll-call votes from 1842 to 1846 are sorted so that we can observe the variation in newspaper coverage across the range of MPs. As described in the notes at the end of the table in book appendix 5, MPs were divided into one of eight possible categories, ranging from very strong protectionist to very strong free trader (the number of MPs in each of these categories is given below its label). Of key importance to this analysis are the very strong and strong protectionists, who were essentially the Non-Peelite Conservatives, and the very weak free traders, who were essentially the Peelites.

Figure 10.3 shows the change in free-trade-oriented newspaper coverage, while figure 10.4 shows the change in protectionist coverage. From figure 10.3, the most dramatic increase in free-trade coverage

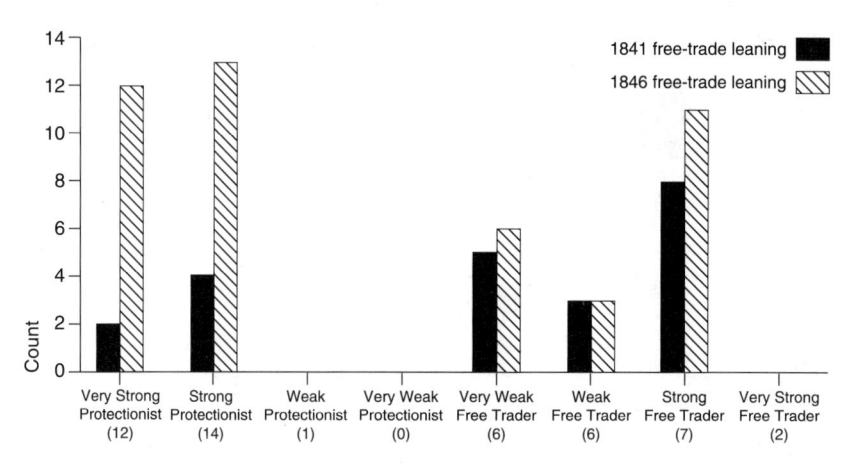

Figure 10.3
Newspaper articles mentioning the League, by MP voting pattern: Free-trade leaning

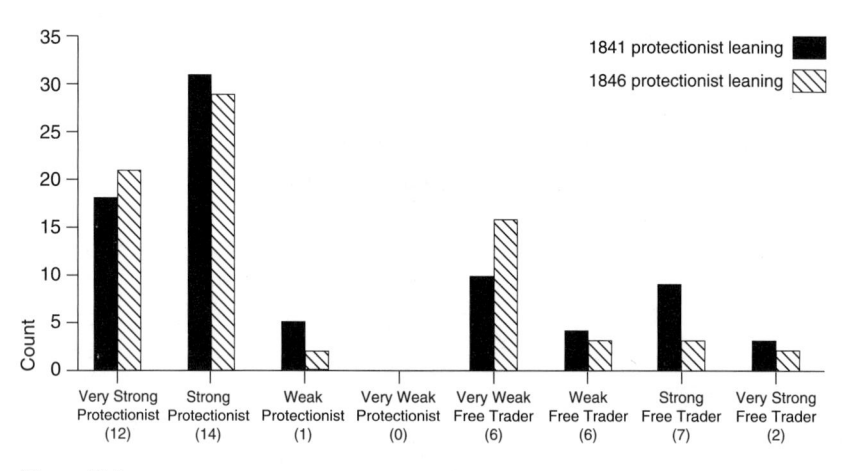

Figure 10.4
Newspaper articles mentioning the League, by MP voting pattern: Protectionist leaning

occurred in the districts represented by Non-Peelite Conservatives (the protectionists). While free-trade newspaper commentaries increased in the districts represented by Peelites (very weak free traders), this increase was only marginal. The free-trade coverage in the districts of strong free traders increased as well, but this is less surprising as it was merely preaching to the converted. Figure 10.4 shows that Non-Peelite Conservatives experienced very little difference in the levels of protectionist coverage from their local newspapers from 1841 to 1846.

Peelites did witness an increase in protectionist-leaning commentaries from 1841 to 1846, and strong and very strong free traders saw a reduction in protectionist-leaning news articles during the time period.

These findings will likely surprise some historians, but they fit well with the argument of this book. In a nutshell, we find that the free-trade ideas to which Non-Peelite Conservatives were exposed increased dramatically as a result of the lobbying campaign of the Anti-Corn Law League. Yet these ideas do not appear to have persuaded these MPs to vote for repeal. Rather, as I have suggested in earlier chapters, they remained wedded to the protectionist interests in their constituencies and to a traditional Conservative ideology in which protection was the route to preserving the interests of the landowning aristocracy in Parliament. As for the Peelites, free-trade ideas increased only marginally, while protectionist ideas increased as well —very likely producing little net overall effect. Yet the Peelites converted dramatically and abruptly to repeal in 1846, which reversed the position of all their previous votes on repeal. Peelites, it would seem, did not experience any dramatic changes in the ideas to which they were exposed in their constituencies from 1841 to 1846, and so it seems unlikely that any change in ideas *outside* Parliament led to their conversion to free trade. Their conversion appears to have been independent of the ideas to which they were exposed, a finding that lends indirect support to the contention that the abrupt conversion of Peelites is best explained as a product of longer-term demand-side pressures, coupled with the short-term supply-side shift in the ideology of Conservatism that took place in the early months of 1846.

Discussion and Conclusion

Two issues remain to be discussed. First, while a small number of biases in the sample have been identified, it is doubtful that any of these significantly affected the results. For example, the overrepresentation of Conservative newspapers might have biased the results *against* finding growth in free-trade ideas, so the growth in these ideas that has been identified by the sample is likely to be even greater than reported here. Moreover, to the extent that borough MPs are overrepresented and county MPs underrepresented *and* free-trade ideas were more prevalent in urban areas (such as boroughs), the findings may overrate the effect of free-trade ideas on MPs. But inasmuch as the evidence of any effect of free-trade ideas on the pivotal Peelite

MPs is minimal, one could conjecture that the actual effect of free-trade ideas on these MPs was almost nonexistent. Finally, the undersampling of MPs who abstained is unlikely to create any bias in the results, since there exists no rationale in the literature to suggest that these MPs were linked in any way by a common reason for failing to vote. Hence, such abstinences might contribute to the overall noise but not contribute to a bias.

The second issue is how well the analysis of this chapter has filled the gaps in the larger argument. The first gap was the lack of firm evidence that the lobbying of the Anti-Corn Law League increased in intensity in the lead-up to repeal, without which it was difficult to argue with confidence that League-sponsored demand-side pressures did indeed nudge Peelites and Liberals toward repeal. From figure 10.1, we find an increase in newspaper coverage of League activity of about 7 percent between 1841 and 1846, with League activity accounting for about 36 percent of the newspaper coverage on trade policy in 1846. (Admittedly, however, coverage of Ireland and the timing of repeal also increased during this time, though this does not detract from the marked increase in coverage of the League.) In short, ideational pressure from League activity did contribute to the out-of-doors, demand-side pressure for repeal. The second gap essentially raised the possibility that this increased intensity in free-trade lobbying—and not the difference in constituency economic makeup that existed between Non-Peelite Conservatives and Peelites—might have accounted for the conversion of Peelites. However, figures 10.3 and 10.4 show that Peelites do not appear to have experienced any dramatic changes in the ideas to which they were exposed in their constituencies, and so it would be difficult to argue that ideas alone explain their conversion to free trade. By weakening this as a plausible alternative, the evidence of this chapter strengthens the argument that the abrupt reversal of the Peelites is best understood as the product of both demand-side pressures (most notably, the increasingly free-trade-oriented interests of their constituents) and the reinterpretation of Conservative ideology that occurred in the early months of 1846.

In the final analysis, Cobden was probably correct in his assessment that the Corn Laws had been repealed too soon. The demand-side pressures that pushed for repeal were gaining momentum in the 1840s, but their force was simply insufficient to account for the success of repeal in the House of Commons. Peelites do not seem to have been converted by the force of economic logic of free trade (as articulated by the League) or by the democratic activism of the League, though these factors very probably helped to move them toward the brink of repeal.

Yet the interesting and unexpected finding of this chapter—namely, that Non-Peelite Conservative MPs experienced the most dramatic increase in free-trade ideas—suggests that staunch protectionists were experiencing fierce lobbying by the League and its supporters. Yet they failed to convert. This is not to say that the efforts of the League were in vain, as this pressure no doubt contributed to the successful passage of the repeal bill in the Lords. In the final analysis, it may be concluded that the free-trade lobbying of the League created an environment in which the interests of key actors could utilize ideas to gain advantage but that it was the interests of these actors (and those of their constituents) that most effectively carried repeal to its successful conclusion.

11 Concluding Thoughts on Repeal and the Road to Democratic Reform in Nineteenth-Century Britain

Introduction

In dissecting Britain's repeal of the Corn Laws, I may have at times stretched the patience of some readers—particularly those with little sympathy for empirical analysis. The first section of this concluding chapter will, I hope, ease the frustration of these readers by providing what might be considered the bottom line in my retelling of the repeal story. This unadulterated version of repeal provides a simple narrative of what gave rise to the repeal legislation and what, in the end, appears to best explain its passage. Yet this simplified account of repeal serves another purpose, and that is to suggest ways in which this book might contribute to the larger historiography on repeal and nineteenth-century British politics. In other words, it addresses the inevitable (and quite important) question of the British historian: "What has this book told us that we did not already know"?[1]

The conclusion then returns to the more theoretical issue of the interaction of interests, ideas, and institutions. In particular, the final section addresses a question often posed by political scientists: if interests are fundamentally important in determining the behavior of political actors, to what extent can ideas be said to have an independent effect? This section also examines how both interests and ideas appear to have shaped the development of the institutions of parliamentary democracy in Britain and how those institutions may have shaped repeal.

The Unadulterated Version of Repeal

The Demand for Free Trade
British industrialization contributed to repeal in three ways. First, it gave rise to pressure from middle-class industrialists for greater

political representation, which in turn resulted in the 1832 Reform Act. While this act had little immediate impact on the control of Parliament by landowning aristocrats, it served to recognize the importance of industrialists to the future of Britain and thereby served as a backdrop to the later debates over free trade. With respect to repeal per se, the 1832 Reform Act—or more specifically, its 40 shilling franchise—allowed the industrialists' lobby, the Anti-Corn Law League, to create free-trade electors. This, together with challenging the qualifications of protectionist electors, made the League's threat of an elected free-trade majority in Parliament a credible one. In short, the Reform Act provided the League with an important tactical advantage in its efforts to repeal the Corn Laws: it gave the industrialists the means to "buy" a free-trade majority in Parliament and, in so doing, posed a threat to the landed basis of Parliament.

Second, with the growth of the cotton textile industry, economic interests in free trade both intensified and spread geographically, which in turn gave rise to the Anti-Corn Law League. Two features unique to Britain's industrialization help explain the timing and organizational success of its free-trade lobbying. First, geographic concentration of the textile industry into Lancashire acted both to concentrate resources available for launching the free-trade campaign and to concentrate the expected benefits accruing from free trade, hence motivating this core of industrialists to bear a disproportionate burden of the lobbying effort. Second, an increase in the number of industries comprising the export sector, combined with geographic deconcentration of export-oriented interests, enhanced the political leverage of the League by broadening its base of support. Its propaganda and voter registration campaigns thereby enjoyed a geographically broader base of support, and the free-trade message of the League appealed to the recently expanded number of interests connected to the export trade.

A third feature of British industrialization was the rapidly emerging capital market, which encouraged diversification of the asset portfolios of some landowners. The policy preferences of landowners on average thus became slightly less protectionist as their incomes became less tied to agricultural rents. MPs representing constituencies with more such diversified landowners were also more likely to support free trade.

As a result of industrialization, then, British industrialists gained momentum in their struggle for free trade while protectionist landowners lost strength. But the battle between the classes did not rely on interests alone, as the League targeted its appeal to the general public by linking free trade to three compelling ideas (a strategy that I have titled "nationalizing the interest"): (1) national prosperity, (2) morality and Christianity, and (3) the injustice of an aristocratic monopoly. The evidence does not suggest that this campaign of ideas pushed the pivotal Peelites over to repeal; rather, its apparent effect was more subtle and indirect. It sought to persuade workers and farmers (who were uncertain of the economic effects of free trade) that repeal would indeed benefit them. It also sought to persuade landowners (who benefited from protection) to support repeal for reasons unrelated to their own self-interest. It thereby sought to create a torrent of public opinion in favor of repeal.

The net effect of these demand-side pressures was twofold. First, it created more support for repeal among Liberal MPs between 1842 and 1846. Second, it widened the division between the two interest-based factions of the Conservative party. Peelites, who represented districts with comparatively more free-trade-leaning interests, faced a conflict between their concern for Conservatism and their representation of constituents who were either borderline protectionist or leaning toward free trade. Non-Peelite Conservatives, who represented mostly agricultural districts, had no motivation to follow Peel as he moved for repeal: both their Conservatism and their representation of rural constituencies pointed toward retaining a firm commitment to protection. In short, *the demand-side pressures brought more Liberals into the repeal camp and brought Peelites nearer to the brink of converting to repeal.*

How Free Trade Was Supplied (or What Economic Interests Alone Fail to Tell Us)

In 1846, Peelites were torn between, on the one hand, representing the increasing free-trade-oriented interests of their constituents and, on the other hand, remaining loyal to a Conservative ideology that sought to defend traditional British institutions, including protection. Agricultural protection was crucial to constitutional conservatism because it "preserved the landed basis of the British constitution" (Gambles 1999, 58). In other words, an economic monopoly was thought to underpin a political monopoly. Moreover, the concept of the "territorial constitution," in which individuals most affected by the policies of government (the landowners) were judged to be the ones most appropriate to determine those policies, was grounded in works of prominent seventeenth- and eighteenth-century writers, and it was this concept that was core to the Conservative ideology.

As Peelites observed the growth of interests linked to manufacturing and trade—partly in their own districts but also throughout the country—the pressure for repeal mounted. For Peelites to justify their support for repeal in terms of the interests of their constituents would, however, wholly cut against the grain of Conservatism. Indeed, most Peelites would have rejected the Liberal notion of legislators as delegates and so would have sought other compelling reasons to justify their abrupt reversal. Perhaps most important, they would seek to square these reasons with their Conservative ideology.

Before 1846, Peelites voted according to their Conservative (protectionist) ideology, but in January 1846, Peel offered them a way to embrace their constituents' interests *and* appear to remain faithful to Conservatism. If protectionism could be legitimately excluded from the umbrella of traditional institutions, then Conservatives who voted for repeal (Peelites) could profess to be adhering to the respected *trustee* mode of representation, rather than caving into popular demand, as a *delegate* might do. Peel characterized repeal as a means to preserve the traditional institutions of the British government—and, in particular, the aristocracy. While Peel offered a plethora of justifications and rationales for repeal, this one in particular resonated with the Peelites because it provided them with the means to endorse repeal. Even though all Conservatives agreed on the preservation of the territorial constitution, Peelites came to believe that repeal constituted a new means to that end. This form of argumentation provided Peelites with the ideological cover to move into the repeal camp. Peelites followed Peel because his rationale for repeal offered a Conservative cover to enable them to align with their increasingly free-trade-oriented constituencies. By trumpeting themselves as loyal to the longer-term preservation of the territorial constitution, and judging that repeal was a necessary concession to ensure this outcome, Peelites could vote as delegates without having to justify themselves as such.

Even with successful passage in the House of Commons in May 1846, however, the repeal legislation faced the prospect of rejection by the House of Lords, an unelected body of aristocratic landowners that feared the growing "democratic tendencies" of the Lower Chamber. Fearing a rejection or amendment to repeal by the Lords, Peel and his Cabinet laid the groundwork for a possible constitutional crisis. Yet such crisis failed to emerge as the Lords—with some resistance—reluctantly accepted repeal. In the end, the Lords acknowledged the danger of opposing the Commons and public opinion more generally—particularly on repeal, where their own economic interests were clearly perceived to be at stake.[2] As a landowning elite, should the Lords reject repeal, they would undoubtedly face accusations of placing economic self-interest above the well-being of the nation. The Lords were, moreover, alarmed by the agitation of the Anti-Corn Law League, and they feared that their rejection of repeal would ignite more radical demands for sweeping democratic reforms, such as universal suffrage and reform of the House of Lords. Hence, they saw their own political self-interest to be tied to repeal. By conceding the economic privilege of protection, they hoped to stave off democratizing reforms even more momentous than the 1832 Reform Act. Repeal was a compromise that preserved, for the time being, the territorial constitution.

Interests, Ideas, and Institutions (Again)

What Do We Know Now That We Did Not Already Know?

Particular aspects of the story above will ring true to historians—namely, the occasional focus on ideas. Indeed, a couple of relatively recent accounts of repeal by political historians will illustrate the importance that they tend to assign to ideas and ideology. But if we compare these accounts to the findings in this book, we can see a frequent omission by some of these authors: by elevating the importance of ideas, they often fail to recognize the motivations given to actors by their interests.

First, most political historians will no doubt acknowledge the importance of the ideas around which the League constructed its nationalizing strategy (namely, free trade as crucial to Britain's prosperity, the religious dimension of free trade, and the emphasis on class conflict). Howe (1997, 36), for instance, notes that by 1846, "the League had successfully turned free trade into a popular moral crusade, converting a 'pocket question' for the cotton lords into a symbol of new community of interest and a new understanding of the nation itself. Free trade rapidly replaced the Corn Laws as a symbol of Britishness." Yet as chapter 3 has suggested, a specific configuration of economic interests account for the initial organizational success of the League, and without this success, no "popular moral crusade" would have emerged. But equally important, the evidence in chapter 10 has shown that however effective the League may have been in fomenting a public opinion in favor of repeal (and in so doing, frightening both MPs and peers with the prospect of more radical agitation), its war of ideas did not appear to account for the abrupt reversal of the Peelites, which is the fundamental key to understanding repeal. So the League's crusade was important—particularly in persuading Liberal MPs and frightening peers—but without integrating this with the interest-based motivations of constituents, one is left with an inadequate account of repeal.

A second example from the political-history literature illustrates the emphasis placed on liberal economic ideology in contributing to the free-trade outcome. In his analysis of European aristocrats in the nineteenth century, Lieven provides one of the clearest statement (by a recent political historian) of the motivations of the pivotal Peelites (Lieven 1992, 232–233):

> What united most of these men was not their backgrounds but their ethos, particularly their attitude to government. They prided themselves on their sense of responsibility and their commitment to the public interest. They were efficient administrators, believers in the most modern ideas of *laissez-faire* economics, and wholly honest and incorruptible public servants—in total contrast to their ancestors, the eighteenth-century spoilsmen. In their political views they were liberal conservatives, enemies of democracy but believers that aristocracy must earn its position, rule efficiently in the general interest and reform abuses.... Above all, many of them came to despise their landowning backbenchers, especially after 1846. The Corn Laws were not the only issue here, though the Peelites saw the Tory stand on this as preferring selfish to national interests, in the process damaging the legitimacy of the ruling class.

As Lieven (1992, 237) explains, repeal of the Corn Laws was part of a larger "spirit of liberal-conservatism in the English high aristocracy" in the mid- to late-nineteenth century, in which "the high aristocracy as a whole believed that liberal tendencies dominated the age in which they lived and that stubborn resistance to these tendencies could only lead to disaster."

This portrayal of the Peelites fits into the theme of Peelites as "independent" MPs or the ultimate trustees (as discussed in chapter 6). This book, however, has argued that in 1846, Peelites voted more in line with the economic interests of their constituents yet enveloped this abrupt reversal into a newly defined Conservatism to eschew any image of catering to constituency demands. At the same time, they, like their colleagues in the Lords, recognized that "stubborn resistance" to repeal (and political reform both before and after repeal) could indeed lead to the type of disaster that was subsequently seen with the French Revolution of 1848. So the fundamental question is whether Peelites acted according to interests or according to ideas. The answer that this book provides is that Peelites voted according to constituency interests (as delegates) but justified their votes in terms of public-spirited Conservatism (as trustees) who sought to maintain the territorial constitution in the wake of agitation that would otherwise lead to more radical and possibly revolutionary change. In short, Peelites acted according to constituency interests in the end, but the means to that end required a prominent role for ideas.

The Fascination with Interests

If historians can be partially blinded by the prominence of ideas, so too can political scientists become mesmerized by the importance of economic interests. As noted in chapter 1, interest-based explanations for repeal divide into two levels—micro-level analyses of key actors or groups (such as industrialists, landowners, and the League) and macro-level analyses of Britain's relative gains from free trade. Micro-level analyses tend to characterize repeal within a simple demand-side model, with no significant role for either ideas or institutions.[3] Macro-level analyses maintain that domestic interests and politics (and thus repeal) were shaped by Britain's concern with its relative position in the international arena, again with scant (or no) attention given to ideas or domestic institutions. But political scientists' preoccupation with economic interests is not unique to the case of repeal, as discussed in the introduction to this book. Indeed, most political scientists will be on a familiar footing as they read the first part of this book, but some will probably question the value of the second part of the book. These scholars may be skeptical about the value added by the extensive attention given to measuring ideas, particularly as distinct from economic interests. They may (quite rightly) ask, "If interests are fundamentally important in explaining the behavior of MPs and peers in nineteenth-century Britain (which you show in part 1 of the book), then to what extent were ideas independent of these interests?" More to the point, are ideas merely epiphenomenal to interests? The blunt answer is that ideas did play an independent and crucially important role in the policy shift to free trade. Most important, even though Peelites voted more in line with constituency interests in 1846, Conservative ideology constrained them from doing so before 1846, and only with a reinterpretation of this ideology did they feel able to support repeal. So in this case, interests inform us of the end (their votes in 1846) but reveal nothing of the means (ideological cover) to that end. Had the Peelites not adapted Conservatism, they may very well have felt too exposed to endorse repeal. It is not unreasonable, then, to conclude that the means (ideological cover) made the particular end (repeal) possible. Pushing the counterfactual a little further, had the Peelites (and thereby the Commons) rejected repeal, Peel's fear of a revolution similar to that seen in France in 1848 may well have erupted in Britain. Interests were the engine that drove repeal, but ideas helped to shape the final outcome.

A second factor given scant attention by political science accounts of repeal is the role of domestic institutions. While ideas may have provided the means to achieve repeal, the institutional context *facilitated* the (relatively) smooth transition of interests into the policy outcome (repeal). More to the point, both the Commons and the Lords had come to recognize that to ensure stability, the wishes of the public (however distasteful) must be acknowledged. Between 1815 and 1846, public officials had become gradually more accepting of the constraints imposed on them by the British public (including the unenfranchised). More MPs came to accept that they served as *delegates* to their constituencies and that as the interests of these constituencies may be seen to shift, so too should public policy. Even more intriguing is that unelected peers also came to accept the limitations on their powers as political actors and, in Lieven's words, recognized that "stubborn resistance" to liberal reform "could only lead to disaster." The institutions of parliamentary democracy in the 1840s had become far more conciliatory to liberal reform than they had been just a few decades before. Thus, while the Lords could very well have rejected repeal, thereby sparking a constitutional crisis (or worse), they chose not to do so. The growing emphasis on MPs as delegates in the Commons and the acquiescence to public opinion in the Lords meant that the engine of economic interests did not erupt into revolutionary fever. In the end, then, economic interests led Britain to repeal, but ideas and institutions delivered the final outcome.

Appendixes

Appendix 1

Summary Table of All Regression Variables and Further Details on Measuring District Trade Orientation

Summary Table of Variables

Table A.1 summarizes all the regression variables used in chapters 3, 5, 6, and 10.

Revisions to DISTPREF (District Trade Preference/Orientation)

I entered my DISTPREF variable into the Aydelotte dataset and in doing so made two main changes: changes resulting from reconciling the two datasets and changes resulting from a review of DISTPREF itself (which I originally constructed in 1988; the original dataset is stored in both the ICPSR and U.K. Data Archives).

It is worth noting that my dataset and Aydelotte's are constructed on different principles. My dataset is a constituency based one for England only, in the sense that there is one entry for each seat (though note that I have included pre- and post-1832 Reform Act seats). I entered into the dataset the names of those Members of Parliament who voted in the first reading on Corn Law in February 1846. One cannot therefore match up the names to earlier (or even in a few cases later) divisions on the Corn Laws included in my dataset because the names of sitting MPs will have changed somewhat. Aydelotte had an entry for each MP sitting in the 1841 to 1847 Parliament—that is, he had more entries than the number of seats (and he covered Scotland, Wales, and Ireland). Nonetheless, Aydelotte's dataset can be constrained to match mine by selecting only those English MPs who voted in the first reading. There are, however, entries for only those English MPs who voted in the first reading (plus a few complicated cases where the MPs turned over during the repeal period). What follows is a description of the changes that resulted from merging Aydelotte's

Table A.1
Summary table of regression variables used in chapters 3, 5, and 6 (and minimally chapter 10)

Variable	Chapter in Which the Variable Is Used and Discussed	Independent and/or Dependent Variable
Subscriptions to the Anti-Corn Law League (in pounds per 100 of total population)	3	Dependent
Subscriptions to the Anti-Corn Law League (in pounds per 100 individuals listed in the town's commercial directory as having an occupation)	3	Dependent
Interest group A: Export-oriented manufacturers and professionals aligned with manufacturing	3	Independent
Interest group B: Interest group A + nonaligned professionals and retail trades	3	Independent
Interest group C: Interest group B + manufacturers supplying domestic markets	3	Independent
Interest group D: Interest group A + manufacturers supplying domestic markets	3	Independent
MP party affiliation (from pollbook data)	5	Independent
MP party affiliation (from W. O. Aydelotte's dataset)	5, 6, 10	Independent and dependent
Portfolio diversification (from death-duty register sample)	5, 6	Independent
Portfolio diversification (from income-tax-return sample)	5, 6	Independent
District economic orientation (formerly DISTPREF)	5, 6, 10	Independent
District (constituency) type (county or borough)	6, 10	Independent
Effect of the 1832 Reform Act	5, 6	Independent
Motions for repeal of the Corn Laws: 11 July 1842 15 May 1843 26 June 1844 10 June 1845 27 February 1846 (1st reading) 15 May 1846 (3rd reading)	5 (1st and 3rd readings only) 6 (all divisions excluding 1st reading) 10 (3rd reading only)	Dependent
1st-dimension coordinate (from NOMINATE)	6	Dependent
2nd-dimension coordinate (from NOMINATE)	6	Independent
MPs' ideology	6	Independent

Appendixes

and my datasets. Some changes resulted from reconciling the two datasets:

1. **W. B. Baring** was recorded in my dataset as an MP for Staffordshire. But in Aydelotte, he was sitting for Thetford. In the 1837 to 1841 Parliament, he did sit for Staffordshire, but he sat for Thetford in the 1841 to 1847 Parliament. I amended my dataset to record him as Thetford. This changes his DISTPREF from 3 to 2.

2. **H. Drummond** was recorded in my dataset as an MP for Surrey County. Drummond became MP for Surrey West in 1847. The H. Drummond who voted in the first reading sat for the Scottish seat of Perthshire, and I had wrongly coded him as Surrey—thereby creating too many seats for Surrey. I therefore deleted this seat from my dataset (it was a DISTPREF 1).

3. **Viscount Ebrington** was recorded in my dataset as an MP for Devon County. But in Aydelotte, he was recorded as sitting for Plymouth. Ebrington sat for the county seat from 1830 to 1839, when he was appointed Lord Lieutenant of Ireland and stood down from his seat. He was elected as an MP for Plymouth in 1841. I have therefore moved Ebrington in my dataset from Devon to Plymouth and thereby corrected the underrepresentation of the latter and overrepresentation of the former (Devon = DISTPREF 1; Plymouth = DISTPREF 4).

4. **G. W. Hope** is recorded in my dataset as the MP for Southampton, which is correct in terms of which seat he occupied in 1846—so this results in no change to my dataset. Aydelotte recorded him as sitting for Weymouth and Melcombe Regis—which is correct in terms of where he sat for immediately after the 1841 election. *(This illustrates a difference between the two datasets. Aydelotte records the first seat occupied in the Parliament, whereas my focus is on 1846. Aydelotte does not have mulitple entries for MPs where they moved constituency, so some care is needed in using his descriptive variables.)* The story is as follows. In the 1841 general election, **Lord Villiers** and **G. W. Hope** were elected for Weymouth and Melcombe Regis. They were unseated on petition and replaced by **Ralph Bernal** and **William Christie** (the losing candidates in the general election). In Southampton, the 1841 election was won by **Lord Bruce** and **Charles Cecil Martyn**. But that election was declared void in 1842, and the subsequent election was won by **George Hope** and **H. St. John Mildmay**. Hope became MP for Southampton. To round off the story, in Cirencester, the 1841 election was won by **Thomas W. C. Master** and **William Cripps**. In 1844, Master resigned and

was replaced by **Lord Villiers**. In the merged dataset, I made the following entries for DISTPREF: **Villiers 2 (Cirencester), Hope 4 (Southampton), Bernal 2 (Weymouth and Melcombe Regis), Christie 2 (Ditto), Mildmay 4 (Southampton)**, and **Cripps 2 (Cirencester)**. These were the MPs sitting for these seats in 1846.

5. **H. Smith (or Smyth)** is recorded in my dataset as MP for Colchester. In the voting record for the first reading, he is recorded as **H. Smith**, but in my source for election records (Smith 1973), he is recorded as **H. Smyth**. These appear to be the same person, but I have entered both spellings (Smith and Smyth) to avoid confusion.

6. **T. H. S. Sotheron** is recorded in my dataset as MP for Wiltshire County. In the 1841 election, the four MPs elected for Wiltshire were **Sir Francis Burdett, Walter Long, John Benett**, and **Sidney Herbert**. In 1844, Burdett died and was replaced by **Sotheron. Sotheron** had been elected for Devizes in the 1841 election, along with **G. H. W. Heneage**. In 1844, Sotheron resigned his seat in Devizes in favor of Wiltshire County, and he was replaced by **W. H. L. Bruges**. My dataset records **Sotheron, Long, Benett**, and **Herbert** as the MPs for Wiltshire County and **Bruges** and **Heneage** as the MPs for Devizes (as they were in 1846). It is more difficult to know how to deal with this in terms of DISTPREF. The question is what entry to make for Sotheron (Wiltshire = 1, Devizes = 2). I thus made no entry.

7. **Sir F. Thesiger** is recorded in my dataset as the MP for Abingdon. In the 1841 election, Thesiger was returned for the Oxfordshire seat of New Woodstock (also known as Woodstock). In 1844, he was appointed solicitor general and had to seek reelection. He did not stand in New Woodstock but instead stood in Abingdon. In 1841, **Thomas Duffield** was elected for Abingdon, but he resigned in 1844 and Thesiger took his place. Thesiger was replaced in New Woodstock by the **Marquis of Blandford** (but here he is also known in the parliamentary divisions as **Lord Churchill**). So for my dataset, the MPs in 1846 were **Thesiger** for Abingdon and **Blandford/Churchill** for New Woodstock. Fortunately, both constituencies are DISTPREF = 2, so none of this matters very much for the merged dataset. Aydelotte had all of these names entered because they all sat in the Parliament.

8. **Alderman William Thomson** (Conservative) is recorded in my dataset as the MP for Westmoreland County. In the 1841 election, the MPs returned for Westmoreland were **Viscount Lowther** and **H. Lowther** (both Conservatives). In September 1841, Viscount Lowther

became a peer. He was replaced in Westmoreland by **William Thompson**. **Thompson** had been elected for Sunderland in the 1841 election along with **David Barclay** (Whig/Liberal). Thompson was replaced in Sunderland by **Lord Howick** (Whig/Liberal). But in 1845, Howick became a peer and was replaced in Sunderland by **George Hudson** (a protectionist Conservative and railway developer "King Hudson"). My dataset records the following members in 1846: Westmoreland (DISTPREF = 1), **H. Lowther** and **William Thompson**; Sunderland (DISTPREF = 5), **Hudson** and **Barclay**. I have made these entries in the merged dataset.

9. **H. Warburton** is recorded in my dataset as the MP for Kendal. **George Wood** was returned for Kendal in the 1841 election. Wood died in November 1843 and was replaced by **Henry Warburton**. Warburton had been elected for Bridport (Dorset) in the 1841 election with **Thomas Mitchell**. He resigned that seat in September 1841 and was replaced by **A. D. R. W. B. Cochrane**. Cochrane resigned in January or February 1846 to fight a by-election as a free-trade Conservative. Cochrane won the by-election, and he voted in the second reading for the repeal of the Corn Laws. But his election was subsequently overturned by petition in favor of his Whig/Liberal opponent **John Romilly**, who voted for repeal in the third reading. In my dataset, **Warburton** is recorded as the MP for Kendal (DISTPREF = 3). In the merged dataset, I have entered DISTPREF = 3 for **Warburton** (even though Aydelotte has him sitting for Bridport—which is DISTPREF = 2—on the grounds that he was sitting for Kendal in 1846) and **Wood**. **Mitchell** is recorded as DISTPREF = 2 (same for Aydelotte). **Cochrane** and **Romilly** are more difficult. In the merged dataset, I have entered Cochrane/Romilly as one, with DISTPREF = 2.

Other changes resulted from a review of DISTPREF itself. In making the above changes I looked more closely at the construction of DISTPREF. I was struck that the coding of DISTPREF at the free-trade end of the scale was sometimes inconsistent between constituencies. This reflects the rather subjective descriptions in Philbin's book, in the sense that Philbin reported verbatim the contemporary descriptions of constituencies, but his reports varied from constituency to constituency in terms of their descriptive detail. For instance, the number of power looms and types of fabrics manufactured might be given for a borough with just a couple of factories, while another borough known to be a large manufacturing center might be described simply as having "extensive manufacturing." This often created a bias against districts that I would predict to have been strongly in favor of free trade (coded as DISTPREF = 5).

I therefore used the data on factory employment by town in the textile, machinery, and cutlery industries in 1838 (from Fang 1978) to construct a measure of factory industrialization by borough. This reveals nothing about employment in counties, whose DISTPREFs are unchanged. This series is as follows:

	Factory Employment in Textiles, Machinery, and Cutlery in 1838	Previous DISTPREF	New DISTPREF
1. Manchester/Salford	48,370	Manchester 5, Salford 4	Manchester 5, Salford 5
2. Stockport	24,072	4	5
3. Leeds	18,317	4	5
4. Oldham	17,967	5	5
5. Bury	14,096	4	5
6. Sheffield	13,541	3	5
7. Rochdale	13,491	3	5
8. Ashton under Lyne	12,836	4	5
9. Bolton	11,269	4	5
10. Bradford	10,896	4	5
11. Macclesfield	10,863	3	4
12. Blackburn	10,820	3	4
13. Preston	9,111	3	4
14. Halifax	7,688	4	4
15. Wigan	6,137	4	4

I first ranked the boroughs in terms of their factory employment in textiles, machinery, and cutlery in 1838. I then assigned a DISTPREF of 5 to the top ten boroughs. Manchester and Salford are treated as one for these purposes because the factory data do not provide a breakdown, but as Salford is a suburb of Manchester it seemed appropriate to give them the same DISTPREF. I assigned a DISTPREF of 4 to the next eleven to fifteen boroughs. The changes are shown above. I then made three further changes:

1. **Liverpool** was moved from DISTPREF = 4 to 5 to reflect its dependency on the cotton trade.

2. **Shrewsbury** was moved from DISTPREF = 5 to 4, which is a good example of subjective exaggeration in Philbin's description of its textile factories. The county in which Shrewsbury resides, Shropshire, does not appear in the top six ranked counties for employment in the textile industries.

3. **Carlisle** likewise was moved from DISTPREF = 5 to 4. In spite of Philbin's description lauding its textile (weaving) activities, it is not listed in the top fifteen centers in Fang (indeed it is not even in the top 30).

The impact of all of this on the overall distribution of DISTPREFs (using voting on the first reading as the key) is as follows:

	Old DISTPREF	New DISTPREF
1	105	105
2	184	184
3	92	83
4	37	36
5	11	22
Total	429	430

The impact is to double the weighting of DISTPREFs equaling 5 from 2.6 percent of the total to 5.1 percent. Overall, the weighting seems about right for the reformed Parliament, which was still heavily weighted toward agricultural constitutencies.

Appendix 2

Speakers 22 January to 15 May 1846 in the Debates on the Customs and Corn Importation Bill

(Listed in order of speaking, with constituency given for first speech only)

22 January
Lord F. Egerton, South Lancashire
E. B. Denison, Yorkshire, West Riding
Sir Robert Peel, Tamworth
Lord John Russell, City of London
W. Miles, East Somersetshire
Viscount Northland, Dungannon, Ireland
Colonel Sibthorp, Lincoln

23 January
J. C. Colquhoun, Newcastle, Staffordshire
Joseph Hume, Montrose, Scotland
Sir Robert Peel
Lord John Russell
D. O'Conor (The O'Conor Don), Roscommon, Ireland
G. Bankes, Dorsetshire
W. S. Crawford, Rochdale
J. Brotherton, Salford

27 January
Sir Robert Peel
Sir R. H. Inglis, Oxford University
A. S. O'Brien, North Northamptonshire
Joseph Hume
H. Liddell, Durham
Captain Rous, Westminster

C. N. Newdegate, North Warwickshire
Viscount Ingestre, South Staffordshire
Lord G. Bentinck, King's Lynn
F. Scott, Roxburghshire, Scotland
Sir J. Tyrell, North Essex
Colonel Sibthorp
Earl of March, West Sussex
Sidney Herbert, South Wiltshire
Mr. Wodehouse, East Norfolk
P. Howard, Carlisle
H. B. Curteis, Rye
J. Benett, South Wiltshire
Mr. Escott, Winchester
Mr. Wakley, Finsbury
T. Gisborne, Nottingham
Colonel Thomas Wood, Breconshire, Wales
Viscount Newport, South Shropshire
Mr. Aglionby, Cockermouth
G. Bankes

3 February
Mr. Wodehouse
Dr. Bowring, Bolton

9 February
Mr. Collett, Athlone, Ireland
H. Goulburn, Cambridge University
Sir Robert Peel
G. Palmer, South Essex
P. Miles, Bristol
Sir W. Heathcote, North Hampshire
W. Lascelles, Wakefield
Lord Norreys, Oxfordshire
Baillie Cochrane, Bridport
Mr. Deedes, East Kent
Sir J. Walsh, Radnorshire, Wales
A. J. B. Hope, Maidstone
Viscount Sandon, Liverpool
Lord John Russell

Appendixes

R. H. Inglis
S. Herbert
Major Fitzmaurice, Buckinghamshire

10 February
Viscount Ebrington, Plymouth
A. S. O'Brien
W. S. Crawford
H. J. Baillie, Inverness-shire, Scotland
Viscount Clements, Leitrim, Ireland
Mr. Lefroy, Longford, Ireland
W. H. Gregory, Dublin, Ireland
Lord Brooke, South Warwickshire
Lord Worsley, Lincolnshire
Sir James Graham, Dorchester
Viscount Clive, North Shropshire

11 February
Lord G. Bentinck
H. Goulburn
Mr. Escott
C. N. Newdegate
A. S. O'Brien
Mr. Wodehouse

12 February
J. C. Colquhoun
C. W. W. Wynn, Montgomery, Wales
G. J. Heathcote, Rutlandshire
W. C. Martin, Newport, Isle of Wight
T. Baring, Huntingdon
Viscount Morpeth, Yorkshire, West Riding
M. Gaskell, Wenlock
J. A. Roebuck, Bath
Sir H. Douglas, Liverpool
H. Hinde, Newcastle on Tyne

13 February
Sir H. Douglas
Viscount Villiers, Cirencester

F. Scott
E. Buller, Stafford
W. Miles
Earl of March
H. Baillie
Viscount Northland
W. B. Ferrand, Knaresborough
Colonel T. Wood, Middlesex
A. S. O'Brien

16 February
Earl of March
Baillie Cochrane
M. Gibson, Manchester
T. P. Halsey, Hertfordshire
F. W. Dickinson, West Somersetshire
Lord C. Churchill, Woodstock
Sir W. Clay, Tower Hamlets
L. W. Buck, North Devonshire
Lord H. Vane, South Durham
Sir J. Tyrell
Mr. James, East Cumberland
Sir Robert Peel
W. Miles

17 February
Lord John Manners, Newark upon Trent
Captain Layard, Carlow Boroughs, Ireland
R. Palmer, Berkshire
Sir C. Napier, Marylebone
Mr. F. Shaw, Dublin University, Ireland
John Bright, Durham
G. Hudson, Sunderland

19 February
Viscount Duncan, Bath
G. Hudson
Alderman Thompson, Westmoreland
Sir W. Molesworth, Southwark

J. Benett
H. Berkeley, Bristol
J. Tollemache, South Cheshire
T. Duncombe, Finsbury
Sir T. Acland, North Devonshire
Lord A. Paget, Lichfield
W. B. Baring, Thetford

20 February
Mr. Cumming Bruce, Elginshire and Nairn, Scotland
Mr. Poulett Scrope, Stroud
C. N. Newdegate
Mr. Barkly, Leominster
P. Bennet, West Suffolk
G. F. Muntz
Benjamin Disraeli, Shrewsbury

23 February
E. Buller
Captain Bateson, Londonderry County, Ireland
M. Gore, Barnstaple
R. A. Fitzgerald, Tipperary, Ireland
Mr. Lockhart, Lanarkshire, Scotland
Sir G. Clerk, Stamford
G. F. Muntz, Birmingham
H. Liddell
Mr. Hutt, Gateshead
Captain Harris, Christchurch
M. Milnes, Pontefract

24 February
M. J. O'Connell, Kerry, Ireland
Colonel Conolly, Donegal, Ireland
Viscount Ingestre
J. S. Trelawney, Tavistock
C. W. Packe, South Leicestershire
H. Goulburn
W. B. Ferrand
W. Miles

26 February
D. R. Ross, Belfast, Ireland
E. B. Denison
J. Brotherton
R. A. Christopher, North Lincolnshire
Mr. E. Cardwell, Clitheroe
Mr. G. Finch, Rutlandshire
H. K. Seymer, Dorsetshire
Mr. C. Villiers, Wolverhampton
Mr. G. Hudson
W. B. Ferrand
Lord John Russell
Colonel Sibthorp

27 February
Mr. G. Bankes
Mr. B. Escott
Captain Gladstone, Ipswich
Richard Cobden, Stockport
Richard Spooner, Birmingham
Mr. P. Borthwick, Evesham
Lord George Bentinck

2 March
Mr. C. Villiers
Colonel Sibthorp
Lord Worsley
Mr. M. Gibson
Mr. B. Escott
Mr. R. Colborne, Richmond
Mr. C. Goring, New Shoreham
John Bright
Mr. G. Palmer
Lord John Russell
Sir W. Jolliffe, Petersfield
Joseph Hume
Mr. P. Borthwick
Marquess of Granby, Stamford

Appendixes

Earl of March
Lord John Manners
Sir A. Brooke, Fermanagh, Ireland
Sir Robert Peel
W. B. Ferrand
M. J. O'Connell
Mr. G. Bankes

3 March
Mr. G. Bankes
Sir Robert Peel
John Bright
C. W. Howard, East Cumberland
Sir John Hanmer, Kingston on Hull
Mr. G. Moffatt, Dartmouth
Mr. G. Finch
H. G. Ward, Sheffield
H. Liddell
Mr. Hutt
Mr. P. Borthwick
Joseph Hume
Lord G. Bentinck
Richard Cobden
Sir T. Acland
Mr. G. Hudson
Lord Worsley
Colonel Sibthorp
Mr. T. Wakley
C. N. Newdegate
Mr. C. Villiers

6 March
Mr. W. O. Stanley, Anglesey, Wales
Colonel T. Wood
A. S. O'Brien
Lord G. Bentinck
Lord Worsley
Sir J. Tyrell

H. B. Curteis
Mr. T. Greene, Lancaster
Lord John Russell
Mr. G. Hudson
Mr. M. Milnes
Mr. Aglionby
Sir Robert Peel
W. Miles
Joseph Hume
Sir A. Brooke
H. N. Burroughes, East Norfolk
T. D. Acland, West Somersetshire
P. Borthwick
Mr. C. Buller, Liskeard
H. G. Ward
Mr. G. Hudson
P. Howard
Alderman Copeland, Stoke on Trent
Sir W. Jolliffe
Mr. G. Finch
Benjamin Disraeli
Mr. C. Villiers
Colonel Sibthorp
Viscount Pollington, Pontefract
D. O'Connell, Cork County, Ireland
John Bright
W. S. Crawford
Mr. C. Goring
Earl of March
Mr. W. Ellis, Leicester

9 March
Sir J. Tyrell
W. Miles
Sir Robert Peel
Mr. E. Cardwell
C. N. Newdegate

Appendixes

W. S. Crawford
Joseph Hume
Colonel Sibthorp
Earl of March
Sir A. Brooke
Mr. P. Scrope
Captain Harris
Mr. P. Howard
Mr. B. Escott
Mr. G. Palmer
R. A. Fitzgerald
Mr. Pierce Butler, Kilkenny County, Ireland
Sir John Rae Reid, Dover
H. Labouchere, Taunton
Mr. G. Finch
Lord G. Bentinck
Mr. W. Ewart, Dumfries, Scotland
Sir G. Clerk
Mr. C. Buller
M. Forster, Berwick upon Tweed
H. Goulburn
Benjamin Disraeli
P. Borthwick
A. J. B. Hope
Mr. B. Hawes, Lambeth
Mr. E. Cardwell
Mr. Aglionby
Mr. W. Williams, Coventry
Dr. Bowring
H. B. Curteis
T. Gisborne
Lord John Russell
Mr. T. Baring
Alderman Copeland
Mr. G. Hudson
Mr. G. Duncan, Dundee, Scotland

13 March
R. Spooner
Sir G. Clerk
C. N. Newdegate
G. F. Muntz
A. S. O'Brien
T. Duncombe
Sir Robert Peel
Alderman Thompson
Mr. E. Grogan, Dublin, Ireland
J. Tollmache
R. H. Inglis
H. Goulburn
Lord George Bentinck
Sir H. Halford, South Leicestershire
T. Gisborne
R. M. Milnes
Sir G. Clerk
Colonel Rolleston, South Nottinghamshire
Mr. E. Strutt, Derby
Mr. W. Ellis
Sir J. Hobhouse, Nottingham
W. Miles
Viscount Ingestre
C. H. Frewen, East Sussex

16 March
J. Plumptre, East Kent
Sir Robert Peel
Colonel Austin, West Kent
F. W. Knight, West Worcestershire
A. J. B. Hope
Alderman Humphery, Southwark
C. H. Frewen
H. Goulburn
Lord George Bentinck
G. W. J. Repton, St. Albans

Appendixes

G. Bankes
Sir G. Clerk
Mr. W. Ellis
J. Brocklehurst, Macclesfield
C. N. Newdegate
Mr. B. Hawes
C. B. Adderley, North Staffordshire
Mr. E. Ellice, Coventry
Lord G. Bentinck
Benjamin Disraeli

17 March
Mr. E. Cayley, North Riding, Yorkshire
Dr. Bowring
Mr. C. Buller
Mr. P. Borthwick
G. F. Muntz
Alderman Thompson
W. Ewart
Mr. E. Cardwell
F. W. Knight
J. P. Allix, Cambridgeshire
W. Miles
Sir Robert Peel
Colonel Sibthorp
Mr. P. Howard
Mr. G. Finch
Mr. H. Goulburn
Sir J. Tyrell
Mr. C. Villiers
Sir J. Trollope, Lincolnshire
P. Borthwick
Sir J. Walsh
H. G. R. Yorke, York
Lord George Bentinck
Cumming Bruce
Sir C. Knightley, South Northamptonshire

Mr. A. Lawson, Knaresborough
Sir G. Clerk
Mr. G. Duncan
Mr. T. A. Mitchell, Bridport
E. Cardwell
Sir J. Hanmer

20 March
Marquess of Worcester, East Gloucestershire
Mr. H. Hinde
Mr. E. Cardwell
Mr. A. Chapman, Whitby
Captain Harris
Mr. G. Palmer
Mr. H. Warburton, Kendal
Mr. P. Borthwick
Joseph Hume
Mr. J. W. Henley, Oxfordshire
Lord George Bentinck
Sir G. Clerk

23 March
Mr. E. Yorke, Cambridgeshire
Sir Robert Peel
Mr. J. Y. Buller, South Devonshire
Mr. F. A. McGeachy, Honiton
C. W. Packe
H. Cholmondley, Montgomery, Wales
H. Vernon, East Retford
Captain Berkeley, Gloucester
R. H. Inglis
Mr. W. Childers, Malton
F. Maule, Perth, Scotland

24 March
Viscount Pollington
J. E. Plumptre
Mr. Hawes
Sir J. Trollope

Appendixes

Sir J. Hanmer
Viscount Ebrington
Mr. Rashleigh, East Cornwall
F. T. Baring, Portsmouth
Mr. F. Shaw
H. Goulburn
Earl of March

26 March
Mr. G. Finch
Lord Rendlesham, East Suffolk
Mr. E. Fellowes, Huntingdonshire
A. E. Fuller, East Sussex
P. Borthwick
Mr. C. Buller
Lord George Bentinck

27 March
Richard Cobden
Sir J. Graham
Mr. E. P. Bouverie, Kilmarnock, Scotland
Mr. J. D. Gardiner, Bodmin
Marquess of Worcester
H. Mildmay, Southampton
Sir Robert Peel
A. S. O'Brien
Lord Palmerston, Tiverton

4 May
Lord George Bentinck
Lord John Russell
Sir Robert Peel
G. Bankes
Benjamin Disraeli
Mr. C. Buller
Colonel Sibthorp
C. W. Packe
P. Bennet

5 May
Lord George Bentinck
Sir H. W. Barron, Waterford City, Ireland
H. Goulburn
Sir F. Thesiger, Abingdon
Captain Layard
J. Stuart, Newark upon Trent
P. Borthwick
G. Finch
W. O. Gore, North Shropshire

8 May
Sir C. Burrell, New Shoreham
Colonel Verner, Armagh County, Ireland
Sir W. Jolliffe
G. Bankes
Earl of Lincoln, Linlithgow Burghs, Scotland
J. Floyer, Dorsetshire
A. S. O'Brien
P. Borthwick
J. W. Henley
J. A. Roebuck
Benjamin Disraeli
S. Herbert
Lord George Bentinck

11 May
Marquess of Granby
M. Gaskell
R. B. Sheridan, Shaftesbury
J. Floyer
W. Miles
Sir J. Graham
Mr. E. Cayley

12 May
C. N. Newdegate
Mr. G. Palmer

Appendixes

R. H. Vyse, Northamptonshire
Captain Polhill, Bedford
J. Benett
J. E. Plumptre
Mr. A. Hastie, Paisley, Scotland
Sir J. Walsh
W. S. Crawford
Mr. F. Scott
Lord Brooke
J. Easthope, Leicester
H. K. Seymer

15 May
J. C. Colquhoun
Sir Robert Peel
Mr. C. Wood, Halifax
P. Bennet
G. Hudson
Marquess of Worcester
M. Gore
Mr. A. Lawson
Mr. Vernon Smith, Northampton
Benjamin Disraeli
Lord John Russell
Sir Robert Peel
Lord George Bentinck
Mr. C. Villiers
Mr. E. Yorke

205 Members Spoke in the Debates on the Customs and Corn Importation Acts
170 English MPs (82.9 percent)
11 Scottish MPs (5.4 percent)
19 Irish MPs (9.3 percent)
5 Welsh MPs (2.4 percent)

Appendix 3　　　　Characteristics of Members of Parliament, 1815 to 1828

318 Characteristics of Members of Parliament

Table A.2
Characteristics of Members of Parliament, 1814 to 1815 and 1826 to 1828

Name	Party	Constituency	District Type	Effect of 1832 Reform Act[a]	Other
1814–1815:					
Mr. Abercrombie	Whig	Calne	Borough	1	
Sir T. Acland	Tory	Devonshire	County	4	
Mr. J. H. Addington	Tory	Harwich	Borough	3	
Alderman Atkins	Tory	London	Borough	3	
Mr. T. Babington	Tory	Leicester	Borough	3	
Mr. H. Bankes	Tory	Corfe Castle	Borough	1	
Mr. Barclay	Tory	Southwark	Borough	3	
Mr. Barham	Whig	Stockbridge	Borough	1	
Mr. A. Baring	Whig	Taunton	Borough	3	
Lord Barnard	Whig	Durham County	County	4	
Mr. Bathurst	Tory	Bodmin	Borough	3	
Lord Binning	Tory	Mitchell	Borough	1	
Mr. Blackburn	Tory	Lancashire	County	4	
Mr. Brand	Whig	Hertfordshire	County	4	
Mr. Broadhead	Tory	Wareham	Borough	2	
Mr. Brooke	Whig	Chippenham	Borough	3	
D. Browne	Whig	County Mayo	County	3	
Sir Egerton Brydges	Tory	Maidstone	Borough	3	
Mr. J. Buller	Tory	Exeter	Borough	3	
Sir F. Burdett	Whig	Westminster	Borough	3	
Sir C. Burrell	Tory	New Shoreham	Borough	3	

Appendixes

Mr. W. Burrell	Tory	Sussex	County	4
Mr. Butterworth	Whig	Coventry	Borough	3
Mr. Calcraft	Whig	Rochester	Borough	3
Mr. C. Calvert	Whig	Southwark	Borough	3
George Canning	Tory	Liverpool	Borough	3
Colonel Carew	Whig	County Wexford	County	3
Mr. Pole Carew	Tory	Lostwithiel	Borough	1
Mr. Cartwright	Tory	Northamptonshire	County	4
Lord Castlereagh	Tory	County Down	County	3
Mr. Cawthorne	Tory	Lancaster	Borough	3
Sir G. Clerke	Tory	Edinburghshire	County	3
Mr. T. W. Coke	Whig	Norfolk	County	4
Sir N. Colthurst	Tory	Cork	Borough	3
Lord Compton	Tory	Northampton	Borough	3
Mr. Courtenay	Tory	Exeter	Borough	3
E. J. Curteis	Tory	Sussex	County	4
Sir W. Curtis	Tory	London	Borough	3
Mr. Daly	Tory	County Galway	County	3
Mr. Hart Davis	Tory	Colchester	Borough	3
Mr. F. Douglas	Whig	Banbury	Borough	3
Mr. W. Douglas	Tory	Dumfries Burghs	Borough	3
Mr. William Elliot	Whig	Peterborough	Borough	3
Mr. Ellison	Tory	Wootton Bassett	Borough	1
Mr. Fawcett	Independent	Carlisle	Borough	3	He regarded himself as a champion of the Independent party.

Table A.2
(continued)

Name	Party	Constituency	District Type	Effect of 1832 Reform Act[a]	Other
Mr. Finlay	Whig	Glasgow Burghs	Borough	4	
W. Fitzgerald	Tory	Ennis (Ireland)	Borough	3	
Mr. Forbes	Tory	Beverley	Borough	3	
Mr. A. J. Foster	Tory	Cockermouth	Borough	3	
J. Foster	Tory	County Louth	County	3	
Sir Frederick Flood	Tory	County Wexford	County	3	
Mr. Fremantle	Tory	Buckingham	Borough	3	
General Gascoyne	Tory	Liverpool	Borough	3	
Mr. Davies Giddy	Tory	Bodmin	Borough	3	
Mr. Gooch	Tory	Suffolk	County	4	
Mr. Gordon	Tory	Staffordshire	County	3	Lord G. L. Gordon, 8 March 1799–1815.
Mr. Gordon	Whig	Staffordshire	County	3	Lord G. L. Gordon II, 31 July 1815–1820.
Mr. Leveson Gower	Independent	Staffordshire	County	3	
Sir James Graham	Tory	Carlisle	Borough	3	
J. P. Grant	Whig	Great Grimsby	Borough	2	
Mr. Grattan	Whig	Dublin	Borough	3	
Mr. Grenfell	Whig	Great Marlow	Borough	1	
Lord A. Hamilton	Whig	Lanarkshire	County	3	
Mr. Harvey	Tory	Norwich	Borough	3	
Sir G. Heathcote	Tory	Rutland	County	3	

Appendixes

Mr. Horner	Whig	St. Mawes	Borough	1	
Mr. Howorth	Whig	Evesham	Borough	3	
Mr. W. Huskisson	Tory	Chichester	Borough	3	
Lord Jocelyn	Tory	County Louth	County	3	
Mr. Gore Langton	Whig	Somerset	County	4	
Mr. Shaw Lefevre	Whig	Reading	Borough	3	
Mr. F. Lewis	Whig	Beaumaris	Borough	3	
Mr. J. G. Lambton	Whig	Durham County	County	4	This MP is described occasionally as Lambert, but there is no Lambert in the Commons at this time.
Lord Lascelles	Tory	Yorkshire	County	4	
Mr. Lockhart	Tory	Oxford	Borough	3	He approved the committee on Corn Laws or 6 June 1814, disagreeing with a petition of his constituents against agricultural protection.
Mr. C. Long	Tory	Haslemere	Borough	1	
Mr. Lushington	Tory	Canterbury	Borough	3	
Mr. Marjoribanks	Tory	Buteshire and Caithnessshire	County	4	
Mr. Marryat	Independent	Sandwich	Borough	3	He claimed to be free of all parties but felt a disposition to vote in favor of those in administration.
Mr. Methuen	Tory	Wiltshire	County	4	
Lord Milton	Whig	Yorkshire	County	4	
C. Monck	Whig	Northumberland	County	4	

Table A.2
(continued)

Name	Party	Constituency	District Type	Effect of 1832 Reform Act[a]	Other
Mr. P. Moore	Whig	Coventry	Borough	3	
Mr. Morritt	Tory	Northallerton	Borough	2	
Sir J. Newport	Whig	Waterford	Borough	4	
Lord Nugent	Whig	Aylesbury	Borough	3	
Lord Ossultoun	Whig	Knaresborough	Borough	3	
Mr. Paget	Tory	Carnarvon Burghs	Borough	3	
Sir H. Parnell	Whig	Queens County	County	3	
Mr. Peel	Tory	Chippenham	Borough	3	
Sir Robert Peel	Tory	Tamworth	Borough	3	
Mr. G. Philips	Whig	Ilchester	Borough	1	
Mr. Ponsonby	Whig	Peterborough	Borough	3	
General Porter	Whig	Stockbridge	Borough	1	
Mr. Portman	Whig	Dorset	County	4	
Mr. Preston	Tory	Ashburton	Borough	2	
Lord Proby	Whig	Huntingdonshire	County	3	He acted generally with Grenville (Whig) but defended the Corn Laws.
Mr. Protheroe	Whig	Bristol	Borough	3	
Sir M. W. Ridley	Whig	Newcastle upon Tyne	Borough	3	
Mr. Robinson	Tory	Ripon	Borough	3	
Sir S. Romilly	Whig	Arundel	Borough	2	
Mr. Rose	Tory	Christchurch	Borough	2	

Appendixes 323

Mr. Round	Tory	Ipswich	Borough	3	
Mr. Horace St. Paul	Tory	Bridport	Borough	3	
John Sebright	Whig	Hertfordshire	County	4	
Sir James Shaw	Tory	London	Borough	3	
Mr. Shiffner	Tory	Lewes	Borough	3	
Alderman C. Smith	Tory	St. Albans	Borough	3	
Mr. John Smith	Whig	Nottingham	Borough	3	
Mr. W. Smith	Whig	Norwich	Borough	3	
Mr. Smyth	Whig	Cambridge University	Borough	3	
Mr. Stephen	Tory	East Grinstead	Borough	1	
Sir John Stewart	Tory	County Tyrone	County	3	
Mr. Wortley Stuart	Tory	Bossiney	Borough	1	
Mr. Home Sumner	Tory	Surrey	County	4	
Mr. Swann	Tory	Penryn	Borough	3	
M. A. Taylor	Whig	Poole	Borough	3	
Mr. T. Thompson	Independent	Midhurst	Borough	2	
H. Thornton	Tory	Southwark	Borough	3	
Mr. Tierney	Whig	Appleby	Borough	1	
N. Vansittart	Tory	Harwich	Borough	3	He was Chancellor of the Exchequer.
Mr. Vyse	Independent	Honiton	Borough	3	He considered himself neutral but was expected to vote for the Liverpool Tory ministry. He voted to reduce the protection price in 1815, though he was convinced of the necessity of protection.

Table A.2
(continued)

Name	Party	Constituency	District Type	Effect of 1832 Reform Act[a]	Other
Sir G. Warrender	Tory	Truro	Borough	3	
Mr. W.P.T.L. Wellesley	Tory	St. Ives	Borough	2	
Mr. Long Wellesley Pole	Tory	Queen's County	County	3	He was a champion of the Corn Bill, 8 March 1815.
Mr. Western	Whig	Essex	County	4	
Mr. Wharton	Whig	Beverley	Borough	3	
Mr. Whitbread	Whig	Bedford	Borough	3	
Mr. Wilberforce	Tory	Bramber	Borough	1	
Colonel Wood	Tory	Breconshire	County	3	
Sir M. Wood	Tory	Gatton	Borough	1	
C. W. Wynn	Tory	Montgomeryshire	County	3	
W. W. Wynn	Tory	Denbighshire	County	4	
Mr. Yorke	Tory	Liskeard	Borough	2	
1826–1828:					
Sir T. Acland	Tory	Devonshire	County	4	
Lord Althorp	Whig	Northamptonshire	County	4	
Mr. G. Bankes	Tory	Corfe Castle	Borough	1	
Mr. C. Barclay	Tory	Dundalk	Borough	3	
Mr. A. Baring	Whig	Callington	Borough	1	
Mr. W. Baring	Independent	Thetford	Borough	3	He was characterized as nonparty but drifted toward the Conservatives.

Appendixes 325

				4 & 3	
Mr. Beaumont	Whig	Northumberland until December 1826; then Stafford	County, borough		
Lord Belgrave	Whig	Chester	Borough	3	
Mr. J. Benett	Whig	Wiltshire	County	4	
Mr. Bernal	Whig	Rochester	Borough	3	
Mr. Birch	Whig	Nottingham	Borough	3	
Mr. Brougham	Whig	Winchelsea	Borough	1	
Sir F. Burdett	Whig	Westminster	Borough	3	
Sir J. Brydges	Tory	Coleraine	Borough	3	
Mr. Byng	Whig	Middlesex	County	3	
Mr. Calcraft	Whig	Wareham	Borough	2	
N. Calvert	Whig	Hertford until 1826; then Hertfordshire	Borough, county	3 & 4	
G. Canning	Tory	Harwich 1822–1826; Newport Isle of Wight 1826–10 April 1827; Seaford 20 April–8 August 1827	Borough, borough, borough	3 3 1	He was Chancellor of the Exchequer and Prime Minister, April to August 1827.
Lord George Cavendish	Whig	Denbighshire	County	4	
Mr. O. Cave	Tory	Leicestershire	County	4	
Sir G. Clerk	Tory	Edinburghshire	County	3	
Lord Clive	Tory	Ludlow	Borough	3	
Mr. C. Cole	Tory	Glamorganshire	County	4	
Mr. J. Cripps	Tory	Cirencester	Borough	3	
Mr. Curteis	Tory	Sussex	County	3	

Table A.2
(continued)

Name	Party	Constituency	District Type	Effect of 1832 Reform Act[a]	Other
Mr. Curtis	Tory	London 1820–1826; Hastings until December 1826	Borough, borough	3 & 3	
Mr. J. C. Curwen	Whig	Cumberland	County	4	
E. D. Davenport	Tory	Cheshire	County	4	
Mr. Dawson	Tory	County Londonderry	County	3	
Mr. W. J. Denison	Whig	Surrey	County	4	
Mr. C. Duncombe	Tory	Newport, Isle of Wight until 1826	Borough	3	
Mr. Ferguson	Whig	Dysart Burghs	Borough	3	
Mr. Fergusson	Whig	Kirkcudbrightshire	County	3	
Lord Folkestone	Whig	Salisbury	Borough	3	
J. L. Foster	Tory	County Louth	County	3	
Mr. T. B. Fyler	Tory	Coventry	Borough	3	
General Gascoyne	Tory	Liverpool	Borough	3	
Mr. Davies Gilbert	Tory	Bodmin	Borough	3	
Mr. Gipps	Tory	Ripon	Borough	3	
Sir T. Gooch	Tory	Suffolk	County	4	
Captain Gordon	Whig	Cricklade	Borough	3	

Appendixes

H. Goulburn	Tory	St. Germains 1812–1818; West Looe 1818–1826; Armagh Borough 1826–1831; Cambridge University from 1831 until his death in 1856	Borough	1812–1826: 1, 1826–1856: 3	He was Chancellor of the Exchequer from January 1828 to 1830 and from 1841 to 1846.
Mr. A. Grant	Tory	Aldborough	Borough	1
Mr. C. Grant	Whig	Inverness-shire	County	3
D. W. Harvey	Radical	Colchester	Borough	3
Mr. J. C. Hobhouse	Whig	Westminster	Borough	3
Lord Howick	Whig	Winchelsea	Borough	1
Mr. Hume	Whig	Aberdeen Burghs	Borough	3
Mr. R. Hurst	Whig	Horsham	Borough	2
William Huskisson	Tory	Liverpool	Borough	3
Mr. J. Irving	Tory	Bramber	Borough	1
Mr. King	Tory	County Sligo	County	3
Sir E. Knatchbull	Tory	Kent	County	4
Mr. R. Leycester	Ind.	Shaftesbury	Borough	2
Sir T. Lethbridge	Tory	Somersetshire	County	4
Mr. F. Lewis	Tory	Ennis to April 1828; Radnorshire from 9 April 1828	Borough, county	3 & 3
Mr. H. T. Liddell	Tory	Northumberland	County	4
Mr. E. J. Littleton	Whig	Staffordshire	County	3
Colonel Maberly	Whig	Northampton	Borough	3
Mr. J. Maberley	Whig	Abingdon	Borough	3

Table A.2
(continued)

Name	Party	Constituency	District Type	Effect of 1832 Reform Act[a]	Other
Mr. J. Marshall	Whig	Yorkshire	County	4	
J. Maxwell	Whig	Renfrewshire	County	3	
Lord Milton	Whig	Yorkshire	County	4	
Mr. J. B. Monck	Whig	Reading	Borough	3	
Mr. P. Moore	Whig	Coventry until 1826	Borough	3	
Lord Morpeth	Whig	Morpeth	Borough	2	
Sir John Newport	Whig	Waterford City	Borough	4	
F. Palmer	Whig	Reading	Borough	3	
R. Palmer	Tory	Berkshire	County	4	
Sir H. Parnell	Whig	Queen's County	County	3	
Mr. Secretary Peel	Tory	Oxford University	Borough	3	
Sir G. Philips	Whig	Wootton Basset	Borough	1	He was baronet from 19 December 1827.
Mr. G. R. Philips	Whig	Steyning	Borough	1	
G. Pigott	Tory	Kinross-shire	County	3	
Mr. E. B. Portman	Whig	Dorsetshire	County	4	
Mr. Spring Rice	Whig	Limerick	Borough	4	
Mr. G. Robinson	Whig	Worcester	Borough	3	
Mr. F. Robinson	Tory	Ripon	Borough	3	He was Chancellor of the Exchequer from 1823 until April 1827.

Appendixes

Lord John Russell	Whig	Huntingdonshire until 1826; Bandon Bridge 19 December 1826–1830	County, borough 3
Sir J. Sebright	Whig	Hertfordshire	County 4
Colonel Sibthorpe	Tory	Lincoln	Borough 3
Alderman C. Smith	Tory	St. Albans	Borough 3
Mr. Stanley	Whig	Lancashire	County 4
Alderman Thompson	Tory	London	Borough 3
C. P. Thompson	Whig	Dover	Borough 3
Colonel Torrens	Whig	Ipswich	Borough 3
Alderman Waithman	Whig	London	Borough 3
Mr. Warburton	Whig	Bridport	Borough 3
Mr. W. Ward	Tory	London	Borough 3
Mr. Western	Whig	Essex	County 4
Mr. T. Whitmore	Tory	Bridgnorth	Borough 3
Mr. Wodehouse	Tory	Norfolk	County 4
Alderman Wood	Whig	London	Borough 3
Colonel Wood	Tory	Breconshire	County 3
J. Wood	Whig	Preston	Borough 3
Sir J. Wrottesley	Whig	Staffordshire	County 3
Sir W. W. Wynn	Tory	Denbighshire	County 4

Sources: Hansard Indexes 27 (1813–1814), 28 (1814), 29 (1814–1815), 30 (1815), 16 (1826–1827), 18 (1828), 19 (1828). Additionally, information was derived from Craig (1973), Thorne (1986), Judd (1955), Philbin (1965), Porritt and Porritt (1909), Stenton (1976), and Gash (1977).
a. The coding of the 1832 Reform Act is described in chapter 5: 1 is continued representation, with seats reduced; 2 is continued representation with no change in seats; 3 is continued representation with seats increased; and 4 is newly created representation.

Appendix 4   Details of Parliamentary Proceedings, 1814 to 1846

Volume 27 (1813 to 1814)

5 April and 25 April 1814 Petitions presented for and against the Corn Laws.

5 May Sir Henry Parnell's motion: "That it is expedient that the exportation of corn, grain, meal, malt and flour, from any part of the United Kingdom, should be permitted at all times, without the payment of any duty, and without receiving any bounty whatever." (c. 666)

13 May Report on Parnell's resolutions on the Corn Laws.

16 May Further consideration of the resolutions.

17 May Report on Corn Trade recommitted.

18 May Report on Corn Trade.

23 May Vote for a Committee to inquire into the Corn Laws, defeated by 99 to 42, majority 57. (c. 997)
Third reading of Corn Exportation Bill 107 to 127, majority 80. (c. 1013)

24 May Corn Importation Bill, petitions, 3 and 6 June.

6 June Committee on the Corn Laws: Vote that the report should be taken into consideration in six months (amendment by General

Gascoyne) passed 116 to 106. Chancellor of the Exchequer on behalf of the government had proposed three weeks. (c. 1102)

Volume 29 (1814 to 1815)

14 and 17 February 1815   State of the Corn Laws, average price of bread (15 February).

22 February   Committee reported on State of the Corn Laws—voted for the House in the Committee. The first three resolutions were agreed. The fourth resolution fixing prices at which wheat shall be imported gave rise to debate. The government proposed 80 s. as the domestic price at which foreign corn was admissible.

23 February   Amendment proposed by Mr. Baring to substitute 72 s. for 80 s., was defeated by 209 to 265, majority 144. (c. 1043)

27 February   Vote for bringing up the report including price of 80 s., passed 235 to 238, majority 197. (c. 1082)

Report to be read passed 193 to 129, majority 164. (c. 1084)

28 February   Mr. Calcraft's amendment to substitute 72 s. for 80 s. defeated by 154 to 135, majority in favor of 80 s., 119. Subsequent resolutions agreed to and leave given to bring in a bill on said resolutions. (c. 1117)

1 March   Corn Bill: Amendment by Mr. Whitbread to delay the bill defeated by 109 to 130. (c. 1126)

3 March   Second reading for the bill regulating the importation of corn. Lambton's amendment that the bill be read a second time in six months time, defeated 218 to 156, majority 152. (c. 1242)

Baring's motion to delay the second reading by a week defeated 215 to 244, majority 171. Bill committed on the following Monday. (c. 1243)

Volume 30 (1815)

8 March 1815   Amendment to delay bringing up the report by six months defeated 168 to 150, majority 118. (c. 69)

Baring's amendment to bring up the report after the Easter recess defeated 206 to 257, majority 149. (c. 77)

For price of 80 s., passed 184 to 178, majority 106. (c. 77)

Baring amendment to delay the third reading defeated 220 to 246, majority 174. (c. 78)

10 March Third reading: Protheroe's amendment to delay the measure by six months defeated 245 to 277, majority 168. (c. 124)

"After the Bill had been read a third time, Mr. Portman proposed by way of rider, the substitution of 76 s. as the protecting price instead of 80 s. On this proposition another division took place. For the Amendment 73, Against 213, Majority against 241."

Baring introduced two motions:

1. Rendering bill liable to be amended or repealed during the present session. This was agreed to.

2. Making the duration of the measure coextensive with the Bank Restriction Act. Negatived without a division.

Bill then passed. (c. 125)

Volume 16 (1826 to 1827)

22 and 28 November 1826 Petitions for and against revision of the Corn Laws presented by Sir T. Lethbridge (protectionist) and Joseph Hume (free trader). (c. 97, c. 143)

1 March 1827 House resolved into committee to consider the acts relative to the trade in corn, moved by George Canning. (c. 758)

Ministerial measures: Revision of duties, when corn was 60 to 61 s. a quarter, the duty was to be £1, and for every shilling the price was raised, the duty was decreased by 2 shillings until 70 shillings. Above 70 shillings, the duty should be 1 shilling for every quarter.

Between 59 and 60 shillings, the duty shall be £1 2 shillings. Under 59 shillings, for every shilling under 59 shillings, the duty was to be increased by 2 shillings. (c. 772–773)

Similar measures for barley, oats, rye, beans, peas, etc.

8 March Committee on Corn Trade Acts.

9 March Whitmore's amendment: When the price of wheat shall be between 50 and 51 s. the quarter, the duty shall be £1 for every quarter. The original resolution had the same duty at the price of 60 shillings. (c. 1100–1101)

Amendment defeated 335 to 350, majority 285. (c. 1122)

Volume 17 (1827)

27 March 1827 Report of Committee on Corn Trade Acts.

Hume's amendment that the duty should be reduced by 1 shilling yearly. From 5 July 1827 to 5 July 1828, the rate shall be 15 shilling a quarter on wheat. The following year it would be 14 shilling, next 13 shilling, etc., until 5 July 1833, when a 10 shilling fixed duty on every quarter of wheat from foreign countries would be permanent, except from Canada. (c. 100)

Hume's amendment defeated 140 to 116, majority 124. (c. 105)

29 March Corn Duties Bill based on the late resolutions, first reading. (c. 132)

2 April Second reading.

Sir T. Lethbridge's amendment that the bill be read six months hence. (c. 177)

Divisions: For the second reading, 243; For the amendment 78, majority 165. (c. 198)

6 and 9 April Further reports on the bill. (c. 286, c. 345)

12 April Third reading passed, no division list or figures (might have passed without division). (c. 391–392)

18 June Corn Trade Committee proposed by Canning, passed 238 to 252, majority 186. (c. 1339)

Volume 18 (1828)

31 March 1828 Committee on Corn Laws. (c. 1379–1411)

Volume 19 (1828)

22 April 1828 Calcraft's amendment to revise the scale of duties to correspond to Canning's scale of duties of 1827. (c. 29)

Amendment defeated 202 to 258, majority 144. (c. 39)

25 April Committee on Corn Laws: Amendment of Benett by which the duty decreased 2 shillings instead of 1 shilling when the price was 62 shillings, till it reached 67 shillings. Defeated 230 to 232, majority 198. (c. 155)

Amendment of Portman: Descending scale at 1 shilling each. Instead of 1 shilling advance in the duty on every shilling of fall in price, it should be 2 shillings. This was the scale of 1827. Defeated 140 to 150, majority 90. (c. 156)

29 April First reading of the Corn Bill.

Hume's amendment (same as his previous one of 27 March 1827): for original resolution 139, Hume's amendment 27, majority 112. (c. 229)

Further amendments defeated.

23 May Third reading (c. 900–902). No figures available in *Hansard*.

Volume 60 (1842)

3 February 1842 Peel's introduction of the consideration of revision of the scale of duties relating to importation of foreign corn. (c. 40)

9 February Ministerial plan relating to duties on import of foreign corn. (c. 202–236)

16 February Amendment against the adoption of the government measure as the principle of the sliding scale, causing price fluctuations, was maintained. Amendment defeated 349 to 226, majority 123. (c. 620)

18 February Villiers's motion for total repeal. (c. 648)

24 February Villiers's motion that all duties cease defeated 393 to 390, majority 303. (c. 1082)

25 February Christopher's amendment to the Ministerial Plan, substituting a more protective scale of duties (c. 1093). Average price of wheat between 50 and 51 shillings a quarter, duty to be 25 shillings. (c. 1103)

25 February Division on the original question, that under 51 shillings, the duty for every quarter of wheat should be 20 shillings. Passed by 306 to 104, majority 202. (c. 1168)

28 February Division on duty of 7 shillings on oats when priced between 19 and 20 shillings a quarter. Passed by 256 to 253, majority 203. (c. 1221)

Volume 61 (1842)

4 March 1842 First reading of Peel's revision of the sliding scale. (c. 44)

9 March Second reading of above. Passed 284 to 176, majority 108. (c. 405)

14 March Committee stage, with Ward's motion for the appointment of a Select Committee on Burdens on Land. (c. 519)

Defeated 230 to 115, majority 115. (c. 572)

Division on the motion that the chairman of the Committee report the progress of the bill, passed 89 to 64, majority 25. (c. 582)

Volume 62 (1842)

7 April 1842 Cobden's amendment to the third reading, that it was "unjust to pass a law to regulate, with a view to raise unnaturally, the prices of food." (c. 27)

Amendment defeated 236 to 286, majority 150. (c. 58)

7 April Amendment by Hindley to adjourn the debate defeated 247 to 268, majority 179. (Division List c. 61–63)

On third reading 229 to 90, majority 139. (c. 63–66)

Various motions regarding bonding and warehousing defeated. Third reading passed. (c. 75)

An amendment by Mr. French, that the measures affecting the importation of flour from foreign countries should be delayed six months, was rejected without a division. (c. 66–68)

Volume 64 (1842)

11 July 1842 Repeal of the Corn Laws motion by Villiers. (c. 1307) Defeated by 231 to 117, majority 114. (c. 1385)

Volume 65 (1842)

22 July 1842 Gibson's amendment that the House should consider the distressed state of the country. (c. 517)

Volume 73 (1844)

12 March 1844 Protective duties, the agricultural interest: Cobden's motion for a Select Committee into the effects of protective duties on tenant farmers and laborers. Defeated 224 to 133, majority 91. (c. 960)

Volume 75 (1844)

25 June 1844 Villiers motion on abolition of the Corn Laws. (c. 1353)

26 June Villiers motion defeated 328 to 124, majority 204. (c. 1549)

Volume 84 (1846)

27 February 1846 Ministerial measures: First reading passed 337 to 240, majority 97. (c. 349; Division List c. 349–354)

2 March Total and Immediate Repeal Motion defeated—vote on the chairman reporting progress defeated 227 to 270. (c. 422–467; Division List c. 467–470)

3 March Total and immediate repeal defeated 265 to 278, majority 187. (c. 527–575; Division List c. 575–578)

Volume 85 (1846)

27 March 1846   Ministerial measures: Second reading passed 302 to 214, majority 88. (c. 265; Division List c. 265–271)

Volume 86 (1846)

15 May 1846   Ministerial measures: Third reading passed 327 to 229, majority 98. (c. 721; Division List c. 721–726)

Appendix 5   Details of Members of Parliament Sampled for Newspaper Analysis

Table A.3
Details on Members of Parliament sampled for newspaper analysis

	Constituency and District Type (1 = county, 2 = borough)	Newspapers and Party	Speaking Record	Party Affiliation	Voting Record[a]	Notes
Sir T. Acland	Devon Co. (North) (1)	North Devon Advertiser (Conservative) North Devon Journal (Liberal)	19 Feb., 3 March	Non-Peelite Cons.	*Strong protectionist:* '42: 2 prot., 2 abstain '43: 2 prot. '44: prot. '45: prot. '46: 2 prot., abstain on 3rd reading	
Col. Austin	Kent Co. (West) (1)	Kentish Independent (Lib.), Kentish Mercury (Neutral), West Kent Guardian (Cons.), Kentish Observer (Cons.), Kent Herald (Lib.), Kentish Gazette (Cons.)	16 March (on hops)	Non-Peelite Cons.	*Very strong protectionist:* '45: prot. '46: 3 prot.	Won uncontested by-election in April 1845

Appendixes

Rt. Hon. F. T. Baring	Portsmouth (2)	*Hampshire Telegraph* (Lib.)	24 March	Liberal	*Weak free trader:* '42: 2 free trade, 2 abstain '43: 1 prot., 1 abstain '44: abstain '45: abstain '46: 3 free trade	Former Chancellor of Exchequer under Whigs; resided outside constituency
P. Bennet	Suffolk Co. (West) (1)	*Bury and Suffolk Herald* (Cons.), *Suffolk Chronicle* (Lib.)	20 Feb., 15 May	Non-Peelite Cons.	*Very strong protectionist:* '46: 3 prot.	Won uncontested by-election in July 1845
Lord G. Bentinck	Kings Lynn (2)	*Lynn Advertiser* (Cons.), *Norfolk Chronicle* (Cons.)	27 Jan., 27 Feb., 6 March, 9 March, 26 March, 4 May, 5 May, 8 May, 15 May	Non-Peelite Cons.	*Strong protectionist:* '42: 3 prot., 1 abstain '43: 1 prot., 1 abstain '44: prot. '45: abstain '46: 3 prot.	Leader of Protectionists
Hon. C. F. Berkeley	Cheltenham (2)	*Cheltenham Chronicle* (Cons.), *Cheltenham Journal* (Cons.), *Cheltenham Looker On* (Cons.), *Cheltenham Examiner* (Lib.), *Cheltenham Free Press* (Lib.)	27 Feb., 3 March	Reformer	*Strong free trader:* '42: 4 free trade '43: 1 free trade, 1 abstain '44: abstain '45: abstain '46: 3 free trade	

Table A.3
(continued)

	Constituency and District Type (1 = county, 2 = borough)	Newspapers and Party	Speaking Record	Party Affiliation	Voting Record[a]	Notes
Dr. Bowring	Bolton (2)	*Bolton Chronicle* (Cons.), *Bolton Free Press* (Lib.)	16 Feb. (interjected), 9 March	Reformer	*Very strong free trader*: '42: 4 free trade '43: 2 free trade '44: free trade '45: free trade '46: 3 free trade	Resided outside constituency
Lord Brooke	Warwick Co. (South) (1)	*Lemington Spa Courier* (Cons.)	10 Feb. (maiden speech in Commons), 12 May	Non-Peelite Cons.	*Very strong protectionist*: '46: 3 prot.	Won uncontested by-election in Nov. 1845
E. Buller	Stafford (2)	*Stafford Advertiser* (Indep.)	23 Feb.	Liberal	*Strong free trader*: '42: 3 free trade, 1 abstain '43: 1 free trade, 1 abstain '44: free trade '45: free trade '46: 2 free trade, 1 abstain (3rd reading)	

H. N. Burroughes	Norfolk Co. (East) (1)	*Norfolk News* (Lib.), *Norfolk Chronicle* (Cons.)	6 March	Non-Peelite Cons.	*Strong protectionist:* '42: 3 prot., 1 abstain '43: 1 prot., 1 abstain '44: abstain '45: prot. '46: 3 prot.
R. A. Christopher	Lincoln Co. (North) (1)	*Boston, Stamford, and Lincolnshire Herald* (Cons.), *Lincolnshire Chronicle* (Cons.), *Lincolnshire, Rutland, and Stamford Mercury* (Indep.), *Lincoln Standard* (Cons.)	26 Feb.	Non-Peelite Cons.	*Very strong protectionist:* '42: 4 prot. '43: 2 prot. '44: prot. '45: prot. '46: 3 prot.
Viscount Clive	Shropshire Co. (North) (1)	*Shropshire Conservative* (Cons.–Old Tory)	10 Feb.	Non-Peelite Cons.	*Very strong protectionist:* '43: 2 prot. '44: prot. '45: prot. '46: 3 prot. Won uncontested by-election in Jan. 1843

Table A.3
(continued)

	Constituency and District Type (1 = county, 2 = borough)	Newspapers and Party	Speaking Record	Party Affiliation	Voting Record[a]	Notes
W. Deedes	Kent Co. (East) (1)	*Kentish Gazette* (Cons.), *Kentish Observer* (Cons.), *Kent Herald* (Lib.), *Kentish Independent* (Lib.), *Kentish Mercury* (Neutral/Indep.), *West Kent Guardian* (Cons.)	9 Feb. (maiden speech in Commons)	Non-Peelite Cons.	*Very strong protectionist*: '45: prot. '46: 3 prot.	Won uncontested by-election in March 1845
E. B. Denison	Yorkshire Co. (West Riding) (1)	*Doncaster Chronicle* (Cons.), *Doncaster Gazette* (Lib.), *Harrogate Advertiser* (Neutral)	26 Feb.	Non-Peelite Cons.	*Strong protectionist*: '42: 3 prot., 1 abstain '43: 2 prot. '44: prot. '45: prot. '46: 3 prot.	

Appendixes 345

F. H. Dickinson	Somerset Co. (West) (1)	Somerset Co. Herald (Cons.), Somerset Co. Gazette (Lib.)	16 Feb.	Peelite	*Very weak free trader:* '42: 3 prot., 1 abstain '43: 2 prot. '44: prot. '45: prot. '46: 3 free trade	
Sir H. Douglas	Liverpool (2)	Liberal papers: *Liverpool Albion, Liverpool Chronicle, Liverpool Journal, Liverpool Mercury, Liverpool Times, Yr Amserau* Conservative papers: *Liverpool Courier, Liverpool Mail, Liverpool Standard* Neutral papers: *Liverpool European Times, Liverpool General Advertiser*	13 Feb.	Non-Peelite Cons.	*Strong protectionist:* '42: 4 prot. '43: 1 prot., 1 abstain '44: prot. '45: prot. '46: 3 prot.	Won uncontested by-election in Feb. 1842; resided outside constituency
Sir J. Easthope	Leicester (2)	*Leicester Mercury* (Lib.), *Leicester Chronicle* (Lib.), *Leicester Journal* (Cons.), *Leicester Advertiser* (Neutral)	11 May	Liberal	*Strong free trader:* '42: 4 free trade '43: 2 abstain '44: free trade '45: free trade '46: 3 free trade	Resided outside constituency

Table A.3 (continued)

	Constituency and District Type (1 = county, 2 = borough)	Newspapers and Party	Speaking Record	Party Affiliation	Voting Record[a]	Notes
Wynn Ellis	Leicester (2)	Leicester Mercury (Lib.), Leicester Chronicle (Lib.), Leicester Journal (Cons.), Leicester Advertiser (Neutral)	6 March	Liberal	*Strong free trader*: '42: 3 free trade, 1 abstain '43: 2 free trade '44: free trade '45: free trade '46: 3 free trade	
G. Finch	Rutland Co. (1)	Lincolnshire, Rutland, and Stamford Mercury (Indep.), Lincoln Standard (Cons.), Boston, Stamford, and Lincolnshire Herald (Cons.), Lincolnshire Chronicle (Cons.)	26 Feb., 6 March, 9 March, 26 March, 5 May	Non-Peelite Cons.	*Very strong protectionist*: '46: 3 prot.	Won uncontested by-election in Feb. 1846

J. Floyer	Dorset Co. (1)	*Sherbourne Journal* (Lib.), *Sherbourne Mercury* (Cons.), *Dorset Co. Chronicle* (Cons.), *Western Flying Post* (Cons.)	8 May, 11 May	Non-Peelite Cons.	*Very strong protectionist*: '46: 3 prot.	Won uncontested by-election in Feb. 1846, when two of the three Dorset Co. MPs resigned
A. E. Fuller	Sussex Co. (East) (1)	*Sussex Advertiser* (Lib.), *Sussex Agricultural Express* (Cons.)	16 March (on hops), 26 March	Non-Peelite Cons.	*Very strong protectionist*: '42: 4 prot. '43: 2 prot. '44: prot. '45: prot. '46: 3 prot.	
T. Gisborne	Nottingham (2)	*Nottingham Journal* (Cons.), *Nottingham Mercury* (Lib.), *Nottingham Review* (Lib.)	27 Jan.	Reformer	*Weak free trader*: '43: 1 prot., 1 free trade '44: free trade '45: abstain '46: 3 free trade	Won a contested by-election in April 1843
M. Gore	Barnstaple (2)	*North Devon Advertiser* (Cons.), *North Devon Journal* (Lib.)	23 Feb., 15 May	Peelite	*Very weak free trader*: '42: 4 prot. '43: 2 prot. '44: prot. '45: prot. '46: 3 free trade	

Table A.3
(continued)

	Constituency and District Type (1 = county, 2 = borough)	Newspapers and Party	Speaking Record	Party Affiliation	Voting Record[a]	Notes
Right Hon. Sir J. Graham	Dorchester (2)	*Dorset Co. Chronicle* (Cons.), *Sherbourne Journal* (Lib.), *Western Flying Post* (Cons.), *Sherbourne Mercury* (Cons.)	10 Feb., 27 Feb. (interrupted), 6 March (interrupted), 27 March, 11 May, 15 May (interrupted)	Peelite	*Very weak free trader:* '42: 4 prot. '43: 2 prot. '44: prot. '45: prot. '46: 3 free trade	Was in Peel's Cabinet as Home Secretary; resided outside constituency
T. P. Halsey	Hertford Co. (1)	*Hertford Co. Herald* (Neutral), *Hertfordshire Co. Press* (Cons.)	16 Feb.	Non-Peelite Cons.	*Very strong protectionist:* '46: 3 prot.	Won uncontested by-election in Jan. 1846 (predecessor became peer)
G. J. Heathcote	Rutland Co. (1)	*Lincolnshire, Rutland, and Stamford Mercury* (Indep.), *Boston, Stamford, and Lincolnshire Herald* (Cons.), *Lincolnshire Chronicle* (Cons.), *Lincoln Standard* (Cons.)	12 Feb.	Reformer	*Strong protectionist:* '42: 2 prot., 2 abstain '43: 2 prot. '44: prot. '45: prot. '46: 3 prot.	

Hon. S. Herbert	Wiltshire Co. (South) (1)	*Wiltshire and Gloucestershire Standard* (Cons.), *Devon and Wiltshire Gazette* (Cons.), *Wiltshire Independent* (Lib.)	27 Jan., 9 Feb., 8 May	Peelite	*Very weak free trader:* '42: 4 prot. '43: 2 prot. '44: prot. '45: prot. '46: 3 free trade
A. Hope	Maidstone (2)	*Maidstone Journal* (Cons.), *Maidstone Gazette* (Lib.)	9 Feb.	Non-Peelite Cons.	*Strong protectionist:* '42: 3 prot., 1 abstain '43: 2 prot. '44: prot. '45: abstain '46: 3 prot.
P. H. Howard	Carlisle (2)	*Carlisle Journal* (Lib.), *Carlisle Patriot* (Cons.), *Cumberland Pacquet* (Cons.)	27 Jan., 6 March, 9 March	Liberal	*Very weak free trader:* '42: 4 abstain '43: 2 prot. '44: prot. '45: prot. '46: 3 free trade	Resided outside constituency
W. Hutt	Gateshead (2)	*Gateshead Observer* (Lib.)	23 Feb., 3 March	Liberal	*Strong free trader:* '42: 3 free trade, 1 abstain '43: 2 abstain '44: free trade '45: free trade '46: 3 free trade

Was in Peel's Cabinet as Secretary at War (appointed May 1845)

Table A.3
(continued)

	Constituency and District Type (1 = county, 2 = borough)	Newspapers and Party	Speaking Record	Party Affiliation	Voting Record[a]	Notes
W. James	Cumberland Co. (East) (1)	Cumberland Pacquet (Cons.), Carlisle Journal (Lib.), Carlisle Patriot (Cons.)	16 Feb.	Liberal	*Weak free trader*: '42: 1 prot., 3 abstain '43: 2 abstain '44: abstain '45: abstain '46: 3 free trade	
Hon. W. Lascelles	Wakefield (2)	Wakefield Journal (Cons.)	9 Feb.	Peelite	*Weak free trader*: '42: 1 free trade, 3 abstain '43: 2 abstain '44: abstain '45: free trade '46: 3 free trade	Resided outside constituency
W. C. Martin	Newport (IoW) (2)	Isle of Wight Observer (Cons.)	12 Feb.	Peelite	*Weak free trader*: '42: 2 prot., 2 abstain '43: 2 prot. '44: prot. '45: prot. '46: 3 free trade	Resided outside constituency

Appendixes

W. Miles	Somerset Co. (East) (1)	*Westonian and Somerset Mercury* (Lib.), *Somerset Co. Herald* (Cons.), *Somerset Co. Gazette* (Lib.)	27 Jan. (twice), 13 Feb., 16 Feb., 25 Feb., 6 March, 9 March, 11 May	Non-Peelite Cons.	*Strong protectionist*: '42: 2 prot., 2 abstain '43: 1 prot., 1 abstain '44: prot. '45: prot. '46: 3 prot.	Sat in constituency where the League actively challenged registers
G. Muntz	Birmingham (2)	*Birmingham Advertiser* (Cons.), *Birmingham Journal* (Lib.), *Birmingham Pilot* (Lib.), *Birmingham Gazette* (Neutral), *Midlands Counties Herald* (Neutral)	20 Feb., 23 Feb.	Reformer	*Strong free trader*: '42: 1 free trade, 3 abstain '43: 2 free trade '44: free trade '45: free trade '46: 3 free trade	Resided outside constituency
G. Palmer	Essex Co. (South) (1)	*Chelmsford Chronicle* (Neutral), *Essex Herald* (Neutral), *Essex Standard* (Cons.)	9 Feb., 9 March, 12 May	Non-Peelite Cons.	*Strong protectionist*: '42: 3 prot., 1 abstain '43: 2 abstain '44: prot. '45: prot. '46: 3 prot.	

Table A.3 (continued)

	Constituency and District Type (1 = county, 2 = borough)	Newspapers and Party	Speaking Record	Party Affiliation	Voting Record[a]	Notes
J. Plumptre	Kent Co. (East) (1)	*Kentish Gazette* (Cons.), *Kentish Observer* (Cons.), *Kent Herald* (Lib.), *Kentish Independent* (Lib.), *Kentish Mercury* (Neutral), *West Kent Guardian* (Cons.)	16 March (on hops), 24 March, 12 May	Non-Peelite Cons.	*Strong protectionist*: '42: 3 prot., 1 abstain '43: 2 prot. '44: prot. '45: prot. '46: 3 prot.	
W. Rashleigh	Cornwall Co. (East) (1)	*Cornwall Roy. Gazette* (Cons.), *West Briton* (Lib.)	24 March	Non-Peelite Cons.	*Very strong protectionist*: '42: 4 prot. '43: 2 prot. '44: prot. '45: prot. '46: 3 prot.	
Lord Rendlesham	Suffolk Co. (East) (1)	*Suffolk Chronicle* (Lib.), *Bury and Suffolk Herald* (Cons.)	26 March	Non-Peelite Cons.	*Strong protectionist*: '43: 2 prot. '44: prot. '45: abstain '46: 3 prot.	Won by-election in April 1843

Appendixes 353

Lord Sandon	Liverpool (2)	Liberal papers: *Liverpool Albion, Liverpool Chronicle, Liverpool Journal, Liverpool Mercury, Liverpool Times, Yr Amserau* Conservative papers: *Liverpool Courier, Liverpool Mail, Liverpool Standard* Neutral papers: *Liverpool European Times, Liverpool General Advertiser*	9 Feb.	Peelite	*Very weak free trader:* '42: 4 prot. '43: 2 prot. '44: prot. '45: prot. '46: 3 free trade	Resided outside constituency
Col. Sibthorpe	Lincoln City (2)	*Lincoln Standard* (Cons.), *Boston, Stamford, and Lincolnshire Herald* (Cons.), *Lincolnshire Chronicle* (Cons.), *Lincolnshire, Rutland, and Stamford Mercury* (Indep.)	27 Jan., 12 Feb. (interjected), 26 Feb., 6 March, 9 March, 2 March, 17 March, 26 March (interruption), 27 March (interrruption)	Non-Peelite Cons.	*Strong protectionist:* '42: 3 prot., 1 abstain '43: 2 prot. '44: prot. '45: prot. '46: 3 prot.	

Table A.3 (continued)

	Constituency and District Type (1 = county, 2 = borough)	Newspapers and Party	Speaking Record	Party Affiliation	Voting Record[a]	Notes
R. Spooner	Birmingham (2)	*Birmingham Advertiser* (Cons.), *Birmingham Journal* (Lib.), *Birmingham Pilot* (Lib.), *Birmingham Gazette* (Neutral), *Midlands Counties Herald* (Neutral)	26 Feb., 27 Feb.	Non-Peelite Cons.	*Very strong protectionist:* '45: prot. '46: 3 prot.	Won by-election in July 1844
Sir J. Trollope	Lincoln Co. (South) (1)	*Wisbech Advertiser* (Neutral), *Boston, Stamford, and Lincolnshire Herald* (Cons.), *Lincolnshire Chronicle* (Cons.), *Lincolnshire, Rutland, and Stamford Mercury* (Indep.), *Lincoln Standard* (Cons.)	17 March, 24 March	Non-Peelite Cons.	*Strong protectionist:* '42: 2 prot., 1 free trade, 1 abstain '43: 2 prot. '44: prot. '45: prot. '46: 3 prot.	See notes below table for information on Trollope's voting record.

Hon. C. Villiers	Wolverhampton (2)	*Wolverhampton Chronicle* (Cons.)	26 Feb., 2 March, 3 March, 6 March, 15 May	Reformer	*Very strong free trader*: '42: 4 free trade '43: 2 free trade '44: free trade '45: free trade '46: 3 free trade	Core member of the League; made annual motion for repeal from 1838; resided outside constituency
H. G. Ward	Sheffield (2)	*Sheffield "Iris"* (Lib.), *Sheffield Independent* (Lib.), *Sheffield Mercury* (Cons.)	13 Feb., 3 March, 6 March	Liberal	*Strong free trader*: '42: 3 free trade, 1 abstain '43: 2 free trade '44: free trade '45: free trade '46: 3 free trade	Resided outside constituency
C. Wood	Halifax (2)	*Halifax Guardian* (Cons.)	15 May	Liberal	*Weak free trader*: '42: 3 free trade, 1 abstain '43: 2 abstain '44: free trade '45: abstain '46: 3 free trade	Became Chancellor of Exchequer in Russell's Government (46 July 1852); Resided about 20 miles from constituency
Marquess Worcester	Gloucester Co. (1)	*Wiltshire and Gloucestershire Standard* (Cons.)	27 March, 15 May	Non-Peelite Cons.	*Strong protectionist*: '46: 3 prot.	27 Feb. 1846, predecessor (F. W. Charteris, Cons., who had been voting protectionist) resigns, and Worcester elected unopposed

Table A.3
(continued)

	Constituency and District Type (1 = county, 2 = borough)	Newspapers and Party	Speaking Record	Party Affiliation	Voting Record[a]	Notes
Lord Worsley	Lincoln Co. (North) (1)	*Boston, Stamford, and Lincolnshire Herald* (Cons.), *Lincolnshire Chronicle* (Cons.), *Lincolnshire, Rutland, and Stamford Mercury* (Indep.), *Lincoln Standard* (Cons.)	10 Feb., 2 March, 3 March	Liberal	*Weak protectionist:* '42: 2 free trade, 2 prot. '43: 1 free trade, 1 prot. '44: prot. '45: prot. '46: 3 prot.	See notes below table for information on Worsley's voting record.

Sources: Aydelotte (n.d.); Brown (1985); Dod's *Parliamentary Companion 1846* (London); *Hansard* indexes; Lee (1976); *Newspaper Press Directory* (1846); Stenton (1976); Wadsworth (1954).

Note: Divisions to evaluate voting pattern (N = number of sampled MPs voting in the division):

1842:
16 February: Motion to go into Committee, rejecting amendment criticizing present Corn Laws and protesting against further legislation founded on the same principles (N = 32).
9 March: Order for a second reading of the Corn Importation Bill (N = 28).
7 April: Third reading of the Corn Law Importation Bill (N = 22).
11 July: Motion to go into Committee of Supply, rejecting Villiers's amendment for repeal of the Corn Laws (N = 25).

1843:
12 May: Motion for adjournment of debate on the Corn Laws (N = 26).
15 May: Villiers's motion for abolition of the Corn Laws (N = 33).

1844:
26 June: Villiers's motion for Committee of the Whole to consider repeal of the Corn Laws ($N = 34$).
1845:
10 June: Villiers's motion for Committee of the Whole to consider abolition of restrictions on corn ($N = 34$).
1846:
27 February: Motion for Committee on Corn Importation to reject delaying amendment (first reading of repeal) ($N = 48$).
27 March: Second reading of the Corn Law Repeal Bill ($N = 48$).
15 May: Third reading of the Corn Law Repeal Bill ($N = 46$).

Notes on the voting records of Trollope and Worsley:

A review of the voting records and parliamentary speeches of Trollope and Worsley for the years 1842 and 1843 (on all bills relating to British trade policy) indicates that both were essentially protectionists who wished to see no alteration in the pre-1842 sliding scale. Their "free-trade" votes were not free trade as such but either protests against Peel's sliding scale or anomalous votes on a procedural amendment to adjourn debate.

a. Classification of voting patterns:

Very strong protectionist/Free trader: During their term always voted and consistently voted protectionist or free trade.
Strong protectionist/Free trader: Mostly voted protectionist or free trade but sometimes did not vote.
Weak protectionist/Free trader: Voted, on balance, protectionist or free trade but several times did not vote and/or once voted for the other side.
Very weak free trader: Consistently voted protectionist before 1846 (Peelite, or Liberal who acted like a Peelite).
Very weak protectionist: Not a relevant category for this sample.

Notes

Chapter 1

1. On the "puzzle-solving" approach to research, see Grofman (2001).

2. While Peel carried the repeal legislation in June 1846, he was defeated shortly thereafter on a coercion bill for Ireland and resigned as Prime Minister. The real reason for his defeat was the Corn Laws, as protectionists retaliated against Peel by opposing the Coercion Bill. In July 1846, Lord Russell formed a Whig administration (in which Whigs, Radicals, and Irish were in a minority) that lasted until the general election of 1847, after which the Whigs returned to govern with an increased number of MPs.

3. An important exception is the work of Austen-Smith and Riker (Austen-Smith and Riker 1987, 1990; Austen-Smith 1990).

4. For references, see Weingast's summary of the important contributions to the exogeneity of institutions (Weingast 2002, 669).

5. Economists, too, have recently pushed the frontiers well beyond the early work of Douglass North by questioning not only the origins and development of institutions but also the causal relationships that drive institutions (Acemoglu 2003; Acemoglu and Johnson 2003; Rodrik and Subramanian 2003).

6. More accurately, roll-call votes are mapped into a two-dimensional space in which the first dimension reflects a liberal-conservative divide over the role of the government in the economy. It is this first dimension that Poole and Rosenthal summarize as "ideology," although they also note that issues that are bundled together will invariably underpin this ideology. They maintain, therefore, that "spatial voting is not inconsistent with voting on the basis of economic interests. Economic interests, though difficult to measure, can influence how issues are mapped onto the space captured by D-NOMINATE. Moreover, members of Congress will express these interests strategically, voting by the use of logrolls, implicit or explicit, in which various interests are packaged. We thus find only a few dimensions of voting, not because legislators are simpleminded with respect to the multitude of issues that arise but because they are strategic actors, seeking to enter into coalitions that further their own or their supporters' interests on the issues." They argue that parties are essential to bundling complex issues into a low-dimensional space (Poole and Rosenthal 1997, 35, 118). Hence, Poole and Rosenthal do not claim that interests and parties do not matter but rather that a spatial model better accounts for the data than do models that attempt to measure interests and party directly.

7. Austen-Smith (1990, 124) noted that "despite the prevalence of institutionalised debate, the issue of when debate or, more generally, speechmaking might be expected to have real effects on legislative decisions does not seem to have been addressed." He argued that, given preferences that were not too dissimilar, legislators' speeches could indeed affect outcomes, although he noted (with Riker) that the information revealed through debate would not necessarily yield socially optimal decisions.

8. This section derives from (Schonhardt-Bailey 1997, 1: 1–51).

9. In 1814, the average price of wheat was 74 s. 4 d. per quarter, but following the war and with a good harvest in 1815, the price dropped to 52 s. 10 d. William Spence noted in 1815 that "thousands of farmers, who but twelve months ago were living in prosperity, are utterly unable to raise money for their taxes merely, and tens of thousands to discharge them are force to sell their produce at less than one half its prime-cost" (Spence 1815, reprinted in Schonhardt-Bailey 1997, 1: 101–118).

10. See also Baring (1815), reprinted in Schonhardt-Bailey (1997, 1: 349–352).

11. See also Huskisson (1814), Spence (1815), and Malthus (1815), all reprinted in Schonhardt-Bailey (1997, 55–74, 101–118, 341–345).

12. Heathcote and Paul (1815), Sussex and Goucester (1815), and Malthus (1815), all reprinted in Schonhardt-Bailey (1997, 1: 55–74, 345–348, 352–354).

13. Ricardo (1822), reprinted in Schonhardt-Bailey (1997, 1: 128–158). J. R. McCulloch, J. S. Mill, and Joseph Hume also supported a fixed duty, although Mill and Hume suggested a lower starting duty (McCulloch 1822, Mill 1825 and 1826, and Hume 1828, all reprinted in Schonhardt-Bailey 1997, 1: 158–165, 165–187, 204–231, 386–393).

14. Canning was Foreign Secretary from 1822 to April 1827, when he became Prime Minister.

15. Canning (1827), reprinted in Schonhardt-Bailey (1997, 1: 355–366).

16. Goderich (1827), reprinted in Schonhardt-Bailey (1997, 1: 366–377).

17. Hilton (1977, 284–286) describes the misunderstanding and disagreement that emerged in an ambiguous rider that Huskisson proposed to Wellington's warehousing amendment to the 1827 bill. In the House of Commons, Huskisson read the correspondence between himself and Wellington to the House of Commons, exposing the source of their disagreement. The keyword in this passage was "thenceforward," which Wellington read as meaning a permanent measure but Huskisson had meant as temporary (Huskisson 1827, reprinted in Schonhardt-Bailey 1997, 1: 377–386).

18. Agitation on trade policy did, however, exist before the League (see Turner 1995; Wordie 2000).

19. More recently Pickering and Tyrrell offer a different look at the League by examining the lives of its members, as well as the regions and towns in which they pursued the cause of repeal (Pickering and Tyrell 2000).

20. According to Prentice, the *Times* "had an influence, for good, beyond that of any other journal" and its leader article gave "fresh impulse to the agitation against the then existing Corn Laws" (Prentice 1968, 1: 136). The *Times* article is reprinted in Schonhardt-Bailey (1997, 2: 117–119).

21. The *Anti-Corn Circular* was published under three titles: (1) *The Anti-Corn Law Circular* 2 (1–57) (16 April 1839 to 8 April 1841) was published in Manchester; (2) *The Anti-*

Bread Tax Circular 3–4 (58–140) (21 April 1841 to 26 September 1843) was also published in Manchester in a larger size; and (3) *The League*, numbering 1 to end (30 September 1843 to 1846), was published in London at the League's Fleet Street office (Fay 1932, 91 n.).

22. Bright (1868), reprinted in Schonhardt-Bailey (1997, 2: 122–129).

23. Gash (1977, 91) explains that "until the Reform Act an elector claiming a vote for the county under the property qualification had to be assessed to the land tax. This necessity was abolished by the act and the way was thus thrown open for a flood of 40 shilling freeholders from the urban and industrial areas to join the county electorate." This feature of the act allowed the League to encourage and actively help arrange purchases of 40 shilling freehold voting qualifications for free-trade supporters.

24. Cobden (1968), reprinted in Schonhardt-Bailey (1997, 2: 119–121).

25. Aglionby (1846), Ashburton (1846), Richmond and Kinnaird (1846), and Sibthorp (1846), all reprinted in Schonhardt-Bailey (1997, 2: 78–80, 82–88).

26. Cayley (1844) and Day (1844), both reprinted in Schonhardt-Bailey (1997, 2: 132–152).

27. Association (1841) and Blackie (1842), both reprinted in Schonhardt-Bailey (1997, 2: 106–107, 153–156).

28. Several authors have sought to understand why Peel shifted toward repeal. Examples include Gash (1951, 1965, 1977), Crosby (1976), Irwin (1989), Jenkins (1999), and McLean (2001). Peel's own ambiguity on this subject complicates the interpretation of his shift toward repeal. As background for his decision to introduce repeal, Peel explained that he "adopted at an early period of my public life, without, I fear, much serious reflection, the opinions generally prevalent at the time among men of all parties, as to the justice and necessity of protection to domestic agriculture.... I had, however, been a willing party, both in 1828 and 1842, to the reductions which took place in the amount of protection fixed by the Corn Law of 1815" (Peel 1857, 3: 98–99). With respect to his more complete conversion to free trade by the 1840s, he remarked, "During the discussions in Parliament on the Corn Law of 1842 I was more than once pressed to give a guarantee (so far as a Minister could give it) that the amount of protection established by that law should be permanently adhered to; but although I did not then contemplate the necessity for further change, I uniformly refused to fetter the discretion of the Government by any such assurances as those that were required from me" (Peel 1857, 3: 101). While this may suggest a conversion by 1842 (or earlier), Peel then confused his readers by noting that between 1842 and the end of 1845, his opinion on protection to agriculture had "undergone a great change" (Peel 1857, 3: 101).

29. Peel (1846), reprinted in Schonhardt-Bailey (1997, 2: 58–72). The itemization of the various tariffs and the lengthy details of the incentives given to agriculturalist have been omitted from the reprinted version.

30. The repeal as a concession argument hinges on a strategy of removing objections to the continuation of aristocratic rule. This might be linked with the rise of the "responsive," benign, and efficiently run state. See, for example, Mandler (1990) and Harling (1996). (I am grateful to an anonymous reviewer for this point.)

31. This was the result of an accident. Peel was sixty-two when he died.

32. Kindleberger cites in this regard the works of Pincus (1972) and Olson (1965), along with others. It should be noted that subsequent works by Pincus (1975, 1977) have received more attention from other authors.

33. Kindleberger (1975), republished in Schonhardt-Bailey (1997, 4: 203–204, 214).

34. Rohrlich (1987), republished in Schonhardt-Bailey (1997).

35. Howe (1992), republished in Schonhardt-Bailey (1997, 4: 186). See also Howe (1997).

36. Irwin (1989), republished in Schonhardt-Bailey (1997).

37. Hilton (1979), republished in Schonhardt-Bailey (1997).

38. For an earlier version of this chapter, see Schonhardt-Bailey (1991a), republished in Schonhardt-Bailey (1997).

39. For an earlier version of this chapter, see Schonhardt-Bailey (1991b), republished in Schonhardt-Bailey (1997).

40. Stein (1984), republished in Schonhardt-Bailey (1997).

41. Cain and Hopkins (1980), republished in Schonhardt-Bailey (1997). See also Gallagher and Robinson (1953) and Semmel (1970).

42. Lake and James (1989), republished in Schonhardt-Bailey (1997).

43. It is often convenient to assume that the world can be divided into economic and political actors, but of course this does not fit reality and certainly was not the reality of nineteenth-century Britain, in which 80 percent of MPs in the 1841 to 1847 Parliament were landowners whose economic interests would most certainly be affected by abolishing protection for agriculture.

44. Milner (1997b, 15) continues that "preferences are a variable; interests are not." This is, for the most part, true; however, in chapter 5 I show that interests are more malleable in cases of policy uncertainty than under normal circumstances.

45. This, essentially, was the approach taken in my Ph.D. dissertation (Schonhardt-Bailey 1991b).

46. Using another analogy, interests speak to the left brain (logical, rational, analytical, objective), while ideas speak to the right brain (intuitive, holistic, subjective).

47. Garrett and Weingast note that "The lesser the distributional asymmetries between contending cooperative equilibria and the smaller the disparities in the power resources of actors, the more important will be ideational factors" (Garrett and Weingast 1993, 186).

48. McGillivray (2004) is an important recent exception.

Chapter 2

1. Some examples of demand-side models include Magee, Brock, et al. (1989), Rogowski (1989), Browne (1995), Adler and Lapinski (1997), Alvarez and Saving (1997), and Adler (2000). On the intersection of demand-side and supply-side models, see Hansen (1990), Shepsle and Weingast (1995), and Remington and Smith (1998).

2. These may include, for example, the conduct of committees, agenda setting, logrolling, or the redefinition of the policy choice within the legislative setting.

3. In particular, rational-choice scholars have sought to demonstrate the existence of stable policy outcomes as a function of specific institutional features that overcome problems of preference aggregation (Shepsle 1979; Shepsle and Weingast 1981).

4. Two-way party distribution (including Irish, Scottish, and Welsh votes) from Aydelotte (n.d.).

5. Strong empirical evidence from the roll-call votes suggests that voting in the 1841 to 1847 Parliament was largely unidimensional (chapter 6).

6. Jones and Erickson (1972, 7–8) note that "the free trade propagandists (i.e., the League) had done their work well and had called into existence an indefinite number of Free Trade Conservatives [Peelites] well before the Corn Law Crisis of 1845–46." However, as they faced strong pressure from their fellow "land-based Conservatives" to support protection, "the Conservative converts to free trade held their views in secret and refrained from joining Lascelles [a Conservative convert to free trade] on the Corn Laws Divisions, which makes the problem of dating their conversions a complex one" (7–8).

7. In this same letter, Cobden describes Hunter as one of his "privy councillors."

8. Manufacturers could, it was argued, move their capital abroad.

9. This conception of land and capital fails to recognize that other factors (such as time) can influence the degree to which both land and capital are "fixed." These issues are addressed in greater detail in chapter 3.

10. Edmund Burke's biography was published in 1833 to 1834 and featured prominently his famous "trustee" speech to his constituents in 1774 (Burke 1996).

11. Studies of political representation have for many years contrasted the "delegate" and "trustee" roles of legislators, where delegates are said to represent the interests (normally economic) of their constituents (Mayhew 1974), and trustees represent what they deem to be the national or wider public interest (Hill 1929; Eulau 1962; Davidson 1969; Uslaner 1999). In the words of a contemporary legislator (Edwards 2003, 352):

Life as a legislator is essentially a balancing act: one is guided first by who one is and what one believes, but also by the interests and preferences of the people he or she represents. Cynics will say that this is because voting against the interests of constituents will likely bring defeat in the next election, but it is also possible to believe that a legislator takes seriously both a "trustee" role as an elected official and a "delegate" role as the voice of the people. I will not say that the desire for reelection is never a factor in legislative decisions. It may not often be a force driving a decision in a particular direction, but it may serve as a brake, causing one to refrain from doing what one might otherwise do. In that case, the calculus is more about intensities and priorities. One asks, "Do I feel as strongly about this issue as I do about others, and if I fall on my sword for this one, will that prevent me from influencing events on matters I care more about?" Again, a matter of balance.

In early to mid-nineteenth-century Britain, a partisan divide emerged between Liberals who generally supported the delegate mode and Conservatives who advocated the trustee mode of representation (in the tradition of Edmund Burke, who is attributed with coining these terms (Burke 1906)). In the wake of the 1832 Reform Act (which, among other things, enfranchised the middle class), Conservative MPs feared that Parliament would become an assembly of "delegates," each protecting the interests of his own locality. In parliamentary debates on reform, Lord Eldon asserted: "To convert a member of the other House of Parliament into the mere representative of the peculiar place for which he was returned, instead of the representative of the whole of the Commons of England, was a perversion of one of the best principles of the constitution" (quoted in Hill 1929, 83–84). In the same vein, Sir Robert Inglis argued (quoted in Hill 1929, 83–84):

This House is not a collection of deputies...as the assemblies in some...continental countries. We are not sent here day by day to represent the opinions of our constituents. Their local rights, their municipal privileges, we are bound to protect, their general interests we are bound to consult at all times; but not their will, unless it shall coincide with our own deliberate sense of right. We are sent here with a large and liberal confidence; and when elected, we represent, not the particular place only for which we are returned, but the interests of the whole empire.

On the other hand, MPs may have voted according to the interests of their constituents, with those from industrial districts supporting repeal and those from agricultural districts opposing it. Supporters of political reform (Liberals/Whigs and Reformers) saw Conservative disdain for "delegates" as a means to protect their own vested interests and to eschew the equality of representation promised in the 1832 Reform Act ("Art. VII-1" 1837; "Postscript" 1846). For them, MPs quite rightly should vote to protect and safeguard the interests of their constituents. Richard Cobden exemplified this motivation for voting. He famously mocked the Conservatives' aversion to representing local interests in his 1844 motion to inquire into the state of agricultural distress experienced by tenant farmers and farm laborers. In his address, he proclaimed that while he was not himself a county member of Parliament (and therefore did not represent an agricultural constituency), he felt a strong sympathy for the interests of tenant farmers and farm laborers, identifying himself "as the advocate of what I conscientiously believe to be the interests of the agriculturalists" (Cobden 1844, col. 863).

12. In British vernacular, "scatter gun."

13. In addition, four Reformer MPs opposed repeal.

14. Similar arguments have been made for other political contexts (Jones 1994, 78–102; Hinich and Munger 1997, 69–71). In figures 2.1 and 2.2, the precise positions of the median MPs are unimportant, as the graphs provide merely an abstract illustrations of the argument.

15. McLean attributes the origins of the term *heresthetics* to Riker (1986).

16. Shepsle endorses McLean's interpretation of Peel as a heresthetician, arguing that by inventing the new dimension of the famine, Peel managed to "repackage" repeal to provide an "unconventional interpretation of what was at stake" (Shepsle 2003, 312). Shepsle suggests that Peel led the Peelites to repeal by "listening" to their territorial constitution argument (Shepsle 2003, 315). This argument rests on the votes of the Peelites in the third division but fails to recognize that they had already voted for repeal in the first and second divisions. Hence, the Peelites had already voted twice to support repeal before Peel recognized the importance of the territorial constitution as an argument of persuasion. Not only does this argument fail to explain the abrupt reversal of the Peelites, but it also skirts around McLean's argument that Peel's introduction of the famine issue constituted a new dimension that shifted the debate toward repeal. The analysis in chapter 7 shows that a new dimension was introduced in the early months of 1846, but this dimension was not the famine. Rather, it was the notion of the territorial constitution.

Chapter 3

1. Some historians have disputed the political importance and effectiveness of the Anti-Corn Law League, arguing that MPs were unwilling to respond to the pressure exerted by the League, that the League was only marginal in terms of effecting repeal of the

Corn Laws, or that the League was counterproductive in that it sparked the emergence of the Anti-League—that is, the protectionist lobby. However, a close examination of MPs' speeches (in chapters 7, 8, and 9), the League's effective registration campaign (chapter 2), and its propaganda campaign (chapter 5) clearly illustrates the political importance and economic clout of the Anti-Corn Law League.

2. For further analysis of the importance of geography in lobbying and political participation, see Hansen (1990), Milner (1997a), and Busch and Reinhardt (1999, 2000, 2003).

3. By 1821, industry had already outdistanced agriculture in proportion of national income by 32 to 26 percent, and by 1831 the gap widened even further to 34.4 and 23.4 percent. Additionally, the proportion of national income derived from trade and transport rose from 15.9 percent in 1821 to 17.4 percent in 1831 and 18.4 percent in 1841 (Mitchell and Deane 1971).

4. Industry and manufacturing interests had organized themselves into business associations and chambers of commerce in the late eighteenth century—long before the Anti-Corn Law League was born in 1838 (see, e.g., Bowden 1925, 172–173; Mantoux 1948, 398–403; Howe 1984, 162–163).

5. In the 1980 article (Lloyd-Jones and LeRoux 1980), the authors list fifteen Manchester cotton firms by name, their number of employees, and their poor-rate assessment (which corresponded with number of employees). Based on poor-rate assessment figures (also listed) for seventy-five other cotton firms in Manchester, the authors then calculate the number of employees for these firms. Some recalculations of their data show the division between medium- and large-size firms to be sensitive to slight changes. In all cases, the proportion of medium-size firms increases dramatically, and in many instances (depending on where the division is made between medium and large) so does the proportion of large firms. Nonetheless, in all cases, the proportion of small firms decreases substantially.

6. Discussion of concentration outside the cotton industry is very limited. Two articles that have addressed the topic: Timmins (1982) and Dutton and Jones (1983) argue that output increasingly became concentrated in a small number of integrated firms.

7. Similar to business organizations, League staff were compensated with salaries and wages for their efforts. However, it should be noted that the broader membership received no clear "selective incentives" other than engraved membership cards indicating by color their subscription amount (McCord 1958, 134, 174).

8. Even the so-called transfer of League headquarters to London in 1843 was effectively nullified by the political necessity of maintaining a central core of staunch free-trade advocates (who, coincidentally, were also key beneficiaries of liberalization). The official move to London was more a strategic propaganda ploy than an actual shift in administrative operations, as McCord (1958, 139–140) explains: "A pressing reason for the move was a desire to break the close identification between the League and Manchester in the public mind, which made the League appear as a sectional movement instead of the nation-wide crusade its leaders conceived it to be. For this reason the move to London in...1843 was made with great parade and emphasis....Nevertheless, this ostentatious move did not indicate a genuine shift of centre...and the control of the League was not materially affected by the change." The move does, however, demonstrate the League's strategy of nationalizing the interest (discussed in the next chapter).

9. The data for figure 3.1 are from Great Britain (1825–1846) and Mitchell (1988). For the IQV, see Healey (1984).

10. For elaboration on the usage of nineteenth-century city directories, see Page (1974), Duggan (1975), Wilde (1976), Shaw (1978), and Timmins (1979).

11. I do not call into question the concentrated political influence of landowners in rural constituencies. Indeed, constituency economic composition (rural versus urban) played a critical role in determining which MPs voted for repeal of the Corn Laws (as seen in chapter 6), even though it is also true that landowner economic interests were not monolithic (as shown in chapter 5). Nevertheless, my primary concern here is the urban constituencies that in the wake of the 1832 electoral reform were strongly influenced by the growing and more widely dispersed export-sector interests.

Chapter 4

1. Kollman's (1998) work constitutes an important exception. Many scholars have, to varying degrees, explored this aspect of interest-group behavior (e.g., Jones 1994; Mitchell 1997; Goldstein 1999), but few have elaborated on it.

2. This chapter builds on a burgeoning literature on the role of ideas and ideology in policy making. A few in political economy include Goldstein (1993), Woods (1995), Hood (1994), Hall (1989), Sikkink (1991), Jacobsen (1995) and Henderson (1986). Other areas of political science—such as foreign policy, electoral choice, legislative studies, public policy, and political theory—have witnessed a similar growth in the literature on ideas and ideology: Goldstein and Keohane (1993), Risse-Kappen (1994), McCormick and Black (1983), Hinich and Munger (1994), Silverman (1985), Grier (1993), Langston (1992), Haas (1992), Sabatier and Jenkins-Smith (1993), Yee (1996), Goodin (1996), Drezner (2000), Legro (2000), Nakano (2000), Walsh (2000), Hansen and King (2001), and Lieberman (2002).

3. To avoid confusion from the outset, I do not use the term *nationalize* in any reference to the nationalization of industries or to the debates surrounding private and public industries.

4. I examined lobbying in three cases of trade policy in the nineteenth and early twentieth centuries—the repeal of the Corn Laws, the tariff-reform challenge to Britain's free-trade policy (1903 to 1906), and Germany's protectionist backlash to the freer trade policies of the early 1890s (Schonhardt-Bailey 2001). In two of these cases—the repeal of the Corn Laws and post-Caprivi Germany—the interest group successfully nationalized the trade-related interest of its members. For the Anti-Corn Law League in Britain, this interest was in free trade, while for the Bund der Landwirte in Germany, the interest was in protection (Schonhardt-Bailey 1998b). In the case of tariff reform in Britain, we find an example of an interest group that tried but failed to nationalize its interest.

5. For a more extensive definitional discussion of ideas and ideology, see Schonhardt-Bailey (2001).

6. Members of such groups may be true believers of the ideology. However, the concern here is not whether group members are true believers but rather how the ideology is used to obfuscate the special benefits.

7. However important nationalizing the interest may be to a group's policy success, its applicability is inevitably limited by the nature of the policy in question. Three types of policies provide less fertile ground for nationalizing the interest: (1) very narrow or localized policies (such as the preservation of a neighborhood woodland), (2) highly special-

ized or technical policies (such as the reserve requirements for commercial banks), and (3) secretive policies (such as military planning and expenditures). Very local policies affect too few people, specialized policies are too difficult to understand, and secretive policies (by definition) lack an open forum for discussion. On the other hand, distributive and redistributive policies (such as international trade, social welfare, and fiscal policy) allow greater scope for nationalizing the interest since the numbers affected are substantial, the issues are fairly intuitive, and they are subject to public debate.

8. See note 7.

9. In figures 4.1a and 4.1b, the horizontal and vertical axes represent an abstract policy space and are thus not intended to be directional (for example, moving northward along the "interests" axis does not signify more interests). Rather, these graphs are intended to convey the relativity between the axes (interests and ideas), not absolutes of either one.

10. Not one of the leading political economists advocated immediate free trade.

11. Meanwhile, Anti-Leaguers (primarily landowners) never fully launched a nationalizing the interest strategy but rather hoped that insider access to members of Parliament (80 percent of whom were landowners themselves) would be sufficient to counter the momentum of the League. A belated attempt was made by protectionists to launch a nationalizing the interest strategy. They hoped at least to delay a Parliamentary decision until after the next general election (Stewart 1971).

12. For articles by Senior, McCulloch, and Villiers, see Schonhardt-Bailey (1997, vol. 2).

13. In the immediate postwar period, political economists clashed repeatedly on whether free trade led to higher or lower wages. Malthus and Spence maintained that lower food prices, resulting from free trade, would lower wages for agricultural labor. Displaced agricultural laborers would then seek employment in industry, thus raising unemployment in industrial areas (Schonhardt-Bailey 1997, 1: nos. 1, 4). In a head-on confrontation, Buchanan found that Malthus arrived at some "rather strange conclusions; for if his reasonings be just, an abundance and low price of provisions would in all cases be a disadvantage to the labourer,—while a scarcity, with its necessary attendant a high price, would be an advantage" (Schonhardt-Bailey 1997, 1: no. 2). Buchanan maintained that Malthus pushed Adam Smith's principle "that the average price of corn regulates the rate of wages" further to argue "that a high money price of corn gives the labourer the same command over the necessaries, *and a greater command* over the luxuries of life" (Schonhardt-Bailey 1997, 1: no. 2):

Now we have always understood, that when corn rose in price, it was only that part of the labourer's wages which was converted into corn, that was supposed to be affected by the circumstance. A rise in the price of corn was always said to be followed by a *corresponding* rise of wages,—in other words, by such a rise as enabled the labourer to consume the same quantity of corn as before: But it was never understood, though Mr Malthus now seems to maintain this doctrine, that this rise of wages added to his power of purchasing *other* articles; nor are we aware, indeed, of any principle on which so startling a theory can be supported.

Freer traders (Ricardo and Torrens) maintained that protection resulted in lower, not higher wages, since it lowered profits for manufacturers and farmers and thereby forced them to cut production costs by reducing wages (Schonhardt-Bailey 1997, 1: nos. 6, 14). In the late 1830s, Torrens stressed that free trade would raise wages by allowing workers to be paid according to their higher productivity relative to foreign labor (Schonhardt-Bailey 1997, 2: no. 25). Porter agreed with Torrens that high food prices did not yield high wages but just the reverse (Schonhardt-Bailey 1997, 2: no. 27). High prices for food were said to have lessened the demand for labor and therefore lessened wages (which rests on the argument that demand for food is price inelastic and that the demand for other goods—notably manufactured goods—is more elastic with respect to food prices). James Pennington rejected the hoopla associated with this issue, arguing that free traders and protectionists alike exaggerated the effects of repeal on corn prices (and on domestic agriculture more generally) (Schonhardt-Bailey 1997, 2: no. 26). He doubted that the quantity of foreign grain available to Britain would be great enough to bring about any significant fall in prices. In defense of the protectionist case, Alison argued that repeal would only temporarily lower prices. Once foreigners became monopoly suppliers of grain to Britain, they would use this opportunity to raise prices (Schonhardt-Bailey 1997, 2: no. 35).

Chartists were drawn to the Mathusian argument, suspecting that the true motive of the industrialists was to obtain lower wages through repeal. Antirepealers were happy to feed this suspicion. League circulars and Anti-League pamphlets were filled with claims and counterclaims about the effect of bread prices on workers wages (Schonhardt-Bailey 1997, 2: nos. 14, 15, 20, 24).

14. Prentice (1968) reported that of the 670 circulars that the League sent to the churches represented at a conference in Edinburgh in 1842, 459 ministers expressed support for immediate repeal of the Corn Laws: "With regard to the opinions of the people, 431 of the ministers stated that their congregations were nearly unanimous in approving of the total abolition of the Corn and Provision Laws, and Free Trade" (Prentice 1968, 1: 290).

15. On the importance of religion and evangelicalism in nineteenth-century British politics, see Hilton (1988).

16. The Corn Laws "made both industrial employers and workmen feel that Government and Parliament existed to serve only the interests of agriculture. Here was an attitude full of potential danger, the possible basis of revolution" (Read 1967, 67). Read continues: "Peel offered repeal of the Corn Laws to the industrial population. And he struck a remarkable response. The workers were deeply impressed that a Prime Minister had made a dramatic intervention on their behalf. Middle-class employers, for their part, were attracted by Peel's determination and success in forcing the landlords who predominated in Parliament to surrender their favourite policy of protection. Here was ample demonstration, in the words of a Manchester journalist a few years later, that 'the owner of ten thousand spindles' was now the political equal of 'the lord of ten thousand acres.'"

17. For instance, the position taken by Ricardo and Mill was contrary to that of Malthus. Thompson (1832), moreover, sought to weaken arguments on rent that were used to defend the Corn Laws. (I am grateful to an anonymous reviewer for noting this.)

18. Torrens, in 1839, recognized a clear division in interests between landowners (who gained from higher food prices) and farmers (who did not gain because of shifting rents). Later (in 1844) he explored the effect of immediate repeal on corn rents as opposed to money rents. He argued that repeal would reduce both types of rent and that neither reduction would save farmers from widespread insolvency and destitution. The League, he argued, was wrong to suggest that farmers would not suffer from repeal, unless repeal was accompanied by a corresponding reduction in money wages and the prices of manufactured goods (Schonhardt-Bailey 1997, 2: nos. 25, 34).

19. For instance, Ian Newbould (1985, 139) argues that because the Liberal party was fragmented in its composition (consisting of Whigs, Radicals, Liberals, and so on), it was deliberately disorganized. In other words, the Whigs eschewed party organization be-

cause it would only enable and encourage the Radical faction to push for further reform measures—measures that undermined the Whig position. He also argues that MPs touted their independent position on issues, resulting in a government that "was never sure of its support." In fact, Newbould quotes Melbourne as saying, "No one knows beforehand what parliament or members of parliament will do or how they will vote."

Norman Gash (1982) argues that the Conservative party similarly lacked organization. There existed (1) "no regular practice of calling party meetings before the start of the parliamentary session" (140), (2) little or no discipline among Conservative peers in the House of Lords, and (3) no real collaboration between Peel (the Conservative leader in the House of Commons) and Wellington (the Conservative leader in the House of Lords). On this last point, Gash quotes Wellington as having said in 1837, "I do not like to interfere in the affairs of the House of Commons, first because I have nothing to say to them; and next, because I really do not understand them" (143). Fourth, Gash notes a growing loss of contact between Peel and his followers between 1841 and 1846, as evidenced by fewer and less satisfying party meetings and as evidenced by Peel's deliberate avoidance of the party process for gaining support for repeal of the Corn Laws. Gash writes, "In 1846..., over the repeal of the Corn Laws, the breach had become so great that Peel seems not even to have considered summoning a party meeting to explain his policy. When Brougham subsequently suggested that the disruption of the party could have been avoided if Peel had taken leading members into his confidence and called a general meeting, Peel merely observed to Aberdeen that if he had done so, he would have failed in his object of carrying the repeal of the Corn Laws—and 'I was resolved not to fail.' No stronger proof is needed of his realization that repeal could not be carried by the ordinary processes of party government" (143–144). Finally, Gash concurs with Newbould that MPs enjoyed and preferred to maintain their status as independent thinkers. Members of Parliament "spoke of 'the gentlemen with whom I usually act' or more informally of 'our friends.' But they did not as a rule talk of being members of a party; and they strove to give the appearance of being independent and unfettered in their parliamentary conduct" (156).

Chapter 5

1. For an excellent discussion of nineteenth-century British investors' responsiveness to fluctuations in investment opportunities, see Michie (1981).

2. These were individuals who were under some compulsion—perhaps impending insolvency—to reinvest flows in a factor that yielded less than other factors.

3. In an ideal world, one would employ not a static model but rather a dynamic one that incorporated future expected returns.

4. Undiversified farmers were enticed by the government to acquiesce to repeal, as evidenced most clearly in the "drainage-loan" portion of the repeal legislation (see Moore 1965). Nevertheless, many "marginal" farmers (grain farmers unable to increase production through advanced farming methods or unable to switch to other forms of farming) left Britain in the wake of repeal hoping to gain better returns for their capital investments in the United States (see Van Vugt 1988).

5. The literature explaining the various linkages between railways and the development of heavy industry in Britain is considerable. For instance, Llewellyn Woodward (1962, 41) wrote that "the railways were one of the results of progress in the iron industry and of

the increased consumption of coal brought about by the use of steam power. They were in turn, the cause of a vast expansion in the metal trades and of a much greater demand for coal. Directly or indirectly they influenced the development of most industries in the country. [In addition,] the railway itself was an article of export; British contractors built lines in every continent and organized companies to buy them." E. Hobsbawm (1962, 63) found that the "immense [coal] industry, though probably not expanding fast enough for really massive industrialization on the modern scale, was sufficiently large to stimulate the basic invention which was to transform the capital-goods industries: the railway. For the mines not only required steam-engines in large quantities and of great power, but also required efficient means of transporting the great quantities of coal from coal-face to shaft and especially from pit-head to the point of shipment. The 'tramway' or 'railway' along which trucks ran was an obvious answer.... Technologically the railway is the child of the mine, and especially the northern English coal mine." He added that "in the first two decades of the railways (1830–1850) the output of iron in Britain rose from 680,000 to 2,250,000 [tons].... The output of coal between 1830 and 1850 also trebled from 15 million tons to 49 million tons. That dramatic rise was due primarily to the railway, for an average each mile of line required 300 tons of iron merely for track" (Hobsbawm 1962, 64).

B. R. Mitchell (1984) sketches the correlation between the rising demand in the iron and coal industries and the railway booms and the subsequent royalties accruing to landowners. Mitchell explains that royalties usually consisted of a fixed rent plus a royalty paid according to the amount of coal extracted. From the early nineteenth century to the 1870s, royalties averaged between 8 percent to 11 percent of coal sales, or 6 d. to 9 d. per ton, or 50 to 180 pounds per acre (see Mitchell 1984, 251–258). Other useful sources that address the linkages between railways and the development of heavy industry (not to mention the large literature simply on railway development) include Cottrell (1980), Thompson (1963), and von Tunzelmann (1978).

6. See Thompson (1963) for a discussion of the mineral incomes of several great landowners (such as the Dukes of Northumberland and Portland, the Earl of Carlisle, Lords Hastings and Rokeby, Sir Matthew White Ridley, and the Earl of Durham) and gentry (such as the Claytons, Crofts, Bates, Edens, Riddells, Wrightsons). He noted that "landowners certainly drew large and increasing incomes from coal, but these were predominantly and increasingly in the shape of royalty and wayleave rents" (Thompson 1963, 264). Some gentry received mineral income equal to half their total income. For further analysis of the incomes of aristocrats, see Beckett (1986, 288–295).

7. One might add that landowners would be more likely to invest in industries (mostly heavy) that had land occupying a larger share of assets (coal, iron, and railways) than such light industries as cotton textiles.

8. Manufacturing and industrial enterprises were not as apt to benefit from the repeal of the Bubble Act since, unlike insurance companies whose ownership was corporate, these firms largely consisted of partnerships (see Michie 1985, 62).

9. J. R. Killick and W. A. Thomas (1970) provide a listing of companies quoted on the Leeds, Liverpool, Manchester, and Newcastle exchanges that clearly illustrates the progressing dominance of railway shares from 1837 to 1847 (see also Thomas 1973).

10. See also Thomas (1973).

11. For general references to this argument, see Moore (1966) and Hobsbawm (1968). For the specific application of this argument to the MPs of 1841 to 1847, see Aydelotte (1962, 290–307). Also see Thomas (1925, 1929).

12. My own test of this hypothesis reveals that a transformation in the incomes of Members of Parliament certainly was occurring, though not at a rate or level sufficient to confirm the hypothesis (Schonhardt-Bailey 1991b).

13. English (1984) argues that death-duty registers offer more complete records of business holdings than do probates. For example, the registers list stocks and shares, industrial machinery, business interests, and residual estate. They offer more detail about the form in which wealth was held at death. Only since 1982 have the registers for the period from 1796 to 1903 been opened to study by researchers. I did find, however, that for later years many registers remain closed, some until the year 2007. Jane Cox describes and explains the contents, format, notations, and abbreviations relevant both to probates and death-duty registers (Cox 1980).

14. Since 1825 and 1846 constitute roughly the critical years before and after the emergence of capital markets and diversification, and since we may assume that an individual would most likely be at his financial peak not at his death but rather a few years prior, 1830 and 1850 appeared to be adequate choices for each time period sample. For details of the sampling technique, see Schonhardt-Bailey (1991b).

15. As it was the final year of the wartime income tax, returns in 1815 dropped sharply due to public resistance to the tax and less stringent collection efforts by the Tax Office (see Hope-Jones 1939, 77, 109). Hence, 1815 was not considered an appropriate year to sample.

16. The real estate estimate for this sample suffers from various coding difficulties. Real estate, usually listed as "charges thereupon" rather than as actual values, creates distortion due to inflated values in some cases and unreported values in others. It is possible that these two distortions may have nullified each other, but without better micro-level data the extent of the distortions is unknown. Moreover, real estate included not only agricultural holdings but also commercial property and sometimes mining interests as well. Finally, while I include "residue" with real estate, not all the residue value could indeed be verified as real estate. The effect of these crosscutting distortions in the estimate of real estate is, again, unknown.

17. Squaring both terms of the equation was considered but dismissed since the result was an increased sensitivity to changes in income levels. In other words, given equal ratios of real estate to non–real estate holdings, squaring the terms multiplied the effect of one's income level—that is, a wealthier individual would be predicted to have an exponentially stronger interest in either free trade or protection for any given ratio of real estate to non–real estate holdings. The unsquared version, being less responsive to changes in income levels, has the advantage of isolating to a greater degree strictly the effects of diversification.

18. A final clarification regarding the diversification indexes should be mentioned. Since the possible scores range from -1 (complete investment in land) to $+1$ (complete investment in trade, industry, and so on), one might surmise that the "perfect," or best, score would be zero. This conclusion might be warranted if one's argument were founded on a nondirectional diversification index in which industrialists investing in land created the same incentive for MPs to vote for free trade as did landowners in industry. Such an index would presumably require one to obtain the absolute values of each score and hypothesize a negative correlation between diversification and free-trade votes (where free trade $= 1$ and protectionism $= 0$). In contrast, the argument here—that landowners were seeking higher returns by investing in industry—necessitates a directional index and hypothesizes a positive correlation between diversification and votes for free trade. The

higher the score of a particular district, the greater the probability of its representative MP voting for free trade. Broadly speaking, diversification need not demonstrate direction. Returns from factor inputs need not be channeled from land to capital; the flow could be reversed. The point is that factor returns—as capital flows—will shift from low- to high-yield sectors of the economy.

19. The content of these divisions is as follows:

- Mr. P. Miles amendment to delay the House from going into committee to consider the Corn Laws by six months, thus forcing a vote on Peel's motion that the House immediately resolve itself into a committee of the whole (Peel's first reading of the Corn Law Repeal) (27 February 1846): ayes = 337; noes = 240.
- Mr. Peel's motion to repeal the Corn Laws, Third Reading (15 May 1846): ayes = 327; noes = 229.

In the earlier article version of this chapter (Schonhardt-Bailey 1991c), I presented a more extensive array of regression results. I have reestimated these here for three reasons. First, I use logistic regression, rather than the original probit, to marry up with later estimations of the roll-call votes (chapter 6) that use logistic regression. Second, I use a revised version of my original DISTPREF variable (originally devised in 1989), which measures the free-trade—protectionist orientation of constituencies more aptly than the previous version (for details of these revisions, see book appendix 1). This is the same measure that is used in chapter 6. Third, having reviewed the multitude of results reported in my original article, it seemed preferable to offer readers a simpler and more intuitive presentation of essentially the same message.

20. Here I use my own measure for MP party affiliation, which is based on pollbook data. Aydelotte (n.d.) devised a different measure for party affiliation that divided Conservatives into Non-Peelite Conservatives and Peelites, depending on how they voted in the final reading of repeal. Aydelotte's measure has clear disadvantages when used in a simple regression model (namely, it overestimates the influence of party) but has advantages in a more complex estimation procedure, as is shown in chapter 6.

21. District economic orientation (coded from Philbin 1965) groups districts into five categories: most protectionist, protectionist-oriented, neutral or no orientation, free-trade oriented, and most free trade (coded 1 to 5, respectively). As examples, a constituency coded as "most protectionist" would produce grain, "protectionist-oriented" would likely be a general agricultural producer, "neutral" would produce primarily for the domestic market, "free-trade oriented" would contain some industries with export outlets, and "most free trade" would have extensive manufacturing or export trade. To this original classification, I added information on factory employment in textiles, machinery, and cutlery from Fang (1978). See book appendix 1 for further details on this variable. (This appendix also describes how I merged my dataset with Aydelotte's.)

22. Electoral reform is a variable that measures the effect of the Reform Act of 1832 on district representation. Constituencies fell into one of four categories: 1 = continued representation, with number of seats reduced; 2 = continued representation, with no change in seats; 3 = continued representation, with number of seats increased; and 4 = newly created representation. Boroughs with reduced representation are considered "quasi-rotten" since an earlier draft of the Reform Bill proposed complete disfranchisement, but the final act allowed them to retain representation, albeit with fewer seats. These quasi-rotten boroughs generally preferred Conservative representatives and protectionist policies, as they tended to be rural or dominated by landowning interests. Boroughs that

received new representation were mostly northern industrial areas and tended to favor Liberals and free trade.

23. If we consider cases of later industrialization (for example, Germany and Japan) in which larger sums of initial capital investment were required, the dominant actors responsible for managing the flow of investment capital were banks. The requirement for larger sums of investment capital created a role for banks as providers and thereby limited the direct involvement of landowners in the diversification of their portfolios (though this does not explain why in some countries banks rather than securities markets were the main source of capital-raising activity). Landowners were able to invest in banks whose role was to mobilize the capital needed for larger units of production and that could pool the risks to an extent that could no longer be done by individuals investing directly. This chapter has found a link between direct investment in industrial capital and a change in trade-policy preferences; however, where the investment link is indirect, via a bank that pools risk by spreading its assets across economic sectors, it is more likely that the trade preferences of asset holders will be more weakly specified (Schonhardt-Bailey and Bailey 1995; Verdier 2002). For a discussion of the link between asset diversification and trade liberalization in the second half of the twentieth century, see Feeney and Hillman (2001).

Chapter 6

1. For instance, Gash (1951), Stewart (1971), Aydelotte (1972), Conacher (1972), Jones and Erickson (1972), and Blake (1974).

2. The arguments of these authors have been outlined in chapter 1. Here the focus is on the specific data and methodology used by these authors. This chapter is a slightly amended version of Schonhardt-Bailey (2003).

3. Of the 1,029 divisions that occurred during the lifetime of this Parliament, Aydelotte sampled 186, or 18 percent. Aydelotte biased his sample toward those divisions that were relatively well attended (that is, in which 200 or more MPs participated) and that were, in Aydelotte's judgment, important and relevant to key problems of the day.

4. Chapter 2 and the footnotes contained therein discuss the trustee and delegate interpretations of representation in greater detail.

5. The concluding sentence from Jones and Erikson (1972: 223) (which Cox also cites) summarizes this independence: "For if there was one attitude that the Peelites popularized and made fashionable, it was that even the most mute back-bencher, when it came to a division, had a duty to vote his conscience and his sense of honor."

6. Another way to evaluate the fit of their model is to see how much NOMINATE improves on a benchmark model by estimating the proportional reduction in error, or PRE, of NOMINATE over the benchmark (Poole and Rosenthal 1997, 30). Here, the APRE, or aggregate proportional reduction in error, for the first dimension is .692 and for the second dimension is .753.

7. Dimensions in roll-call votes are essentially abstractions that capture the structure of voting across a wide set of topics. Low dimensionality (particularly relative to the range of issues) can suggest a greater role for ideology. If, for instance, a high percentage of votes can be correctly classified with just one dimension, it is likely that a single left-right (liberal-conservative) ideological continuum is a good predictor of the votes. Further

dimensions may capture other ideological divisions or may reflect cleavages in interests. Moreover, while an ideological dimension may reflect party loyalties, party may comprise just one element of this dimension. Hence, ideology and party are not necessarily synonymous.

8. Hall (1989), Goldstein (1993), Goldstein and Keohane (1993), Yee (1996), Drezner (2000), Legro (2000), Nakano (2000), and Walsh (2000).

9. The data used in this chapter may be obtained from ⟨http://personal.lse.ac.uk/SCHONHAR/⟩.

10. For a recent application of NOMINATE to parliamentary voting (including that of the 1841 to 1847 British Parliament), see Poole (2005).

11. Scores for the Aydelotte's "Big scale" and NOMINATE's first dimension are, moreover, highly correlated, with a bivariate correlation of .82.

12. Economic growth and structural change within constituencies are indirectly measured in two ways. The first indicates the "type" of district—either county or borough (this is coded as 0 and 1, respectively). This measures the urban/rural split—with boroughs defined as the urban interest (in the context of repeal more likely to favor free trade) and counties as the rural interest (more likely to favor protection for agriculture) (Vincent 1967). This variable is subject to some misspecification in that, despite electoral reform, some boroughs were still "rotten," while others remained intimately linked to a rural economic structure. Likewise, a few counties were not entirely rural but rather had an economic base closely tied to mining or manufacturing industries. The second measure is district economic orientation, which is used as a control variable in chapter 5 and is explained there.

In Schonhardt-Bailey (1994), I find that each district type (borough versus county) can exhibit a unique slope coefficient. That is, MPs from districts with similar economic orientations but different district types might vary in their propensity to vote for free trade or to affiliate with a particular party. Specifically, the combined effect of district type and district economic orientation may in itself reveal a more subtle distinction between borough and county MPs' voting behavior. An interaction term is therefore included to measure this independent effect. As a predictor of repeal, the expected sign for this variable is negative, meaning that for borough MPs the effect of district economic orientation on votes should taper off toward the higher end of the scale (4 and 5), while county MPs who represented more industrial districts are more likely to vote for free trade. It should be noted that district type takes on the values of 0 for county and 1 for borough and therefore that the distinction between urban and rural *county* is lost in the interaction term. However, cross-tabulations reveal that no county MP scored 4 or 5 for district economic orientation.

A final variable, electoral reform, measures the effect of the 1832 Reform Act on district representation. This variable is used as a control in chapter 5 and is explained there. (See book appendix 1 for a summary of the variables used in regressions in chapters 3, 5, and 6.)

13. Overall partisanship by electors had declined markedly in 1847 relative to 1841. An analysis of split votes (where electors in double-member districts split their votes between the two major parties, voting for both a Conservative and a Liberal) and of nonpartisan plumping rates (where electors used only one of their two votes for a candidate when a candidate of the same party was available) reveals that the 1841 election was far more partisan than was the 1847 election (Cox 1987).

Notes

14. Poole and Rosenthal use a dynamic version in their study of the U.S. Congress.

15. The program used to generate the NOMINATE scores includes only those legislators who cast at least twenty-five votes.

16. Owing to the considerable turnover in MPs during 1841 to 1847, the Aydelotte dataset contains 815 MPs (the total number of MPs who sat at some point during the life of the Parliament), while only 658 MPs sat in Parliament at any one time (and only 656 after the disfranchisement of Sudbury in 1844). Hence the 590 English MPs (reduced to 483 after deducting those who failed to cast at least twenty-five votes) include members who sat for a short period and ones who sat for the entire Parliament. (See book appendix 1 for details on the merging of Aydelotte's and my datasets.)

17. A rank-order list of MPs by the first-dimension coordinates provides some support for trade policy as the underlying force to the first dimension. The three leading free traders—Richard Cobden, John Bright, and Charles Villiers, who consistently voted for free trade—are at the top of the list, with Cobden in the lead. Conversely, protectionist MPs are at the bottom.

18. Four critical motions for repeal are analyzed, all of which reflected annual attempts by Charles Villiers, MP, to repeal the Corn Laws. The dates for these motions are 11 July 1842, 15 May 1843, 26 June 1844, and 10 June 1845. The percentage of votes correctly classified, PRE, and errors for each division, are as follows: 1842: 97.5 percent, .963, 7 errors; 1843: 97.9 percent, .972, 8 errors; 1844: 98.0 percent, .972, 7 errors; and 1845: 98.3 percent, .975, 5 errors.

19. While their procedure allows the analysis of individual roll-call votes (Poole, Rosenthal, et al. 1999), Poole and Rosenthal note that their estimates of roll-call outcomes are less reliable than are their estimates for the spatial locations of legislators or the cutting lines. Hence, certain roll calls will exhibit a large number of misclassified votes, while others will have few or no errors.

20. There appears to be a decline in the classification success of both the one-dimensional and two-dimensional models over the course of the Parliament. For instance, the percentage of votes correctly classified in the one-dimensional model drops from 97.28 percent in 1841 to 84.84 percent in 1847 and for the two-dimensional model from 98.12 percent to 88.65 percent. A time-series test of this apparent trend (in which I use the percentage of votes correctly predicted in a monthly count of divisions from the beginning of the Parliament) shows a statistically significant negative time trend (at 1 percent) and a statistically significant autoregressor (at 5 percent). Hence, while the spatial positions of MPs classify the votes in the early years of the Parliament quite well, their classification success falls over time and particularly in 1846 and 1847.

21. These spatial positions are thus measured across an array of policy issues.

22. This classification is from Aydelotte (n.d.).

23. The content of the second dimension is more ambiguous than that of the first. For instance, a density plot for the second dimension (not shown here) shows no clear divides or clusters among the party groups, and mean scores of 0.076 for Non-Peelite Conservatives, −0.605 for Peelites, and 0.000 for both Liberals and Reformers are hardly illuminating. Nonetheless, an extensive analysis of NOMINATE results by issue area—economic, political reform, social legislation (with factory legislation as a subset), Ireland, religion, and other legislation—reveals that the content of the second dimension is the conflict over factory legislation.

24. A two-tailed *t*-test for equality of means for the Peelites and Non-Peelite Conservatives indicates that the difference is significant at the 1 percent level.

25. Not included in the total of nineteen are the Corn Laws scale, the Big scale, and the Conservative party scale (for which the differences in the means of the two groups are statistically significant at the 1 percent level). Differences in the means for the two groups in the Landed Interest, Religion, and Enlarged Canada Wheat scales are all statistically insignificant. Differences in the means for the Working-Class Distress scale are significant at 5 percent, while those for the remaining fifteen scales are significant at the 1 percent level.

26. The differences in means for McLean's three revised Canada Wheat scales are significant at the 5 percent level, while those for his remaining revised scales are significant at the 1 percent level.

27. Regressing the two blocks of Conservatives on four constituency interests variables obtains a weak but significant correlation. All the predictors except electoral reform are significant at 1 percent, and overall the model correctly predicts 75 percent of the cases.

28. Their voting behavior on trade policy up to 1846 could even be described as adhering to a sense of "false consciousness" (Bawn 1999).

29. A simple test of means finds that just the death-duty diversification variable is statistically significant at 1 percent.

30. Four other models of parliamentary voting were tested. Model 1 predicts votes from constituency characteristics plus the party affiliation of the MP. (The diversification variables are not included since missing data would reduce considerably the number of cases.) For the final repeal vote, this model correctly predicts 96.4 percent of the votes, with 16 errors. From 1842 to 1844, MP party affiliation appears to swamp the regressions (as one would expect, given high levels of partisanship following the 1841 election), but in 1845 and 1846 the constituency-interest variables become statistically and substantively significant. Model 2 contains the NOMINATE coordinate 1 as the single predictor. For the 1846 vote, 93.93 percent votes are correctly predicted, with twenty-five errors. This model performs better in the previous divisions, predicting between 97 to 98 percent of the votes. The decline in predictive success of this model substantiates the earlier finding regarding the poorer performance of the spatial model in 1846. Model 3 adds the second-dimension coordinate to model 2. For 1846, 94.42 percent of the votes are correctly predicted, with twenty-three errors. As with model 2, the predictive success prior to 1846 is around 98 percent. The second-dimension coordinate is not significant until the final vote in 1846—a finding that recurs in the model presented in table 6.4. This finding is discussed in note thirty-four below. Model 4 is the "kitchen-sink" model, which includes all the variables from models 1 and 3. In 1846, it correctly predicts 98.05 percent of the votes, with eight errors. In the previous votes, this model obtains 98 to 99 percent predictive success. But as with many "kitchen-sink" models, all the regressions suffer from severe multicollinearity. Collinearity is particularly problematic between party affiliation and the first-dimension coordinate but is also a problem between the economic-interest variables and both party affiliation and coordinate 1. This suggests that free-trade-oriented constituencies tended to elect Liberal MPs (who, in turn, generally supported free trade), while protectionist-oriented constituencies tended to elect Conservative MPs (who supported protection). But the problems of collinearity make it clear that model 4 is inappropriate for accurately measuring ideology, constituency interests, and MP party affiliation.

31. Figure 6.6 resembles more closely a traditional left-right ideological continuum, while figure 6.2 reflects more the partisan component of the first-dimension coordinate.

32. A model that follows the Kalt and Zupan (1990) method (by including party affiliation in the first and only regression) obtains the same overall percentage correctly predicted as model 4 (discussed in note 30) and results in zero errors for the observed yeas and eight for the observed nays. This model was, however, considered inappropriate for reasons discussed in the section on methodological approaches.

33. Data limitations described in the chapter mean that this model actually explains seventy-seven of the eighty-two Peelites for which I have data. There are four further English Peelites who failed to vote frequently enough to calculate their NOMINATE coordinates and twenty-eight more who were Irish, Scottish, or Welsh (areas for which equivalent economic-constituency data are not available). In sum, of Aydelotte's original 815 MPs, 600 voted in the third reading of repeal. Of these, 241 were Non-Peelite Conservatives (NPCs), 114 Peelites (Ps), 153 Whig/Liberals (WLs), 77 Reformers (Rs), and 15 Irish Repealers (IRs). Of the 590 for which data are available for constituencies, only 446 voted in repeal, and of these, 193 were NPCs, 86 Ps, 106 WLs, and 61 Rs. Of the 483 for which constituency data *and* NOMINATE coordinates were available, 412 voted in repeal, and of these 171 were NPCs, 82 Ps, 101 WLs, and 58 Rs.

34. At first glance, the statistical significance of the second-dimension coordinate is puzzling, as it clearly lessens the predictive success of the model in 1846. The one-dimensional model misclassifies seventeen votes (with a PRE of .905) while the two-dimensional model mis-classifies twenty-two votes (with a PRE of .877). But does the second dimension lie behind the split between the Peelites and the Non-Peelite Conservatives? If so, is there a causal relationship between the apparent split between Peelites and Non-Peelite Conservatives on the second dimension and the split on repeal? In a nutshell, the answer is yes, but the direction of causality runs in the opposite direction—from the split on repeal to the split on the second dimension.

First, the content of the second dimension is clearly factory legislation. Analyzed according to issue areas, the first dimension correctly classifies 92 to 97 percent of the votes on economic issues, political reform, Ireland, and religion but only 83 percent of the votes on social legislation and 86 percent on other legislation. A large subset within social legislation is factory reform. For this subset, the first dimension correctly classifies just 70 percent of the votes. Adding the second dimension to the model for this subset increases the classification success to 93 percent. In comparison, the addition of the second dimension improves the classification success by less than 1 percent in each of the remaining issue areas.

Second, a correlation does indeed exist between the two Conservative factions and the second dimension (yielding a Pearson's r of .54). This requires a closer look, particularly at those divisions on factory legislation where the second dimension is important (where it increases the predictive success over the one-dimensional model by 20 percent or more). Cross-tabulations of the votes on factory legislation leading up to the critical vote on repeal show that 31 to 55 percent of Non-Peelite Conservatives (but only 18 to 34 percent of Peelites) voted yea (that is, *for* factory legislation). Repeal exacerbated this cleavage between Non-Peelite Conservatives and Peelites. Beginning just days after the final vote on repeal, the percentage of Non-Peelite Conservatives voting for factory legislation increased to between 74 and 96 percent, while Peelite support remained low at between 10 and 39 percent. This trend continued through the end of the Parliament.

What, then, shaped the split on factory legislation, and how is that related to Repeal? Peel reported to the Queen in 1844 that agricultural MPs opposed the government's effort to curtail factory legislation, "partly out of hostility to the Anti-Corn Law League, partly from the influence of humane feelings" (Jenkins 1999, 114). Landowners retaliated against the League's accusations of selfishly protecting their agricultural incomes by pointing to the unwillingness of industrialists to improve poor working conditions in factories. Repeal simply magnified this resentment toward the League, as the votes of Non-Peelites demonstrate. In a nutshell, hostility toward repeal shaped the cleavage on the second dimension, not vice versa.

Further evidence that the second dimension is not driving the results in this chapter can be found in the content analysis of *all* the debates on Repeal in 1846, as analyzed in chapter 7. This analysis clearly shows that factory legislation was *not* a theme in the debates on trade.

35. The interpretations of the probabilities given below are consistent with those of the omitted years.

36. This sets aside differences between the geographic constituency and the election constituency (Fenno 1978; Uslaner 1999), as well as questions arising from the limited franchise. Aggregate measures of constituency interests include those of the disenfranchised, and if these were found to differ from those of the franchised, they may introduce a bias to the measurement of constituency interests. Such a bias is, however, unlikely as the interests of the disenfranchised (which include free-trade-oriented industrial workers and protectionist-oriented rural laborers) may simply mirror those of the franchised (namely, industrial capitalists and landowners).

37. The motivations of MPs are invariably difficult to capture from roll-call analysis. Ideally, researchers would use content analysis to evaluate the written and verbal explanations given by MPs for their positions. This is precisely the direction in which this book moves in part 2.

38. In a cross-tabulation of party affiliation and the electoral fate of MPs in the 1847 election, 49 percent of Non-Peelite Conservatives were returned to Parliament (with or without a contest), while 45 percent of Peelites were similarly returned. And similarly, where a contest occurred, 67 percent of Non-Peelites won, while 64 percent of Peelites won.

Chapter 7

1. For a discussion of the reporting of parliamentary debates in the early nineteenth century, see Aspinall (1956) and Gordon (1983, 232–233).

2. In his memoirs, Peel refrained from summarizing the proceedings in Parliament and instead referred his readers to the parliamentary debates on repeal: "It is the most complete account in point of fullness of detail, and presents a record of the views and motives of those who took part in the discussion, less liable to objection on the score of partiality than any which could be given by one who was himself so actively engaged and took so deep an interest in that discussion" (Peel 1857, 287). More generally, the reporting of Parliamentary debates improved considerably during the first half of the nineteenth century, particularly with the introduction of shorthand around 1812. Cobbett (*Parliamentary History*) provided regular reports of current debates from 1803, while Hansard assumed control in 1812. Hansard continued as a private enterprise until it began to receive public funding in 1855 (Keir 1948). Nonetheless, dating back to the late eighteenth century, MPs were wary of the presence of newspaper reporters and other "strangers" in the House, and until 1875, any MP could order the gallery to be cleared—though during debate, this occurred rarely (and not during the Corn Law debates). Until 1853, moreover, the

House of Commons cleared the Strangers Gallery for divisions. In 1852, provision was made for reporters, which reflected a more relaxed attitude among MPs in allowing reporters to be present during debates (Aspinall 1949).

3. Subsequent divisions on this bill invariably suffer from a degree of bandwagoning.

4. Some recent examples include Jenkins-Smith, Clair, et al. (1991), Kahn (1992), Hill, Hanna, et al. (1997), and Finkel and Geer (1998).

5. "Taken together, the program realizes a complex *descending hierarchical classification* combining elements of different statistical methods like segmentation (Bertier and Bouroche 1975), hierarchical classification and dichotomization based on reciprocal averaging or correspondence analysis (Hayashi 1950; Benzecri 1981; Greenacre 1993), and the theory of dynamic clouds (Diday, Lemaire et al. 1982)" (Kronberger and Wagner 2000, 306).

6. For Alceste, "statements" are defined as "contextual units." The program automatically determines contextual units with reference to punctuation and the length of the statement up to a maximum of 250 characters. The description of Alceste follows Kronberger and Wagner (2000).

7. Through its dictionary, Alceste prepares the text by reducing different forms of the same word (in the form of plurals, suffixes, and so on) to the root form and transforms irregular verbs to the indicative, thereby producing a matrix of reduced forms. It also subdivides the corpus into "function words" (articles, prepositions, conjunctions, pronouns, and auxiliary verbs) and "content words" (nouns, verbs, adjectives, and adverbs). The content words are understood to carry the meaning of the discourse, and the final analysis is based on these. (Content words are sometimes referred to as the "meaningful words.")

8. The term *class* is used for descending hierarchical classification analysis, while the term *cluster* is used for the more traditional ascending cluster analysis (Kronberger and Wagner 2000, 308).

9. The debates begin on 22 January (after the Queen's speech) and were focused on the forthcoming measures of the government. Peel's speech, which introduced repeal, followed on 27 January.

10. The electronic version of these debates was obtained in pdf format with support from the Nuffield Foundation (Schonhardt-Bailey 1999), and the text file (ready for analysis with Alceste) was obtained with support from the LSE Staff Research Fund and Suntory and Toyota International Centre for Economics and Related Disciplines (STICERD). My research assistant, Gordon Bannerman, photocopied the debates for scanning and converted the pdf files into readable text files.

11. See Allum (1998) for an analysis of different corpora of textual data using Alceste, along with a detailed interpretation of Alceste results.

12. Plurals and conjugation endings are reduced to a single form, and nonce words are eliminated from the analysis. The leaves a smaller word count, which is analyzed by the program.

13. These are deemed passive as they do not contribute to either the calculation of the word classes or the factors in the correspondence analysis.

14. The speeches of all MPs contain tags for the name of the MP, his party affiliation (from Aydelotte n.d.), and the timing of the speech. Tags for constituency characteristics are included for only the English MPs.

15. The official vote tallies from Hansard are: first reading, 337 to 240; second reading, 302 to 214; third reading, 327 to 229; and Villier's failed motion, 265 to 78.

16. In total, 205 MPs spoke in the 1846 debates on repeal, and of these, 170 (83 percent) represented English constituencies, 11 (5 percent) Scottish, 19 (9 percent) Irish, and 5 (2 percent) Welsh. See book appendix 2 for the full list of MPs who spoke in the debates.

17. The dollar sign can be inserted in the text by the user to override the automated construction of ECUs, thereby closing an ECU where the user deems necessary. For instance, this symbol is inserted at the end of each speech to ensure that the text of each speaker is identified separately.

18. A contextual unit is equivalent to one or more successive ECUs. The two calculations are done with two different parameters for the selected number of words per contextual unit to check the reliability of the classes and the stability of the results (Reinert 1998, 14).

19. A simple analogy is given to explain the relationship between contextual units, ICUs and ECUs: "a contextual unit is to an ICU what a paragraph is to a chapter, and to an ECU, what a paragraph is to a sentence" (Reinert 1998, 11).

20. This compares favorably with Laver and Benoit's percentage of words scored, which ranged from 81 to 94 percent (Laver and Benoit 2002, 16–17).

21. The minimum chi-squared value for selecting a word is set at 20, which is the top threshold set in Alceste. Smaller text files have lower thresholds, down to a minimum of 2. The smaller word count in the Lords debates (chapter 9) requires a lower χ^2 threshold of 8. For simplicity, table 7.2 truncates the word lists to just one page, thereby giving the top thirty-three for each class.

22. The standard report lists the top twenty ECUs for each class, ranked by chi-squared association. However, a separate file is produced that lists all the ECUs for each class.

23. Twelve of the top twenty typical ECUs for this class make an explicit link between wages and prices.

24. See chapter 4, note 13.

25. As Louis XVI's controller-general, Turgot enacted policies of free trade in corn to Paris (1776) (Cobban 1974, 104–112).

26. Further ECUs from this class illustrate how Non-Peelite Conservatives considered Peel's motion as a betrayal of the party's commitment to protection, made explicit in the election of 1841:

(42) ... and the House of Commons had chosen the right hon. baronet as the leader of that party. And now, in 1846, they were called upon to pass the very same measure nay a far stronger and more sweeping measure than that which their constituents had returned them to oppose and put down. Rightly or wrongly, that had taken place; and by what measure of political expediency could such a change be justified?

Some Non-Peelite Conservatives maintained that their prospects in the aftermath of repeal (as a "Protection Party") would be enhanced as a result of their adherence to their protectionist pledges:

(39) ... This protection party, who have honestly stood by their pledges, and not broken their faith, who have not participated in the disgrace of breaking the faith of parliament, of dishonoring the parliament of this country; I am much mistaken, I say, if this party

will not come back to this house greatly strengthened by the support of those constituencies that have been betrayed during the present session.

27. A loose interpretation of the distribution of classes from table 7.1 would suggest that MPs spent about 31 percent of their speaking time engaging in parliamentary rhetoric (though this includes the timing of repeal, as discussed below).

28. Peel's legislation retained small duties on grain until 1 February 1849, after which a uniform registration duty of 1 s. per quarter was instituted. This registration duty was repealed in 1869.

29. While correspondence analysis is well established in the French literature (see Benzecri 1973) and the journal *Cahiers de l'Analyse des Données*, its use has spread with the publication of English applications (Greenacre and Underhill 1982; Greenacre 1984, 1993; Weller and Romney 1990). Correspondence analysis has only recently received attention by political scientists (Blasius and Thiessen 2001). Correspondence analysis using numerical data is available in several major statistical packages, including BMDP, SPSS, and SAS.

30. For this, correspondence analysis uses the "chi-squared distance," which resembles the Euclidean distance between points in physical space. However, in correspondence analysis, each squared difference between coordinates is divided by the corresponding element of the average profile (where the profile is a set of frequencies divided by their total). The justification for using the chi-squared concept is that it allows one to transform the frequencies by dividing the square roots of the expected frequencies, thereby equalizing the variances. This can be compared to factor analysis, where data on different scales are standardized. Greenacre (1993, 36) provides further geometric reasons for using the chi-squared distance in correspondence analysis.

31. Correspondence analysis usually refers to the "inertia" of a table, which can also be called "association" (Weller and Romney 1990). A corresponding chi-squared value can be obtained by multiplying the association value by the total n of the table.

32. The association and chi-squared statistic may be interpreted geometrically as the degree of dispersion of the set of rows and columns (or profile points) around their average, where the points are weighted.

33. Factors 3, 4, and 5 account for the following percentages of association—respectively, 18.3, 12.2, and 8.3.

34. Greenacre (1993, 14) notes that the geometry of profiles greater than three require the "barycentric coordinate system" for plotting and that the dimensionality of this system is always one less than the number of elements (here, classes) in the profile.

35. The sequence of the debates is first reading, total and immediate repeal, second reading, and third reading. The dates of the divisions in 1846 were, respectively, February 27, March 3, March 27, and May 15.

36. Urban MPs, particularly those representing industrial centers, were more likely to support free trade, while county MPs represented more agricultural districts and therefore were more protectionist leaning (Schonhardt-Bailey 1994). These tags were given to all MPs who spoke in the debates.

37. Owing to data limitations, these tags were assigned to the English MPs only and so do not capture these characteristics for Welsh, Scottish, or Irish MPs. (See book appendix 2 for further information on these MPs.)

38. The cut-off for this chi-squared value is 2.

39. The tag with the highest chi-squared value is "first reading" (33.3), while "Peelite" is the next highest (11.2), excluding the names of various MPs.

40. Landowners were by no means united in their support for protection. For example, those with diversified portfolios were more likely to benefit from repeal and so were less wedded to protection (as is shown in chapter 5).

Chapter 8

1. Supply-side theories of policy making may highlight the institutional setting in which legislators operate (Krehbiel 1991; Cox and McCubbins 1993; Krehbiel 1998; Stewart 2001) or the ideas that influence policy makers (Baumgartner and Jones 1993). To recap, the argument from chapter 2 is that a shift in constituency demands was necessary but not sufficient to convert a majority of MPs to repeal. Even if all Liberal MPs voted for repeal, it could not have passed without the support of some Conservative MPs. To push the wavering Conservatives to free trade, the definition of repeal required reinterpretation so that it could be seen to be compatible with Conservative ideology. Peel provided this reinterpretation when he introduced the repeal legislation, and Peelites latched onto this reinterpretation as political and ideological cover for their free-trade votes. By trumpeting themselves as loyal to the longer-term preservation of the territorial constitution and acceding that repeal was a necessary concession to ensure this outcome, Peelites could vote as delegates without having to justify themselves as such.

2. Book appendix 3 is compiled in part from Porritt and Porritt (1909), Judd (1955), Philbin (1965), Craig (1973), Stenton (1976), Gash (1977), and Thorne (1986).

3. All representative ECUs in this chapter are drawn from the top twenty of each class (ranked according to chi-squared values).

4. But see Fetter (1980).

5. The logic of this argument rests on Ricardian theory of rent, which the Anti-Corn Law League exploited in an attempt to divide the interests of landowners and tenant farmers (see chapter 4).

6. See chapter 4 for the landowners' rebuttal to the rent argument.

7. Notably, such an alliance would have to have overcome serious differences in reformist strategies.

8. From 2006, the data will also be available from the Interuniversity Consortium for Political and Social Research and the United Kingdom Data Archive.

9. A further two factors are required to account for the total association for 1814 to 1815, with factor 3 accounting for 17.9 percent and factor 4 for 16.9 percent. One further class is required to make up the remaining 22.2 percent association for 1826 to 1828. Four further factors are needed to account for the total association for 1842 to 1844, with each, consecutively, accounting for 16.0 percent, 10.3 percent, 9.4 percent, and 6.5 percent. Moreover, as noted in the previous chapter, the dimensionality of each coordinate system is one less than the number of classes.

10. See book appendix 4 for a detailed legislative schedule.

11. A fifth category—creating new representation for the constituency—does not apply during this prereform period.

12. For a detailed description of this district-economic-orientation variable, see chapter 5 and book appendix 1.

13. Notably, Peelite speeches provide support for an ideal point some distance away from that of the Non-Peelite Conservatives, while their votes up to 1846 (chapter 6) suggest an ideal point on par with their Conservative colleagues. The findings of this chapter together with those of chapter 6 illustrate a juxtaposition of speeches and votes. This underpins figure 2.1, where the ideal points of the two factions were some distance apart but both were positioned on the right-hand side of the cut point. The introduction of the second dimension (figure 2.2) then allowed Peelites to vote more according to what might be described as their true preferences.

Chapter 9

1. Before 1860, the Lords vetoed a number of public policy bills "in which taxation was incidentally involved, [but] they ... respected bills exclusively relating to matter of supply and ways and means" (Cocks 1964, 840). That is, inasmuch as repeal clearly "involved" taxation, the Lords possessed the authority to reject it outright (unlike, say, the budget). The Lords' veto power was limited by the Commons in 1860; however, as Erskine May's authoritative treatise explains: "Before 1860 it was not unusual for the repeal or imposition of separate classes of duties or taxes to be effected by separate bills, but the rejection by the Lords in that year of the Paper Duties Repeal Bill led the Commons to adopt the practice of including all the fiscal changes of each year in a general or composite bill" (Cocks 1964, 840). Thus, by incorporating fiscal proposals into the budget, the Commons eliminated the possibility of a Lords' veto on these proposals.

2. Often, narratives of repeal and the rise of free trade devote considerable attention to the activities of the League and the long and acrimonious debate in the Commons. Far less attention is given to the shorter debate in the Lords. The description of Armitage-Smith is one of the older examples of this tendency, describing the repeal bill as having "passed quickly through the Lords by the Duke of Wellington" (Armitage-Smith 1898, 90).

3. Gash notes that while the failure of the House of Lords to obstruct repeal is "one of the most surprising aspects of the [Corn Law] crisis," this "phenomenon ... has received less attention than it deserves" (Gash 1965, 47).

4. There are, however, very good studies on the Lords more generally, including Weston (1970), May (1979), and Gash (1990).

5. Commentary from *The Times* offers some flavor of the climate of democracy years before repeal, focusing particularly on the Anti-Corn Law League's agitation. Armitage-Smith (1898, 82) cited a lead article on 18 November 1843 in which *The Times*

admitted the growing importance of the League. After recording the subscriptions and the persistence of the agitators, it continued: "These are facts important and worthy of consideration. No moralist can disregard them, no politician can sneer at them, no statesman can undervalue them: he who collects opinions must chronicle them. He who frames laws must to some extent consult them. The League may be a hypocrite—a huge Trojan horse of sedition. But the League exists.... A new power has arisen in the State.... We acknowledge that we dislike gregarious collections of cant and cotton men. But we cannot but know that whatever is the end of this agitation, it will expire only to bequeath its violence and its turbulence to some successor."

6. Turberville (1974, 408) illustrates this point by estimating the concentration of economic wealth in mid-nineteenth-century Britain: "as much four-fifths of the surface of the United Kingdom was in the hands of no more than 7,000 persons, that twenty-eight dukes owned 158 separate estates, comprehending just under four million acres; that thirty-three marquesses owned 121 estates, totally rather more than 1,500,000 acres; that one hundred and ninety-four earls, in 634 estates, were possessed of nearly 5,900,000 acres; that two hundred and seventy viscounts and barons owned 680 estates, whose combined acreage was 3,780,000. In other words five hundred and twenty-five members of the nobility were possessed of rather more than fifteen million acres, which was not much less than half the total acreage of the country."

7. See, for example, Craig (1973) and Vincent and Stenton (1971).

8. For instance, Lords for which party affiliation is known, since they previously sat as MPs, were Lord Brougham (Liberal MP for Southwark in 1832 to 1835, defeated at Leeds in 1835); Earl Fitzwilliam (Liberal MP for Northamptonshire in 1832 to 1833 as Viscount Milton); and Earl of Malmesbury (as Viscount Fitzharris, Conservative MP for Wilton in June to October 1841).

9. Opposition speeches came from the Duke of Richmond, Lord Brougham, the Marquis of Londonderry, and the Earl of Ripon. On a handful of other occasions, however, debates took place on the first readings of bills received from the Commons (Gordon 1983, 497).

10. A peer could appoint a colleague to vote on his behalf (with or without conditions), though no one peer could possess more than two proxy votes. Smith (1992, 43–44) characterizes the proxy system as a means to maintain party strength:

In general, the use of proxies in this period became more an instrument to maintain party strengths, irrespective of actual attendance, than a means by which individual peers sought to compensate for unavoidable absence or to salve their consciences for nonperformance of their duties. As the Upper House came more to mirror the parties in the House of Commons, and as the diminished "influence of the Crown" no longer gave the government of the day a powerful lever to keep the Upper House in line, the party whips and managers gave more attention to the organisation of the proxy system and tried to induce their supporters to nominate proxies before the start of each session as a safeguard against non-attendance.... [Earl] Fitzwilliam defended the practice as being a remedy for lords who were unable to attend because of illness or necessary duty, and pointed out the lords gave their proxies to people with whose views they tended to agree and that if the proxy-holder was influenced by the debate he would use his judgement whether to use the proxy.... The proxy system came under increasing attack from the press and public during the middle years of the nineteenth century and their use diminished sharply after 1850.

11. In a letter to his wife dated 15 May, Cobden (Morley 1881, 382) registered the same fear:

There is at last a prospect of reading the Bill a third time to night. The Protectionists promise fairly enough, but I have seen too much of their tactics to feel certain that they will not have another adjournment. There is a revival of rumours again that the Lords will alter the Bill in committee, and attempt a fixed-duty compromise, or a perpetuation of the reduced scale. It is certain to pass the second reading by a majority of thirty or forty, but it is not safe in the committee, where proxies don't count.

12. A number of amendments were proposed in the Lords after the second reading. For instance, on 11 June, the Earl of Stanhope attempted to delay the House going into Committee by six months; on 15 June, the Duke of Buckingham proposed a fixed duty of 10 s. per quarter, instead of Peel's proposed 1 s. after 1849; on 16 June, the Earl of Wicklow proposed a lower fixed duty of 5 s.; and further amendments were proposed by Lord Ashburton on 22 June and the Duke of Richmond on 25 June. Majorities opposed to these amendments ranged from approximately twenty to thirty.

13. More specifically, "When a protest has been drawn up by any Lord, other Lords may either subscribe it without remark, if they assent to all the reasons assigned in it; or they may signify the particular reasons which have induced them to attach their signatures" (Gordon 1983, 482–483).

14. The first protest attracted no further signatures, while the second was signed by thirteen other peers (although most of these agreed with only a few of Stanhope's seven reasons).

15. Putting this into context, Smith (1992, 45) notes that "Only 10 protests, 9 before 1850, were signed by more than twenty peers; the great majority (279 out of 373) were signed by five peers or less, including 148 signed by only one individual."

16. Some minor speeches occurred with the amendments of early June, but these have not been included in the analysis since the protectionist opposition is viewed as having died with the safe passage of the second reading.

17. Recall from chapter 7 that the program uses the presence or absence of words in each ECU to calculate matrices on which to build the classification process. Table 7.3 in chapter 7 provides examples of ECUs, with each three- or four-digit reference designating a given ECU in the text. The program conducts two preliminary analyses, each using slightly different lengths for the contextual unit. It then opts for the length that allows the greater proportion of ECUs to be successfully classified relative to the total available.

18. It should be noted that the longer time frame given to debating repeal in the Commons may, of itself, have afforded MPs the luxury of "theorizing."

19. It seems evident that the outcome of a possible dissolution was entirely uncertain: the Whigs feared a protectionist victory, while the protectionists feared a return of free traders.

20. Recall from chapter 7 that correspondence analysis aims to account for a maximum amount of association along the first (horizontal) axis. The second (vertical) axis seeks to account for a maximum of the remaining association, and so on. Hence, the total association is divided into components along principal axes. The resulting map provides a means for transforming numerical information into pictorial form. It provides a framework for the user to formulate her own interpretations, rather than providing clear-cut conclusions.

21. Factors 3 and 4 account for 19.5 and 14.4 percent of the total association, respectively. Recall from chapter 7 that, as the number of classes is five, the "dimensionality" of the coordinate system is four, or one less than the number of classes.

22. While the tag for Wellington is statistically significant for three classes (parliamentary rhetoric, Peel as trustee, and the House of Lords), the χ^2 value for each of these is relatively small (2, 8, and 14, respectively).

23. Unlike the Commons, the Lords represented no particular constituencies, and so the same sort of argument advanced in chapter 5 would not apply to the Lords. Virtually all of the Lords were landowning aristocrats with no allegiances to any particular geographic locality, and so variations in portfolio diversification across the country would not affect any one of the Lords more than another. One might conjecture that Lords who supported repeal were *themselves* more diversified in their portfolios, but neither the secondary literature nor my own preliminary investigation of this possibility suggests that much weight should be given to an economic interest-based interpretation of the voting in the House of Lords.

Chapter 10

1. Brown (1985, 47) notes that "no newspaper advanced from a provincial base to swamp the country."

2. While the data in this and other chapters are chiefly from English districts, some readers may find it useful to compare this newspaper sample with the larger population of U.K. newspapers.

3. Class newspapers appear to have been specialist newspapers, such those for railways and the arts, that are not predominantly political in their content.

4. Once again, as this book does not attempt to cover the whole of the United Kingdom, this comparison between England and the United Kingdom is for information only.

5. On completing the electronic version of the 1846 debates for chapter 7, it became evident that the indexes in *Hansard's Parliamentary Debates* had failed to include twenty-three English MPs who spoke during the repeal debates. Nineteen of these MPs gave very short speeches and sometimes only interjections (which, no doubt, contributed to their omission in the indexes). Taken as a whole, these MPs represented a variety of constituencies and party affiliations, and so there appears to be no pattern to their exclusion from the indexes (beyond their own verbal brevity). Hence, any bias that might occur from their exclusion from the sampling frame is likely to be minimal.

6. These summaries were completed by my research assistant, Gordon Bannerman, and are available by request. All newspapers were obtained from the British Library's Newspaper Library at Colindale. I am sincerely grateful for the assistance given by the staff at Colindale.

7. In a small number of cases, a newspaper was not available during these six-month time periods (newspapers came and went and so were not always available in a smooth timeline). In these handful of cases, the data were assigned to the nearest time period rather than simply discarded.

8. In making the distinction in types of coverage, a *speech* was deemed to consist of an actual speech made outside of Parliament to constituents (generally of party associations or interested bodies), letters to party associations or to a newspaper directly, and election addresses. Newspaper *comment* would, in contrast, relate to newspaper editorials, reports, articles, and so on. In short, comments included any material relating to trade policy that did not emanate from the MP himself. Reports of Protection or Anti-Corn Law meetings at the local and national levels were designated as comment, though most of this material related to the editorial comment of newspapers.

9. The data were in a form that was not appropriate for more intensive statistical analysis.

Chapter 11

1. George Jones, a colleague of mine, posed this question years ago when I presented my research in a seminar at the LSE. This portion of the conclusion addresses his question.

2. One might argue that it was the perception of economic disaster that mattered more than the reality, as Britain entered the so-called golden age of farming in the aftermath of repeal.

3. My earlier work on repeal (Schonhardt-Bailey 1991b, 1994) fits this description precisely. The present book, in contrast, represents the work of a reformed (but not repentant) rational choicer.

References

Acemoglu, D. (2003). "Root Causes: A Historical Approach to Assessing the Role of Institutions in Economic Development." *Finance and Development* (June): 27–30.

Acemoglu, D., and S. Johnson. (2003). "Unbundling Institutions." Working Paper No. W9934, National Bureau of Economic Research (NBER).

Acemoglu, D., and J. A. Robinson. (2005). *Economic Origins of Dictatorship and Democracy.* Cambridge: Cambridge University Press.

Adler, E. S. (2000). "Constituency Characteristics and the 'Guardian' Model of Appropriations Subcommittees, 1959–1998." *American Journal of Political Science* 44(1): 104–114.

Adler, E. S., and J. S. Lapinski. (1997). "Demand-Side Theory and Congressional Committee Composition: A Constituency Characteristics Approach." *American Journal of Political Science* 41(3): 895–918.

Aglionby, M. (1846). *The Battle for Native Industry: The Debate upon the Corn Laws* (vol. 1, 101–102). H. o. Commons. London, Office of the Society for the Protection of Agriculture and British Industry.

Allum, N. C. (1998). *A Social Representations Approach to the Comparison of Three Textual Corpora Using Alceste*. London: London School of Economics and Political Science.

Alvarez, R. M., and J. L. Saving. (1997). "Deficits, Democrats, and Distributive Benefits: Congressional Elections and the Pork Barrel in the 1980s." *Political Research Quarterly* 50(4): 809–831.

Anderson, G. M., and R. D. Tollison. (1985). "Ideology, Interest Groups, and the Repeal of the Corn Laws." *Journal of Institutional and Theoretical Economics* 141(2): 197–212.

Anderson, K. (1992). "Agricultural Trade Liberalization and the Environment: A Globabl Perspective." *World Economy* 15(1 January): 153–172.

The Annual Register, or a View of the History and Politics of the Year 1846. (1847). London: Rivington.

Armitage-Smith, G. (1898). *The Free Trade Movement and Its Results.* London: Blackie.

"Art. VII-1. Corrected Report of the Speech of Lord John Russell at the Dinner Given at His Election for Stroud; and 2. Prospects of the Country under a New Parliament." (1837). *Quarterly Review* 118: 519–564.

Ashburton, L. (1846). *The Battle for Native Industry: The Debate upon the Corn Laws* (vol. 1, 108–110). H. o. Lords. London, Office of the Society for the Protection of Agriculture and British Industry.

Aspinall, A. (1949). *Politics and the Press, c. 1780–1850*. London: Home and Van Thal.

Aspinall, A. (1956). "The Reporting and Publishing of the House of Commons' Debates, 1771–1834." *Essays Presented to Sir Lewis Namier*. Ed. A. J. P. Taylor and R. Pares. London: Macmillan.

Association, M. A.-C. L. (1841). *Anti-Bread Tax Tracts for the People, 3*. Manchester: Gadsby.

Austen-Smith, D. (1990). "Information Transmission in Debate." *American Journal of Political Science* 34(1): 124–152.

Austen-Smith, D., and W. H. Riker. (1987). "Asymmetric Information and the Coherence of Legislation." *American Political Science Review* 81(3): 897–918.

Austen-Smith, D., and W. H. Riker. (1990). "Asymmetric Information and the Coherence of Legislation: A Correction." *American Political Science Review* 84(1): 243–245.

Aydelotte, W. O. (1962). "The Business Interests of the Gentry in the Parliament of 1841–1847." *The Making of Victorian England*. Ed. G. K. Clark. London: Methuent.

Aydelotte, W. O. (1967). "The Country Gentlemen and the Repeal of the Corn Laws." *English Historical Review* 82(322): 47–60.

Aydelotte, W. O. (1972). "The Distintegration of the Conservative Party in the 1840s: A Study of Political Attitudes." *The Dimensions of Quantitative Research in History* (319–346). Ed. W. O. Aydelotte, A. G. Bogue, and R. W. Fogel. Princeton: Princeton University Press.

Aydelotte, W. O. (n.d.). *British House of Commons, 1841–1847*. Ann Arbor: Inter-University Consortium for Political and Social Research.

Baack, B. D., and E. J. Ray. (1983). "The Political Economy of Tariff Policy: A Case Study of the United States." *Explorations in Economic History* 20: 73–93.

Bailey, A., and C. Schonhardt-Bailey. (2005). *Explaining the Volcker Revolution of 1979: Testing Theories with Transcripts*. Washington, DC: American Political Science Association.

Bailey, A. J. (1984). *The Impact of the Napoleonic Wars on the Development of the Cotton Industry in Lancashire: A Study of the Structure and Behaviour of Firms during the Industrial Revolution*. Cambridge: Cambridge University.

Baldwin, R. (1989). "Measurable Dynamic Gains from Trade." Working Paper No. 3147, National Bureau of Economic Research, Cambridge, MA.

Baldwin, R. E. (1985). *The Political Economy of U.S. Import Policy*. Cambridge: MIT Press.

Baring, A. (1815). *Parliamentary Debates* (vol. 3, cols. 69–73). H. o. Commons. London: Hansard.

Barnes, D. G. (1930). *A History of the English Corn Laws from 1660–1846*. London: Routledge.

Bates, R. H., and A. O. Krueger. (1993). "Generalizations Arising from the Country Studies." *Political and Economic Interactions in Economic Policy Reform: Evidence from Eight Countries*. Ed. R. H. Bates and A. O. Krueger. Oxford: Basil Blackwell.

References

Bauer, M. (2000). "Classical Content Analysis: A Review." *Qualitative Researching with Text, Image and Sound: A Practical Handbook* (131–151). Ed. M. W. Bauer and G. Gaskell. London: Sage.

Baumgartner, F. R., and B. D. Jones. (1993). *Agendas and Instability in American Politics*. Chicago: University of Chicago Press.

Bawn, K. (1999). "Constructing 'Us': Ideology, Coalition Politics, and False Consciousness." *American Journal of Political Science* 43(2): 303–334.

Beckett, J. V. (1986). *The Aristocracy in England 1660–1914*. Oxford: Basil Blackwell.

Bell, D. (1960). *The End of Ideology*. New York: Free Press.

Benzecri, J.-P. (1973). *L'Analyse des Donnees. Tome 1: La Taxinomie. Tome 2: L'Analyse des Correspondances*. Paris: Dunod.

Benzecri, J.-P. (1981). *Pratique de l'analyse des donnees: linguistique et lexicologie*. Paris: Dunod.

Bertier, P., and J. M. Bouroche. (1975). *Analyse des donnees multidimensionnelles*. Paris: Presses Universitaires de France.

Biagini, E. F. (1992). *Liberty, Retrenchment and Reform: Popular Liberalism in the Age of Gladstone, 1860–1880*. Cambridge: Cambridge University Press.

Blackie, T. (1842). *To the Members of the Corn-Law Convention, to Be Held in Edinburgh*. Edinburgh: Elder.

Blake, R. (1974). *The Conservative Party from Peel to Churchill*. London: Fontana/Collins.

Blasius, J., and V. Thiessen. (2001). "Methodological Artifacts in Measures of Political Efficacy and Trust: A Multiple Correspondence Analysis." *Political Analysis* 9(1): 1–20.

Blyth, M. (2002). *Great Transformations: Economic Ideas and Institutional Change in the Twentieth Century*. Cambridge: Cambridge University Press.

Blyth, M. (2003). "Structures Do Not Come with an Instruction Sheet: Interests, Ideas, and Progress in Political Science." *Perspectives on Politics* 1(4): 695–706.

Bohrnstedt, G. W., and D. Knoke. (1994). *Statistics for Social Data Analysis*. Itasca, IL: Peacock.

Bowden, W. (1925). *Industrial Society in England towards the End of the Eighteenth Century*. New York: Macmillan.

Brazill, T. J., and B. Grofman. (2002). "Factor Analysis versus Multidimensional Scaling: Binary Choice Roll-Call Voting and the U.S. Supreme Court." *Social Networks* 24: 201–229.

Briggs, A. (1959). *The Age of Improvement 1783–1867*. London: Longman.

Bright, J. (1845 (1868)). "Speech at an Anti-Corn Law League Meeting, Covent Garden Theatre." *Speeches on Questions of Public Policy by John Bright, M.P.* (vol. 2, 153–162). Ed. J. E. T. Rogers. London: Macmillan.

Broadbridge, S. A. (1970). *Studies in Railway Expansion and the Capital Market in England 1825–1873*. London: Cass.

Brock, W. R. (1941). *Lord Liverpool and Liberal Toryism*. London: Frank Cass.

Brown, L. (1959). "The Chartists and the Anti-Corn Law League." *Chartist Studies*. Ed. A. Briggs. London: Macmillan.

Brown, L. (1985). *Victorian News and Newspapers*. Oxford: Clarendon.

Browne, W. (1995). *Cultivating Congress: Constituents, Issues, and Interests in Agricultural Policymaking*. Lawrence: University Press of Kansas.

Browne, W. P. (Ed.). (1992). *Sacred Cows and Hot Potatoes: Agrarian Myths in Agricultural Policy*. Boulder: Westview Press.

Browne, W. P. (2001). *The Failure of National Rural Policy: Institutions and Interests*. Washington, DC: Georgetown University Press.

Brugidou, M. (1998). "Epitaphs. François Mitterrand's Image: An Analysis of an Open Question Asked on His Death." *Revue Française de Science Politique* 48(1): 97–120.

Brugidou, M. (2000). "The Discourse of Demands and Action in [French] Trade Union Press Editorials (1996–1998)." *Revue Française de Science Politique* 50(6): 967–992.

Burke, E. (1906). "Speech to the Electors of Bristol." *The Works of the Right Honorable Edmund Burke* (vol. 2). New York: Oxford University Press.

Burke, E. (1996). "Mr Edmund Burke's Speech to Bristol Voters, November 3, 1774." *The Writings and Speeches of Edmund Burke. Vol. 3, Party, Parliament, and the American War 1774–1780* (64–70). Ed. W. M. Elofson and J. A. Woods. Oxford: Clarendon Press.

Busch, M., and E. Reinhardt. (1999). "Industrial Location and Protection: The Political and Economic Geography of U.S. Nontariff Barriers." *American Journal of Political Science* 43(4): 1028–1050.

Busch, M., and E. Reinhardt. (2000). "Geography, International Trade, and Political Mobilization in U.S. Industry." *American Journal of Political Science* 44(4): 703–719.

Busch, M., and E. Reinhardt. (2003). "Industrial Location and Voter Participation in Europe." Working Paper, Queen's University and Emory University.

Cain, P. J., and A. G. Hopkins. (1980). "The Political Economy of British Expansion Overseas, 1750–1914." *Economic History Review* (2nd series) 33(4): 463–490.

Canning, G. (1827). *Parliamentary Debates* (vol. 30, cols. 758–772). H. o. Commons. London: Hansard.

Caves, R., and R. Jones. (1985). *World Trade and Payments*. Boston: Little, Brown.

Caves, R. E. (1976). "Economic Models of Political Choice: Canada's Tariff Structure." *Canadian Journal of Economics* 9: 278–300.

Cayley, E. S. (1844). *Reasons for the Formation of the Agricultural Protection Society: Addressed to the Industrious Classes of the United Kingdom* (179–180). A. P. Society. London: John Ollivier.

Chaloner, W. H. (1968). "Introduction to the Second Edition." *History of the Anti-Corn Law League* (vol. 1, v–xxii). Ed. A. Prentice. London: Cass.

Chaloner, W. H. (1970). "The Agitation against the Corn Laws." *Popular Movements, c. 1830–1850* (135–151). Ed. J. T. Ward. London: Macmillan.

References

Coates, D., and M. Munger. (1995). "Legislative Voting and the Economic Theory of Politics." *Southern Economic Journal* 61: 861–873.

Cobban, A. (1974). *A History of Modern France*. Vol. 1, 1715–1799. Harmondsworth: Penguin.

Cobbett, W. (Ed.). (1803). *Cobbett's Parliamentary History*, vols. 1–36.

Cobden, R. (1844). *Parliamentary Debates* (vol. 73, cols. 862–895). London: Hansard.

Cobden, R. (1853 (1968)). "Speech at Manchester Free Trade Hall, 24 October 1844." *History of the Anti-Corn Law League* (149–152). Ed. A. Prentice. London: Cass.

Cocks, S. B. (Ed.). (1964). *Erskine May's Treatise on The Law, Privileges Proceedings and Usage of Parliament* (17th ed.). London: Butterworth.

Conacher, J. B. (1972). *The Peelites and the Party System, 1846–52*. Newton Abbot: David & Charles.

Cottrell, P. L. (1980). *Industrial Finance 1830–1914: The Finance and Organization of English Manufacturing Industry*. London: Methuen.

Cox, G., and M. McCubbins. (1993). *Legislative Leviathan: Party Government in the House*. Berkeley: University of California Press.

Cox, G. W. (1987). *The Efficient Secret: The Cabinet and the Development of Political Parties in Victorian England*. Cambridge: Cambridge University Press.

Cox, J. (1980). *The Records of the Prerogative Court of Canterbury and the Death Duty Registers: A Provisional Guide*. London: Public Record Office.

Craig, F. W. S. (Ed.). (1973). *Henry Stooks Smith, The Parliaments of England, from 1715 to 1847*. Chichester: Political Reference Publications.

Crosby, T. L. (1976). *Sir Robert Peel's Administration, 1841–1846*. Newton Abbot: David & Charles.

Davidson, R. H. (1969). *The Role of the Congressman*. New York: Pegasus.

Davis, R. (1979). *The Industrial Revolution and British Overseas Trade*. Leicester: Leicester University Press.

Day, G. G. (1844). "*The Speech of Mr George Game Day of St Ives, at Huntingdon, . . . , on the Occasion of Forming an Anti-League Association for the County of Huntingdon.*" 31st ed. (The People's Edition) (166–177). A. P. Society. London: John Ollivier.

Defoe, D. (1702). *The Original Power of the Collective Body of the People of England*. London.

Diday, E., J. Lemaire, et al. (1982). *Elements d'analyse des donnees*. Paris: Dunod.

Disraeli, B. (1905). *Lord George Bentinck: A Political Biography*. London: Constable.

Dougan, W. R., and M. C. Munger. (1989). "The Rationality of Ideology." *Journal of Law & Economics* 32: 119–142.

Drezner, D. W. (2000). "Ideas, Bureaucratic Politics, and the Crafting of Foreign Policy." *American Journal of Political Science* 44(4): 733–749.

Duggan, E. P. (1975). "Industrialization and the Development of Urban Business Communities: Research Problems, Sources, and Techniques." *Local Historian* 11: 457–465.

Dutton, H. I., and S. R. H. Jones. (1983). "Invention and Innovation in the British Pin Industry, 1790–1850." *Business History Review* 57: 175–193.

Duverger, M. (1961). *Political Parties: Their Organization and Activity in the Modern State.* London: Methuen.

Edwards, M. (2003). "Political Science and Political Practice: The Pursuit of Grounded Inquiry." *Perspectives on Politics* 1(2): 349–354.

Eichengreen, B. (1998). "Dental Hygiene and Nuclear War: How International Relations Looks from Economics." *International Organization* 52(4): 993–1012.

English, B. (1984). "Probate Valuations and the Death Duty Registers." *Bulletin of the Institute of Historical Research* 58(135): 80–91.

"The EU's Coming Wrangle for Reforms and Spoils." (1999). *The Economist*: 33.

Eulau, H. (1962). "The Legislator as Representative: Representational Roles." *The Legislative System.* Ed. J. C. Wahlke, H. Eulau, W. Buchanan, and L. C. Ferguson. New York: Wiley.

Fang, H.-T. i. (1978). *The Triumph of the Factory System in England.* Philadelphia: Porcupine Press.

"Farmer Franz Fischler Digs In." (1998). *The Economist*: 52.

Fay, C. R. (1932). *The Corn Laws and Social England.* London: Cambridge University Press.

Feeney, J., and A. L. Hillman. (2001). "Privatization and the Political Economy of Strategic Trade Policy. *International Economic Review* 42: 535–556.

Fenno, R. F. (1978). *Home Style: House Members in Their Districts.* Boston: Little, Brown.

Fetter, F. W. (1980). *The Economist in Parliament: 1780–1868.* Durham: Duke University Press.

Finkel, S. E., and J. G. Geer. (1998). "A Spot Check: Casting Doubt on the Demobilizing Effect of Attack Advertising." *American Journal of Political Science* 42(2): 573–595.

Gabel, M. J., and J. D. Huber. (2000). "Putting Parties in Their Place: Inferring Party Left-Right Ideological Positions from Party Manifestos Data." *American Journal of Political Science* 44(1): 94–103.

Gallagher, J., and R. Robinson. (1953). "The Imperialism of Free Trade." *Economic History Review* (2nd ser.) 6(1): 1–13.

Gambles, A. (1999). *Protection and Politics: Conservative Economic Discourse, 1815–1852.* Woodbridge, Suffolk: Royal Historical Society, Boydell Press.

Garrett, G., and B. R. Weingast. (1993). "Ideas, Interests, and Institutions: Constructing the European Community's Internal Market." *Ideas and Foreign Policy: Beliefs, Institutions, and Political Change* (173–206). Ed. J. Goldstein and R. O. Keohane. Ithaca: Cornell University Press.

Gash, N. (1951). "Peel and the Party System, 1830–50." *Transactions of the Royal Historical Society* (5th ser.) 1: 47–69.

Gash, N. (1965). *Reaction and Reconstruction in English Politics, 1832–1852.* Oxford: Oxford University Press.

Gash, N. (1977). *Politics in the Age of Peel: A Study in the Technique of Parliamentary Representation, 1830–1850*. Hassocks: Harvester Press.

Gash, N. (1982). "The Organization of the Conservative Party, 1832–1846, Part 1: The Parliamentary Organization." *Parliamentary History* 1: 137–159.

Gash, N. (1990). *Wellington: Studies in the Military and Political Career of the First Duke of Wellington*. Manchester: Manchester University Press.

Gatrell, V. A. C. (1977). "Labour, Power, and the Size of Firms in Lancashire Cotton in the Second Quarter of the Nineteenth Century." *Economic History Review* (2nd ser.) 30(1): 95–139.

Geddes, B. (2003). *Paradigms and Sand Castles: Theory Building and Research Design in Comparative Politics*. Ann Arbor: University of Michigan Press.

Godek, P. E. (1985). "Industry Structure and Redistribution through Trade Restrictions." *Journal of Law and Economics* 28: 687–703.

Goderich, V. (1827). *Parliamentary Debates* (vol. 17, cols. 984–999). H. o. Lords. London: Hansard.

Goldstein, J. (1993). *Ideas, Interests, and American Trade Policy*. Ithaca: Cornell University Press.

Goldstein, J., and R. O. Keohane (Eds.). (1993). *Ideas and Foreign Policy: Beliefs, Institutions, and Political Change*. Ithaca: Cornell University Press.

Goldstein, K. M. (1999). *Interest Groups, Lobbying, and Participation in America*. Cambridge: Cambridge University Press.

Golob, S. R. (2003). "Beyond the Policy Frontier: Canada, Mexico, and the Ideological Origins of NAFTA." *World Politics* 55(3): 361–398.

Goodin, R. E. (1996). "Institutionalizing the Public Interest: The Defense of Deadlock and Beyond." *American Political Science Review* 90(2): 331–343.

Gordon, S. C. (Ed.). (1983). *Erskine May's Treatise on The Law, Privileges, Proceedings and Usage of Parliament*. London: Butterworths.

Gray, P. (1999). *Famine, Land and Politics: British Government and Irish Society 1843–1850*. Dublin: Irish Academic Press.

Great Britain, Public Record Office. (1825–1846). *Exports, Produce and Manufactures of the United Kingdom*. Cust. 9. London.

Greenacre, M. J. (1984). *Theory and Applications of Correspondence Analysis*. London: Academic Press.

Greenacre, M. J. (1993). *Correspondence Analysis in Practice*. London: Academic Press.

Greenacre, M. J., and L. G. Underhill. (1982). "Scaling a Data Matrix in Low-Dimensional Euclidean Space." *Topics in Applied Multivariate Analysis*. Ed. D. M. Hawkins. Cambridge: Cambridge University Press.

Grier, K. B. (Ed.). (1993). *Public Choice: Empirical Studies of Ideology and Representation in American Politics*. Special issue of Public Choice.

Grofman, B. (Ed.). (2001). *Political Science as Puzzle Solving*. Ann Arbor: University of Michigan Press.

Groseclose, T., S. D. Levitt, et al. (1999). "Comparing Interest Group Scores Across Time and Chambers: Adjusted ADA Scores for the U.S. Congress." *American Political Science Review* 93(1): 33–50.

Grossman, G., and E. Helpman. (1988). "Product Development and International Trade." Working Paper, Princeton, Princeton University.

Haas, P. (Ed.). (1992). *Knowledge, Power, and International Policy Coordination*. Special Issue of *International Organization* 46 (Winter).

Hall, P. A. (Ed.). (1989). *The Political Power of Economic Ideas: Keynesianism across Nations*. Princeton: Princeton University Press.

Hall, P. A. (1997). "The Role of Interests, Institutions, and Ideas in the Comparative Political Economy of the Industrialized Nations." *Comparative Politics: Rationality, Culture, and Structure* (174–207). Ed. M. I. Lichbach and A. S. Zuckerman. Cambridge: Cambridge University Press.

Hansard's Parliamentary Debates. (1846). (3rd ser.). London: T.C. Hansard.

Hansen, R., and D. King. (2001). "Eugenic Ideas, Political Interests, and Policy Variance: Immigration and Sterilization Policy in Britain and the U.S." *World Politics* 53(2): 237–263.

Hansen, W. L. (1990). "The International Trade Commission and the Politics of Protectionism." *American Political Science Review* 84(1): 21–46.

Harling, P. (1996). *The Waning of 'Old Corruption': The Politics of Economical Reform in Britain, 1779–1846*. Oxford: Clarendon Press.

Hawke, G. R., and J. P. P. Higgins. (1981). "Transport and Social Overhead Capital." *The Economic History of Britain since 1700* (vol. 1). Ed. R. Floud and D. McCloskey. Cambridge: Cambridge University Press.

Hayashi, C. (1950). "On the Quantification of Qualitative Data from the Mathematico-Statistical Point of View." *Annals of the Institute of Statistical Mathematics* 2. 35–48.

Healey, J. F. (1984). *Statistics: A Tool for Social Research*. Belmont, CA: Wadsworth.

Heathcote, G., and H. S. Paul. (1815). *Parliamentary Debates* (vol. 30, cols. 69–73). H. o. Commons. London: Hansard.

Heckman, J. J., and J. M. Snyder. (1997). "Linear Probability Models of the Demand for Attributes with an Empirical Application to Estimating the Preferences of Legislators." *RAND Journal of Economics* 28(0): S142–S189.

Henderson, D. (1986). *Innocence and Design: The Influence of Economic Ideas on Policy*. Oxford: Basil Blackwell.

Hill, K. Q., S. Hanna, et al. (1997). "The Liberal-Conservative Ideology of U.S. Senators: A New Measure." *American Journal of Political Science* 41(4): 1395–1413.

Hill, R. L. (1929). *Toryism and the People, 1832–1846*. London: Constable.

Hilton, B. (1977). *Corn, Cash, Commerce: The Economic Policies of the Tory Governments 1815–1830*. Oxford: Oxford University Press.

Hilton, B. (1979). "Peel: A Reappraisal." *Historical Journal* 22: 585–614.

Hilton, B. (1988). *The Age of Atonement*. Oxford: Clarendon Press.

Hilton, B. (1998). "Comments on Kinealy and Schonhardt-Bailey." *Free Trade and Its Reception 1815–1960: Freedom and Trade* (vol. 1, 82–85). Ed. A. Marrison. London: Routledge.

Hinich, M. J., and M. C. Munger. (1994). *Ideology and the Theory of Political Choice*. Ann Arbor: University of Michigan.

Hinich, M. J., and M. C. Munger. (1997). *Analytical Politics*. Cambridge: Cambridge University Press.

Hirst, F. W. (Ed.). (1903). *Free Trade and Other Fundamental Doctrines of the Manchester School*. London: Harper.

Hix, S. (2000). *Nations vs. Parties vs. Ideology: Voting Behavior in the European Parliament, 1994–2000*. Washington, DC: American Political Science Association.

Hobsbawm, E. J. (1962). *The Age of Revolution 1789–1848*. New York: New American Library.

Hobsbawm, E. J. (1968). *Industry and Empire*. London: Weidenfeld and Nicolson.

Holland, B. (1980). *The Fall of Protection, 1840–1850*. Philadelphia: Porcupine Press. (Originally published in 1913).

Hood, C. (1994). *Explaining Economic Policy Reversals*. Buckingham, England: Open University Press.

Hope-Jones, A. (1939). *Income Tax in the Napoleonic Wars*. Cambridge: Cambridge University Press.

Howe, A. (1984). *The Cotton Masters, 1830–1860*. Oxford: Oxford University Press.

Howe, A. (1992). "Free Trade and the City of London, c. 1820–1870." *History* 77(254): 391–410.

Howe, A. (1997). *Free Trade and Liberal England, 1846–1946*. Oxford: Clarendon Press.

Hume, J. (1828). *Parliamentary Debates* (vol. 17, 208–217). H. o. Commons. London: Hansard.

Hume, J. D. (1996). "Corn Laws. The Evidence of James Deacon Hume before the Committee of the House of Commons on the Import Duties." *Free Trade: The Repeal of the Corn Laws*. Ed. C. Schonhardt-Bailey. Bristol: Thoemmes Press. (Originally published in 1839).

Huskisson, W. (1814). "*A Letter on the Corn Laws.*" London: Ridgway.

Huskisson, W. (1827). In *Hansard's Parliamentary Debates* (vol. 17, cols. 1324–1335). H. o. Commons. London: Hansard.

Irving, R. J. (1984). "The Capitalisation of Britain's Railways, 1830–1914." *Journal of Transport History* (3rd ser.) 5(1): 1–24.

Irwin, D. A. (1989). "Political Economy and Peel's Repeal of the Corn Laws." *Economics and Politics* 1: 41–59.

Irwin, D. A., and R. S. Kroszner. (1999). "Interests, Institutions, and Ideology in Securing Policy Change: The Republican Conversion to Trade Liberalization after Smoot-Hawley." *Journal of Law and Economics* 62: 643–673.

Jackson, J. E., and J. W. Kingdon. (1992). "Ideology, Interest Group Scores, and Legislative Votes." *American Journal of Political Science* 36: 805–823.

Jacobsen, J. K. (1995). "Much Ado about Ideas: The Cognitive Factor in Economic Policy." *World Politics* 47(2 January): 283–310.

Jenkins, J. A. (2000). "Examining the Robustness of Ideological Voting: Evidence from the Confederate House of Representatives." *American Journal of Political Science* 44(4): 811–822.

Jenkins, T. A. (1999). *Sir Robert Peel*. London: Macmillan Press.

Jenkins-Smith, H. C., G. K. S. Clair, et al. (1991). "Explaining Change in Policy Subsystems: Analysis of Coalition Stability and Defection over Time." *American Journal of Political Science* 35(4): 851–880.

Jones, B. D. (1994). *Reconceiving Decision-Making in Democratic Politics: Attention, Choice, and Public Policy*. Chicago: University of Chicago.

Jones, W. D. (1956). *Lord Derby and Victorian Conservatism*. Athens: University of Georgia Press.

Jones, W. D., and A. B. Erickson. (1972). *The Peelites, 1846–1857*. Columbus: Ohio State University Press.

Judd, G. P. (1955). *Members of Parliament 1734–1832*. New Haven: Yale University Press.

Kahn, K. F. (1992). "Does Being Male Help? An Investigation of the Effects of Candidate Gender and Campaign Coverage on Evaluation of U.S. Senate Candidates." *Journal of Politics* 54(2): 497–517.

Kalt, J. P., and M. A. Zupan. (1990). "The Apparent Ideological Behavior of Legislators: Testing for Principal-Agent Slack in Political Institutions." *Journal of Law and Economics* 33: 103–131.

Keir, D. L. (1948). *The Constitutional History of Modern Britain 1485–1937*. London: Black.

Kellett, E. E. (1934). "The Press." *Early Victorian England, 1830–1865* (vol. 2, 1–98). London: Oxford University Press.

Kennedy, P. (1992). *A Guide to Econometrics* (3rd ed.). Oxford: Basil Blackwell.

Killick, J. R., and W. A. Thomas. (1970). "The Provincial Stock Exchanges: 1830–1870." *Economic History Review* (2nd ser.) 23(1): 96–111.

Kindleberger, C. P. (1975). "The Rise of Free Trade in Western Europe, 1820–1875." *Journal of Economic History* 35(1): 20–55.

Kinealy, C. (1998). "Peel, Rotten Potatoes and Providence: The Repeal of the Corn Laws and the Irish Famine." *Free Trade and Its Reception 1815–1960* (vol. 1, 50–62). Ed. A. Marrison. London: Routledge.

King, G., R. O. Keohane, et al. (1994). *Designing Social Inquiry: Scientific Inference in Qualitative Research*. Princeton: Princeton University Press.

King, G., M. Tomz, et al. (2000). "Making the Most of Statistical Analyses: Improving Interpretation and Presentation." *American Journal of Political Science* 44(2): 347–361.

Kirchheimer, O. (1990). "The Catch-all Party." *The West European Party System* (50–60). Ed. P. Mair. Oxford: Oxford University Press.

References

Koford, K. (1989). "Dimensions in Congressional Voting." *American Political Science Review* 83(3): 949–962.

Kollman, K. (1998). *Outside Lobbying: Public Opinion and Interest Group Strategies*. Princeton: Princeton University Press.

Koss, S. (1981). *The Rise and Fall of the Political Press in Britain*. Vol. 1, *The Nineteenth Century*. London: Hamilton.

Krehbiel, K. (1991). *Information and Legislative Organization*. Ann Arbor: University of Michigan.

Krehbiel, K. (1998). *Pivotal Politics: A Theory of U.S. Lawmaking*. Chicago: University of Chicago Press.

Kronberger, N., and W. Wagner. (2000). "Keywords in Context: Statistical Analysis of Text Features." *Qualitative Researching with Text, Image and Sound: A Practical Handbook* (299–317). Ed. M. W. Bauer and G. Gaskell. London: Sage.

Krugman, P. (1988). *Endogenous Innovations, International Trade, and Growth: Problem of Development*. Buffalo: State University of New York.

Lahlou, L. (1996). "A Method to Extract Social Representations from Linguistic Corpora." *Japanese Journal of Experimental Social Psychology* 36: 278–291.

Lahlou, S. (1998). *Penser manger*. Paris: Presses Universitaires de France.

Laitin, D. D. (2002). "Comparative Politics: The State of the Subdiscipline." *Political Science: State of the Discipline* (630–659). Ed. I. Katznelson and H. V. Milner. New York: Norton and American Political Science Association.

Laitin, D. D., J. A. Caporaso, et al. (1995). "The Qualitative-Quantitative Disputation: Gary King, Robert O. Keohane, and Sidney Verba's 'Designing Social Inquiry: Scientific Inference in Qualitative Research.'" *American Political Science Review* 89(2): 454–481.

Lake, D. A., and S. C. James. (1989). "The Second Face of Hegemony: Britain's Repeal of the Corn Laws and the American Walker Tariff of 1846." *International Organization* 43(1): 1–29.

Langston, T. S. (1992). *Ideologues and Presidents*. Baltimore: Johns Hopkins University Press.

LaPalombara, J., and M. Weiner. (1990). "The Origin of Political Parties." *The West European Party System* (25–30). Ed. P. Mair. Oxford: Oxford University Press.

Laver, M., and K. Benoit. (2002). *Locating TDs in Policy Spaces: Wordscoring Dail Speeches*. Dublin: Trinity College.

Laver, M., K. Benoit, et al. (2002). *Placing Political Parties in Policy Spaces*. Dublin: Trinity College.

Laver, M., K. Benoit, et al. (2003). "Extracting Policy Positions from Political Texts Using Words as Data." *American Political Science Review* 97(2): 311–331.

Laver, M., and J. Garry. (2000). "Estimating Policy Positions from Political Texts." *American Journal of Political Science* 44(3): 619–634.

Lavergne, R. P. (1983). *The Political Economy of U.S. Tariffs*. Toronto: Academic Press.

Lee, A. J. (1976). *The Origins of the Popular Press in England, 1855–1914*. London: Croom Helm.

Legro, J. W. (2000). "The Transformation of Policy Ideas." *American Journal of Political Science* 44(3): 419–432.

Levitt, S. D. (1996). "How Do Senators Vote? Disentangling the Role of Voter Preferences, Party Affiliation, and Senator Ideology." *American Economic Review* 86(3): 425–441.

Lieberman, R. C. (2002). "Ideas, Institutions, and Political Order: Explaining Political Change." *American Political Science Review* 96(4): 697–712.

Lieven, D. (1992). *The Aristocracy in Europe, 1815–1914*. London: Macmillan.

Lijphart, A. (1990). "Dimensions of Ideology in European Party Systems." *The West European Party System* (253–265). Ed. P. Mair. Oxford: Oxford University Press.

Lipset, S. M., and S. Rokkan. (1990). "Cleavage Structures, Party Systems, and Voter Alignments." *The West European Party System* (91–138). Ed. P. Mair. Oxford: Oxford University Press.

Lloyd-Jones, R., and A. A. LeRoux. (1980). "The Size of Firms in the Cotton Industry: Manchester 1815–1841." *Economic History Review* (2nd ser.) 33(1): 72–82.

Lloyd-Jones, R., and A. A. LeRoux. (1982). "Marshall and the Birth of Firms in the Early Nineteenth-Century Cotton Industry." *Business History* 24(1): 141–155.

Macintyre, A. (1989). "Lord George Bentinck and the Protectionists: A Lost Cause?" *Transactions of the Royal Historical Society* 5: 141–165.

Magee, S. P., W. A. Brock, et al. (1989). *Black Hole Tariffs and Endogenous Policy Theory: Political Economy in General Equilibrium*. Cambridge: Cambridge University Press.

Mair, P. (1990). "Introduction." *The West European Party System* (1–24). Ed. P. Mair. Oxford: Oxford University Press.

Malthus, T. (1993). "The Grounds of an Opinion on the Policy of Restricting the Importation of Foreign Corn." *The Economics of the Manchester School*. Vol. 1, *The Economic Background* (1–48). London: John Murray (Routledge Thoemmes Press). (Originally published in 1815).

Mandler, P. (1990). *Aristocratic Government in the Age of Reform: Whigs and Liberals 1830–1852*. Oxford: Clarendon Press.

Mantoux, P. (1948). *The Industrial Revolution in the Eighteenth Century*. London: Johnathan Cape.

May, G. H. L. L. (1979). *The Victorian Constitution: Conventions, Usages, and Contingencies*. London: Duckworth.

Mayer, W. (1984). "Endogenous Tariff Formation." *American Economic Review* 74(4): 970–985.

Mayhew, D. R. (1974). *Congress: The Electoral Connection*. New Haven: Yale University Press.

McCarty, N., K. T. Poole, et al. (2001). "The Hunt for Party Discipline in Congress." *American Political Science Review* 95(3): 673–698.

McCord, N. (1958). *The Anti-Corn Law League, 1838–1846*. London: Unwin University Books.

McCormick, J. M., and M. Black. (1983). "Ideology and Senate Voting on the Panama Canal Treaties." *Legislative Studies Quarterly* 8(1): 45–63.

McCulloch, J. R. (1822). "Agricultural Distress: Causes—Remedies." *Edinburgh Review* 36: 452, 468–477, 481–452.

McGillvray, F. (2004). *Privileging Industry: The Comparative Politics of Trade and Industrial Policy*. Princeton: Princeton University Press.

McKeown, T. J. (1987). *The Politics of Corn Law Repeal Reconsidered*. Chicago: American Political Science Association.

McKeown, T. J. (1989). "The Politics of Corn Law Repeal and Theories of Commercial Policy." *British Journal of Political Science* 19: 353–380.

McLean, I. (1995a). "Interests and Ideology in the United Kingdom Parliament of 1841–7." *Contemporary Political Studies 1995* (vol. 1) (1–20). Ed. J. Lovenduski and J. Stanyer. Belfast: Political Studies Association of the United Kingdom.

McLean, I. (1995b). "Railway Regulation as a Test-bed of Rational Choice." *Preferences, Institutions and Rational Choice* (134–161). Ed. K. Dowding and D. King. Oxford: Clarendon Press.

McLean, I. (2001). *Rational Choice and British Politics: An Analysis of Rhetoric and Manipulation from Peel to Blair*. Oxford: Oxford University Press.

Michie, R. C. (1981). *Money, Mania and Markets: Investment, Company Formation and the Stock Exchange in Nineteenth-Century Scotland*. Edinburgh: Donald.

Michie, R. C. (1985). "The London Stock Exchange and the British Securities Market, 1850–1914." *Economic History Review* (2nd ser.) 38(1): 61–82.

Mill, J. S. (1825). "The Corn Laws." *Westminster Review* 3: 394–420.

Mill, J. S. (1826). "Corn Laws." *Westminster Review* 16: 373–404.

Milner, H. (1997a). "Industries, Governments, and the Creation of Regional Trade Blocs." *The Political Economy of Regionalism*. Ed. E. D. Mansfield and H. V. Milner. New York: Columbia University Press.

Milner, H. (1997b). *Interests, Institutions, and Information: Domestic Politics and International Relations*. Princeton: Princeton University Press.

Milner, H., and K. Kubota (2005). "Why the Move to Free Trade? Democracy and Trade Policy in the Developing Countries." *Industrial Organization* 59(1): 107–143.

Mitchell, B. (1984). *Economic Development of the British Coal Industry 1800–1914*. Cambridge: Cambridge University Press.

Mitchell, B. R. (1988). *British Historical Statistics*. Cambridge: Cambridge University Press.

Mitchell, B. R., and P. Deane. (1971). *Abstract of British Historical Statistics*. Cambridge: Cambridge University Press.

Mitchell, N. J. (1997). *The Conspicuous Corporation: Business, Public Policy, and Representative Democracy*. Ann Arbor: University of Michigan.

Moore, B. (1966). *Social Origins of Dictatorship and Democracy*. Boston: Beacon Press.

Moore, D. C. (1965). "The Corn Laws and High Farming." *Economic History Review* (2nd ser.) 18(3): 544–561.

Morgan, E. V., and W. A. Thomas. (1962). *The Stock Exchange: Its History and Functions*. London: Elek Books.

Morley, J. (1881). *The Life of Richard Cobden*. London: Chapman and Hall.

Nakano, K. (2000). "The Role of Ideology and Elite Networks in the Decentralisation Reforms in 1980s France." *West European Politics* 23(3): 97–114.

Namier, L. B. (1930). *England in the Age of the American Revolution*. London: Macmillan.

Nelson, D., and E. Silberberg. (1987). "Ideology and Legislator Shirking." *Economic Inquiry* 25: 15–25.

Newbould, I. (1985). "Whiggery and the Growth of Party 1830–1841: Organization and the Challenge of Reform." *Parliamentary History* 4: 137–156.

Newspaper Press Directory. (1846). London: Charles Mitchell.

Noel-Jorand, M. C., M. Reinert, et al. (1995). "Discourse Analysis and Psychological Adaptation to High Altitude Hypoxia." *Stress Medicine* 11: 27–39.

North, D. (1990). *Institutions, Institutional Change and Economic Performance*. Cambridge: Cambridge University Press.

Norton, J. E. (1950). *Guide to the National and Provincial Directories of England and Wales, Excluding London, Published before 1856*. London: Offices of the Royal Historical Society.

"Not All as Cosseted as Consumers Say." (1998). *The Economist*: 59.

Noury, A. (2000). *Ideology, Nationality, and Euro-Parliamentarians*. Washington, DC: American Political Science Association.

Olson, M. (1965). *The Logic of Collective Action*. Cambridge: Harvard University Press.

Page, D. (1974). "Commercial Directories and Market Towns." *Local Historian* 11: 85–88.

Pahre, R. (1997). "British Hegemony and the Repeal of the Corn Laws." *The Rise of Free Trade* (vol. 4, 481–502). Ed. C. Schonhardt-Bailey. London: Routledge.

Peel, S. R. (1846). "Motion That the House Resolve Itself into a Committee of the Whole House on the Customs and Corn Importation Bills." *The Battle for Native Industry: The Debate upon the Corn Laws* (vol. 1, 91–97). H. o. Commons. London: Office of the Society for the Protection of Agriculture and British Industry.

Peel, S. R. (1857). *Memoirs of the Right Honourable Sir Robert Peel*. London: John Murray.

Peltzman, S. (1984). "Constituent Interest and Congressional Voting." *Journal of Law and Economics* 27: 181–210.

Perkin, H. (1969). *The Origins of Modern English Society 1780–1880*. London: Routledge & Kegan Paul.

Philbin, J. H. (1965). *Parliamentary Representation, 1832 England and Wales*. New Haven: Yale University Press.

References

Pickering, P. A., and A. Tyrell. (2000). *The People's Bread: A History of the Anti-Corn Law League*. New York: Leicester University Press.

Pierson, P., and T. Skocpol. (2002). "Historical Institutionalism in Contemporary Political Science." *Political Science: State of the Discipline*. Ed. I. Katznelson and H. V. Milner. New York: Washington, DC: Norton and American Political Science Association.

Pincus, J. (1972). *A Positive Theory of Tariff Formation Applied to Nineteenth-Century United States*. Palo Alto: Stanford University.

Pincus, J. J. (1975). "Pressure Groups and the Pattern of Tariffs." *Journal of Political Economy* 83: 757–778.

Pincus, J. J. (1977). *Pressure Groups and Politics in Antebellum Tariffs*. New York: Columbia University Press.

Plumb, J. H. (1967). *The Growth of Political Stability in England 1675–1725*. London: Macmillan.

A Political Parody on Tubal Cain. (1846). London: Rye.

Pollins, H. (1954). "The Marketing of Railway Shares in the First Half of the Nineteenth Century." *Economic History Review* (2nd ser.) 7(2): 230–239.

Poole, K. T. (2005). *Spatial Models of Parliamentary Voting*. New York: Cambridge University Press.

Poole, K. T., and H. Rosenthal. (1991). "Patterns of Congressional Voting." *American Journal of Political Science* 35(1): 228–278.

Poole, K. T., and H. Rosenthal. (1997). *Congress: A Political-Economic History of Roll Call Voting*. Oxford: Oxford University Press.

Poole, K. T., H. Rosenthal, et al. (1999). "Voteview for Windows V2.0.0.: Roll Call Displays of the U.S. Congress, 1789–1988." Princeton: Princeton University and Carnegie-Melon University.

Porritt, E., and A. G. Porritt. (1909). *The Unreformed House of Commons* (2 vols.). Cambridge: Cambridge University Press.

"Postscript." (1846). *Quarterly Review* 77: 603–610.

Prentice, A. (1968). *History of the Anti-Corn Law League* (vol. 1–2). London: Cass. (Originally published in 1853).

Prest, J. (1977). *Politics in the Age of Cobden*. London: Macmillan.

Read, D. (1967). *Cobden and Bright: A Victorian Political Partnership*. London: Arnold.

Reinert, M. (1983). "Une methode de classification descendante hierarchique: application a l'analyse lexicale par contexte." *Les Cahiers de l'Analyse des Données* 8(2): 187–198.

Reinert, M. (1993). "Les 'mondes lexicaux' et leur 'logique' a travers l'analyse statistique d'un corpus de recits de cauchemars." *Langage et société* 66: 5–39.

Reinert, M. (1998). *ALCESTE users' manuel* (English version). Toulouse: Image.

Remington, T. F., and S. S. Smith. (1998). "Theories of Legislative Institutions and the Organization of the Russian Duma." *American Journal of Political Science* 42(2): 545–572.

"Report from the Select Committee on Votes of Electors." (1846). *Parliamentary Papers VIII.*

Ricardo, D. (1822). "On Protection to Agriculture." *The Works and Correspondence of David Ricardo.* Vol. 4, *Pamphlets and Papers 1815–1823* (210–222, 228–231, 235–266). Ed. P. Sraffa. London: Murray and Cambridge University Press.

Richardson, L. E., and M. C. Munger. (1990). "Shirking, Representation, and Congressional Behavior: Voting on the 1983 Amendments to the Social Security Act." *Public Choice* 67: 11–34.

Richmond, D. O., and L. Kinnaird. (1846). *The Battle for Native Industry: The Debate upon the Corn Laws* (vol. 1, 104–107). H. o. Lords. London: Office of the Society for the Protection of Agriculture and British Industry.

Riker, W. H. (1986). *The Art of Political Manipulation.* New Haven: Yale University Press.

Risse-Kappen, T. (1994). "Ideas Do Not Float Freely: Transnational Coalitions, Domestic Structures, and the End of the Cold War." *International Organization* 48(2): 185–214.

Rodrik, D., and A. Subramanian. (2003). "The Primacy of Institutions (and What This Does and Does Not Mean)." *Finance and Development* (June): 31–34.

Rogowski, R. (1989). *Commerce and Coalitions: How Trade Affects Domestic Political Alignments.* Princeton: Princeton University Press.

Rohrlich, P. E. G. (1987). "Economic Culture and Foreign Policy: The Cognitive Analysis of Economic Policy Making." *International Organization* 41(1): 61–92.

Ruppel, F. J., and E. D. Kellogg (Eds.). (1991). *National and Regional Self-Sufficiency Goals.* London: Rienner.

Sabatier, P. A., and H. C. Jenkins-Smith (Eds.). (1993). *Policy Change and Learning: An Advocacy Coalition Approach.* Boulder: Westview Press.

Sartori, G. (1990). "The Sociology of Parties: A Critical Review." *The West European Party System* (150–184). Ed. P. Mair. Oxford: Oxford University Press.

Schattschneider, E. E. (1960). *The Semisovereign People: A Realist's View of Democracy.* New York: Holt, Rinehart & Winston.

Schonhardt-Bailey, C. (1991a). "Lessons in Lobbying for Free Trade in 19th-Century Britain: To Concentrate or Not." *American Political Science Review* 85(1): 37–58.

Schonhardt-Bailey, C. (1991b). "A Model of Trade Policy Liberalization: Looking Inside the British 'Hegemon' of the Nineteenth Century." *Ph.d. dissertation.* Los Angeles: University of California.

Schonhardt-Bailey, C. (1991c). "Specific Factors, Capital Markets, Portfolio Diversification, and Free Trade: Domestic Determinants of the Repeal of the Corn Laws." *World Politics* 43(4): 545–569.

Schonhardt-Bailey, C. (1994). "Linking Constituency Interests to Legislative Voting Behavior: The Role of District Economic and Electoral Composition in the Repeal of the Corn Laws." *Parliamentary History* 13: 86–118.

Schonhardt-Bailey, C. (Ed.). (1997). *The Rise of Free Trade* (4 vols.). London: Routledge.

Schonhardt-Bailey, C. (1998a). "Interests, Ideology and Politics: Agricultural Trade Policy in nineteenth-Century Britain and Germany." *Free Trade and Its Reception, 1815–1960*. Vol. 1, *Freedom and Trade* (63–81). Ed. A. Marrison. London: Routledge.

Schonhardt-Bailey, C. (1998b). "Parties and Interests in the 'Marriage of Iron and Rye.'" *British Journal of Political Science* 28: 291–332.

Schonhardt-Bailey, C. (1999). *Ideas and Interests in Parliamentary Debates on Trade Policy, 1814–1846*. Bicester: Bell & Howell Micromedia.

Schonhardt-Bailey, C. (2001). "The Strategic Use of Ideas: Nationalizing the Interest in the Nineteenth Century." *International Trade and Political Institutions: Instituting Trade in the Long Nineteenth Century* (146–197). Ed. F. McGillivray, I. McLean, R. Pahre, and C. Schonhardt-Bailey. Cheltenham, UK: Elgar.

Schonhardt-Bailey, C. (2003). "Ideology, Party and Interests in the British Parliament of 1841–1847." *British Journal of Political Science* 33: 581–605.

Schonhardt-Bailey, C. (2005). "Measuring Ideas More Effectively: An Analysis of Bush and Kerry's National Security Speeches." *PS: Political Science and Politics* 38(3): 701–711.

Schonhardt-Bailey, C., and A. Bailey. (1995). "The Buck in Your Bank Is Not a Vote for Free Trade: Financial Intermediation and Trade Preferences in the United States and Germany." *Preferences, Institutions, and Rational Choice*. Ed. K. Dowding and D. King. Oxford: Clarendon Press.

Searle, G. R. (1993). *Entrepreneurial Politics in Mid-Victorian Britain*. Oxford: Oxford University Press.

Semmel, B. (1970). *The Rise of Free Trade Imperialism*. Cambridge: Cambridge University Press.

Shaw, G. (1978). "The Content and Reliability of Nineteenth-Century Trade Directories." *Local Historian* 13: 205–207.

Shepsle, K. (1979). "Institutional Arrangement and Equilibrium in Multidimensional Voting Models." *American Journal of Political Science* 23: 27–59.

Shepsle, K. (1985). "Comment." *Regulating Policy and the Social Sciences*. Ed. R. Noll. Berkeley: University of California Press.

Shepsle, K. A. (2003). "Losers in Politics (and How They Sometimes Become Winners): William Riker's Heresthetic." *Perspectives on Politics* 1(2): 307–315.

Shepsle, K. A., and B. R. Weingast. (1981). "Structure-Induced Equilibrium and Legislative Choice." *Public Choice* 37: 503–519.

Shepsle, K. A., and B. R. Weingast. (1995). "Positive Theories of Congressional Institutions." *Positive Theories of Congressional Institutions* (5–38). Ed. K. A. Shepsle and B. R. Weingast. Ann Arbor: University of Michigan.

Sibthorp, C. (1846). *The Battle for Native Industry: The Debate upon the Corn Laws* (vol. 1, 98–100). H. o. Commons. London: Office for the Protection of Agriculture and British Industry.

Sikkink, K. (1991). *Ideas and Institutions: Developmentalism in Brazil and Argentina*. Ithaca: Cornell University Press.

Silverman, L. (1985). "The Ideological Mediation of Party-political Responses to Social Change." *European Journal of Political Research* 13: 69–93.

Smith, C. (n.d.). "Tracts on the Corn Trade and Corn Laws." 2(72).

Smith, H. S. (1973). *The Parliaments of England* (2nd ed.). Ed. F. W. S. Craig. Chichester: Political Reference Publications.

Smith, E. A. (1992). *The House of Lords in British Politics and Society, 1815–1911*. London: Longman.

Snyder, J. M. (1992). "Committee Power, Structure-Induced Equilibria, and Roll Call Votes." *American Journal of Political Science* 36(1): 1–30.

Snyder, J. M., and T. Groseclose. (2000). "Estimating Party Influence in Congressional Roll-Call Voting." *American Journal of Political Science* 44(2): 193–211.

Snyder, J. M., and T. Groseclose. (2001). "Estimating Party Influence on Roll Call Voting: Regression Coefficients versus Classification Success." *American Political Science Review* 95(3): 689–698.

Spence, W. (1815). *The Objections against the Corn Bill Refuted; and the Necessity of this Measure, to the Vital Interests of Every Class of the Community, Demonstrated*. London: Longman, Hurst, Rees, Orme & Brown.

Stasavage, D. (2003). *Public Debt and the Birth of the Democratic State: France and Great Britain, 1688–1789*. Cambridge: Cambridge University Press.

Stein, A. (1984). "The Hegemon's Dilemma: Great Britain, the United States, and the International Economic Order." *International Organization* 38: 355–386.

Stenton, M. (Ed.). (1976). *Who's Who of British Members of Parliament, 1832–1885* (vol. 1). Hassocks: Harvester Press.

Stewart, C. (2001). *Analyzing Congress*. London: Norton.

Stewart, R. (1971). *The Politics of Protection: Lord Derby and the Protectionist Party, 1841–1852*. Cambridge: Cambridge University Press.

Stone, L. (1965). *The Crisis of the Aristocracy 1556–1641*. Oxford: Oxford University Press.

Sussex, D. o., and D. o. Goucester. (1815). *Parliamentary Debates* (vol. 30, cols. 263–265). H. o. Lords. London: Hansard.

Taylor, A. J. (1949). "Concentration and Specialization in the Lancashire Cotton Industry, 1825–1850." *Economic History Review* (2nd ser.) 1–3: 114–121.

Taylor, M. (1995). "Public Petitioning in the Nineteenth Century: A Reinterpretation." Unpublished manuscript.

Thomas, J. A. (1925). "The House of Commons, 1832–1867: A Functional Analysis." *Economica* 13(2): 49–61.

Thomas, J. A. (1929). "The Repeal of the Corn Laws: 1846." *Economica* 25(2): 53–61.

Thomas, J. A. (1939). *The House of Commons 1832–1901: A Study of Its Economic and Functional Character*. Cardiff: University of Wales Press.

Thomas, W. A. (1973). *The Provincial Stock Exchanges*. London: Cass.

References

Thompson, F. M. L. (1963). *English Landed Society in the Nineteenth Century*. London: Routledge and Kegan Paul.

Thompson, T. P. (1832). *The True Theory of Rent: In Opposition to Mr. Ricardo and Others; Being an Exposition of Fallacies on Rent, Tithes, &c. in the Form of a Review of Mr. Mill's Elements of Political Economy/by the Author of the Catechism on the Corn Laws* (9th ed.). London: Pub. for the proprietors of the *Westminster Review* by Robert Heward.

Thorne, R. G. (1986). *The History of Parliament: The House of Commons 1790–1820* (5 vols.). London: Seeker & Warburg, for the History of Parliament Trust.

Timmins, G. (1979). "Measuring Industrial Growth from Trade Directories." *Local Historian* 13: 349–351.

Timmins, J. G. (1982). "Concentration and Integration in the Sheffield Crucible Steel Industry." *Business History* 24: 61–78.

Tomz, M., J. Wittenberg, et al. (2001). *CLARIFY: Software for Interpreting and Presenting Statistical Results, Version 2.0*. Harvard University, Cambridge, MA, ⟨http://gking.harvard.edu⟩.

Turberville, A. S. (1974). *The House of Lords in the Age of Reform, 1784–1837, with an Epilogue on Aristocracy and the Advent of Democracy, 1837–1867*. Westport, CT: Greenwood Press.

Turner, M. J. (1995). *Reform and Respectability: The Making of a Middle-Class Liberalism in Early Nineteenth-Century Manchester*. Manchester: Published for the Chetham Society by Carnegie Publishing.

Uslaner, E. M. (1999). *The Movers and the Shirkers: Representatives and Ideologues in the Senate*. Ann Arbor: University of Michigan Press.

Van Vugt, W. E. (1988). "Running from Ruin? The Emigration of British Farmers to the U.S.A. in the Wake of the Repeal of the Corn Laws." *Economic History Review* (2nd ser.) 41(3): 411–428.

Verdier, D. (1997). "Between Party and Faction: The Politics behind the Repeal of the Corn Laws." *Rise of Free Trade*. Vol. 4, *Free Trade Reappraised: The New Secondary Literature* (309–338). Ed. C. Schonhardt-Bailey. London: Routledge.

Verdier, D. (2002). *Moving Money: Banking and Finance in the Industrialized World*. Cambridge: Cambridge University Press.

Vincent, J., and M. Stenton. (Eds.). (1971). *McCalmont's Parliamentary Poll Book: British Election Results, 1832–1918*. Brighton: Harvester Press.

Vincent, J. R. (1967). *Pollbooks: How Victorians Voted*. Cambridge: Cambridge University Press.

Voeten, E. (2000). "Clashes in the Assembly." *International Organization* 54(2): 185–215.

von Tunzelmann, G. N. (1978). *Steam Power and British Industrialization to 1860*. Oxford: Oxford University Press.

Wadsworth, Alfred P. (1954). "Newspaper Circulations, 1800–1954." In *Proceedings of the Manchester Statistical Society, 1954*. Manchester: Manchester Statistical Society.

Walsh, J. I. (2000). "When Do Ideas Matter? Explaining the Successes and Failures of Thatcherite Ideas." *Comparative Political Studies* 33(4): 483–516.

Waxman, C. I. (Ed.). (1968). *The End of Ideology Debate*. New York: Funk and Wagnalls.

Weingast, B. R. (2002). "Rational-Choice Institutionalism." *Political Science: State of the Discipline* (660–692). Ed. I. Katznelson and H. V. Milner. New York: Norton and American Political Science Association.

Weller, S. C., and A. K. Romney. (1990). *Metric Scaling: Correspondence Analysis*. London: Sage.

Weston, C. C. (1970). *English Constitutional Theory and the House of Lords 1556–1832*. New York: AMS.

Wilcox, C., and A. Clausen. (1991). "The Dimensionality of Roll-Call Voting Reconsidered." *Legislative Studies Quarterly* 16(3): 393–406.

Wilde, P. (1976). "The Use of Business Directories in Comparing the Industrial Structure of Towns." *Local Historian* 12: 152–156.

Winters, L. A. (1990). "Digging for Victory: Agricultural Policy and National Security." *World Economy* 13(2): 170–190.

Woods, N. (1995). "Economic Ideas and International Relations: Beyond Rational Neglect." *International Studies Quarterly* 39(2): 161–180.

Woodward, S. L. (1962). *The Age of Reform, 1815–1870*. Oxford: Oxford University Press.

Wordie, J. R. (Ed.). (2000). *Agriculture and Politics in England, 1815–1939*. Basingstoke: Macmillan.

Yee, A. S. (1996). "The Causal Effect of Ideas on Policies." *International Organization* 50(1): 69–108.

Index

Abercrombie, 318
Acemoglu, D., 30
Acland, T., 305, 307–308, 318, 324, 340
Adderley, C. B., 311
Addington, J. H., 318
Aglionby, M., 302, 308, 310
Agricultural Protection Society, 13
Agriculture, 73, 368n16. *See also* Landowners
　activism and, 78–79
　class conflict and, 210–212
　Corn Laws and, 1–2 (*see also* Corn Laws)
　domestic production and, 244–246
　efficiency and, 171
　food self-sufficiency and, 198, 200, 218
　grain trade and, 198–202, 205, 208, 213–214
　high farming and, 163–171
　highway system and, 171
　House of Lords and, 238, 244–246
　insolvency and, 110–111
　interest groups and, 78–79
　national income proportion and, 365n3
　ownership distribution and, 110
　Parliamentary debates and, 163–171, 244–246
　pauperism and, 171
　portfolio diversification and, 107–126, 369n4
　prices and, 163–171, 195
　rents and, 103, 195
　tenant farmers and, 110–111
　wages and, 163–171, 208–210
Alceste, 159–161, 185, 216, 241, 274, 379n6, 379n7
Allix, J. P., 312
Allum, N. C., 159–160

Althorp, 324
American League to Abolish Capital Punishment, 76–77
Americans for Democratic Action (ADA), 134
Anderson, G. M., 20, 31, 129, 229
Anderson, K., 78
Annual Register, The, 239
Anti-Anti-Corn Law League, 17, 212–213, 215–216
Anti-aristocracy, 25, 81, 102–104
Anti-Corn Law Circular, 12
Anti-Corn Law League, 14–18, 45, 284, 287, 365n8
　argument gaps and, 265–266, 280–281
　aristocracy and, 25, 28–30, 102–104
　Chartists and, 100–102, 264
　class conflict and, 210–212
　concentration and, 56–59
　deconcentration and, 56–59, 64–70
　demand-side models and, 34–39
　democratic change and, 25–26
　economic interests and, 20–21, 23
　electoral strategy of, 96
　exports and, 64–69
　House of Commons and, 109
　House of Lords and, 228–234, 247, 259–260
　Lancashire and, 35–39, 57
　leadership and, 81
　League machine and, 11–13
　lobbying and, 27, 49–50, 95–106
　moral issues and, 99–102
　nationalized interest and, 75, 80, 82, 94–106, 263
　national prosperity and, 96–99
　newspaper influence and, 263–281

Anti-Corn Law League (cont.)
   organizational management of, 56–57
   Parliamentary debates and, 158, 178,
      191–192, 222 (see also Parliamentary
      debates)
   political agenda of, 11–18
   subscription increase of, 105
   textile industry and, 20–21, 23
   voting and, 153, 187
   wages and, 163–171
Aristocracy, 1, 20, 28–30, 70
   class conflict and, 102–104, 210–212
   export interests and, 63
   nationalized interest and, 102–104
   portfolio diversification and, 107–126
   repeal and, 153
   resistance to, 25, 81, 102–104
   territorial constitution and, 40–44
   trustees and, 171–174
Ashburton, L., 40
Ashworth, H., 230
Aspinall, A., 193–194
Atkins, 318
Austen-Smith, 8, 360n7
Austin, 311, 340
Aydelotte dataset, 42, 375n16
   DISTPREF variables and, 293–299
   voting and, 128–131, 137

Baack, B., D., 53
Babington, T., 318
Bailey, A., 56, 160
Baillie, H., 303–304
Baldwin, R., 50–51, 53
Bankes, G., 301–302, 306–307, 311, 314–315, 324
Bankes, H., 318
Barclay, David, 297, 318
Barclay, G., 324
Barham, 318
Baring, A., 318, 324
Baring, F. T., 313, 341
Baring, T., 303, 310
Baring, W., 295, 305
Barkly, 172–173, 305
Barnard, 318
Barnes, D. G., 9
Barron, H. W., 314
Bates, R. H., 76
Bateson, 305
Bathurst, 318
Bauer, M., 159

Baumgartner, F. R., 32
Bawn, K., 32
Beaumont, 325
Belgrave, 325
Bell, D., 81
Benett, J., 296, 302, 305, 315, 325
Bennet, P., 305, 314, 316, 341
Benoit, K., 8, 159–160
Bentinck, George, 256, 341
   agriculture and, 186
   Parliamentary debates and, 239, 302–303, 306–316
Berkeley, Captain, 313
Berkeley, C. F., 341
Berkeley, H., 305
Bernal, Ralph, 295–296, 325
Biagini, E. F., 100
Big Scale, 131
Binning, 318
Birch, 325
Blabouchere, H., 309
Blackburn, 318
Blackie, Thomas, 100
Blyth, M., 3, 86
Board of Trade, 10
Bohrnstedt, G. W., 123
Borthwick, P., 306–308, 310–311, 313–315
Bouverie, E. P., 314
Bowring, Dr., 302, 310–311, 342
Brand, 318
Brazill, T. J., 180
Briggs, A., 115
Bright, John, 11, 96, 163, 175, 212
   nationalized interest and, 101–103
   Parliamentary debates and, 222–223, 305, 307, 309 (see also Parliamentary debates)
Broadbridge, S. A., 114
Broadhead, 318
Brock, W. R., 31, 129
Brocklehurst, J., 311
Brooke, A., 303, 307–309, 315, 318, 342
Brotherton, J., 301, 306
Brothwick, P., 312, 314
Brougham, 325
Brown, L., 264, 266–267
Browne, D., 318
Browne, William, 79
Bruce, Cumming, 295, 305, 312
Bruges, W. H. L., 296
Brugidou, M., 160
Brydges, Egerton, 318

Brydges, J., 325
Bubble Act, 113
Buck, L. W., 304
Buller, C., 308–309, 311, 314
Buller, E., 304–305, 342
Buller, J., 313, 318
Burdett, Francis, 296, 318, 325
Burke, Edmund, 40–41
Burrell, C., 315, 318
Burrell, W., 319
Burroughes, H. N., 308, 343
Busch, M., 51
Butler, Pierce, 309
Butterworth, 319
Byng, 325

Cain, P. J., 21
Calvert, C., 319
Calvert, N., 325
Canada, 238
Canning, George, 10, 199, 319, 325
Capital
  capital market development and, 112–115
  fixed, 110
  flow allocation and, 109–110
  portfolio diversification and, 107–126
Caporaso, J. A., 3
Cardwell, E., 306, 309–310, 312
Carew, Pole, 319
Carlisle, 299
Carlow, 175
Cartwright, 319
Castlereagh, 319
Causality, 2, 5–6
Cave, O., 325
Cavendish, George, 325
Caves, R., 51, 108
Cawthorne, 319
Cayley, E., 311, 315
Chaloner, W. H., 11, 13
Chapman, A., 312
Chartists, 6, 13
  class conflict and, 211
  middle class and, 264
  nationalized interest and, 100–102
Cheshire, 55
Childers, W., 313
Chi-square criterion, 161
Cholmondley, H., 313
Christianity, 96, 100
Christie, William, 295–296
Christopher, R. A., 306, 343

Churchill, C., 296, 304
Civil liberty, 99
Civil unrest, 199–200
Class
  aristocracy and, 102–104 (*see also* Aristocrcacy)
  conflict and, 28–30, 210–212
  gentry and, 63, 70
  middle, 153, 264, 283–284
  Parliamentary debates and, 210–212
Clausen, A., 133
Clay, W., 304
Clements, 303
Clergy, 70, 102
Clerk, G., 172–173, 305, 309–313, 319, 325
Clive, 303, 325, 343
Coal, 112, 114
Coates, D., 128
Cobden, Richard, 19, 35, 39, 280–281
  House of Lords and, 229–230
  League machine and, 11–12, 15–16 (*see also* Anti-Corn Law League)
  middle class and, 264
  nationalized interest and, 96, 98–99
  Parliamentary debates and, 222, 306–307, 314
  voting and, 163, 185
Cochrane, A. D. R. W. B., 297
Cochrane, Baillie, 302, 304
Coke, T. W., 319
Colborne, R., 307
Cole, C., 325
Collective action, 52–53
Collett, 302
Colquhoun, J. C., 301, 303, 316
Colthurst, N., 319
Combe, G., 230
Committee on the Import Duties, 97, 105
Common Agricultural Policy (CAP), 78
Comparativists, 3–5
Compton, 319
Computer-assisted content analysis, 4, 159–161.
Concentration
  19th century Britain and, 54–56
  Anti-Corn Law League and, 56–59
  collective action and, 52–53
  geographical representation and, 50–51
  industrialists and, 50–59
  interest group theory and, 50–54
  Lancashire and, 54–56
  liberalization and, 52–54

Conolly, 306
Conservative Party, 1, 6, 13, 24–26, 28, 105
　aristocracy and, 28–30
　demand-side models and, 32–39
　economic interests and, 132–154
　electoral connection and, 174–175
　House of Lords and, 235–236
　ideology and, 25, 132–154, 285–290
　Lancashire and, 35–39
　Members of Parliament (MPs) free trade voting patterns and, 115–126
　middle class and, 264
　newspaper influence and, 263–281
　NOMINATE technique and, 131, 133–139, 146
　Parliamentary debates and, 157–189, 221–222 (see also Parliamentary debates)
　Peelites and, 32, (see also Peelites)
　portfolio diversification and, 108
　regression analysis of votes of, 147–149
　shirking and, 149–151
　social foundations of, 42
　split of, 127
　supply-side models and, 40–44
　territorial constitution and, 18, 40–41, 285
　trustees and, 171–174
Consolidated Fund, 15, 171
Copeland, 308, 310
Corn Law Convention, 100
Corn Laws, 1–2, 27, 107, 284–288, 293. See also Repeal
　1815 and, 9–11
　Act of 1822 and, 9–10
　anti-aristocracy and, 102–104
　Anti-Corn Law League and, 11–30 (see also Anti-Corn Law League)
　argument gaps and, 265–266, 280–281
　aristocracy and, 28–30
　class conflict and, 210–212
　Conservative Party split and, 127
　demand-side pressure and, 33–39
　dual purpose of, 9
　grain trade and, 9–10, 198–202, 205, 208, 213–214
　House of Commons and, 230
　House of Lords and, 233 (see also House of Lords)
　Ireland and, 175–177
　Members of Parliament (MPs) free trade voting patterns and, 115–126
　methodology and, 4–5
　moral issues and, 99–102
　Napoleonic Wars and, 9
　newspapers and, 274, 276, 280–281
　Parliamentary debates and, 160, 192, 199–200, 222 (see also Parliamentary debates)
　Peel and, 14–16 (see also Peel, Robert)
　petitions and, 199–200
　prices and, 195
　rents and, 195
　shirking and, 149–151
　sliding-scale tariffs and, 9–11
　specific-factors model and, 108–109
　taxes and, 102
　wages and, 208–210
Correspondence analysis, 180–184
　Parliamentary debates and, 216–223
Cotton textile industry, 20–23, 365n5. See also Industry
　concentration and, 54–56
　demand-side pressure and, 33–39
　Europe and, 59–60
　Lancashire and, 54–56, 65, 68
Cottrell, P. L., 55, 113
Courtenay, 319
Cox, G., 31–32, 128–129
Crawford, W. S., 301, 303, 309, 315
Credit cards, 77
Cripps, J., 325
Cripps, William, 295–296
Crosby, T. L., 13
Cuncombe, C., 326
Curteis, H. B., 302, 308–309
Curteis, E. J., 319, 325
Curtis, W., 319, 326
Curwen, J. C., 326
Customs Department, 97

Dalhousie, 237
Daly, 319
Davenport, E. D., 326
Davidson, R. H., 7
Davis, R., 59–60
Dawson, 326
Death-duty registers, 116–121, 124
Deconcentration
　19th century Britain and, 54–56
　Anti-Corn Law League and, 56–59, 64–70
　empirical testing and, 64–69
　export-sector, 59–63
　industrialists and, 54–59
　interest groups and, 54
Deedes, 302, 344

Index

Defoe, Daniel, 40
Delegate role, 7, 127–128, 363n11
Demand-side models, 31
  Anti-Corn Law League and, 34
  Lancashire and, 35–39
  nationalized interest and, 75–106 (*see also* Nationalized interest)
  Parliamentary debates and, 157–189 (*see also* Parliamentary debates)
  pressure and, 33–39
  repeal and, 32
Democracy, 25–26, 134, 259
Denison, E. B., 301, 306, 344
Denison, W. J., 326
Derbyshire, 55
Dickinson, F. H., 345
Dickinson, F. W., 304
Direct London-Exeter railroad, 113
Direct Western Railway, 113
Disraeli, Benjamin
  Parliamentary debates and, 305, 308, 310–311, 314–316
  voting and, 173–174, 185–186
DISTPREF variables, 293–299, 372n19
Dorchester, 173
Dougan, W. R., 128, 149
Douglas, F., 319
Douglas, H., 304, 345
Douglas, W., 319
Drummond, H., 295
Duffield, Thomas, 296
Duncan, G., 305, 310, 312
Duncombe, T., 305, 310
Durham, 175
Duverger, M., 81, 105

East Anglia, 119
Easthope, J., 316, 345
Ebrington, 295, 303, 313
Economic interests, 287–289
  British political environment and, 28–30
  comparative politics and, 3–5
  concentration and, 50–59
  Conservative Party and, 132–154
  Corn Laws and, 1–2 (*see also* Corn Laws)
  current debates and, 3–9
  demand-side models and, 31–39
  House of Commons and, 227–228
  individual preference and, 83–95
  Industrial Revolution and, 59–60
  institutions and, 132–154
  interactive effects and, 2
  London Stock Exchange and, 112–113
  measuring methods for, 133–139
  Members of Parliament (MPs) and, 139–141
  methodology and, 3–5
  middle class and, 153, 264
  nationalized interest and, 75–106 (*see also* Nationalized interest)
  national prosperity and, 96–99
  NOMINATE technique and, 133–139
  Parliamentary debates and, 224 (*see also* Parliamentary debates)
  pauperism and, 171
  Peelite/Non-Peelite schism and, 141–146
  portfolio diversification and, 107–126
  relevance and, 23–25
  repeal and, 20–21
  roll-call voting and, 7–9
  specific-factors model and, 107–126
  supply-side models and, 31–33, 40–44
  taxes and, 102
  territorial constitution and, 40–41
Edinburgh Chartist Association, 100
Egerton, F., 301
Eichengreen, B., 3
Electoral connection, 31, 174–175, 203–204
Elementary context unit (ECU)
  newspapers and, 273
  Parliamentary debates and, 162–163, 171, 176–178, 194–208, 212, 241, 244–248, 273, 380n26
Ellice, E., 311
Elliot, William, 319
Ellis, Wynn, 309, 311, 346
Ellison, 319
Enfranchisement, 81–82
Environmental issues, 77, 92
Equations, 134, 189, 371n17
Equilibrium tariff model, 109
Erickson, A. B., 129
Escott, B., 302–303, 306–307, 309
Essex, 173
Eulau, H., 7
European Union (EU), 78
Ewart, W., 309, 312
Exports
  Anti-Corn Law League and, 64–69
  deconcentration and, 59–69
  gentry and, 63
  heavy goods and, 71
  landed aristocracy and, 63
  manufacturers and, 71–73
  semiexports and, 71, 73

Factor analysis, 133
Factor-ownership distribution, 109
Fang, H.-T.i., 54
Fawcett, 319
Fay, C. R., 9
Fellowes, E., 313
Ferguson, 326
Fergusson, 326
Ferrand, W. B., 304, 306–307
Finch, G., 306–309, 312–314, 346
Finlay, 320
Fitzgerald, R. A., 305, 309, 320
Fitzmaurice, 303
Flood, Frederick, 320
Floyer, J., 315, 347
Folkestone, 326
Food self-sufficiency, 198, 200, 218
Forbes, 320
Formal methods, 3–5
Forster, M., 310
Foster, A. J., 320
Foster, J., 320, 326
Free trade, 363n6
  argument gaps and, 265–266, 280–281
  capital market development and, 112–115
  civil liberty and, 99
  constituent pressure and, 31–39
  deconcentration and, 54–69
  demand for, 283–287
  demand-side models and, 32–39
  equilibrium tariff model and, 109
  grain trade and, 198–202, 205, 208, 213–214
  House of Lords and, 229 (*see also* House of Lords)
  imperialism and, 21
  interest groups and, 50–54
  lobbying and, 49–74
  Members of Parliament (MPs) voting patterns and, 115–126
  morality of, 99–102
  nationalized interest and, 75–106 (*see also* Nationalized interest)
  newspapers and, 266–271, 274–281
  Parliamentary debates and, 157–189, 223 (*see also* Parliamentary debates)
  Peel and, 32–33
  portfolio diversification and, 107–126
  pressure timing and, 53–54
  prices and, 163–171
  roll-call voting and, 152–153 (*see also* Roll-call voting)
  supplying of, 285–287
  supply-side models and, 32–33, 40–44
  territorial constitution and, 40–42
  wages and, 367n13
Fremantle, 320
French Revolution, 15–16, 172, 288–289
Frewen, C. H., 311
Fuller, A. E., 314, 347
Fyler, T. B., 326

Gabel, M. J., 159
Gallagher, J., 21
Gambles, A., 40–41, 285
Gardiner, J. D., 314
Garry, J., 159–160
Gascoyne, 320, 326
Gash, Norman, 40, 42, 235, 258, 368n19
Gaskell, M., 173–174, 303, 315
Gatrell, V. A. C., 54–55
Geddes, Barbara, 7
Gentry, 63, 70
Gibson, M., 304, 307
Giddy, Davies, 320
Gilvert, Davies, 326
Gipps, 326
Gisborne, T., 302, 310, 347
Gladstone, 306
Godek, Paul, 52
Goldstein, J., 82
Golob, S. R., 3
Gooch, 320, 326
Gordon, S. C., 194, 236, 320, 326
Gore, M., 305, 347
Gore, W. O., 314, 316
Goring, C., 307, 309
Goulburn, H., 41, 302–303, 306, 310–314, 327
Government securities, 113
Gower, Leveson, 320
Graham, James, 173, 237, 303, 314–315, 320, 348
Grain trade, 198–202, 205, 208, 213–214
Grant, A., 327
Grant, C., 327
Grant, J. P., 320
Grattan, 320
Gray, P., 176
Great North Railway, 113
Greenacre, M. J., 180, 252
Greene, T., 308
Gregory, W. H., 303
Grenfell, 320

Index

Grofman, B., 180
Grogan, E., 310
Groseclose, T., 7, 133
Grossman, G., 53
Guttman scaling analysis, 131, 134, 137

Halford, H., 310
Hall, P. A., 4
Halsey, T. P., 304, 348
Hamilton, A., 320
Hanmer, John, 7, 312–313
Hansard's Parliamentary Debates, 233–236, 271, 386n5
Hansen, W. L., 52
Harris, 305, 309, 312
Hart David, 319
Harvey, D. W., 320, 327
Harwood, Philip, 99
Hastie, A., 315
Hawes, B., 310–311, 313
Hawke, G. R., 114
Heathcote, G. J., 303, 320, 348
Heathcote, W., 302
Heckman, J. J., 133
Heckscher-Ohlin model, 109
Helpman, E., 53
Heneage, G. H. W., 296
Henley, J. W., 313, 315
Herbert, Sidney, 296, 302–303, 315, 349
Higgins, J. P. P., 114
High farming, 163–171
Hill, R. L., 7, 219
Hilton, Boyd, 9, 20, 229, 360n17
  demand/supply-side perspective and, 31
  Parliamentary debates and, 195, 198, 203
  voting analysis and, 129, 176
Hinde, H., 304, 312
Hinich, M. J., 80
Hirst, F. W., 103
Historical institutionalism, 5–6
Hobhouse, J., 311, 327
Hobsbawm, E. J., 199
Holland, 233, 239
Hope, A., 296, 303, 310–311, 349
Hope, G. W., 295
Hope-Jones, A., 119
Hopkins, A. G., 21
Horner, 321
House of Commons, 238. *See also* Members of Parliament (MPs)
  1846 Parliamentary debates and, 256–258
  Corn Bill and, 230, 236
  debate analysis and, 239–258
  Duke of Wellington and, 232–233
  repeal and, 227–228
  Select Committee of, 9
House of Lords, 1–2, 383n1, 385n12. *See also* Members of Parliament (MPs)
  1846 Parliamentary debates and, 256–258
  agriculture and, 238, 244–246
  Alceste analysis and, 241
  Anti-Corn Law League and, 228–234, 247, 259–260
  Cobden and, 229–230
  debate analysis of, 239–258
  democratic reform of, 259
  Duke of Wellington and, 232–233, 235, 255–260
  empirical transformation and, 257–258
  influences on, 231–236
  international trade and, 241–244
  landowners and, 229, 231–236
  Lord Palmerston and, 235
  Lord Stanley and, 233–238, 255–256, 261
  newspaper influence and, 263–281
  Peel and, 233–239, 255–259, 286–287
  peer influence and, 231–236
  political process and, 236–239, 259–260
  protectionism and, 249
  proxies and, 236–239
  Queen's government and, 229, 233
  Reform Act and, 228, 230–231
  rhetoric and, 241
  role of, 247–248
  rubber stamping of decisions and, 228–229
  sliding scale and, 233
  territorial constitution and, 227, 258
  theme identification and, 240–241
  trustees and, 233–236, 246–247
  Twelve-point Protest and, 249
  understanding conversion of, 228–231
  Upper Chamber, 239–240, 259, 263–264
  voting record of, 260–261
Howard, C. W., 307
Howard, P., 302, 308–309, 312, 349
Howe, A., 19–20, 31, 56–57, 99, 104, 287
Howick, 297, 327
Howorth, 321
Huber, J. D., 159
Hudson, George, 297, 305–306, 308, 310, 316
Hume, James Deacon, 97–98, 105
Hume, Joseph, 301, 307–309, 313, 327

Humphery, 311
Hunter, T., 39, 230
Hurst, R., 327
Huskisson, William, 9–10, 203, 213, 219–220, 321, 327
Hutt, W., 305, 307, 349

Ideas, 2, 45–46, 287–289
 comparative politics and, 3–5
 current debates and, 3–9
 demand-side models and, 31–39
 ideology and, 25–27
 individual preferences and, 83–95
 methodology and, 3–5
 nationalized interest and, 75
 newspaper influence and, 266–281
 policy making and, 132
 relevance and, 25–27
 supply-side models and, 31–33, 40–44
 voting and, 7–9, 132
Ideology, 366n2
 argument gaps and, 265–266, 280–281
 collective action and, 76–77
 Conservative Party and, 25, 132–154, 285–290
 demand-side models and, 31–39
 equilibrium level for, 81–82
 free-trade and, 17, 19–20
 ideas and, 25–27
 individual preferences and, 83–95
 institutions and, 81–82
 interest groups and, 76–77
 Kalt-Zupan method and, 134–135
 landowners and, 132–133
 leadership and, 80–81
 measuring methods for, 133–139
 Members of Parliament (MPs) and, 8
 middle class and, 264
 nationalized interest and, 76–77
 NOMINATE technique and, 131, 133–141, 146–149, 152
 Parliamentary debates and, 192–193 (see also Parliamentary debates)
 Peelite/Non-Peelite schism and, 141–146
 Peelites and, 286
 policy making and, 132
 relevance and, 25–27
 reputation building and, 149–151
 residualization approach and, 133
 roll-call voting and, 7–9, 128–132
 Schattschneider and, 76–77
 shirking and, 128, 149–151

territorial constitution and, 40–42
 vacuum of, 81–82
Independent Affiliation, 217, 219
 Parliament member characteristics and, 319–329
Individual preference
 changing of, 86–95
 nationalized interest and, 83–95
 self interest and, 87–92
 two extremes of, 84–86
 uncertainty and, 90–92
Industrial Revolution, 59–60
Industry, 16, 20–21, 373n23
 coal, 112, 114
 concentration and, 54–59
 deconcentration and, 54–69
 demand-side pressure and, 33–39
 export-sector, 59–63
 firm size and, 56
 free trade and, 283–284 (see also Free trade)
 House of Commons and, 108–109
 interest group theory and, 49–54
 iron, 59, 112, 114
 leadership and, 80–81
 liberalization and, 52–53
 manufacturers, 71, 73, 76–77, 98, 264
 middle class and, 283–284
 minerals, 111
 mining, 111, 114
 national income proportion and, 365n3
 organization and, 80–81
 Plug Strikes and, 101
 portfolio diversification and, 108–126
 protectionism and, 108 (see also Protectionism)
 semifinished products and, 60
 steel, 112, 114
 taxes and, 102
Ingestre, 302, 306, 311
Inglis, R. H., 301, 303, 310, 313
Initial context unit (ICU), 162, 241
Insolvency, 110–111
Institutions, 287–290
 comparative politics and, 3–5
 current debates and, 3–9
 demand-side models and, 31–39
 endogenous, 4–6
 enfranchisement and, 81–82
 exogenous, 4
 historical institutionalism and, 5–6
 identifying relevant, 27–28

Index

ideology and, 81–82
interactive effects and, 2
methodology and, 3–5
nationalized interest and, 81–82, 104–105
protectionism and, 41–42
rational-choice, 5–6
Reform Act and, 104–105
relevance and, 27–28
repeal and, 21–22
roll-call voting and, 7–9
shirking and, 149–151
supply-side models and, 31–33, 40–44
Verdier on, 21–22
weak party system and, 105
Integration, 3
Interest groups, 70
  Anti-Corn Law League and, 64–69 (*see also* Anti-Corn Law League)
  collective action and, 76–77
  deconcentration and, 54–60
  endogeneity and, 49–54, 83–95
  equilibrium level for, 81–82
  export issues and, 59–69
  ideology and, 76–77
  individual preferences and, 49–54, 83–95
  liberalization and, 52–54
  member benefits and, 76–77
  nationalized interest and, 75–106 (*see also* Nationalized interest)
  policy of, 78–80
  positive externalities and, 78–80
  Schattschneider and, 76–77, 82–83
  theory of, 49–54
  women's rights and, 81
  workers' rights and, 81
International trade, 177–178, 241–244
Investment, 373n23
  flow allocation and, 109–110
  portfolio diversification and, 107–126
  specific-factors model and, 109–110
Ireland, 177, 239, 293
  agriculture and, 175–176
  potato famine, 33, 130, 246
Iron, 112, 114
Irving, J., 327
Irwin, D. A., 128, 229

Jackson, J. E., 128, 133
James, W., 21, 229, 304, 350
Jenkins, J. A., 7
Jocelyn, 321
Joint-stock companies, 111, 113

Jolliffe, W., 307–308, 315
Jones, B. D., 32
Jones, R., 108
Jones, W. D., 129, 233

Kalt, J. P., 7, 128, 131, 133–135, 151–152
Kellett, E. E., 268
Kennedy, P., 270
Keohane, R. O., 3
Killick, J. R., 114
Kindleberger, C. P., 19–20, 31, 128, 229
Kinealy, C., 176
King, G., 3, 147, 327
Kingdon, J. W., 128, 133
Kirchheimer, O., 80, 82
Knatchbull, E., 327
Knight, F. W., 311–312
Knightley, C., 312
Knoke, D., 123
Koford, K., 133
Koss, S., 267
Krehbiel, K., 32
Kronberger, N., 160, 188–189
Kroszner, R. S., 128
Krueger, A. O., 76
Krugman, P., 53

Lahlou, S., 160
Laitin, D. D., 3–5
Lake, D. A., 21, 229
Lambton, J. G., 321
Lancashire
  Anti-Corn Law League and, 57
  cotton textile industry and, 54–56, 96
  demand-side models and, 35–39
  export issues and, 65, 68
Landowners, 285, 367n11
  anti-aristocracy and, 102–104 (*see also* Aristocracy)
  class conflict and, 210–212
  control of Parliament by, 108–109
  export interests and, 63
  House of Lords and, 229, 231–236, 239
  ideology and, 132–133
  insolvency and, 110–111
  nationalized interest and, 95, 102–104
  ownership distribution and, 109–110
  portfolio diversification and, 107–126
  railroads and, 113–114
  rent theory and, 103
  taxes and, 102
  territorial constitution and, 40–44

Langton, Gore, 321
LaPalombara, J., 105
Lascelles, W., 302, 321, 350
Laver, M., 8, 159–160
Lavergne, R. P., 50–51, 53
Lawson, A., 312, 316
Layard, 175, 304, 314
Leadership, 80–81
Lee, A. J., 268
Lefevre, Shaw, 321
Lefroy, 303
Leominster, 172–173
LeRoux, A. A., 55–56
Lethbridge, T., 327
Levitt, S. D., 7, 133
Lewis, F., 321, 327
Leycester, R., 327
Liberalization, 52–54
Liberal Party, 13, 19–20, 285, 288, 368n19
 demand-side pressure and, 34–39
 House of Lords and, 235–236
 Lancashire and, 35–39
 Members of Parliament (MPs) free trade voting patterns and, 123, 125
 newspapers and, 266, 269
 NOMINATE technique and, 131, 133–139, 146
 roll-call voting and, 129
 territorial constitution and, 44
Liddell, H., 301, 305, 307, 327
Lieberman, R. C., 3
Lieven, D., 288
Lijphart, A., 82
Lincoln (Earl of), 315
Lipset, S. M., 82
Littleton, E. J., 327
Liverpool, 299
Lloyd-Jones, R., 55–56
Lobbying
 anti-aristocracy and, 102–104
 Anti-Corn Law League and, 27, 49–50, 95–106
 argument gaps and, 265–266, 280–281
 deconcentration and, 54–69
 individual preferences and, 49–69, 83–95
 interest-group theory and, 50–54
 newspaper influence and, 266–281
 organization of, 77
 Peelites and, 131–132
Lockhart, 305, 321
London Guildhall Library, 71
London Stock Exchange, 112–113

Long, Walter, 296, 321
Lower Chamber, 286
Lowther, H., 296–297
Lushington, 321

Maberley, J., 327
McCarty, N., 7
McCord, N., 11, 13, 18, 35, 57, 74, 229–230
McCubbins, M., 32
McCulloch, J. R., 97, 192
McGeachy, F. A., 313
Macintyre, A., 41
McKeown, Timothy, 31, 115, 128–130, 229
McLean, I., 2, 14
 demand/supply side perspective and, 32–33, 44
 House of Lords and, 229, 232–233, 239, 258
 voting analysis and, 128–130, 137, 174
Malthus, T., 98, 103, 163
Manchester Association, 57
Manners, John, 304, 307
Manufacturers. *See* Industry
March (Earl of), 302, 304, 307, 309, 313
Marjoribanks, 321
Markets
 Anti-Corn Law League and, 11–13
 capital market development and, 112–115
 Corn Laws and, 9–11 (*see also* Corn Laws)
 demand-side models and, 32–39
 export-sector deconcentration and, 59–63
 free trade, 10–13, 17, 19–20, 31–39 (*see also* Free trade)
 grain trade and, 198–202, 205, 208, 213–214
 international trade and, 177–178, 241–244
 sliding-scale tariffs and, 9–11
Marquess of Granby, 307, 315
Marquess of Worcester, 312, 314, 316, 355
Marquis of Blandford, 296
Marryat, 321
Marshall, J., 328
Martin, W. C., 303, 350
Martyn, Charles Cecil, 295
Master, Thomas W. C., 295
Maule, F., 313
Maxwell, J., 328
Mayer, W., 109
Mayhew, D. R., 7, 31
Melcombe Regis, 295
Members of Parliament (MPs), 26–27, 45, 289–290. *See also* Specific Party

Index

1814–1844, 331–338
1841–1847, 128–132, 135–139, 149–152
anti-aristocracy and, 103–104
argument gaps and, 265–266, 280–281
Bubble Act and, 113
characteristics of, 318–329
constituent pressure and, 31–39, 265
debate and, 8, 192 (*see also* Parliamentary debates)
demand-side models and, 31–39
DISTPREF variables and, 293–299
economic interests and, 139–141
exports and, 63
free trade voting patterns of, 115–126
House of Commons and, 227–233, 236, 238–258
House of Lords and, 227–261 (*see also* House of Lords)
ideological schisms in, 141–146
Lancashire and, 35–39
landowner control, 108–109
methodological issues and, 4–5
nationalized interest and, 82
newspaper influence and, 263–281
NOMINATE technique and, 131–141, 146–149
personal ideology and, 8, 128, 130–131
religion and, 129
roll-call voting and, 7–8, 128–132
supply-side models and, 40–44
territorial constitution and, 40–44
trustee role of, 5, 171–174, 233–236, 246–247
Methuen, 321
Michie, R. C., 113
Middle class, 153, 264, 283–284
Mildmay, H., 295–296, 314
Miles, P., 302
Miles, W., 301, 304, 306, 308–309, 311–312, 315, 351
Military, 73
Mill, J. S., 103
Milner, H., 23, 52
Milnes, M., 305, 308
Milnes, R. M., 310
Milton, 321, 328
Minerals, 111
Mining, 111, 114
Mitchell, Thomas, 297, 312
Moffatt, G., 307
Molesworth, W., 305
Monck, C., 321

Monck, J. B., 328
Monopolies, 21, 102–104, 224
Moore, P., 322, 328
Moral issues, 285, 287–288
  free trade and, 99–102
  national prosperity and, 96–99
  Parliamentary debates and, 202 (*see also* Parliamentary debates)
  repeal and, 153
Morgan, E. V., 113
Morley, J., 15, 39, 230
Morpeth, 303, 328
Morritt, 322
Much Wenlock, 173
Multidimensional scaling, 133
Munger, M., 80, 128, 149
Muntz, G. F., 305, 310, 312, 351

Naimer, L. B., 40
Napier, C., 304
Napoleonic Wars, 9
National Association of Manufacturers, 76–77
Nationalized interest, 366n7
  Anti-Corn Law League and, 75, 80, 82, 94–106, 263
  aristocracy and, 102–104
  conditions for, 77–83
  description of, 76
  enfranchisement and, 81–82
  ideas and, 75
  individual preference and, 83–95
  insiders and, 82
  institutions and, 81–82, 104–105
  interest groups and, 75
  leadership and, 80–81
  morality of, 99–102
  national prosperity and, 96–99
  organization and, 80–81
  positive externalities and, 78–80, 96–104
  Schattschneider and, 76–77, 82–83
  self interest and, 87–92
National security, 92
Nelson, D., 149
Neoclassical growth theory, 53, 374n12
Neoclassical trade theory, 108–109
Newdegate, C. N., 302–303, 305, 308–311, 315
New Gravesend Railway, 113
Newport, John, 199, 302, 322, 328
Newsletters, 77

Newspapers
　Alceste and, 274
　Anti-Corn Law League and, 271–272, 275–281
　competition among, 266–267
　content analysis of, 267–281
　Corn Laws and, 274, 276, 280–281
　demerits of, 267–271
　free trade and, 279–281
　local, 266–267
　London, 270
　merits of, 267–271
　MP districts and, 269
　Parliamentary debates and, 269–271
　partisan affiliation of, 268–269
　provincial, 267–271, 274–279
　public information and, 263–264
　sampling details for, 340–357
　underlying interests and, 270–271
Noel-Jorand, M. C., 160
NOMINATE technique, 152, 373n6, 376n30, 377n33
　ADA ratings and, 134
　classification rate and, 131
　criticism of, 133–134
　dimensionality and, 131
　equations for, 134
　factor analysis and, 133
　Guttman scaling technique and, 131, 134, 137
　Kalt-Zupan method and, 134–135
　low dimensionality tendencies of, 133–134
　multidimensional scaling and, 133
　Parliament of 1841–1847 and, 135–139
　Parliamentary debates and, 180
　regression analysis of votes and, 146–149
Non-Peelite Conservatives, 24, 32, 377n34
　argument gaps and, 266
　Conservative Party split and, 127
　demand-side pressure and, 34–39
　electoral connection and, 174–175
　ideology and, 132–133
　Members of Parliament (MPs) free trade voting patterns and, 116–126
　newspapers and, 266, 271, 277–279, 281
　NOMINATE technique and, 136–139
　Parliamentary debates and, 221–222, 226 (*see also* Parliamentary debates)
　Peelite ideology and, 141–146
　portfolio diversification and, 108
　regression analysis of votes of, 147–149

roll-call voting and, 129–130
shirking and, 149–151
territorial constitution and, 43–44
trustees and, 173–174
Norreys, 302
North, Douglass, 27
Northland, 301, 304
Norton, J. E., 71
Nuclear energy, 77
Nugent, 322

O'Brien, A. S., 301, 303–304, 308, 310, 314–315
O'Connell, D., 309
O'Connell, J., 306–307
O'Conor, D., 301
Olson, M., 50–52, 77
Ossultoun, 322

Packe, C. W., 306, 313–314
Paget, A., 305, 322
Pahre, 21, 229
Palmer, F., 328
Palmer, G., 302, 307, 309, 312, 315, 351
Palmer, R., 304, 328
Palmerston, 314
Parliamentary debates, 191, 378n2, 383n13, 386n8
　1814 to 1815, 194–200
　1826 to 1828, 200–204
　1842 to 1844, 204–212
　1846, 163–187, 256–258
　agriculture and, 163–171, 175–176, 244–246
　Alceste and, 159–161, 185, 216
　anti-Anti-Corn Law League and, 212–213, 215–216
　argument gaps and, 265–266, 280–281
　basic statistics for, 193–194
　civil unrest and, 199–200
　class conflict and, 210–212
　computer-assisted content analysis and, 159–161
　correspondence analysis and, 180–184, 216–223
　discourse of, 178–184
　electoral connection and, 174–175, 203–204
　elementary context units (ECUs) and, 162–163, 171, 176–178, 194–208, 212, 241, 244–248, 273, 380n26
　food self-sufficiency and, 198, 200, 218

Index

grain trade and, 198–202, 205, 208, 213–214
House of Lords and, 228–229, 239–258 (*see also* House of Lords)
initial context unit (ICU) and, 162, 241
international trade and, 177–178, 241–244
Ireland and, 175–176
liberal ideology and, 192–193
matrix decomposition for, 188–189
maximum chi-square criterion and, 161
methodological analysis of, 158
newspapers and, 269–271
NOMINATE technique and, 180
Peel and, 157–158, 213–214, 218–220, 222, 226, 301–304, 307–314, 322, 328, 378n2
petitions and, 199–200
political economy and, 202–204
prices and, 163–171, 195
public opinion and, 203–204
rents and, 195
repeal timing and, 176–177
territorial constitution and, 224
textual analysis and, 192
theme identification and, 161–167, 194, 240–241
theme linkages and, 178, 184–187, 214–223, 249–256
time comparison of, 223–225
tree graphs and, 179, 214–216
trustees and, 158, 171–174, 187–188, 233–236
wages and, 163–171, 208–210
word-distribution patterns and, 160–161
Parliamentary Papers, 119
Parliamentary rhetoric, 176–177, 195–198, 204, 241
Parnell, H., 322, 328
Partisanship, 31
Pauperism, 171
Peel, Robert, 1–2, 6, 13, 45–46, 106, 263
class fury and, 18
Conservative Party and, 24–25, 28, 127
death of, 16–17
demand-side pressure and, 33–39
free trade and, 19–20, 32–33
grain trade and, 213–214
House of Lords and, 233–239, 255–259, 286–287
ideology and, 151–152
Irish potato famine and, 130
mutual concession and, 14–15
Parliamentary debates and, 157–158, 213–214, 218–220, 222, 226, 301–304, 307–314, 322, 328, 378n2
political tactics of, 14–17, 32–33, 361n28
protectionism and, 41–42
repeal motion of, 14–17
resignation of, 239, 359n2
sliding scale and, 213–214, 233
supply-side models and, 40–44
Tamworth Manifesto and, 42
territorial constitution and, 18–19, 40–44
trustees and, 171–174, 246–247
Peelites, 32, 191–192, 263–264, 285
argument gaps and, 265–266
Conservative Party split and, 127
constituents and, 265
electorial connection and, 174–175
ideology and, 286, 289–290
indepedence and, 288–289
Members of Parliament (MPs) free trade voting patterns and, 115–126
middle class and, 264
NOMINATE technique and, 131–132, 136–139
Non-Peelite ideology and, 141–146
Parliamentary debates and, 157–189, 221–222, 226 (*see also* Parliamentary debates)
regression analysis of, 147–149
roll-call voting and, 128–132, 147–149
rural constituency and, 147–148
shirking and, 149–151
territorial constitution and, 40–41
Peltzman, S., 7, 128, 149
Perkin, H., 264
Petitions, 199–200
Philippe, Louis, 39
Philips, G., 322
Philips, G. R., 328
Philips, Sir G., 328
Pierson, P., 5
Pigott, G., 328
Pincus, J., 51–52, 54
Plug Strikes, 100–101
Plumb, J. H., 111
Plumptre, J., 311, 313, 315, 352
Polhill, 315
Policy, 366n4
American agricultural, 78–79
Common Agricultural Policy and, 78
Conservative Party and, 25–26
Corn Laws and, 1–2 (*see also* Corn Laws)

Policy (cont.)
  free trade, 31–39 (*see also* Free trade)
  ideas and, 132
  ideology and, 132
  income tax and, 119
  individual preferences and, 83–95
  liberalization and, 52–54
  nationalized interest, 75–106 (*see also* Nationalized interest)
  Parliamentary debates and, 157–189, 182
  portfolio diversification and, 107–126
  predicting outcomes of, 83
  territorial constitution and, 40–42
Political economy, 202–203
Political Parody on Tubal Cain, A, 106
Politics
  Anti-Corn Law League and, 11–13 (*see also* Anti-Corn Law League)
  aristocracy and, 28–30
  comparative, 3–5
  computer-assisted content analysis and, 159–161
  concession and, 17–19
  constituent pressure and, 31–39, 133
  Corn Laws and, 1–2 (*see also* Corn Laws)
  delegate role and, 127–128
  demand-side models and, 31–39
  electoral connection and, 31
  free trade voting patterns and, 115–126
  historical institutionalism and, 5–6
  House of Lords and, 231–239 (*see also* House of Lords)
  interest-group theory and, 50–54
  lobbying and, 49–74
  Members of Parliament (MPs) free trade voting patterns and, 116–126
  national prosperity and, 96–99
  newspaper influence and, 263–281
  Parliamentary debates and, 157–189, 219 (*see also* Parliamentary debates)
  partisanship and, 31
  Peel's sliding scale and, 213–214
  portfolio diversification and, 110–111
  positive externalities and, 78–80
  rational-choice institutionalism and, 5–6
  registration campaigns and, 12–13
  representation models and, 127–128
  residualization approach and, 133
  roll-call voting and, 7–9
  shirking and, 149–151
  specific-factors model and, 107–108
  territorial constitution and, 40–42
  trustee role and, 127–128
Pollington, 309, 313
Pollins, H., 113–114
Ponsonby, 322
Poole, K. T., 7, 128, 131, 133
Porter, 322
Portfolio diversification, 369n4, 371n18
  aggregate-level, 116
  Bubble Act and, 113
  capital formation and, 108–126
  capital market development and, 112–115
  in economic history, 111–115
  export sector and, 108
  factor-ownership distribution and, 109–110
  geographical analysis of, 116–126
  government securities and, 113
  income tax and, 119–121
  intensification of, 107
  London Stock Exchange and, 113
  Members of Parliament (MPs) voting patterns and, 115–126
  minerals and, 111
  mining and, 111, 114
  Non-Peelite Conservatives and, 108
  political interpretation and, 110–111
  railroads and, 113–115
  specific-factors model and, 107–108, 111–126
  stocks and, 109–110
  technology and, 113
Portman, E. B., 322, 328
Prentice, Archibald, 228–229
  Anti-Corn Law League and, 11–12, 15, 29, 35
  repeal documentation and, 17–18
Pressure-groups, 53–54
Prest, J., 39
Preston, 322
Prices, 360n9
  agriculture and, 163–171, 195
  protectionism and, 163–171
Proby, 322
Professionals, 73
Propaganda tracts, 13
Protectionism
  Anti-Corn Law League and, 11–13 (*see also* Anti-Corn Law League)
  Corn Laws and, 1–2, 9 (*see also* Corn Laws)
  electoral connection and, 174–175

Index

endogenous protection literature and, 49–54
House of Lords and, 249
ideology and, 151–154
institutions and, 41–42
majority voting and, 109
members of Parliament (MPs) and, 24
nationalized interest and, 82, 106
NOMINATE technique and, 136–141
Parliamentary debates and, 157–189
Peel and, 41–42
prices and, 163–171
shirking and, 149–151
specific-factors model and, 108–111
supply-side models and, 32–33, 40–44
Tamworth Manifesto and, 42
trustees and, 158, 171–174, 187–188
Twelve-point Protest and, 249
Protestant establishment, 132
Protheroe, 322
Public opinion, 203–204

Quadruple Alliance, 21
Quarterly Review, 231
Queen's government, 229, 233

Radicals, 239
Railroads, 113–115, 369n5
Rashleigh, W., 313, 352
Rational-choice institutionalism, 5–6
Ray, E. J., 53
Read, D., 97–99, 102
Reform Act, 121, 284, 287, 372n22
  demand-side models and, 35
  House of Lords and, 228, 230–231
  institutional environment and, 104–105
  middle class interests and, 153
  Parliamentary debates and, 218, 225
  political arena for, 6, 8, 12, 18, 27, 30
  specific-factors model and, 109
  supply-side models and, 40–44
Reformers, 136–137
Registration campaigns, 12–13
Reid, John Rae, 309
Reinert, Max, 160
Reinhardt, E., 51
Religion, 96, 100, 129, 285
Rendlesham, 313, 352
Rents, 103, 195
Repeal, 46, 107, 289–290
  1815 and, 9–11
  Anti-Corn Law League and, 11–13, 96 (see also Anti-Corn Law League)
  argument gaps and, 265–266, 280–281
  aristocracy and, 153
  British political environment and, 28–30
  Bubble Act and, 113
  concession and, 17–19
  Conservative Party split and, 127
  demand-side pressure and, 32–39
  economic interests and, 20–21
  explanations of, 17–22
  free trade and, 19–20, 283–287
  House of Commons and, 227 (see also House of Commons)
  House of Lords and, 227–261 (see also House of Lords)
  institutions and, 21–22
  interest groups and, 75 (see also Interest groups)
  momentum for, 2, 14–17
  moral issues and, 153
  NOMINATE technique and, 137 (see also NOMINATE)
  Parliamentary debates and, 176–177, 191–226 (see also Parliamentary debates)
  political arena and, 17–19
  puzzle of, 1–2
  regression analysis of votes and, 146–149
  rhetoric and, 176–177
  roll-call voting and, 8–9, 128–132
  shirking and, 149–151
  sliding scale and, 9–11
  supply-side models and, 40–44
  territorial constitution and, 18, 40–44
  timing of, 176–177
  unadulterated version of, 283–287
  wages and, 163–171
Repton, G. W. J., 311
Residualization approach, 133
Ricardo, David, 9–10, 19, 103, 163, 192. *See also* Specific-factors model
Rice, Spring, 328
Richardson, L. E., 128, 149
Ridley, M. W., 322
Riker, W. H., 8
Robinson, G., 322, 328
Robinson, J. A., 30
Robinson, R., 21
Roebuck, J. A., 304, 315
Rohrlich, P. E. G., 19–20, 31, 129, 229
Rokkan, S., 82

Roll-call voting, 7–9, 152
  1841–1847 Parliament and, 128–132
  Conservative Party and, 128–132
  constituency interests and, 129–132
  dimensionality and, 131
  ideology and, 153–154
  Liberal Party and, 129
  mapping of, 359n6
  motives in, 139–141
  NOMINATE technique and, 133–141, 146–149 (*see also* NOMINATE)
  regression analysis of, 146–149
  shirking and, 149–151
Rolleston, 311
Romilly, John, 297, 322
Rose, 322
Rosenthal, H., 7, 128, 131, 133
Ross, D. R., 306
Round, 323
Rous, 302
Ruppel, F. J., 78
Rural values, 92
Russell, John
  free trade and, 235, 258
  Parliamentary proceedings and, 301, 303, 306–308, 310, 314, 316, 329
Russia, 175

St. Paul, Horace, 323
Sandon, 303, 353
Sartori, G., 80
Schattschneider, E. E., 76–77, 82–83, 106
Schonhardt-Bailey, C., 17
  concentration and, 63, 70–71
  demand/supply-side perspective and, 31, 35
  lobbying issues and, 63, 70–71
  nationalized interest and, 81–82, 100, 103, 105
  Parliamentary debates and, 225, 229
  portfolio diversification and, 113, 121
  voting analysis and, 128–130, 160
Scotland, 113, 135, 293
Scott, F., 302, 304, 315
Scrope, Poulett, 305, 309
Searle, G. R., 16, 18–19, 35
Sebright, John, 323, 329
Select Committee of the House of Commons, 9
Senior, Nassau, 97
Seymer, H. K., 306, 316
Shaw, F., 305, 313

Shaw, James, 323
Shepsle, Kenneth, 2, 25, 79, 91, 364n16
Sheridan, R. B., 315
Shiffner, 323
Shipping, 111
Shirking, 128, 149–151
Shrewsbury, 173, 299
Sibthorp, C., 206, 301–302, 306, 308–309, 312, 314, 329, 353
Silberberg, E., 149
Skocpol, T., 5
Sliding-scale tariffs, 9–11, 213–214, 233
Smith, Adam, 213
Smith, C., 9, 323, 329
Smith, E. A., 230, 238
Smith, H., 296
Smith, John, 323
Smith, Vernon, 316
Smith, W., 323
Smyth, 323
Snyder, J. M., 7, 133
Sotheron, T. H. S., 296
Specific factors model
  capital formation and, 108–111
  Corn Laws and, 108–109
  equilibrium tariff model and, 109
  House of Commons and, 108–109
  income redistribution and, 109
  investment and, 109–110
  ownership distribution and, 109–110
  political interpretation and, 107–111
  portfolio diversification and, 111–126
  protectionism and, 108–111
  Reform Act and, 109
  standard applications of, 108–109
  stocks and, 109–110
Spence, W., 163
Spooner, Richard, 306, 310, 354
Stamford, 172–173
Stanhope, Earl, 238
Stanley, W. O., 308, 329
  House of Lords and, 233–238, 255–256, 261
Starvation, 33
Steel, 112, 114
Stein, A., 21, 229
Stephen, 323
Stewart, C., 32
Stewart, John, 323
Stewart, R., 186, 235
Stockport, 212
Stocks, 109–110

Index

Bubble Act and, 113
capital market development and, 112–115
London Stock Exchange and, 112–113
Members of Parliament (MPs) free trade voting patterns and, 115–126
railroads and, 113–115
technology and, 113
Stolper-Samuelson theorem, 109
Stone, Lawrence, 111
Strutt, E., 311
Stuart, J., 314
Stuart, Wortley, 323
Sumner, Home, 323
Supply-side models, 45–46, 154, 382n1
Parliamentary debates and, 157–189 (*see also* Parliamentary debates)
political perspective and, 31–33
repeal and, 40–44
shift and, 40–44
territorial constitution and, 40–44
Swann, 323

Tamworth Manifesto, 42
Tariff Reform, 81
Taxes, 238
Corn Laws and, 102
income, 119–121, 125, 141
Taylor, A. J., 55
Taylor, M. A., 323
Technology, 113–115
Territorial constitution, 18, 285
aristocracy and, 40–41
defense of, 42
House of Lords and, 227, 258
Liberal Party and, 44
Parliamentary debates and, 224
supply-side models and, 40–44
Textile industry, 20–21, 23
Thesiger, F., 296, 314
Thomas, W. A., 31, 113–114, 129
Thompson, C. P., 329
Thompson, T., 323
Thompson, William, 296–297, 305, 310, 312, 329
Thornton, H., 323
Tierney, 323
Tollemache, J., 305
Tollison, R. D., 20, 31, 129, 229
Tollmach, J., 310
Tomz, M., 147
Torrens, 103, 163, 192, 219–220, 329, 368n18

Tory Party, 217, 219, 239. *See also* Conservative Party
Parliament member characteristics and, 318–329
Trade. *See* Free trade, International trade, Protectionism
Tree graphs, 179, 214–216
Trelawney, J. S., 306
Trollope, J., 312–313, 354
Trustees, 127–128, 286
House of Lords and, 233–236, 246–247
Parliamentary debates and, 171–174 (*see also* Parliamentary debates)
Peel and, 246–247
role of studies on, 363n11
Turberville, A. S., 231–232, 384n6
Tyrell, J., 173–174, 302, 304, 308–309, 312

Unemployment, 238
United Kingdom
aristocracy and, 28–30 (*see also* Aristocracy)
class conflict and, 28–30, 210–212
concentration in, 54–59
deconcentration in, 54–56
food self-sufficiency and, 198, 200, 218
as hegemonic leader, 229
Industrial Revolution and, 59–60
Parliament and, 1–2 (*see also* Members of Parliament (MPs))
population growth and, 9, 11
specific-factors model and, 107–108
Tariff Reform era and, 81
territorial constitution and, 18, 40–44, 224, 227, 258, 285
United States, 21–22
agricultural policy and, 78–79, 175
roll-call voting and, 7–8
Upper Chamber, 239–240, 259, 263–264
Urban development, 111
Uslaner, E. M., 7, 134

Vane, H., 304
Vansittart, 323
Verdier, D., 21–22, 128–129, 229
Verner, 315
Vernon, H., 313
Villiers, Charles, 11, 97, 295–296
House of Commons and, 257
Parliamentary issues and, 212, 222, 304, 306, 308–309, 312, 316, 355
voting analysis and, 162–163, 177

Viner, 107–108. *See also* Specific-factors model
Voeten, E., 133
Von Tunzelmann, G. N., 54
Voting, 45–46, 152–153, 384n10
  1841–1847 Parliament and, 128–132
  argument gaps and, 265–266, 280–281
  constituents and, 265
  demand-side models and, 32–39
  free trade ideology and, 19–20
  House of Lords and, 260–261
  ideas and, 132
  Members of Parliament (MPs) free trade voting patterns and, 115–126
  middle class and, 264
  motives in, 139–141
  newspaper influence and, 263–281
  NOMINATE technique and, 131, 133–141, 146–149 (*see also* NOMINATE)
  Parliamentary debates and, 157–189 (*see also* Parliamentary debates)
  political representation models and, 127–128
  protectionism and, 41–42
  regression analysis of, 146–149
  roll-call, 7–9 (*see also* Roll-call voting)
  shirking and, 149–151
  tariff protection and, 109
Vyse, R. H., 315, 323

Wages, 367n13
  agriculture and, 163–171, 208–210
  Anti-Corn Law League and, 163–171
Wagner, W., 160, 188–189
Waithman, 329
Wakley, T., 302, 308
Wales, 119, 135, 293
Walsh, J., 303, 312, 315
Warburton, H., 297, 313, 329
Ward, H. G., 307–308, 355
Ward, W., 329
Warrender, G., 324
Waxman, C. I., 81
Weiner, M., 105
Weingast, B. R., 5
Wellesley, W. P. T. L., 324
Wellington, Duke of, 10, 229
  House of Commons and, 232–233
  House of Lords and, 232–233, 235, 255–260
Western, 324, 329
Weymouth, 295

Wharton, 324
Whig-Liberal Party, 136–137, 151, 186, 222, 297. *See also* Liberal Party
Whig Party, 217, 219, 223, 239, 368n19
  House of Lords and, 235–236
  Parliament member characteristics and, 318–329
Whitbread, 324
Whitmore, T., 329
Wilberforce, 324
Wilcox, C., 133
Williams, W., 310
Winters, L. A., 78
Wittenberg, J., 147
Wodehouse, 302–303, 329
Women's rights, 81
Wood, Alderman, 329
Wood, C., 316, 355
Wood, Colonel, 324, 329
Wood, George, 297
Wood, J., 329
Wood, M., 324
Wood, Thomas, 302, 304, 308
Workers' rights, 81
Worsley, Lord, 206, 303, 308, 356
Wrottesley, J., 329
Wynn, C. W., 303, 324
Wynn, W. W., 324, 329

Yorke, E., 313, 316, 324
Yorke, H. G. R., 312

Zupan, M. A., 7, 128, 131, 133–135, 151–152